Rivers of Light

Claire Myers Owens portrait by Minnie Smith, New Haven, CT, c. 1940s. From Blagg-Huey Library, Woman's Collection, Texas Woman's University, Denton, Texas. Published with permission.

RIVERS *of* LIGHT

The Life of Claire Myers Owens

Miriam Kalman Friedman

Syracuse University Press

Syracuse, New York 13244-5290

First Edition 2019

19 20 21 22 23 24 6 5 4 3 2 1

∞ The paper used in this publication meets the minimum requirements of the American National Standard for Information Sciences—Permanence of Paper for Printed Library Materials, ANSI Z39.48-1992.

For a listing of books published and distributed by Syracuse University Press, visit www.SyracuseUniversityPress.syr.edu.

ISBN: 978-0-8156-3633-5 (hardcover) 978-0-8156-1107-3 (paperback)
978-0-8156-5479-7 (e-book)

Library of Congress Cataloging-in-Publication Data

Names: Friedman, Miriam Kalman, author.
Title: Rivers of light : the life of Claire Myers Owens / Miriam Kalman Friedman.
Description: First edition. | Syracuse : Syracuse University Press, 2019. | Includes bibliographical references and index.
Identifiers: LCCN 2018061078 (print) | LCCN 2019008894 (ebook) | ISBN 9780815654797 (E-book) | ISBN 9780815636335 (hardcover : alk. paper) | ISBN 9780815611073 (pbk. : alk. paper)
Subjects: LCSH: Owens, Claire Myers. | Authors, American—20th century—Biography.
Classification: LCC PS3529.W436 (ebook) | LCC PS3529.W436 Z58 2019 (print) | DDC 813/.52 [B]—dc23
LC record available at https://lccn.loc.gov/2018061078

Manufactured in the United States of America

To those women coming of age in the twenty-first century:
the rights of freedom, opportunity, and autonomy you now enjoy were bravely obtained by feminists and activists in the nineteenth and twentieth centuries. Guard these rights as if your identity and self-determination depend on them—because they do. I dedicate this book to the "Tellectinas" of today, tomorrow, and forever.

And to

Carolyn A. Carney, Tellectina Exemplar

Contents

Illustrations

Acknowledgments

TWO YEARS AGO, my friend and colleague Carolyn Carney called to say: "I need a project. Let's bring Claire back to life." I was astonished. The manuscript had sat for over ten years in disarray after an earlier attempt to publish. Carolyn assured me she would rescue the endnotes, and together we decided to go back to the earliest draft of the manuscript. She helped me forget the painful experience of the past and celebrate the joy of creation. Because of her encouragement, you are now reading this book. So first and foremost, I thank Carolyn for her eagle eye, her enduring patience, her expertise in research and American history, and her loyal friendship.

The late Ruthe Winegarten introduced me to Elizabeth Snapp, about whom you will read in the introduction, and who has been part of this project since its inception. Dale Spender's Women Studies Institute in London, which I attended through a grant from Sally Bingham, helped me launch this project in the right direction. Truly a life work, this biography owes to the cooperation and endorsement of Elizabeth Snapp, then director of the Blagg-Huey Library at Texas Woman's University (TWU). She made my discovery of Claire Myers Owens feasible and each project fun. As director, she ran the library, archive, and Woman's Collection with professionalism and dignity, as a place of honor and a tribute to scholarship, as did her staff, especially Dawn Letson and Glenda Kallman. I also thank Kimberly Johnson, current director of libraries at TWU, along with members of her excellent staff, especially Shelia M. Bickel and Kristin Clark for their expertise and cooperation. Shelia's extraordinary efforts offered immeasurable support.

Every biographer joyfully thanks the friends and colleagues of their subjects. All "Claire people" welcomed me into their homes and inner circles with generous hospitality, sharing their personal memories; they have celebrated each phase of this rebirth of the amazing Claire. Because they are numerous, I thank them as a group: Dr. Kenneth Ring, John White, Audrey Fernandez, Dwain Wilder, Raul daSilva, Margaret Lee Braun, Geoffrey Lister, Larry McSpadden, and Dr. Jean Houston, as well as Linda and Ed Stewart.

I have enjoyed enthusiastic support over the years from colleagues, friends, and professors, especially Drs. Janet Freedman, Joan Weimer, Peggy Brown, Paula Joyce, and Larry Campbell, and my BFF, ever-loyal Linda Comess. Special thanks to Dr. Lynette Carpenter for the card graced by the photograph, *The West Wind, 1915*, by Anne Brigman and to Lauren Lean at the George Eastman Museum in Rochester, New York.

Professor Tim Redman and I have stayed in touch since he chaired my doctoral committee at University of Texas at Dallas. I salute him as scholar, mentor, and friend and honor him as a biographer who loves the process.

Among my cherished colleagues at Tarrant County College in Fort Worth, I thank Drs. Ruth McAdams and Pauline Griffith as well as Maureen Hockenberger and Carolyn Carney.

I thank Carol Hoffman, an expert reader and lifelong friend; Denise and Steve Estrin, Terry and Dr. Vikram Jayanty, and Harriet and Gary Hoffman for their continued interest and support. Dawon Washington told me Claire would see print in my lifetime; he was right!

My Mussar group—Marcia and Michael Nichols, Babs Rosenfeld, Heather Westendarp and Naomi Wittlin—provides enthusiastic support, as do my lifelong friends Dottie Unger, Judy Osborn, Ann Plantowsky, and Paula Pozmantier (among too many others to name.) Thanks to Jenna Blum for our discussion of independent women, like Claire and Blum's June Bouquet, who struggle against the "man trap" to balance their autonomy with their connections to the men in their lives.

My husband, Dr. Robert H. Friedman—my truly beloved Bobby—reentered my life in 2003. He has believed in this project and sustained and encouraged my efforts through all its ups and downs. His pride in my work reflects the bonds of our love.

My daughter, Pepi Harris Wucher, and son, Earl Kalman Harris, likely consider Claire a second mother; with no children of her own, she must have been their "Godsent Godmother," for her values and spirit influenced my insights as a mom, and now, as a grandmother. My wonderful family members include Pepi, James, Miles, and Eli Wucher; Earl, Debbie, Lindi, and Cooper Harris; Karen, Walt, and Eliana Friedman-Elliston; Lori and Zeke Perales; Kara, Levi, and Sam Newman; and my "bonus son," Ben Friedman, who found my reprint of Claire's novel, *The Unpredictable Adventure*, in Northwestern University's library, an amazing moment for me. To the entire Kalman/Rose, Harris/Rice/Polishuk, and Friedman/Borger/Grosman/Davis families: I celebrate us.

Working with Syracuse University Press has been an honor and delight. Alison Maura Shay, acquisitions editor, offered kind guidance and brilliant insights. Kelly L. Balenske has added pleasure to the energy of this process. Thanks as well to Suzanne Guiod, editor-in-chief, Lynn Wilcox, Mona Hamlin, Brendan Missett, and Kay Steinmetz. I also extend my gratitude to Alene Ross Levy and Karen Friedman for their assistance with proofreading and to Cathy Goddard for indexing.

And now, joyfully: Claire, the story she wrote with her life.

Rivers of Light

Introduction

The Wind

> It was the first of those strange beautiful frightening experiences which were to change my whole life eventually.
>
> —Claire Myers Owens, *Awakening to the Good*

I HOLD IN MY HAND a photograph of a woman dancing nude on a beach. Sunlight caresses the water with the same playfulness that her feet caress the sand. She is tall and slender, one foot poised as if ready to leap. The wind dances through the light veil she holds above her head, as if it will lift her, carry her out over the ocean, over the dark cliffs, into a shimmering heaven. The photograph, titled *The West Wind, 1915*, by Anne Brigman, graces a greeting card that sits on a shelf in my study.[1] Perhaps what attracts me to this picture is the way it echoes a particularly passionate moment in the life of Claire Myers Owens, a moment on a Long Island beach in 1930 with her second husband, George Wanders:

> Quickly I dropped my clothes to the ground, with every layer discarding layers of artificial civilization. It was the first time in my life I had gone swimming without a suit. . . .
>
> I ran along the firm edge of the sand laughing and dancing, my wet hair streaming out behind me. The sun pressed its fertile kiss emphatically on top of my head . . . as I danced, I sang at the top of my lungs. . . . Swinging my arms high, improvising the steps as I went, I danced faster and faster. . . . The brief occasional touch of

> my feet to the earth only accented the beat of the music. Surely I was dancing in rhythm with the moving waves, the recurrent sun, the seasonal earth, and the unknown universe—in harmony with all natural things.
>
> Then suddenly everything changed.
>
> For abruptly all sense of bodily motion ceased, all physical sensation, all conscious contact with the sand, for the earth itself no longer existed. Nor did the sky, or sun or sea nor love nor giving in marriage nor even husbands.
>
> I was alone in the universe with the universe.[2]

Themes and images in this passage resonate in Claire's writings and repeat throughout her life: the dance of ecstasy, the drive toward freedom, the fusion with nature, the mystical sense of universal oneness. But there was another Claire, exemplified in her portrait rendered in rich pastel colors—a woman in her early forties wearing a tailored gray suit, a pink silk blouse, and a hat of pink roses, caught in a dignified pose holding a book, seated beside a table stacked with two more, her chin thrust at a confident angle, her eyes intelligent, her smile enigmatic.[3]

Claire Myers Owens: writer, lecturer, adventurer, seeker of enlightenment, mystic, clairvoyant, and *grande amoureuse*. Her story lies between these two images—the nymph dancing on the beach and the lady—encompassing each, transcending both. Further ironies associated with the Brigman photograph, *The West Wind, 1915*, both in its title and in its date, expand our understanding of the complexity of and distance between the nymph and the lady.

In 1915, Clairene Myers was a nineteen year old attending the College of Industrial Arts (CIA), now Texas Woman's University (TWU), in Denton. There, the perfume exuded by the honey locust tree prompted the same realization of oneness with the natural world sparked by the sun and wind on the beach. A series of passages illuminating these events comprise her 1958 memoir, *Awakening to the Good—Psychological or Religious?* The chapter "Wind" captures the enormous power of her first remembered experience at age ten in her family garden, when a strong wind erupted out of a clear blue sky:

> Suddenly a bubbling spring of mysterious joy welled up inside me. I commenced to run, to race with the wind, against the wind, over the green grass, over the flowerbeds, between the madly swaying bushes. I flung my arms up. . . .
>
> Faster and faster I danced. For once I was free. Free to be my natural animal self. Free from my mother's daily don'ts. From the satin-lined prison of lady-like decorum. . . . Free from the admonishing voices of teachers. . . . *And from the sin I never felt.*
>
> Stung into a delicious frenzy, I flung myself with renewed vigor into this orgy. Never had I felt so ecstatically happy in my life! Why? I did not know. I did not care.
>
> Mind you a norther is not a storm. It is a freak of nature. A cold streak of wind. It does not rain. It blows. It cuts through a warm sunny day like a sharp knife through a ripe melon. It is incredibly sudden, brief and exciting. It is gone almost before it arrives. You never forget it—if you were ever ten in Texas [emphasis mine].[4]

Dancing herself into a frenzy, this modern young Sufi becomes one with the wind. But wind does not bring oneness; Claire herself does that. Each of her ecstasies allows her to discard "layers of artificial civilization" to break free of the "satin-lined prison of lady-like decorum . . . and from the sin [she] never felt." And here we witness a glaring paradox: the nymph is free, the lady, restricted. Yet in the world of Claire's birth, the world of the Bible Belt South at the turn of the century, sexuality and intellectuality are both forbidden to women; they are not seen as polarities. The only role open to a woman is that of lady in a culture where *lady* means "belle" and where *female* means "feminine"—the opposite of both the intellectual achievement the portrait implies and the freedom to dance naked on a windswept beach.

The image of the wind in these passages becomes a metaphor for the way Claire Myers Owens used the turbulence in her life as both stimulus and obstacle in her psychological journey toward self-discovery and wholeness. For Claire, wholeness became a matter of balancing the sensual with the intellectual, the nymph with the lady to discover the woman. These moments, the events she called "small ecstasies," are harbingers of a life filled with mystical insights that would climax in her spontaneous Great Awakening in 1949, an event that significantly altered her life course along with the focus and genre of her writing. Whereas she began her career writing short stories, novels, book reviews, and magazine columns about her life as a woman, she ended it writing memoirs and scholarly explorations of her ecstatic experiences and her life as a "sentient being" in search of what she called "the good." In retrospect, everything she wrote was autobiographical, in tandem with her effort to provide a scientific explanation for mystical phenomena, to articulate the ineffable. In her work, as in her life, she sought resolution through mediating within the tension of opposites.

Her description of the norther in the passage above is distinctive of her southern roots—a Texan by birth, a northeasterner by choice—that informed her worldview and that functioned as both stimulus and obstacle to the adventure that makes Claire Myers Owens's life unique. To understand Owens and to appreciate her as the protagonist of her life, who transformed ordinary circumstances into an extraordinary adventure, one must understand the significance of the underlying dichotomies that shape the nature of her struggle. The struggle is built on a paradox, rooted in the Texas soil of her southern heritage.[5]

In the years after the Civil War, the lives and roles of white, middle-class, privileged women changed in significant ways. The paradoxical image of woman as submissive, beautiful, charming, modest, and innocent, while remaining a strong, dependable, wife, mother, and domestic manager, haunted the women of Owens's generation as much as it did that of her mother's and grandmother's.

Consistent with so-called pedestal values, this culturally defined image of a white "lady," particularly in the South, coalesced to create a creature who, lacking the capacity for rational thought, developed a highly efficient intuition, which allowed her to be a competent homemaker—wife and mother. "Part of [the southern lady's] charm lay in her innocence. The less a woman knew of life, Ellen Glasgow once remarked bitterly, the better she was supposed to be able to deal with it."[6] A lady was expected to inhabit the private domain and leave "important" matters in the public domain to the men. Naturally, we cannot assume that "being a southern woman meant the same thing to all or even most women."[7] Specifically, Claire's maternal influences and paternal values clearly placed the roots of her childhood in the deep southern mores that accepted "ladylike decorum" as an ideal, and white as the default race. All other races, which in Texas at the turn of the century would have mainly included black and Hispanic people, were defined as "other." Whiteness and privilege were invisible norms to families in young Clairene's middle-class social circles. As a white female, living in the segregated state of Texas, Claire enjoyed privilege, though she would not have realized it. Claire would have seen herself as the norm, conditioned to see herself as white and therefore separate from the "other." Claire would have unconsciously believed, as Debby Irving puts it, "white was the raceless race—just plain, normal, the one against which all others were measured."[8]

Nevertheless, privilege imposed social and familial expectations Claire experienced as limitations. As Roxane Gay points out, "accusations of privilege imply we have it easy."[9] But Claire's intellectual curiosity to explore the world outside her small Texas town set her apart from her peers and created friction between her and her family—friction that informs her life, her loves, and the impetus for her adventures, both spiritual and emotional.

Biography and the Biographer

When Penelope Niven, biographer of Carl Sandburg, James Earl Jones, and Edward Steichen, speaks of "coming to biography" she refers to a process common to the field. Most biographers report an initial moment of discovering their subject as one that defies logic and thrusts them into an unfamiliar and sacred realm. Niven quotes Sandburg's comment to Amy Lowell regarding his biography of Lincoln and hers of Keats: "Ain't it hell the way a book walks up . . . and makes you write it?—Don't you feel almost predestinarian?"[10]

My own "predestinarian" story begins in 1988, with a portrait—the painting described above that hung in Elizabeth Snapp's office at Texas Woman's University. Snapp, who as director of the Blagg-Huey

Library helped develop their extensive Woman's Collection and archival holdings, agreed to assist me in my search for a "lost woman writer" I could rediscover. My model was Elaine R. Hedges's famous reprint of Charlotte Perkins Gilman's *The Yellow Wallpaper.* Snapp began pointing out some of the interesting women whose papers are held in the archives. But my eyes kept focusing on the wall above her head.

The presence of the woman in the portrait, painted by Minnie Smith in the 1940s, cast a spell over me the moment I walked into the room. "Claire Myers Owens," Snapp volunteered, noticing my distraction. "She graduated from here in 1916 with a degree in domestic science and left Texas to do social work. She worked at a coalmine in Alabama for a short stint, then started a cooperative community in the Blue Ridge Mountains of Virginia. Ultimately she settled in the Northeast—New York City, New Haven, Rochester—where she wrote books and reviews, studied transpersonal psychology, and took up Zen Buddhism at age seventy-three."

"Books? What kind of books?" I asked, my eyes locked with Claire's.

"Oh, three or four autobiographies and a fantasy novel banned by the New York Public Library."

Banned? My heart skipped a beat. Banned books are written by "bad" women. Feminist researchers *love* "bad" women. Without even searching, I had found my subject! "Could I see her work—read her books?"

Elizabeth Snapp's answer discouraged me. The Owens papers were closed because only eleven boxes had been catalogued. The bulk of the papers, photos, manuscripts, audio and visual cassettes, and other memorabilia still sat in the huge packing boxes in which they had arrived four years earlier. Snapp, who had been the driving force behind the collection of Owens's papers, tried to interest me in other collections, but I listened with only half an ear. I was mesmerized by that painting, which followed me home that day and haunted my dreams that night. What seduced me? The skill of the artist—the soft, lovely mauves, greens, and purples? The power of the subject—her dignity tempered by stunning beauty? Who was this woman? What secrets lay behind that enigmatic smile, that insolent tilt of the chin?

The next morning, as if not of my own volition, I called Elizabeth Snapp to ask again if I might just browse through the available documents and read that banned book. This time she said yes. Years later, Snapp, who had communicated with Claire at the end of her life and had collected the papers from her Rochester apartment after her death, told me she believes Claire influenced her change of heart. Today we both accept that Claire Myers Owens chose me to write her life the moment I walked into Snapp's office.[11]

That moment marks the call to adventure, which transformed my life as a southern woman, my heritage as a Jew, my roles as mother, wife, daughter, sibling, and friend, and my consciousness of my unconscious. Equally important to writer and scholar, that moment informs my methodology—a system that merges intellectual pursuit with intuition. The experience of bonding with my subject, measured against research into the complex themes of her writing and the cultural and historical milieu from which they arise, comprises the thin line I learned to walk between objectivity and subjectivity. This bond exemplifies Ray Monk's argument that biography as a project comprises moments of "understanding that consist of seeing connections" both within the subject's life and between the subject and the biographer.[12] Ultimately, my journey parallels my subject's journey; the themes of our lives intersect.

Biography is a personal art. Objectivity and subjectivity wrestle for front-row seats at its performance. In the last thirty years, feminist scholars have deemed valid their personal attachment to subjects, often present from the beginning and intensifying as their projects proceed, challenging the "illusion of objectivity."[13] This merging of souls and mirroring of quests creates what Liz Stanley calls a "living relationship" that starts out "complex and becomes more . . . complex over time." The feminist approach, proscribed by traditional scholars, "suggests that writing a woman's life requires an active, not a neutral, voice from the biographer."[14]

Ultimately, as Carol Kolmerten puts it, "we all want to hear about the lives of 'real' people, their obstacles and how they overcame them."[15] Some of these real people, like Claire Myers Owens, were not famous in their own time, but their lives provide patterns of development that reveal the paradox of heroic moments in ordinary life choices. Feminists do not assume Owens, or other biographical subjects, must meet arbitrary definitions of appropriate behavior or measure up to standards outside their milieu to be considered among the "women worthies."[16]

My philosophical approach to Owens's life embraces that expressed by Linda Wagner-Martin: "One of the most difficult problems facing the biographer of women is to make what may be only moderate achievement as important to the reader as it was to the subject."[17] Periodically, I would ask myself, what is moderate achievement for women? How do we define a female heroic? How do we designate "women worthiness," or might we stretch and redefine the boundaries of "exceptional" achievement?[18] How do we consider these values in the context of my subject's life span? This biography explores and illuminates these questions.

During the first several years after my discovery and ensuing investigation of Owens's papers, I published journal articles, a chapter in an anthology, an entry in *The New Texas Handbook*, and presented numerous conference papers, with a goal to republish Owens's 1935 novel, *The Unpredictable Adventure*,[19] a utopian fiction, which Carol Farley Kessler considers "the most significant of the nine utopias published by US women during the 1930s."[20] When Syracuse University Press republished the book in 1993, with my preface, afterword, and glossary translating her ingenious anagrams, I thought I was done with Claire Myers Owens. I was wrong, for she was not done with me, and through a series of twists and turns of fate—synchronicities—I decided to write her full biography.

Thus, discovering Claire became my own "unpredictable adventure." I have come to appreciate Liz Stanley's metaphor of biography as a "process of reverse archeology": "The accumulation of layers of knowledge and complexity" rather than the stripping away of debris to reveal the "real" person beneath.[21] The deeper I dug, the more complicated Owens seemed and the more baffling our relationship became. Rather than unveiling her life, she continually fluttered beyond my grasp by, paradoxically, expanding my horizons. Validated by acceptance of the feminist conundrum of the "inter-twining of biographer and subject," I allowed her life to expand my own.[22]

Together still, we glide, spiraling toward richer and broader interpretations of what some might call reality but which Owens called the cosmos, or Ultimate Reality, or Universal Mind. However, this aspect of my journey became complicated by my own biases; I was highly skeptical about my belief in a higher power or God and frequently embarrassed by her passionate search for spiritual meaning. Her association with the "weird" branches of psychology and her final embrace of Zen Buddhism terrified me—what was I taking on? How would I be perceived as a scholar? Who would take me seriously? In the end, I laid my doubts aside and simply studied the material, allowing my discovery of Claire to put me in touch with my own spirituality.

The Project of Claire Myers Owens

The question remains: why Claire Myers Owens? What makes her ordinary life extraordinary? How do I justify recovering her work, retelling her stories, writing her life? From the beginning, what struck me about the young Clairene Myers was her courage to leave Texas in search of her self, though she repeatedly claimed she had no idea what that meant. Groomed to become a privileged southern belle by her mother and grandmother—fundamentalist Baptists who defined themselves by their connections to the antebellum South and a fabled aristocracy—at age twenty she sought freedom, certitude, and self-definition in a wider, less restricted world. I wanted to understand how she knew what she knew and place her in the historical context of her generation, both within the southern culture from whence she came and in the northeastern culture she joined. As it turned out, my goals were part of the feminist impulse to celebrate that "rare woman" who, to paraphrase Carolyn Heilbrun, recognizes in herself a special gift without definition and writes herself a life beyond convention, thus avoiding a "blunted female destiny." In most cases, such women's choices are motivated by their "dissatisfaction . . . with appropriate gender assignments." Claire's struggles with gender roles and patriarchal codes comprise the predominant theme of her fiction and life choices during the first half of her life, a struggle Heilbrun defines as the pattern of the "unwomanly woman" who lives "the quest plot men are expected to live."[23] For Clairene, there were no established patterns of female autonomy, no women on whom to model her drive toward independence. She had to catapult herself into a wider world she knew only from books and write herself into a new identity.

As our "living relationship" continues, my notion of Claire has evolved to embrace not only her significant contributions as a feminist writer, which attracted me from the beginning, but also her calling as a mystic and spiritual guide, which I found so disconcerting at first. In telling a life, we extend our lives into our subjects' lives as they extend their lives into ours.

Other biographers experience similar connections. All of her life, historian Emily Bingham heard her great aunt Henrietta Bingham (1891–1968) described by family alternately as a "magical physical presence with a muse-like influence," and as a "mess and embarrassment, a 'three-dollar bill,' . . . fascinating but dangerous." When Emily found a trunk full of Henrietta's papers and memorabilia forgotten in the attic of her familial home, her curiosity evolved into a need to redefine her aunt as a real woman, rather than an enigmatic subject of family lore. Emily describes the biography she wrote as "emphatically a work of non-fiction," which readers may finish with a sense having glimpsed a life from "the end of the street" while being unable to completely overtake it. "True history," she explains, "true life is often that way." And yet, as with my relationship to Claire Myers Owens, pinning down a life, discovering its truth, may be as illusive as a dream but as valuable as a crown of rare jewels. Enigmatic women may defy concrete definitions, but their presence in our lives is surely transformative.[24]

During the first half of her life, Claire was a woman of many names and in her New York years, she used all of them. She was born Clairene Lenore Allen Myers, and her given name, Clairene, stuck until she was well into her thirties, when she began to call herself Claire, the name she used on publications. Each time she married, she incorporated her husband's name when she published. Furthermore, early in the 1930s when she started submitting novels, she adopted the name Claire Myers Spotswood, exploiting her connections to the eighteenth-century governor of Virginia, Alexander Spotswood—whose roots connect her to Martha Washington—even though her books rebelled against exploiting such lineage. In several documents of that period, her name appears in multiple variations. She even adopted the male pseudonym, Clarence Myers.

As a feminist, I cringe at the thought of referring to her as Owens in discussions directed at periods or accomplishments that occurred before her marriage to H. Thurston Owens in 1937. Indeed, it was not until 1958, with the publication of her first memoir at age sixty-two that she became professionally and permanently identified as Claire Myers Owens. Therefore, I call her Clairene during her early years, Claire during her middle years, and Owens only when describing periods when that was her name or when referring to the Claire Myers Owens Collection in the Texas Woman's University archive. I refer to her both as Claire and as Owens during this period, designating Owens as her professional persona and Claire as her authentic personal self.

Organization and Method

This biography addresses Claire Myers Owens's life, beginning with her southern ancestors and parents and her childhood in Temple, Texas. Her departure from Texas in 1916 marks her defining moment as a New Woman and adventurer, capturing the early struggles of a young woman "educated enough to have had a choice and brave enough to have made one."[25] Although Owens never identified as a feminist, *The Unpredictable Adventure: A Comedy of Woman's Independence*—modeled after James Branch Cabell's Jurgen series but with a feminist heroine—along with several unpublished novels and an assortment of short stories, reveals her struggle to define herself as a "thinking woman" without sacrificing her feminine charms or sexuality.

Her Great Awakening at age fifty-four initiated a dramatic shift in Owens's lifestyle, goals, and interests and spawned two autobiographies illuminating her search for "the good" inherent in the human spirit: *Awakening to the Good* (1958} and *Discovery of the Self* (1963). Her life as a spiritual journey shifted at age seventy-three, when Owens, recently widowed, took up Zen Buddhism with a group of Yale University graduates, members of the 1970s counterculture, and moved from New Haven to Rochester. *Zen and the Lady* (1979) captures her connection to Zen. Friends and colleagues claim she developed extraordinary capacities of clairvoyance and extrasensory perception as a result of her meditative practice.

Owens's life story provides a model of a self-defined woman whose spirit of adventure remained as courageous and passionate in old age as it had been in her youth. Because Owens's fiction and nonfiction are predominantly autobiographical, I struggle to separate fiction from fact in both genres. Sometimes the characters and events presented in real life seem fictional, and the fictional ones seem real, and indeed, are real—thinly disguised men and women, places and events, which shaped her life and stimulated her observations. Owens wrote to piece her own life together, to create understanding. Her autobiographies and fictions are "autographic" to use Jeanne Perreault's term.[26] As Owens writes, she creates a new self; she connects to the past in order to understand her present and to transform it into ballast for future adventures. Her writing is transformative in the true sense of the word: she becomes the person in her stories, and the person she creates becomes the real Claire Myers Owens.

Throughout this biography, I refer to a 1979 interview Claire Myers Owens did with Professor Kenneth Ring, a leader in the transpersonal psychology movement during the 1970s and 1980s, and into the present. The interview informs my insights and understandings of Claire's journey into the vast arena that has become the modern human-potential movement, now often conflated with what has come to be known as New Age.

Dr. Ring's interview, along with his subsequent willingness to teach and guide my insights, helped me weave the loose threads of Claire's journey into a chronological tapestry, to bring Owens's perceptions to my interpretation of her early years, and to verify Owens's technique of infusing her fictions with real life events. To paraphrase Anais Nin, her life is indeed her art, and her art her life.

1. *The West Wind, 1915*, by Anne Brigman. Digital positive from the original gelatin silver negative in the George Eastman Museum's collection. Courtesy of George Eastman Museum.

Thus, I confront a final conundrum: all biographers and autobiographers create fictions through which, according to Carol Kolmerten, we search for "facts, insights, illuminated moments that will suddenly reveal to readers the 'truth.'"[27] Our own, individual truths, that is. Ultimately, I write in hopes that this new narrative will find its way into the hearts and minds of those in search of stories to live by, stories that invite new patterns of living, that inform creative choices, and contribute, in Claire Myers Owens's honor, to a discovery of "the good" within the human spirit.

1

Smug Harbor

1896–1912

> Smug Harbor, a large and prosperous seaport on the south coast of Err [where] the fog rolled in from the Dead Sea in such thick white clouds that it was impossible to see anything clearly.
>
> —Claire Myers Spotswood, *The Unpredictable Adventure*

"I WAS BORN IN THE DEEP SOUTH, in the heart of Texas. Most people think of Texas as a western state full of cowboys and large ranches. But that's the western part of the state. I never saw a live cowboy in my life." Claire Myers Owens's voice bounces with youthful vibrancy as she speaks during a 1979 taped interview with Professor Kenneth Ring in her home after the release of her last published book, *Zen and the Lady.* Central Texas at the turn of the twentieth century was known as the Black Belt, in reference to its rich soil good for growing cotton. "Half our town was black," she adds, acknowledging the double meaning of the word, especially in that part of the country. "But our whole town was submerged in old southern traditions."[1]

Born in Rockdale, Texas, on February 11, 1896, Clairene Lenore Allen Myers grew up in nearby Temple. Neither place was much of a town. Cotton farms prevailed; streets were unpaved, muddy, and residents were imbued with a provincial southern mentality. Claire's maternal grandmother, Laura Elizabeth Smith Allen, considered herself an "exile of Virginia," though she was born in Tennessee and reared in Harris County, Texas. Claire's mother, Susan Allen Myers, shared her own mother's goal: to ensure that Clairene would grow up to be a proper southern belle—a lady. Together they tried to inculcate in her "not just the ways of a southern aristocracy—but southern values in the days before emancipation, the days of the antebellum South."[2]

The family Bible records the date of Susan Allen's marriage to Coren Lee Myers as June 30, 1893, in Fort Worth, Texas. Coren was twenty-nine, and Susie was twenty-four, typical ages for marriage at the turn of the twentieth century. Susie taught first grade before her marriage. Professor C. L. Myers, as he was called, taught in a one-room structure from 1881 until 1885, when he became principal of Troy High School, a position he held until 1890.[3] Their first child, Coren Douglas, his "mother's favorite," was born in 1894, a year after the Myerses' marriage, and two years later, Clairene Lenore was born. There were no other children and no other pregnancies recorded, though years later Susan would write her daughter that she "knew nothing scientifically about birth control."[4]

Clairene's father, the dominant force in the family, influenced her spirit of ambition and adventure. So fierce was his intellect, so stanch his strong but gentle attitude, her father held the family in his "iron hand with a velvet glove." A "born teacher," Myers eventually left education and went into business to provide a more affluent lifestyle for his family. "He would say honor, honesty, and justice were the most important things in the world."[5] For southerners like Mr. Myers, honor defines the link between society and the individual.[6]

Inherent in the concept of honor lies a sense of noblesse oblige, which separates gentlemen from those considered members of an inferior class.[7] Generous by nature, Myers learned to count on his wife's keen ability to judge people's character. When he loaned money he trusted everybody, "sometimes to his sorrow." Often, he would bring the borrower home to let his more skeptical wife pass judgment: "She could see through people like a pane of dirty glass."[8]

Susan was also involved in civic work, and a group of men once offered to nominate her for governor. "My father wouldn't have that at all," Claire would say. Susan demurred in respect to her husband's wishes for she was "exceedingly conventional."[9]

For southern women, such self-suppression was part of the norm. Though placed on a pedestal, women were expected to bow to the decisions the men in their lives made on their behalf. Men considered endearing women's ability to suffer in silence. As Bertram Wyatt-Brown put it, "Men were not would-be patriarchs. They were the real thing."[10]

Throughout her life, Claire loved telling stories of her mother's ingenuity. One story reveals the underlying paradox that sustains contradictory southern values. "My mother liked to cook and was an expert." But at that time, in that culture, it was considered demeaning for a "lady to do her own work." Ladies left the cooking to their black servants. But Susan Myers was enterprising: "She formed a gourmet club and [the members] cooked all sorts of Cordon Bleu dishes."[11]

On March 6, 1914, Susan Myers organized the Housekeepers Club, inviting "24 Temple women to come to her home at 3 p.m." The club's mission, "the social enjoyment and mutual improvement of its members," apparently included creating unusual menus and serving monthly dinners. Susan was elected the first president, serving in that capacity for eleven years. In 1915, they sponsored a similar club for younger women, the Domestic Science Club.[12]

Through her civic leadership, Susan Myers influenced Temple. As president of the Women's Civil League, in 1915, she issued an unfavorable report following "a sanitary survey of the city," which stated that "unless remedial measures are adopted, there is a danger of much unnecessary illness and probably deaths this winter."[13]

Thus, although a "democratic," civic-minded woman, Susan adhered to the old southern traditions. Friendly toward those who shared her belief system, she was intolerant of those with different values. Once a ball was given by a banker, the "richest man in town—the only one with a ballroom in his house." Clairene wanted to attend, but her mother would not allow it: Susan "saw his wife picking cotton in a field *barefooted*"—a disgrace according to the rigid social standards of their times with its class distinctions and codes for proper female behavior.[14]

An immaculate housekeeper, Susan Myers rarely lifted a finger to do any of the actual work, employing black servants whom she managed with aloof kindness and proficiency. If her attitude seems inconsistent with her identity as an ethical person, it should be noted that her values, rooted in both southern and Baptist traditions, fully supported the prevailing racist views of southern whites. As Rufus Spain points out, "The Baptist view of race was the Southern view.[15] Susan Myers was a strong influence on Claire's life; she wanted her to be a lady above everything else.

As an adult, Claire had to discard many contradictory ideas by recognizing their limitations and defining a place for herself in the modern world. Yet, ironically, the title *Zen and the Lady*, which she published in her eighties, reflects the way old southern values haunted her throughout her life.

Indeed, the influence of both parents on Claire is inestimable. As a businessman with real estate holdings, her father, known for his fairness, had a steady stream of tenants coming to the house for advice on their own legal and business matters. Claire's pride in Myers's ethical standards and outrage at southern injustice shines through in memoirs and interviews during her later years: "If a black man had a case against a white man," Claire would paraphrase her father, "it was lost before it began, merely because he was black." Holding such values in the early 1900s distinguished Myers from his milieu, leading Claire to see him as advanced for his time.[16] In the turn-of-the-twentieth-century South, for Myers "to stand for equal rights and protection under the law for all citizens was not liberal or conservative, but 'radical.'"[17]

Bertram Wyatt-Brown explains the South's paradoxical embrace of slavery and of a code of honor by pointing out that honor came first; slavery was instituted to perpetuate the South and its values. Slavery became interconnected with power and prestige, with ownership of slaves as proof of a man's worth.[18]

In this post–civil rights era, people "tend to think that segregation was maintained by virulent racists. . . . Therein lies the danger. . . . Human goodness can coexist alongside great evil."[19] In truth, the

Myerses would not have seen segregation as evil or even inhumane, though Claire struggled to make sense of it far into her adult years.

In her autobiographical, unpublished novel "Amanda Mann," written in the 1970s and 1980s, Amanda, a surrogate for young Clairene, asks her grandmother if she had approved of slavery. The grandmother answers: "Certainly not. No good Southerner did, but we were caught up in the system."[20]

Susan Myers was the product of Old South values, romanticized through the memories of her mother, Laura Elizabeth Smith Allen. Born June 16, 1845, in the Milam District of Texas, Laura moved at age seven with her family and their slaves to a farm in Harris County, Texas. Laura was proud of her lineage and her Virginia roots. Her mother, Charlotte Mary Payne, Claire's great-grandmother, claimed to be a descendant of Martha Washington and of Alexander Spotswood, who became the first governor of Virginia in 1710.

As an adult, Claire spent many hours collecting genealogical information documenting her roots. Complex and convoluted, her findings are difficult to follow, but are corroborated for the most part by Claire's cousin Mary Roper. "Great-grandmother Charlotte Payne was sister to Mary Roper's mother," Claire wrote in a journal. "My great-great-grandmother and great-great-grandfather [are] Catherine Dandridge and Dr. Nathan Payne. We are related to Martha Washington . . . a daughter of John Dandridge. Catherine Dandridge was either a niece or cousin of John D. My great-grandmother, Charlotte Mary Payne [Laura's mother] had a sister named Dorothia (ea) [*sic*] Spotswood Dandridge Payne. Thus great-great-grandmother Catherine Dandridge is second cousin to Martha Washington."[21]

Fact or legend, the story informed the family's self-definition as aristocracy, with connections to English nobility and to Martha Washington.

On June 4, 1866, Laura Smith married B. F. Allen, a man whose lineage seemed to measure up to Laura's expectations. In 1874, they moved to Rockdale. They had three children, Robert, Laura Lee, and Susan, born November 13, 1869. In "Amanda Mann," the grandmother, modeled on Laura, wore long dresses and nineteenth-century style throughout her life.[22]

In 1880, when Susie was eleven, Laura became a Baptist when she converted at a tent revival amid the usual frenzy of devotion marked by shouted vows and bursts of song. Perhaps Laura's attraction to religion reflected her yearning for excitement and her nostalgia for the glory of Old Southern traditions missing from rural Texas. Perhaps her firm connections to her Virginia heritage and her commitment to the church arose out of the need to fill a social gap. In many ways, Claire's passionate approach to life and her hunger for excitement linked her to Grandmother Allen. Unfortunately, the passions that bound them together were the very same qualities that would ultimately create the chasm that pulled them apart.

In "Amanda Mann," Claire describes Amanda's grandfather as a "tall slender man with the delicate, sensitive face of a poet, not a farmer." This semifictional grandfather taught her that "good breeding will enable you to meet emergencies, that it was one of the marks of an aristocrat." In the story, when Amanda asks her grandmother why Grandfather looked so sad, she answers, "He never recovered from Lee's surrender; the whole war just seemed to break his heart forever." The war story that most impressed his granddaughter purported that "he never killed a man and that once he gave a drink of water from his canteen to a Yankee soldier."[23]

This intimate, autobiographical portrait reveals that young Clairene felt the same kinds of oppression from her grandmother as she did from her mother. Claire often complained that neither her mother nor her grandmother ever kissed or hugged her. Only her Mammy—the black woman who fed and bathed Clairene and her older brother, Coren—openly expressed affection for the children.

Coren Lee Myers's roots were as deeply embedded in southern soil as his wife's; his lineage tied him to Virginian ancestors, "professional people, lawyers and doctors, teachers and preachers."[24] Born in Tennessee on September 23, 1864, Myers arrived in Texas in 1880, to apply for jobs as a high school teacher. In 1889, in commemoration of her son's twenty-fifth birthday, his mother sent a poem signed "Emma S." in tribute to Coren Lee, "a youth to noble manhood grown," who roams in distant lands "amid the world's great busy throng."[25]

To his mother, Myers's leaving Tennessee and settling in Texas was as fearful a journey into the unknown as Clairene's would be to her parents a generation later. And yet Emma Myers's poem reveals a celebration of her son's courage, something Clairene never received from her parents when she left on her own journey into the "world's busy throngs."

The mutual love and respect the Myerses felt for one another surfaces in multiple letters they exchanged during Myers's travels in the early years of their marriage and Clairene's childhood. In 1899, he traveled to Salado for a summer teaching seminar and wrote: "Dear Sweetheart, How I miss my sweetheart and my nice little man and sweet little Clairine [*sic*]. Kiss each one of them for me . . . and say, Oh how I do love them!"[26]

Each letter details his activities. In one, he enclosed a "M. O. for $5.00"; in another he wished "the children were here to ride on my back." This kind of family environment usually fosters security and self-confidence in children, a sense of true belonging and strength in identity. Nevertheless, puzzling as it seems, Clairene sensed herself an outsider almost from the beginning of her life, perhaps in reaction to the contradictory structure of the cultural and familial beliefs her bright intelligence detected at an early age. Her sensitivity to the conflicting ethical values endorsed by her parents, her keen awareness of the hypocrisy, set up a series of personal and public contradictions it would take a lifetime to understand and to resolve.

Remarkable in the nature of Claire Myers Owens's quest for resolution of the paradoxes that haunted her throughout life are her early calculations of the distance she will travel—to rebel against her heritage—even as she strives to honor the sense of moral integrity it instilled within her.

An 1899 letter from Clairene's grandmother Laura Allen to her daughter Susan—then living about sixty miles north of Rockdale in Troy—regarding their mutual concern for three-year-old Clairene during an illness, reveals the bonds of love and care established early in her life. Laura longs to be two places at once, to come to Clairene's aid, while honoring her husband's feelings that "this time [she] should stay home." Of course, in the Allens and the Myerses' world, women did as their husbands told them; it was part of the "natural" order even when there was disorder. Still, Laura executed her duty as matriarch, sending Susan explicit instructions of care: "Attend closely to bathing her & watch for soreness in her bowels the right side especially, use Lard & Turpentine to rub the bowels. Keep up her strength if possible. It will require all of your time . . . you must not neglect yourself or you will get down."[27]

Laura signs off, "Your anxious Mother." Papa scrawls "a few words" on a torn piece of lined tablet addressed to Miss Myers: "Dear Sweet Clairene, I would like to see your beautiful dollie. Has it hair? . . . Be sweet Little Lady & take your medicine just as the Dr. says to. Grand Pa & Gma loves you."

The words of endearment expressed by Clairene's grandfather, B. F. Allen, appropriate at age three, echo in future letters from beaux, fiancés, and husbands, who often addressed her in a similar affectionate, but diminutive manner: "My Own Little Lady"; "Little Girl"; "Little Loreli"; "Little Claire de Lune"; "Little Moonbeam." But Claire was anything but little. A photograph taken on the porch of a frame house in Cameron, Texas, in the early 1900s, shows Clairene only an inch or so shorter than her brother, Coren.

Though Clairene was tall and slender during her adolescence and young adulthood, photographs reveal a round, cherubic face highlighted by deep, mischievous dimples, which held the promise of sensuality tempered with wit. Her personality matched her looks. Gregarious and outgoing, she had a large presence; she made a deep impression, the epitome of southern beauty and charm.[28]

Within the context of the southern tradition, perhaps such pet names are the norm. Nevertheless, these diminutives had an effect on Clairene's childhood psyche with repercussions in adulthood—a stigma for a girl whose goal is to become an intellectual woman, a writer, and an adventurer.

2. Coren Douglas Myers and Clairene Lenora Allen Myers in Cameron, Texas, early 1900s. Photograph courtesy of the TWU Woman's Collection.

Coren Lee Myers was fond of telling his daughter that she was born in the shape of a question mark and, Claire claims, he "could answer any question." Though most men would not discuss ideas with a female, Clairene and her father shared many conversations on such topics as Jeffersonian democracy, justice, freedom, and religion. He was her mentor, teacher, advisor, and role model. His questioning of religion inadvertently taught Clairene to doubt the validity of the fundamentalism her mother and grandmother followed. Yet, their relationship demonstrated Myers's paradoxical attitude toward women. As a southern gentleman, he held the chauvinistic belief that only "one in ten thousand women has a mind." As evinced in his relationship with his wife, he believed in separate spheres for men and women. And yet, he responded to his daughter's curiosity, allowing her to become his protégée in matters of deep philosophical questioning.[29]

Claire considered him religious, in a "genuine sense": "He stopped going to church and he took to the woods" to her mother's and

3. Susan Allen Myers and Coren Lee Myers, Claire's parents. Photograph courtesy of the TWU Woman's Collection.

grandmother's dismay, for they were both "ardent Baptists—even fundamentalists." He called the woods his cathedral and he would "literally tramp through them; he knew every spring, lake, and river." Throughout her life, Claire cherished their "very beautiful relationship."[30]

In the summer of 1912, her sixteenth year, Clairene wrote in her diaries of afternoons spent with her father: "Papa and I went fishing out to the river. I waded and fished, drank out of cold springs . . . had a good time."[31] Other entries record times when her friend Robbie McKnight accompanied them, and Mr. Myers taught the girls to row.

On August 29, she described a family trip from Temple to Rockdale to visit her maternal grandparents, during which "we discovered both our back tires were punctured. These we fixed with much pumping from all of us. We were just getting ready to move on again when we heard something like a cat spitting . . . and again our tire was down. Papa borrowed a horse."[32] The Myers family slept in a motel and continued the next day. The fact that the Myerses owned a car during the early part of the century, when most people still traveled by horse and carriage, testifies to their elite financial position. The fifty-mile journey, which takes less than an hour to drive today, would have taken much longer at the time, even without car trouble. In 1906, concrete and gravel began to replace dirt streets within the town limits, but most city streets and highways were unpaved dirt roads. During the wet seasons the "bottomless mud streets held prisoner many wagons and buggies sometimes for months. . . . In derision some called the city 'Mud.'"[33]

Years later, Claire would speculate that, in the Freudian sense, her love for her father affected her life and her relationship with her mother, making her reluctant to marry. "The daughter can be a rival to the wife; that's what happened in my family and that's why my mother never loved me."[34]

Thus, looking back on her childhood, Claire notes that her father's teachings of Jeffersonian principles—freedom and democracy for all—collided with her mother's and her maternal grandmother's belief in the "caste system of the aristocracy." Both women believed "breeding and family lineage were the most important things in the world—not so much money as systems."[35]

At eighty-three, Claire Myers Owens could appreciate what her parents and grandmother were trying to teach her. But in her youth, she rebelled against all of their values and ran away. Both consciously and unconsciously, she struggled with the underlying paradox of their southern manners, decorum, and the strong sense of who you are and where you came from that informed their priorities. It took Claire eighty years to reconcile these three very distinct influences. During her years immediately after college, as a rebel she left Temple, Texas—her Smug Harbor, as she later called it—to seek her destiny in a wider world. During her middle years, she embraced the upper-class lifestyle through her marriage to her third husband, H. Thurston Owens, and then satirized domesticity in a novel. Her last published book reflected her attempts to modify the Zen life she adopted in her seventies to suit her individual perceptions of spirituality.

Essentially, her father influenced her in ways that are most apparent in her life choices. The two matriarchal influences became those tendencies she most wanted to transcend and fueled her drive toward a future free of authoritative restrictions; the patriarchal influence became the one she most wanted to emulate. Clairene spent much of her youth and early adulthood torn between her need to express herself as an intellectual and satisfy her hunger for knowledge and adventure, and her need to please these two matriarchs and affirm the connections among the three women.

2

A Bundle of Contradictions

1909–1913

> I want to be on the stage and be a renouned [*sic*] actress . . . I wouldn't mind being an authoress either and I expect to write a book someday. I dreaded to write this diary at first but now I hate to stop.
>
> —Clairene Myers, diary

BY EARLY ADOLESCENCE, Clairene's intellectual curiosity had merged with her mischievous spirit. At fifteen, she and her like-minded friend Robbie McKnight sent their handprints to Catherine Cooke, an editor and "palmist" at the *Ladies' Home Journal.* According to Ms. Cooke, Claire's "near-square" handprint revealed her to be "a bundle of contradictions, independent yet exhibiting moments of utter embarrassment." In retrospect, Cooke's assessment becomes an eerie prophecy: "You have a remarkable gift of words—I should think that you would not only be a delightful conversationalist, but that you might write, and write very cleverly too. . . . You are a believer in self-help. You are interested in all the new movements of the day. You have a strong bent towards the occult sciences—you would read hands very cleverly if you mastered signs."[1]

Claire's lifelong attraction to the occult began with her early moments of ecstatic union with nature, climaxed with a Great Awakening at age fifty-four, and evolved into an interest in psychology and ultimately Zen at the end of her life. An enthusiastic conversationalist,

Claire was surrounded by friends and lovers in her youth, and colleagues-become-friends encircled her in adulthood. Her autobiographies, though not traditional self-help books, were written to help others attain spiritual insights.

Cooke further described Clairene as "an ardent and lovable partisan, [with a] strong and positive will." Indeed, Claire appeared strong and positive, willful and stubborn throughout her life; from her earliest years, she had the capacity to dedicate herself to movements and projects in which she believed. Usually art-centered, women-centered, or concerned with the latest theories in psychological discovery, her personal interests and writings seem to define the concept of "serious fun." And as Cooke prophesized, she was "always on the go, out for a good time . . . a little capricious in affairs in the heart, yet flirtation after flirtation is recorded in your palm."

Flirtatious. Intellectual. Willful. Serious. Capricious. Contradictory. As literary editor of the Temple High School yearbook for 1913, Clairene coauthored her own "class prophecy." Narrated as a conversation between herself and a former schoolmate, the opening paragraphs introduce themes of women's rights and suffrage:

> "After all, Clairene, when we view our life-time of utter devotion to the cause in the light of this advanced age, we can find . . . no tinge of regret for our part in this great woman's battle."
>
> "Yes, Bab, and ah, the relief that comes to us now that the victory is won!"[2]

Interestingly, these two "ladies of uncertain age," converse "in the boudoir of an apartment on the one hundred and first floor of the magnificent Home for Superannuated Suffragettes." Already dreaming of a sophisticated future in a city of skyscrapers, Clairene imagines she and her friend's mature features will be marked by their "noble character, strengthened yet softened by a life of valiant struggle." All this from a girl in a town whose streets were still dirt.

Clairene's preoccupation with profiles and prophesies forecasted a taste for personality testing in her adult life, both as a subject searching for self-understanding and as a researcher into early psychological studies, and it portended the talent for clairvoyance she exhibited in her later years. Her "affairs of the heart" were varied and fascinating. She was as much a belle in her eighties as she was in her teens, though even then she was serious and focused. Her writing career and her personal quest for self-discovery formed the foundation of all her relationships, capricious or otherwise.

A 1912 diary entry records a time when her teacher Miss Holt told Clairene's fortune, and again the predictions ring true: she was "very fond of art and music," and while not a spendthrift, she would "help someone in need."[3] Her love of art, music, and literature is apparent in all of her writing. Her generosity became legend among her friends; when she died, everyone she knew was given at least one thousand dollars and many received even more.[4] In 1975, when she met Kenneth Ring at the beginning of his professional career, she bought him a typewriter so he could work more efficiently. Miss Holt's fortune also found Clairene decisive, confident, benevolent, and at least at that time, "not a flirt," but inclined to be argumentative, to stick to her point, and not "give in until disproved."[5] Her tenacity kept her in a state of high involvement with people and projects during her youth and throughout her life.

Embroiled in the emotional turbulence of adolescence, teetering on the cusp of adulthood, Clairene walked the line between two worlds: the domestic and the public spheres. The former, open and acceptable in the society of her day, offered opportunities embraced by her family. The public sphere, which promised the future she desired, was closed, but not completely. For during the first two decades of the twentieth century, forces were at work that would open doors for a young woman like Clairene. Her adolescent diaries reflect her struggle to integrate the selves produced by those two worlds—fragments of wholeness that she sought through her passions, her writing, her living, her loving, and her "bent for the occult."

During adolescence, Clairene's mercurial quality kept her ecstatic one day, morose the next; preoccupied with boys one month, disinterested the next; intense, unpredictable, hard on herself. "I'm kind of mad at everything and everybody but I'm sure it's all my own fault," she wrote in 1911. Feeling different on the inside from her outside persona, she chastised herself for being "so everlasting conceited." Because she did things well, easily, and naturally, she did not "see how people stand me at all . . . I just don't like myself." She was at a "sunk down place in the road looking forward [to] where things are all bright and shiny and [I] see visions of my future self which won't be if I don't hurry . . . I've simply got to get better someday. It feels as if the Lord couldn't leave me this way all the time."[6]

To further complicate matters, she remained haunted by the desire to please her parents and teachers. Her need to fit in sabotaged her drive to excel and to express herself creatively. Her strength of character and keen intelligence created emotional turbulence that kept her spinning, like the young Sufi dancing with the wind, against the wind, moving forward and backward almost at the same time.[7]

In February, for her birthday, her parents gave her a hand-painted vase, encouraging her taste for the artistic. Yet, when she and her friends discovered a diary embossed in gold, "My High School Days," which she described as "Superspringarlic! . . . perfectly grand," her mother—ironically, given the title—told her she could not have it until college. Clairene desperately longed for the day when she would go off to college, "where I want to be," but she saved her money, as she had previously for a two-dollar Kodak, and bought the diary herself. In her erratic, adolescent way, she only filled in a few pages before going back to the plain, lined notebooks.[8]

Her emotions, in a constant state of flux, moved between childhood wishes and adolescent fantasies. Her diary records plans to go see her friend "Mag this summer," in 1910, and her reluctance: "[Mag] is so grown up and crazy about the boys that I don't want to go much. . . . If it wasn't for my love of going to strange places (Kileen [*sic*] is a fine city) I don't think I would go at all." Killeen may have seemed a "fine city" as compared to Temple and Rockdale during that century's first decade, especially to a fourteen-year-old girl who looked forward, even at this age, to finishing college so she could, "Travel! Oh, that's what I long to do." Unlike her female classmates, her heart was set on a different future from the ones they envisioned:

> Agnes, Ernestine, Marie, Katie & Ada are daffy over the other sex. . . . No one has changed more than I have. Six months ago this diary would have been little else than things about boys. . . . Now, my ambitions are high, but since one never rises above his ambitions I want mine to be high. I want to be famous . . . I want to be on the stage and be a renouned [*sic*] actress . . . I wouldn't mind being an authoress either and I expect to write a book someday. I dreaded to write this diary at first but now I hate to stop. . . . I am going to save this until I am grown and then I will like to know what I thought when I was an eighth-grade school girl.[9]

Like Virginia Woolf who, in *A Writer's Diary*, sends a message from her younger self to an older self, so Clairene writes to Claire:[10] "Look here," she seems to say: "I was not just a frivolous school girl. I had thoughts and opinions." Most significantly, in the passage above, she underlined, "I expect to write a book someday," confirming the accuracy of the Cooke handprint analysis and an innate sense of her own destiny.

In fact, she had already written her first book, at age eight, "Miss Mary and Mr. Charles." "I didn't know people had last names," she told Ken Ring in 1979. "And the day after she was married, Miss Mary found a beautiful little baby. Oh I was so ignorant, you have no idea!" she added with a laugh. "I still have it, tied up with pink ribbons."[11]

Tucked carefully away now in the archive in Denton, the little book conveys its own special magic as a relic of childhood innocence, viewed through the lens of contemporary feminist consciousness. Miss Mary and Mr. Charles, which she cut out from popular magazines, appear on the front cover as adults. Miss Mary wears a long pale-pink dress with a fitted bodice and leg-o'-mutton sleeves with deep ornate cuffs, matching collar, and a lofty hat with purple blossoms. Mr. Charles is dressed in a brown plaid suit and bowler and sports a thin mustache that bears an uncanny resemblance to the mustache worn by Claire's mysterious lover in the 1920s.[12]

At eight, her creativity expresses a preoccupation with beauty, fashion, and love. Dreaming of marriage was a belle's role in life, and she had embraced it. Although in many ways that idealized image of love and the sanctity of the male-female bond stayed with Claire all her life, by adolescence her focus had changed. She wanted to experience life, to travel, study, and work in the world. Time after time, passion for intellectual pursuit propelled her toward freedom. And time after time, in "flirtation after flirtation," love catapulted her back to the domestic scene.

Today we might read "Miss Mary and Mr. Charles" as an illustration of the influence fairy tales have on the formation of a young girl's imagination. Certainly in later life, Claire confirmed their negative impact: "[At] first I was strongly influenced by fairy tales. Psychologists today say they are very good for people. . . . [But] I took them too literally. . . . I think this had a very bad effect on me. I was romantic for years . . . as most southern girls were who were brought up at that time."[13] By southern, she means white, middle class, and privileged. There is no evidence in her early writings that she wondered what girls her age of color or of working class parents were thinking or doing. White was, indeed, the "raceless race."[14]

In *The Unpredictable Adventure*, protagonist Tellectina (appellation for intellectual woman) at age ten regularly climbs into Andersen's or Grimm's[15] boats and sails happily out to Romantz Isle. By age thirteen, however, in a conversation with her ribald and worldly Aunt Sophistica, she realizes that she has outgrown those little boats and that, while the island was a place "where virtue was always rewarded and wickedness always punished . . . the great world out there looks far more beautiful." That world—which the author calls Nithking (anagram for *thinking*)—is forbidden and unladylike because, as Sophistica explains, "all interesting things are."[16]

For Clairene, as for her fictional persona, the shift from fairy tales to worldly knowledge represented a movement beyond the usual rite of passage between childhood and maturity because it took her into a land her foremothers did not inhabit or endorse. After all, the charm of southern women lay in their perpetual innocence.[17] White middle-class mothers trained their daughters to be paragons of virtue, and virtue meant submissiveness, not intellect or will.

The pictures and captions depicting childhood in "Miss Mary and Mr. Charles" reflect a preoccupation with the mother figure, foreshadowing Claire's concerns in her later written reflections. No father figure appears in the childhood scenes; fathers are not associated with domesticity and therefore do not enter the child's imagination. Mrs. Christian, the mother figure in the novel, is standoffish, cold, and unsympathetic to her daughter's passionate nature. A passage that captures the "wind incident," described in nonfictional terms in *Awakening to the Good*, here depicts Tellectina celebrating the arrival of the first norther of autumn. Despite warnings from both parents, Tina darts into the garden where she stands "amid the frenzied swaying of trees and shrubs—motionless, expectant, breathless. . . . The wind quickened the child's pulse, drawing her irresistibly into the wild autumn bacchanalia. . . . Delirious with this strange fearful ecstasy, she abandoned herself to the orgy with all the fervor of a whirling young dervish."[18]

The child recognizes this rite of passage as overtly sexual and therefore forbidden territory: "Something's wrong with me," she thinks. "There's something queer about all this . . . joy." The novel explores the dichotomy between proper Puritan behavior—synonymous to proper Baptist behavior—practiced by citizens of Err, and pagan or heathen behavior practiced by citizens of Nithking. When Tellectina asks her aunt why "you never hear anything about Nithking in Smug Harbor," Sophistica explains that not only is Nithking "forbidden country, it is a forbidden subject."[19]

To Tellectina, thinking is an erotic adventure as volatile and liberating as the wind itself. Intellectual and erotic freedom lie on the same path and both foster ecstatic experiences. Mrs. Christian is exasperated by her daughter's passion: "She does everything to excess. She studies too hard, reads too much, and even plays too violently," she tells her husband, who recommends "moderation."[20] "Daughter," Mr. Christian exclaims, "can't you run more . . . quietly? It would be just as much fun."

In life, Susan Allen Myers was a formal woman, undemonstrative and, in the face of Clairene's exuberance, cold. Although as an adult Claire often remarked that her mother never loved her, she seemed to recognize the tight bonds between them. In the 1920s and 1930s, Mrs. Myers expressed love in letters that reveal deep and abiding concern for her daughter's welfare after she left home. After all, to Mrs. Myers the world outside Temple was evil and dangerous.

Letters offer advice, in the same tone found in Laura's 1899 letter regarding three-year-old Clairene's illness: kind, polite, instructional, at times affectionate, but never laced with the effusive love someone of Claire's nature would have found comforting. Mixed messages became part of the normal line of communication between mother and daughter. Perhaps this explains the letter Clairene wrote to her mother on January 3, 1912, during her junior year in high school, the month before her sixteenth birthday. Susan Myers had gone to her parents' home in Rockdale to assist her mother. Clairene and Coren Douglas were left in charge, and the daughter assumed domestic responsibility in her mother's place. She reported on the weather—it was eight degrees—and wondered how to plant pansies: "I just love to do the housekeeping and cooking all by myself. . . . I don't care if I never see another history or Latin or anything just so I learn to cook and sew! I'm going to make one of those lap writing desks like Mrs. Stirt's. I think I've told every word I know so I say good by."[21]

The letter demonstrates the polite consideration mother and daughter typically showed one another on the surface. However, given Clairene's taste for intellectual and creative projects, this seems an attempt to please and console. After all, she planned to sew a "lap writing desk"! In this letter, which prefigures the ones she will write home in the 1930s during her marriage to George Wanders, Clairene seeks to assure her mother and grandmother that she will become the proper young lady they have groomed.

Her love for sports surfaces in her diaries, especially when highlighting her involvement with basketball: "Fun is no name [for it] and the grandest exercise (all I get too). Elected Captain of Sophomore team but I fear I made a very poor one." One entry imagines the "one real desperate love affair" she will have in college: "He will be coming off the baseball diamond. He will have a perfect nose and almost perfect ears . . . fleshy but a fine athlete." Just as the subject of sports and boys weave throughout her diaries, so does the subject of cooking—a source of ambivalence and disdain most of her life.[22]

At eighty-three, Claire recalled that her mother and grandmother were adamant that she do nothing around the house and, "sit on a cushion and sew a fine seam." However, the teen diaries indicate that domestic duties were part of every young girl's formal education. At sixteen she was "glad [she] was cook for three weeks; it taught [her] so much." She and her friend Ernestine made fudge together and set buttonholes in their princess slips. They shopped for supplies for domestic science class. Clairene took these assignments seriously. The paradox holds: girls were expected to know how to cook and sew so that as adults they could supervise an efficiently run household.[23] Reality was another story. Private letters and diaries suggest more pragmatic considerations.

The tenor of matriarchal teachings left the impression that proper ladies lived in idle splendor. Except for the very wealthy, the reality for most women in both the pre– and post–Civil War South was hard work. Most women played an actual physical role in the domestic scene. Otherwise, how might we explain Susan's rush to her mother's aid in an emergency? Or Clairene's assumption of domestic chores in her mother's absence? Or for that matter, Laura's indispensable presence on her farm, which necessitated her guilt-laden letter apologizing for not coming to Clairene's aid when she was ill at age three? There was much more to being a woman in the rural South than just pleasing a man, even if men seemed to be in charge of what "mattered."

Clairene's father signed her report cards, which year after year indicate perfect attendance and conduct. Devoted to her studies, she rhapsodized when she was exempt from all exams, "including Latin!" though she took the English exam, which was "easy." In 1910, the first year she "disliked school," her diary began to reflect the pressure of adolescence. The refrain, "Haven't time, no have to study" rings in her ears. By 1911, she "hates to be treated indifferently by boys," and felt she was "getting worse every day" because she failed to live up to her projected level of accomplishments. Although she worried about "getting lazier," that same year she observed, "Mama, Miss Hanover, and Robbie all got after me for studying so much and hard." The following year she was proud of her summer accomplishments, having "read twelve good books, [made] eight garments, three handkerchiefs and two doilies, cooked about six meals and learned five pieces of music."[24]

In high school she wrote themes, which she kept in folders.[25] The writing is smooth and eloquent, displaying a mastery of language beyond her years. From an early age, Clairene used the tools of fiction, claiming, with an air of false modesty, to have "no idea" why her English teacher would read her themes aloud in class.[26]

The thematic import of her research papers anticipates future concerns. "Our First Suffragette" presents a biographical portrait of Margaret Brent (c. 1601–c. 1671), a woman who gained influence with Maryland governor Leonard Calvert. On the governor's deathbed, he whispers, "I make you my sole executrix, take all and pay all," which Margaret heroically interprets to mean that she must distribute state wealth for the benefit of the people of Maryland. Though the end of the story is missing, Margaret Brent provided a perfect role model for the young southern belle struggling to break free of restrictive gender models. Brent became a businesswoman of considerable executive ability whose femininity is limited to one scene. Though she has many suitors who vie for her hand, she refuses all and works for the public good.[27]

An essay arguing against high school fraternities and sororities because they build up a "cast of distinction between those eligible to be members" and those excluded, based on wealth and beauty rather than intelligence or integrity, reveals Clairene's advanced social conscience. However, her essay, "The Character of the Negro," reinforces negative stereotypes. While all her work reflects the limited resources available for her research, these two themes reveal her perceptions of the injustice of class, but not of race.

Her 1912 diary opens on Clairene's sixteenth birthday, a milestone especially for one being groomed as a belle: "February 11, 1912. And I am sixteen today! Sweet Sixteen! I think it deserves to be written with capitals," she writes as if she expects someone someday will notice. "I have always thought—till now—that I would simply be 'It' when I was sixteen. However, I find there's no change at all." Subsequent entries show she was still characteristically hard on herself.[28]

However, she began to be less ambivalent about her interest in boys, recording February 12: "I got a real nice letter from Luther this morning . . . the first real letter I ever received from a boy. I'm glad it came when I was just sixteen; it makes it so romantic." As Claire told Kenneth Ring years later, girls "had to be besieged by beaux" day and night or they were considered a "complete failure."[29] Another 1912 diary entry points to the contradictions embedded in school policy: "On rainy days when everyone stops in the locker room, Mr. Procter and Miss Mitchell won't let a boy and girl look at each other even."

Susan, and perhaps many of the other mothers of her class and region, would have supported such policies: "My mother was exceedingly Puritanical; [the family] didn't believe in drinking or dancing or cards, and sex of course was the supreme sin in the world. In fact, they hardly mentioned the word. They'd spell it sometimes." Girls of Claire's generation were taught that sex was pleasant for men but not for women. "When I discovered years later that sex could be a delight for women, I was the most surprised person in America." Socially girls were taught to be belles, with their future tied to marriage and children. "I'd read a lot of books and I knew there was a bigger life than that, a world greater than a small southern town. I wanted to see Paris and London. Books saved my life; they made my life."[30]

Dickens, Thackeray, and George Eliot taught her there was more to life than that which existed in Temple, a.k.a. Smug Harbor. Other writings confirmed the staid teachings of her heritage. The story "When Nightwood Was in Flower" by Thomas Nelson Page, a southerner who wrote about Virginia plantation days, further imbued her with restrictions. Thus, her love of reading, like her love for her family, prevailed, pulling her in several directions through her aspirations for a "bigger life" of travel, adventure, and career.

Missing from her diary entries are her feelings for her brother Coren Douglas. His senior picture in the 1912 Temple High School

4. Clairene Myers senior picture, Temple High School, Press Club, 1913. Photograph courtesy of the TWU Woman's Collection.

year book shows a kind, handsome face, a dignified smile and soft, wavy hair a shade lighter than his sister's. As Coren Douglas was less accomplished in high school than Clairene, the caption lists no memberships or athletic activities but simply states, "In a certain sense all men are prophets."

Clairene's senior picture the following year credits her many achievements. In 1913, Clairene Myers was literary editor, secretary of the senior class, president of the Press Club, and a member of the Girls' Glee Club. She played on the basketball team in 1910, 1911, and 1912. "You are fresh and sweet as the first flower," reads the caption, ironically implying a delicate beauty rather than highlighting her athletic and intellectual proclivities. And yet, 1913 marked the founding of the first Girls' Debating Society at Temple High School, with Clairene Myers elected president. Its mission statement claimed a feminist agenda: "In this great modern age of the rising superiority of women, we hear constantly of the weaker sex equaling and immediately surpassing their masculine competitors."[31]

Susan Myers, who attended Baylor College for Women in Belton, Texas, wanted her daughter to attend Sophie Newcomb College in New Orleans, then a finishing school for girls. Clairene longed to attend the University of Texas in Austin to pursue a bachelor's degree in literature and philosophy. She turned to her father for support. But Myers held to his southern definition of female propriety and insisted she attend the all-woman College of Industrial Arts in Denton, where he enrolled her in the domestic science program. Again, her father's actions present something of a paradox: His teachings ignited in her a deep love and respect for knowledge, ethics, and universal justice. But her father was more a southern gentleman than a freethinker when it came to the women in his family. His belief in the Southern Code of Honor, with its strict gender roles that reinforce male authority, narrowed the options for both his wife and his daughter. Furthermore, the domestic training he prescribed for Clairene reinforced the paradox. She would be educated to become a lady, following in her mother's footsteps. But like her mother, who loved to cook and to experiment with gourmet recipes, she would be expected to defer those skills to servants. Interestingly, as the future Claire Myers Owens, she would be only too happy to do so.

3

Rote Hill

1913–1916

> Always strive to keep the unseen above the seen—
> for they're the only things that matter.
>
> —Clarence Myers, "Gaily Bedight"

WHEN CLAIRENE MYERS arrived in the fall of 1913, the College of Industrial Arts in Denton, Texas, was celebrating its ten-year anniversary. She entered the seventy-acre campus, situated on "gently rolling" land that commanded a "fine view of town and country," through red-brick gates facing Bell Avenue. There stood two stately brick buildings: the yellow-brick academic arts building, currently known as the Old Main, and Stoddard Hall, Clairene's home for the next three years. An imposing red-brick structure with a front porch filled with chairs, Stoddard, the first state dormitory in Texas, held 150 students.[1] A scattering of other buildings included several stately structures and a few temporary buildings amid a natural landscape rich with trees and sloping lawns.

The founding of the College of Industrial Arts, which became Texas Woman's University in 1957, has its roots in the history of women's education.[2] The Morrill Act of 1862 provided for new state colleges that would offer practical training in agriculture and engineering. Educational opportunities for women grew as a result of private women's colleges established in the East, and the admission of women to new state colleges in the West.

A. J. Rose, worthy master of the State Grange and Patrons of Husbandry, led the campaign in Texas for separate state colleges for women. In 1889, pointing to the success of Texas A & M, Rose argued: "Do [girls] not need an industrial college too, where they can receive a practical education, which will prepare them for some vocation in life, in order that they may not work in the cotton fields from necessity? Certainly the State will not do less for her girls than her boys."[3]

A long battle ensued, joined by the Women's Christian Temperance Union in 1893. Helen Stoddard, president of the Texas chapter of the WCTU, petitioned the legislature, arguing it was "sane and reasonable [and] the best protection a parent could give his daughter," for "worthy young women" deserved a college education.[4]

On January 1, 1903, the cornerstone was laid for the College of Industrial Arts, the first college for women in Texas. In February 1903, the first president, Cree T. Work, who also taught psychology, addressed the State Farmers' Congress of Texas, emphasizing that education designed for men was not necessarily appropriate for women, though the "women's sphere" was equally as large as the "men's sphere." President Work forcefully defended the rights of women to enter suitable occupations other than homemaking: "The cry has been raised that women are encroaching upon the occupations of men, taking their places and causing reduced wages." He asked, "who gave the male sex the monopoly of all industry outside the home?" and asserted that women should be "permitted to do that which is suited to their nature."[5]

President Work, concluding that men *assumed* the monopoly and still *claimed* it, coined the college motto, "We learn to do by doing." Work promised to promote "culture of the highest order, scholarship of the most efficient kind, and domestic and industrial training of the most modern and practical type" to prepare women for work in the "industrial and commercial world if they so choose." Freedom of choice had come to the women of Texas!

Or had it? Was this an example of the contradictions between appearance and reality so common to southern culture? In many ways, the College of Industrial Arts stands as a monument to the changing conditions in education for women in the South. Its history marks an important first for women. In addition to appointing Helen M. Stoddard, for whom the dorm was named, as secretary for the first Board of Regents, Governor Joseph D. Sayers appointed Mary Eleanor Brackenridge of San Antonio as vice president, and Mrs. Cone Johnson of Tyler as a member—the first three women to serve as regents of a Texas institution.[6] However, the curriculum reinforced the limited vocations offered to women, for as Work told the Farmers' Congress, "education designed for men was not necessarily appropriate for women."

On September 23, 1903, the College began its first term. Enrollment was open to "all white girls of good moral character," age sixteen and over, who could demonstrate "abilities"—there was an entrance exam—and good attitudes. One hundred and seventy-three students from three states and sixty-six counties attended. By 1914–15, Clairene Myers's middle year, enrollment had grown to 866, making the College of Industrial Arts, with its university-trained faculty of sixty, the largest college for women in Texas. In 1916, the State Department of Education recognized the College of Industrial Arts as "a college of the first class."[7]

The class of 1916, which arrived for a three-year program in domestic science in the fall of 1913, could choose to pursue a diploma in household arts, fine and applied arts, or literature. Academic subjects included education and philosophy, English and literature, biology and geology, history and social science, Latin and modern language, and manual arts, which included rural arts and music. Vocational courses took one year and included dressmaking, millinery, photography, typewriting, bookkeeping, and shorthand.

According to Miss Corabel Weimer, director of the Domestic Science Department, the "rapidly expanding" Food and Cookery Department showed increasing "public favor." Using a "scientific approach to homemaking," courses raised "home conditions to a higher, healthier plane," leading to "general social betterment." Theoretically, such training would "not only equip young women for the home," but also prepare them "to earn a livelihood," which meant teaching. Ultimately, the program intended to create "a deepened and more extensively organized home." Ironically, while established to enlarge the women's sphere, the College of Industrial Arts, elevated household chores to a fine art and science, attempting to bring dignity to domestic drudgery.[8]

In later years, writing her "Autobiography," Claire remembered the kitchen as a scientific lab, where "we weighed everything in grams." They studied every aspect of food production, care, preparation, cooking, serving, composition, digestion, and assimilation.[9]

The first day Clairene and her classmates were shown into the laboratory-kitchen and then into a more formal dining area. "Since this is a state college," they were told, "you will be entertaining the Governor and senators. You will learn to cook formal dinners Russian style and simple family meals, learn the duties of hostess, host, elder daughter, and maid." The instructor explained that great cooking was a gift from God, and that at graduations "young men of Texas line up outside ready to marry any CIA [College of Industrial Arts] girl."[10]

Clairene was jolted by the conflicting values the course of study promoted. So deeply had the aristocratic system been embedded in her "very bones" that her "body bristled like a cat" the first time she walked into the lab-kitchen. She had been taught that "women never did menial work." Her grandmother, mother, and their friends had "cooks and washer women." To Clairene, learning to cook, even with a view of teaching it later, seemed contradictory. Since good southern belles never performed the actual chores, she considered it outrageous to be required to learn to do them in college. Nevertheless, she found the analytical theory "easy and delightful" and was the only student who passed the written test.[11]

Clairene found gourmet feasts at the College everywhere *except* the kitchen. In writings, she frequently described the profound impact of her studies: Greek mythology, architecture, drama, geology—learning was one of life's great adventures.

In Clairene's first novel, "Gaily Bedight," authored by one "Clarence" Myers, the chapter titled, "A Germ is Planted" fictionalizes Clairene's college years and implies that society considered the pursuit of knowledge a disease. Yet, the protagonist, Sibyl Randolph, whose life mirrors Clairene's, finds biology "thrilling." Botany and bacteriology strike her "dumb with wonder."[12]

This coming-of-age novel traces Sibyl's development over a three-year period, illuminating her liberation from the narrow Christian background of her childhood. Although Sibyl was brought up to believe in God, "the scientific truth about mankind"—evolution—freed her from ignorance. The Greek myths re-create a romantic world of gods and nymphs that seemed real. She realized that at one time people took those beliefs seriously, just as Christians did in her time. While Sibyl had been taught that ethics had to do with good and evil, college taught Sibyl there were no absolutes. One must "always strive to keep the unseen above the seen—for they're the only things that matter." Such transformative information disturbed Sibyl's sense of certainty.

Chemistry and physics amazed her with explanations regarding natural phenomena such as "why water boiled, why toast browned, why soap lathered, why the fishing pole looked bent in the water." Her "hands would grow cold" with excitement; she felt as if she had arrived at a carnival. Writing English papers made her "high on words."[13] A teacher who "broke the rules" and read aloud an essay from the *Atlantic Monthly* became her role model because she exhibited an independent sense of humor with an interest in the artistic.

But this was the South, and Sibyl, like Clairene, learned the hard way that to be a serious student—if you were a girl—was to be considered a "grind," open for ridicule by girls and avoidance by boys. It was not ladylike to be intellectual, learned, or scholarly. Claire explained years later she had to conceal her enthusiasm, even from her fiancé during her senior year. In her fiction and in her memoirs, only the faculty respect knowledge.[14]

In her second novel, *The Unpredictable Adventure*, Claire Myers "Spotswood," writing in the 1930s, called the college Rote Hill, and modeled it after a health spa where young ladies came to be cured of "cerebral lethargica," a form of sleeping sickness with symptoms including imagination and daydreams. As in "Gaily Bedight," the author satirizes hunger for knowledge as a disease. The protagonist Tellectina, an appellation for intellectual woman, finds the cure in a drug obtained from lead pencils, called Cianite Vitigrew (creative writing)—a cure her parents consider unacceptable. However, Tellectina discovers that Rote Hill is not a health spa, but a "carnival" full of magic "to keep you thrilled for the rest of your natural life."[15]

When Aunt Sophistica comes to visit, Tellectina asks, "Why . . . did no grown-up person tell me that there was magic in ideas?"

"Ideas don't wake most persons up," Sophistica answers, "they put them to sleep."[16]

But college awakened more than just ideas for Clairene. In the novel, the author expresses this awakening as a magical transformation that occurs on Tellectina's first night away from home. Through a process at once fantastic and deeply metaphorical, Tellectina observes a "mysterious incident." Sitting quietly on the marble rim of a fountain after dinner, trying to collect herself from the overwhelming experience of being away from home and of living in a house full of girls, she hears "someone calling softly through the dusk." Tellectina finds herself magnetically drawn toward a young, handsome boy "lying on top of the high stone wall" that borders the campus. To her amazement, she notices herself "flashing her eyes at him in the most unaccountable fashion."

> As he advanced toward her, the most extraordinary thing happened. Slowly, subtly, surely, half of the girl's inner self stirred, tugged at her other self—loosened—uncoiled its tendrils from about her mental self like a vine being torn away from its support, and suddenly wrenched itself free. . . . She saw to her amazement that standing immediately in front of her and completely concealing her from the boy's view was another girl who had emerged mysteriously out of her own being—out of her own body; a girl who looked and sounded like herself yet was not herself; a stranger touching her so closely that she could feel the blood dancing in the other's veins; while Tellectina herself was left behind, sufficiently detached and intact coolly to observe the interloper.[17]

The youth introduces himself as Andrew Mereboy. "With a toss of her head and a flash of her black eyes," Tellectina responds "in a voice that sounded like her own but was not her own" that he can try calling her Femina Christian. Smitten, Andrew's response envelops her with a "sensation more delicious than she had ever dreamed existed." Frightened by both the boy and the mysterious Femina, Tellectina flees to her room, only to realize the other girl has come with her. Leaning against the doorpost, the bewildered Tellectina murmurs: "Dear Lord what have you done to me? Must I be divided into two people just because I think one thing and feel another? Which am I?"[18]

The clue to the characterization lies in the full name of the protagonist: Tellectina Femina Christian, which embodies the protagonist's psychological identity. Tellectina, the intellectually curious, aggressive, male-*modeled* self is pitted against the passive, ladylike, nurturing, seductive, and male-*identified* self—the ideal woman. Once Femina appears, she exists as if she were a separate character. From this moment on in the novel, the protagonist operates as a woman divided against herself, split by society, which separates her thinking self from her emotional self, alienating her mind from her body. The two "natural sisters" emerge and converse with one another as separate selves, each arguing with and tricking the other in an effort to win control.

Because the novel is set in the fantastic, the conceit seems plausible. Neither persona, however, can develop into natural wholeness because each has been split off from the other through the moralistic upbringing represented by their surname. *Christian* functions as a superego, or patriarchal conscience, by structuring the two personae who appear, disappear, divide, and reunite throughout the novel.[19]

Indeed, the focus of the adventure itself comes to represent not just a journey of self-discovery, or a quest for certitude, though these are both central, but a passionate drive to achieve psychological wholeness. The seeds for such a struggle, both in the novel and in Claire's life—sown by a culture steeped in traditional gender role identification—blossom in the dichotomy underlying Claire's, and the fictional Tellectina's, self-definition. That inner voice that whispered in her high school diaries begins to shout insights that allow her to visualize the split. Such a dichotomy was surely nurtured in this girl's college where contradictions were blatant, where studies were secondary to femininity, and career secondary to social life and domestic obligations. For here, with the exception of some progressive teachers, girls were educated to become ladies.

Clairene and her dear "friend for life," Clare Ousley, latched on to those rare opportunities for growth. Daughter of Clarence Ousley of Fort Worth,[20] a member of the College of Industrial Arts Board of Regents and later Democratic candidate for the Senate from Texas, Clare Ousley was the only student Clairene found who enjoyed discussing her studies. She had spent much of her youth in Washington, DC due to her father's career as a politician, an editor, and owner of several Texas newspapers; Clare seemed sophisticated to the provincial girl from Temple. A passage in the "Autobiography" reveals Clairene's response to her new friend: "When most girls looked at you, half their minds were elsewhere; but Clare looked you straight in the eye, was totally aware, her face came alive in response to your personality." A "stimulating, heartwarming, and rare" friendship of trust, acceptance, admiration, and fierce loyalty evolved.[21]

Three editions of the *Daedalian*, 1914–16, published during their stay, document the two girls' college careers.[22] Both were active in the Chaparral Literary Club and the Press Club; both served on the editorial board of the *Lass-O*, a weekly student publication. Between 1913 and 1916, Clairene joined the tennis team and served as president of the Temple Club and the Press Club. Clare Ousley was president of the *Lass-O*, while serving as secretary of the Press Club. During Clairene's senior year, she acted in the *Merchant of Venice*. In 1915, for the Press Club, she contributed a reading titled, "The Significance of the Quarterly," and in April 1916, she delivered a paper entitled, "Alfred Noyes—Playwright—Man—Poet."

"The Demonstration Cottage," an essay Clairene wrote her senior year, brought high acclaim from her English teacher.[23] As in her high school portrait of Margaret Brent, she chose the format of a short story to portray a tough-minded businessman who has decided against sending his daughter to the College of Industrial Arts. Given Clairene's interest in pursuing a course of study outside the domestic sphere,

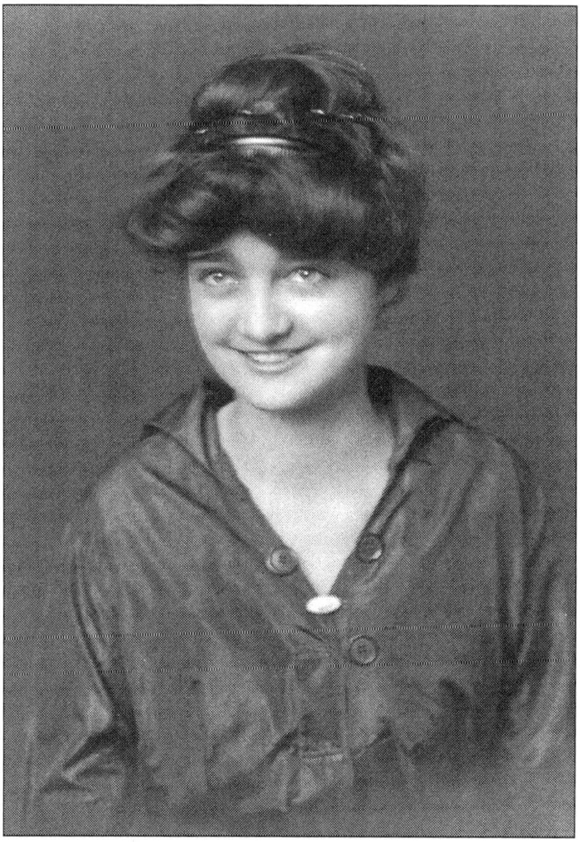

5. Clairene Myers, College Press Club. Verso inscription: "Miss Clairene Myers of Temple. Press Club President, 1916." College of Industrial Arts, 1916. Photograph courtesy of the TWU Woman's Collection.

ironically, she created a narrator who plays devil's advocate. Teachers kept a copy of the essay for publication in the *Daedalian*. The significance of the paper lies in Clairene's success in composing an argument in defense of a system she believed to be absurd.

Clairene found life in the dorm a revelation. While sharing food from home, the girls held lively discussions about sex, speculating on stories of white slavery.[24] Speaking to strangers, she learned, might land you in a "fancy house in South America." Whereas in her "Autobiography" Claire wrote that they spoke of boys but not sex "exactly," other writings indicate they wondered about "that thing between men's legs" and what husbands and wives did in bed. Wild guesses ensued with no satisfactory answers.

If in her preteen and high school years she was a "bundle of contradictions," then in college she was a "bundle of emotions," longing for fulfillment of desires she had neither the maturity nor the knowledge to name. In the "Autobiography" she describes the following encounter with a girl named Rosalie who came into her dorm room: "'I can't sleep unless I do this. I always do it with my roommate.' She placed her hand on my breast. A cold wave of revulsion swept through me. I did not want to hurt her feelings so I turned over nonchalantly and her hand slipped off." At the time, she wondered about other girls who slept in the same beds on Saturday nights and about those who seemed to court one another with flowers and candy. Such behavior gave her a "squeamish" feeling, though she didn't understand why.[25]

At that time, gender distinction was considered "natural" and therefore scandalous when people did not follow expected patterns. Homosexuality, even with current laws addressing gender identity, may still be considered "unnatural."[26] Clairene's revulsion arises from her lack of understanding gender differences; nothing could have prepared her for sexual advances from another girl.

Other writings portraying this period deal with the results of sexual repression during the 1910s and 1920s. *The Unpredictable Adventure* describes a similar scene between Tellectina and a girl named Tommy, who is described as "mannish" and named in the style of the novel to suggest the stereotypical tomboy image. In life as in art, such dilemmas, incomprehensible in their day, are left unresolved: both in the 1910s, when the incident occurred, and in the 1930s when Claire Myers "Spotswood" wrote about it.[27]

As Lillian Faderman suggests in her book *Surpassing the Love of Men*, the idea that two people could engage in "venereal activity" in the absence of the male sex was unimaginable. And since women were thought to have "no sex drive," there could be no sexual relationship between them. "Sound women were asexual."[28]

Social decorum implied prohibition of sexual expression and kept discussions veiled in mystery. But Tellectina and Femina in *The Unpredictable Adventure* and Sibyl in "Gaily Bedight" know one thing for sure: kissing boys is wrong, though they all wonder why because it feels so right. As Sibyl observes: "Oh, dear Lord, how can it be wrong to let Owen put his arm around me when I *want* it so! . . . Oh if I only had someone to talk to . . . I want to be good and pure always—please God, help me not to let Owen even hold my hand." The tension between her sexual longings and the admonitions against them keep her in a state of confusion.

In *The Unpredictable Adventure*, Tellectina's longing for something "unnamed" translates into "a sweet, unfamiliar ache that plagued her body," becoming almost unbearable on moonlit nights when drawn irresistibly by the potency of the moonlight. "Its beauty awakened hopes of a fabulous, unattainable happiness and stirred memories of sorrows she had never known. . . . Was there any beauty on earth so compelling? . . . Some day she would find perfect love. . . . But love was not enough. She longed . . . for adventure . . . the fullness of life . . . to taste all the beauty [and] even the cruelty of life! Only to miss nothing!"[29]

For Tellectina, as for Clairene during college, available love meant limited freedom—settling for a traditional lifestyle back home. Liberating love existed "out there," in the unknown awaiting her future self. Longing for the love out there merges with her yearning for adventure and becomes an amorphous call.

In "Gaily Bedight," knowledge stimulates ecstasy; Sibyl describes a three-fold awakening she undergoes after she entered college: the passion aroused by her beau, the aesthetic awakening aroused by her response to the arts—literature and music—and finally her delight in intellectual stimulation, like a "carnival": "Now her mind leapt up and grasped ideas which heretofore it had been unable to reach. Oh the joyous adventure of walking through the house of knowledge."

Sibyl's dreams for the future, her sense of adventure, are palpable; she lies awake at night filled with longing: "The great beautiful world, how it called her. 'Come—Come.' It is the call irresistible—and youth replies: 'Yes, I am coming—I am coming to you, World! someday!'"

Although Clare Ousley shared Clairene's thirst for adventure and high ideals, her high school friend Robbie McKnight took a more skeptical view. Robbie's parents refused to allow her to attend either the University of Texas in Austin or the College of Industrial Arts and instead sent her to a small college in Eureka Springs, closer to Temple. Robbie's letters to Clairene often reflect her feelings of being left out, and eventually Clairene became something of a role model. But in 1914, Robbie warned Clairene against overreaching: "Beautiful as your ideals always are they *are* too high. . . . If you continue to keep your ideals in the clouds, you're going to be hurt." Robbie's "opinions about certain things," meaning boys, had "changed since last year."[30] Since most girls' thoughts about boys were unmentionable, she dropped the subject here, but picked it up in future correspondence.

Her senior year, Clairene was elected delegate to a state convention in Dallas, with all expenses paid by the Press Club. She wore a beautiful yellow evening gown her mother sent for the occasion. She "made a little speech," and met Alden Evans, a junior at a Dallas university and a part-time reporter for the *Dallas News*. He had dark eyes and hair and when he came to see Clairene on the weekends in Denton, the girls teased her that he would be taken for a Jew.[31]

In the chapter "Flowers" in *Awakening to the Good*, Claire describes Alden's presence at one of her early altered-state experiences that recalls the wind experience of her childhood and anticipates future moments of ecstasy. "We arrived at a wild wooded part of the campus where I had never been before. An overpowering fragrance rushed out to greet us. There standing alone against a clump of green trees stood an incredibly beautiful white tree . . . covered with a profusion of white blossoms."[32]

Alden positioned her for a picture with the flowering honey locust tree as background: "I stood motionless, speechless for a long moment, staring at this incredible sight. Never in my life had I beheld such

6. Clairene at the locust tree on CIA campus. Here she had one of her many "small ecstasies." Photograph courtesy of the TWU Woman's Collection.

an enchanting tree. Never had I inhaled such a—a provocative perfume . . . deeply disturbing. . . . This scent possessed a life, a meaning of its own!" Recalling Shelley's description of "Flowers so sweet the sense faints picturing them," she wonders if the fragrance could be an "elusive messenger from some indescribable other world?"[33]

In the Ring interview, Claire remembered this moment as a confrontation with her own innocence, her sense of the purity and universal oneness of all humanity.[34] The fragrance evoked an image of pre-existence, convincing her that at one time she had been completely enlightened and in perfect bliss.

Naturally she did not discuss the incident with Alden at the time; he would not have understood. He understood little of Clairene, the girl he professed to love and determined to marry, despite her protestations. Her writings give various accounts of her reluctant engagement. Near the end of her senior year in college, Alden gave her a small diamond solitaire, which she tried to refuse, explaining she wanted "to see the world, and had applied for a social work job in an Alabama coal-mining town." He wrote her a letter urging her to reconsider: "A mining camp is no place for a lady. . . . This little ring will bind you to me. I don't want to lose you. I think that would kill me . . . I give you a year in Alabama."

The letter cloys for her affection and sympathy, moving from accusations to assertions for control and veiled threats:

> Jan. 23, 1916
>
> Darling Little Girl
>
> You don't know how bad I want to be with you. . . . I looked all through your letter . . . for the place where you said you loved me but it isn't there. . . . Precious Girl, you hurt this old boy [saying] . . . you hadn't turned out to be the girl I want and maybe you have disappointed me. . . . *Write me the day you get this.* I don't care where you are going, what you have planned . . . how busy you are. Don't write just a note . . . *a note won't do I must have a letter.* I'll know when I mail this, look up the schedules, determine when it gets to you and when the answer is due. I love you. Are you mine?[35]

Though at the time Clairene could not articulate the fears such love provoked, she understood that Alden's intensity would smother her sense of independence. "I didn't want to get married; I wanted to live!" she explained to Ken Ring, laughing at her early foreboding that marriage would mean the end of living. But at the time it did not seem funny. While she agreed to wear the ring to pacify Alden, she dismissed its significance when her friend Clare Ousley was shocked to see it.

Years later, when she portrayed the Alden-Clairene engagement in *The Unpredictable Adventure*, she depicts Clare Ousley and Tellectina as shocked by the ring, for only Femina knows of it: "It's really news to me, too," Tellectina tells Clare. "But I don't intend to allow her [Femina] to marry for years yet. We must both see the world before we settle down to pots and pans and babies!" Thus, the conflict becomes obvious: a woman must resist society's expectations to live out the marriage plot, as Carolyn Heilbrun terms it, and embrace the spirit of adventure only an independent—single—woman can adopt.[36]

"In our senior year Clare Ousley and I had this feeling that we wanted to go out and 'save the world overnight.' I wanted to abolish poverty and suffering," Claire told Ring. When she left college, and ultimately Texas, she left with a "wind of desire" and no clear plan: "I didn't attend the commencement week parties but rather went to Alabama and got a job in a mining camp. The urge was so great I had no control over it. My father disinherited me legally; I thought he was the one person who would understand . . . I remember my mother crying, 'Why do you want to leave home? A lady never leaves home, we'll give you a horse of your own, a new automobile.'"[37]

She knew her decision was a terrible blow to her family, but felt as if she had not decided it herself; rather as if something decided it for her. What could have provoked her need to leave the cocoon-like world of her childhood? What events led her to break free of the constricted atmosphere of the South, she wondered years later. In part, she felt she had been influenced by those early intellectual discussions with her father; in part by the books she had read since early childhood.[38] No matter the conflict her decision would cause in her family, Clairene's determination to leave was a matter of self-preservation.

A conversation between the fictional Sibyl and her mother, Mrs. Randolph, in "Gaily Bedight," re-creates the kinds of conversations that might have passed between Clairene and her mother.

Mrs. Randolph tries to convince Sibyl to postpone leaving because, with three years of college and one summer term, she "never had a chance to enjoy life!" Of course, traditional mothers might not have defined learning as enjoyable, a "carnival." Rather, Mrs. Randolph plans a "nice debut" followed by "a lovely home wedding," since she had come to accept that her daughter would object to a church ceremony. Despite her diamond engagement ring, Sibyl explains that she doesn't intend to marry and settle down. She wants to see the world first.[39]

When Sibyl receives notification that she has been accepted for a job, both parents are outraged. "I can't for the life of me see why any girl wants to work for a living when she doesn't have to!" Sibyl's mother exclaims. Sibyl answers: "I want to live by my own efforts—to be independent economically and every other way too," adding that she finds it humiliating to take money from her father. In a rare moment of honesty, Mrs. Randolph concurs: "Yes, it is humiliating—but it's a thing I've had to do all my married life . . . account for every penny." The possibility for the two women to bond passes, however, since the mother cannot condone her daughter's unorthodox behavior.

Sibyl's father mandates, if his daughter defies them, he will expect her to be self-supporting and "act exactly like a son." "From now on," he tells her, "never expect help or money from me."

Likewise, Claire's father, whose courage as a "noble adventurer" had been celebrated by his mother's poem, turned a cold heart against his daughter. Claire often recalled that her father legally disinherited her and refused ever to speak to her again. However, several times during the twenty years between 1916 when she left and 1936 when he died, Mr. Myers rescued his daughter with expressions of loving care accompanied by a check. His behavior left her in conflict: "As much as I loved my father, I didn't want to be under his thumb. I wanted . . . freedom and I would have to support myself."[40]

The freedom she sought was more than just financial independence or the right to decide when and whom to marry. Freedom meant self-discovery—"the freedom to be myself"—though she often claimed it would be years before she fully understood what that impulse meant.

Many college students speak of a "wind of desire, a wind of change," she noted later in life. But Clairene had "never read anything about a lady going out to work . . . never read anything about social service." She defined herself as "a small-town girl," way behind the times, preoccupied with "dancing and having pretty clothes and going to parties."[41]

However, her novels and the "Autobiography" contradict this assertion.[42] In sociology classes she had learned about the slums of New York, the mountaineers, and "those moon light schools in Carolina." In "Gaily Bedight," Sibyl and Marion (a.k.a. Clare Ousley) discuss their future: "I want to work—to be independent and support myself like a man," Sibyl says. Marion agrees: "We must!" The novel implies that as college students, the two girls shared the same high

7. Clairene and Alden on the Myers's porch, Temple, Texas, 1916. Photograph courtesy of the TWU Woman's Collection.

ideals about helping the less fortunate as well as ideas of rebellion, which arose from a sense that there was more to learn in college than housekeeping skills.

In leaving, it becomes clear that Clairene, like Sibyl, abandoned her responsibility to honor the family claim as she rushed to fulfill a destiny the folks back home considered reckless. Each time Claire left Temple, her guilt was enormous, but the call of the world was larger still.

The "Autobiography" and novels indicate that just as she had been impatient to leave home for college, Clairene was impatient to leave college for "that great wide beautiful world" that beckoned her. Faced with the moment of choice, she was torn; however, she realized she must find the courage to leave. As Sibyl describes her flight from her parental home, "I don't know why—but something *pulls* me—*pulls* me!"[43]

4

Be Wise

1916–1917

> Throw yourself into this expedition with a whole heart—half measures are for puny people.
>
> —Aunt Sophistica
>
> Claire Myers Spotswood, *The Unpredictable Adventure*

LEAVING SMUG HARBOR to explore the land of Nithking (anagram for *thinking*), Tellectina in *The Unpredictable Adventure* becomes the archetypal hero who heeds what the famed mythologist Joseph Campbell terms "the call to adventure" and sets off to explore the unknown. Unlike Clairene, when Tellectina leaves Smug Harbor, she is not alone in her quest. Rather, her indomitable Aunt Sophistica, the "protective figure" who arms the adventurer with the fruits of her own knowledge, gives her an inspiring send-off.[1]

The send-off provides an opportunity to satirize both the cultural and the religious injunctions against freedom. Reversing truisms common to Tellectina's—and Clairene's—fundamentalist background, Sophie advises her protégée *not* to be careful, as Tina expects, but to "be wise and rush in where fools fear to tread," not to let conscience be her guide, but desire: "Throw yourself into this expedition with a whole heart—half measures are for puny people. Abandon yourself recklessly to the passion of living. . . . Be the grand[e] amoureuse of life . . ."[2]

Clairene never had such a supportive mentor, never had such liberating advice, only an innate dynamic drive toward freedom and a passion to discover her true self. This need to be herself, though it would take her "many years to fully understand what that meant," became one of the central themes of Claire's life, expressed metaphorically in her poetic descriptions of her whirl in the Texas wind, her reaction to the perfume of the honey locust flower, and in similar altered states of consciousness, those "small ecstasies."[3] The odyssey of self-discovery on which Clairene embarked at age twenty, parallels the journey of self-realization reflected in her spiritual life. The former is a search for self-definition in a social and cultural context. The latter, the "small ecstasies"—ineffable, spontaneous moments that transcend material reality and allow the infusion of the eternal into the present—generate a link between her inner, unconscious self and her exterior persona.

As Claire indicates in her autobiographical passages describing the Texas wind, the faster she danced, the freer she became: "Free to be my natural animal self. Free from my mother's daily don'ts. From the satin-lined prison of lady-like decorum. . . . Free from the admonishing voices of teachers. . . . And from the sin I never felt." The "tantalizing voice" of the north wind calls her to "fairer fields of fulfillment" and promises "impossible delights."[4] These paranormal events function as both metaphors of and stimuli to Claire's ability to define herself against the traditions of her native culture, to leave the domestic sphere and enter the wide world in search of fulfillment and delight.

Armed with a spirit of rebellion and a sense of destiny, at age twenty Clairene became part of a movement that began during the middle of the nineteenth century and progressed with significant impact on both European and American culture in the early years of the twentieth century. For when Clairene Myers left home that summer of 1916, she became one of the New Women of her generation.[5]

The New Woman, an expression created by the news media at the turn of the century, "seemed to be everywhere and no where." Originally modeled after the 1860s generation of feminist suffragists, by the 1890s the New Woman discarded the traditions of chastity before marriage and motherhood and became unconventional.

The subject of the "woman question" that buzzed through media and social circles at the turn of the twentieth century, the New Women threatened to turn the world upside down.[6] In the United States, New Women were university educated and sexually independent proponents of the "single standard" who insisted that marriage was not women's only option for a fulfilling life. Challenging male supremacy in art, the professions, and the home, the image engendered intense hostility and fear.[7]

One New Woman Claire would come to admire, Edna St. Vincent Millay (1892–1950), rebelled against traditional women's roles. Born in Maine, Millay, who called herself Vincent, grew up in poverty. A Vassar graduate, she became an icon of Bohemian lifestyles in New York's Greenwich Village, where Claire would settle in the 1920s. Millay's poetry and prose rose to high acclaim; in 1923, she received a Pulitzer Prize in poetry, the first woman to earn the prestigious award. Though her family did not object to her unorthodox behavior, her refusal to conform to separate sexual mores for women became legend in Greenwich Village. Once women gained the right to vote in 1920, exceptional women from all over the country felt empowered to carve out separate identities and to create independent lifestyles.[8]

Young women like Clairene, rare in the South, began to seek worldly success, experimenting with alternative lifestyles. Although Clairene's education had not encouraged a public career, college exposed her to the progressive ideas of her time. The lessons of her study and the ideas she and Clare Ousley explored, coalesced with a sense of justice nurtured by her father, led to her brief interest in settlement house work. Her sense of entitlement helped her resist the protestations of her family, friends, and fiancé. This right to seek her destiny, along with her yearning for excitement, travel, and worldly knowledge, provided the impetus to "be wise and rush in" to an opportunity she had anticipated since childhood.

"Gaily Bedight" captures the enormous sense of relief Clairene must have felt. As the taxi speeds down Michigan Avenue in Chicago, Sibyl's heart sings: "At last, at last you're free! . . . Ah, Life—the great Adventure that held such infinite possibility of happiness!"[9]

"Gaily Bedight" is the only extant document in the archives that details her summer in Chicago; several of the characters, particularly Karl, a fictionalized version of her first husband, Leo Saidla, resurface in her subsequent accounts of her life in New York City. A letter dated July 13, 1916, from Alden Evans addressed to Clairene Myers at 955 Grand Ave., Chicago Commons, then a settlement house for new immigrants, provides concrete evidence that Clairene went to Chicago before her job began in Alabama.[10] According to the events described in "Gaily Bedight," Chicago marks the first stage of her lifelong journey, replete with motifs that describe moments of self-insight, loss of innocence, and coming of age.

At dinner the first evening, Sibyl, "initiated into a new world," reflects on the central question of her mission: "What was important . . . erudition, culture, worldly experience?" Were the "values in her upbringing" the only correct ones? She vows to define a new "scale by which life can be measured" other than money and social position.[11]

In place of family responsibility, Sibyl experiences the full weight of autonomy, its ballast and its burden: "With all supporting background removed, she now stood or fell according to her own merits." Yet Sibyl seems remarkably comfortable living "alone in the mysterious city [filled with] the joy of being an individual and not a part of anything else." Stripped bare of her cultural ties, "instinct directs her thoughts" and reveals, in the midst of the "dim yearnings and unconscious stirrings of youth," an innate sense of destiny or even predestiny: "No man can be what he wills but is what he was—potentially at birth—and before birth even."[12]

At the settlement house located in Chicago's Little Poland, Sibyl's small room overlooks the "dull red roofs and blackened chimneys of innumerable tenements." Uncharacteristically shy at the dining table that first evening, "aware of her youth and ignorance, she dared not speak." The veils of her innocence fall away one by one: She is impressed by a man who lived seven years in Europe, but shocked by his disrespectful treatment of his aged mother. She is "surprised to hear people actually converse about the 'single standard'—her favorite theory to embrace," though she had never dared to "broach the subject." She is baffled by the position taken by a woman lawyer—"how wonderful that a woman could be a lawyer"—in favor of the double standard. Women, the lawyer believes, as "vessels through which every human being must pass," should keep their vessel "clean and pure." "How," wonders Sibyl, "could such an 'advanced woman' be so old-fashioned?"[13]

Training consists of two weeks of lectures on charity and poverty, after which participants are assigned to "investigate" families living in tenements. Sibyl's job is to send children to the country, to find work for fathers, distribute clothes and money, and send the sick to clinics. Socially and professionally her initiation has begun; more veils of innocence fall away. When Sibyl reads the case histories, she finds "a mass of details concerning too many childbirths, too expensive funerals, drunkenness, deserted wives, child labor, fathers without work—dirt, disease, and poverty, poverty—poverty."[14]

Though pity "wrung her heart," Sibyl, revolted by the filth, finds she cannot bear to touch the children, nor enter another "evil smelling hole!" Her reactions, echoing Jacob Riis's 1890 study, *How the Other Half Lives*, confronts this unfamiliar territory,[15] but ends in a reinforcement of stereotypes: the Italians are "inveterate liars," the Poles, "cold and taciturn," the Irish, "voluble and quarrelsome."[16]

As Sibyl observes this world, she struggles to liberate herself from "smugness" concerning decent social standards. Ultimately, she sympathizes with the immigrant workers; outraged that employers "didn't pay them a living wage," she declares social work "an intrusion on their privacy."[17]

Although she is not homesick, she experiences a "hitherto unknown loneliness" at once "nourishing and disturbing." She does not want to go to the theater or gossip with the other trainees. She connects feelings of longing to a woman's "natural need for love," realizing that beneath her search for career lies the quest for an ideal lover: "Always from the very day she is born the woman begins to wait . . . for her ideal lover; and consciously or unconsciously tests every man who crosses her path."[18]

As Simone de Beauvoir observed, for women, love is a religion: "It is agonizing for a woman to assume responsibility for her life"; even those who choose independence "dream of a *grand amour*, a soul searing love."[19] In the throes of independent living, Sibyl's fantasies turn to love for relief, demonstrating a significant theme in the author's life, as in the protagonist's quest; this need sets up dichotomies between the emotional and the intellectual, love and work, commitment to a man and the need for autonomy. The characters Claire portrayed in her novels seek not to escape love but to avoid marriage—not to do without men but to create male-female relationships based on a single standard.

The divided self, personified in *The Unpredictable Adventure* through the characterization of the Tellectina-Femina split, manifests in "Gaily Bedight" as an inner tug toward traditional femininity, overlaid with modern ideas so contradictory that the protagonist herself remains unaware of her motives. A new platonic friendship with the "effeminate" Karl provides the resolution between Sibyl's higher idealistic drives and her lower libidinal ones. "Sibyl desired romance yet a part of her nature hungered after just this sort of thing, which had no bearing on sex whatsoever."[20]

Even as the veils of innocence fall away, new ones appear to restrict her vision. As she and Karl walk to Lake Michigan in the darkness, the fact that they are strangers adds to the magic of the encounter; they pour out their inmost thoughts. "Never had she met so responsive a person." Sibyl feels this stranger understands her and will not misinterpret her actions. But she seems incapable of understanding his reserve, and his manner leaves her confused. When they lie together on the cement at the water's edge, he places his cap beneath her cheek and when that's too rough, his hand. His sophistication dazzles her. Flattered by the attentions of this "learned" man, annoyed that he resists her attempts to seduce him by moving "her lithe young body close against him," she feels relief when he talks on without responding to her sexually.[21]

During another outing, Karl takes her to a museum where she confronts nude statues: "People in her hometown condemned the nude even in art" which she finds "ridiculous."[22] She stands looking at a bronze Mercury from "cap to heel, forcing herself to seem neither amazed nor self-conscious though she is both." Later they stroll by a lagoon—she finds all water romantic—and she exclaims to herself, "Was this not romance!" as if to convince herself that this is a perfect relationship. Disappointed to discover that Karl had been a minister, a profession she associates with the narrow-mindedness of her childhood religion, she begs him never to speak of it again, "determined that he should be as wonderful a person as she wished him to be," and remains unaware of her own contradictory responses.[23]

On Sundays she receives letters and the "customary box of roses" from her fiancé, who vows eternal love and begs her to hasten home. She sobs with guilt at her disloyalty to this "good wholesome clean man." But how could she be happy with him? He does not "care whether I have any brains at all." Yet knowing that he loves her becomes "a problem that constantly tore at her heart"; she begs God to make her good, pure, and beautiful inside.[24]

Given the letters that document Clairene and Alden's actual long-distance relationship, it is easy to see how they would wreak havoc upon a young girl's psyche. A letter dated July 13, 1916, reflects Alden's confusion and his manipulative techniques: "My Own Little Girl: —I got the best letter from you today, Sweetheart. . . . You were a little careless or I would have received it long before now." He likes that it was so "Clairene-like." Alternating admonitions and declarations of love become his signature style throughout their courtship: "I am the same Alden, doing the same things in the same way, loving the same little girl. . . . *But honestly Clairene, you and I ought to be just a little more careful . . . don't you think you should know me a little better every day? . . . and that I learn a little more about the real Clairene*" (emphasis mine).[25]

Extrapolating from characterizations of this relationship in *The Unpredictable Adventure* and in "Gaily Bedight," telling anyone about the "real Clairene" was a fruitless endeavor. No one could understand what she was saying. Not only Alden, but most of the men Clairene met would "not have cared if she had a brain or not"—no one except Karl, the fictionalized version of Leo Saidla. Leo/Karl reappears in later sections of her novels and plays an important role in Clairene's New York adventure.

Back home, after training in Chicago, Clairene and Alden took up where they left off. Her brief stay prior to leaving for Alabama replicated the period prior to leaving for Chicago earlier that summer. Alden came to visit and had a marvelous time. Apparently, Clairene did too. The day after he returned to Fort Worth, where he had become a reporter for the *Fort Worth Star Telegram*, he wrote, his "Own Darling Girl" that he would truly give his life for "'Just a little love a little kiss'" [his quotes]. During the two days he spent with her, "*Everything* was beautiful, lovely, grand" and he was the happiest man in the world. "Forever and ever Clairene and Alden will love each other just as they do now."[26]

This letter details his work day, scattered with promises to "*make good*." But he wants to be successful only to please *her*; his success depends on *her* returning his feelings. Her letter indicates how happy she had been during their visit, while other letters express her refusal to commit. Was she leading Alden on? Was she playing belle to the hilt? Or was she as confused as he?

Since Clairene uses quotes from actual letters in her fiction, putting Alden's words in the fictional fiancé's letters, it is probable that Sibyl's response reflects Clairene's feelings. When Sibyl's fiancé asks that she promise to be true and not let another man kiss her or even touch her "little finger," Sibyl replies, "No, my dear—I won't promise anything." Yet she is filled with happiness when he promises his fidelity.

As for her parents, Sibyl's sense of adventure obliterates her guilt: though "saddened by the sorrow of the lonely people she was leaving . . . the real adventure was to work—to be independent . . . there stood Life, the Great Shining Knight, beckoning her." And once again she answers the call, "I'm coming! I'm coming!"[27]

One source of Clairene's power to resist her family and fiancé lies in her innate sense of feminism, expressed in "Gaily Bedight." On the train to the mining camp, Sibyl writes her fiancé that she was the only woman in the car and a battery of men's eyes was constantly upon her. He answers that "it is not customary for *nice* young women to travel alone . . . so if you *will* be independent and unconventional—you must expect men to stare."

Sibyl's reply provides a glimpse into Clairene's feminist views: "If a woman is capable of working and supporting herself, she is also capable of going where and doing what she sees fit—and alone—as any man does who works and supports himself. And I intend to: it is high time [that silly tradition] was broken down!"[28]

A subsidiary of United States Steel, the Tennessee Coal Mine and Railroad Company employed fifty college-educated girls in their various locations; five girls were assigned to the location to which Clairene was sent, the Wennonah Mines in Bessamer, Alabama, near Birmingham.[29]

Life in the mining camp, as portrayed in the novel, breaks down more of Sibyl's illusions, though it reinforces her conviction concerning the single- and double-standard conundrum. The employees, for the most part, are social workers who answer to the superintendent of the Welfare Department, a woman she soon discovers to be unjust and hypocritical. Sibyl is the only one from the South; the others are from the Northeast with degrees from such prestigious colleges as Vassar and Bryn Mawr. Distressed by competition, back-stabbing, and constant bickering among the employees, Sibyl is surprised that "college girls—who surely represented the best in modern women, were petty, jealous, and personal, and as quarrelsome as all other women."[30]

In life, the lessons Clairene learned proved profound. When Claire told this part of her story to Kenneth Ring, her voice vibrated with enthusiasm:

> The company was doing welfare work. They said this was not a humanitarian project but just good business to keep people happy so they wouldn't leave the mines. . . . So we had a clubhouse for them and dances. . . . Some of the mining boys had brought sheet music. Well, I couldn't sight-read the music, play [the organ], and sing at the same time . . . so I told them to sing and I would play. And they didn't say a word, and then I realized the men couldn't read. So I would sing a line and they would sing after me. When they came

> to the dances, they would have a gun . . . on one hip and a bottle of moonshine on the other. Our senior social worker used to . . . hide them during the dances. They'd whirl you around until they'd nearly kill you . . . their breath had such a strange odor . . . and they said, "Why that was the moonshine."[31]

Ironically, after training in Chicago, after traveling across the country, after breaking free of tradition, what was waiting for Clairene at the mining camp was her great nemesis: cooking. One of her first assignments was to teach cooking classes to the women. Once, cooking popovers on an oil stove: "They didn't pop. I'd never even seen an oil stove. I was supposed to entertain these women and they were sitting there chewing snuff." They were older and knew far more about cooking than she did. They never came back. "I'm afraid my cooking class was a great failure," she mused. Perhaps their disinterest lay in their lack of trust in this educated, yet naïve, young woman.[32]

In "Gaily Bedight," Sibyl finds it becomes increasingly difficult to throw herself into the work; she doesn't care "whether these stupid miner girls ever learn to cook or sew or not! I'm not interested in *anybody's* cooking food or sewing clothes. Bah!"[33] Her quilting classes "failed utterly"; the women were "lethargic creatures who sat obstinately in their dirty little houses breeding children and expectorating snuff. Uplifting them was a difficult task." Perhaps her fiancé and her parents were right. Given her revulsion of the Chicago tenements and of the "dirty miners" and their families, a lady could find no place in the real world.

As Janet L. Freedman points out in her history of consciousness-raising, until the women's and human rights movements of the 1960s and 1970s, class advantages were invisible; race, gender, ethnicity, education, affluence, and more were all unearned advantages Claire was unaware she possessed. She had been reared in a world of white, middle-class privilege.[34] Her experiences in social work in Chicago and Alabama initiated her to the way the other half lived. Life in the real world she had longed for in high school and college came with lessons she had not envisioned.

Though often repulsed, she found compassion and connection through her exposure to the children of the miner families. With them, she momentarily transcended the grime of their realities. The kindergarten seemed to hold its own special magic, where "dirty little miner children [blossomed] forth like fragrant little flowers. They danced and laughed and played together in perfect harmony. Invariably if another adult entered the room, however, the spell was broken—the petals closed and they became merely quarrelsome [and] obstinate."[35]

Later in life, Claire puzzled over their remarkable transformation from wild and undisciplined "urchins": "Something we did brought out the best in the children; there was never a problem of discipline, not once," though as they sang nursery rhymes, the children "chewed tobacco like mad."[36]

They would take nature walks in the woods. Ordinarily when they saw a bird, they shot at it, but not when Clairene was in charge. When the maid came in with cocoa or other things they needed, the children accepted her; but when anyone from the office in Birmingham came in there would be a great disruption. "There was a kind of spell on us I don't understand, but we just loved each other." That unique bonding between teacher and child triggered yet another magical moment, another "small ecstasy." As Clairene recalled in *Awakening to the Good*, "On a balmy April day" she witnessed an incredible spectacle. While the children blew bubbles in the air—beautiful and iridescent—the homeliest little girl sat down next to her and "suddenly I just felt such love for these children, for the goodness that they had manifested the whole year. I saw auras . . . like colored envelopes . . . [and] I saw an image like a little kernel of wheat . . . realizing there was a kernel of good not just in these children but in everyone in the world but it was all covered over . . . I was convinced from that moment forever after that people had innate goodness.[37]

As Professor Ring observed, this moment was like a "kernel" of her later experiences, fostering a perception of the world, of nature, and of people that would influence the even deeper experiences she would have throughout her life. This intimation of the miracle of innocence, revealed to her as an inherent property of all life, broke through her consciousness as a result of the purity of the children and her own innocence. The mining camp played an important step in her initiation, a second glimpse into the real world beyond her childhood. The message inherent in this kernel of knowledge, combined with the intuitive insights of the ecstatic event, introduced an element of optimism that informed her entire life journey and rescued her from bouts with depression. However, at the time, she could only wonder at the implications of that quality inherent in humanity she came to call "the good."

Messages from home arrived regularly, especially from Alden. One dated January 12, 1917, opens with a disclaimer: surely he must have been "non composmentis" when he wrote all of his previous letters or he would not have failed to say "anything nice in a single one of them." Clairene accused Alden of not understanding her letters; his retaliation accused her of writing infrequently or being inattentive. Most of his quibbles involved his concerns for his "girl's" well-being. Evidently, she had offered to try again—he agreed she should.[38]

His letters maintain an accusatory tone, even as they shift to explanations of his having been unfaithful. He claims he would not have told her except he thought she might find out about the "Amarillo girl." He admits he has "done some things with other girls" but not "the worst"—only "things for the fun of it." He offers to give up all girls except her.[39]

Most likely, Clairene had been seeing other men too, including Leo Saidla. She did not promise to be faithful when Alden asked her to. Still, breaking up with Alden was no easy task. Like a boomerang, his letters consistently twisted her words and hurled them back with plans for their future together. "I want to live a certain life, be a certain kind of a man, and all with the girl of my choice. . . . Play fair," he implores, "you always have, tell me, tell me, and tell me now."[40]

Miraculously, she did. While he was writing one letter, a letter arrived from Clairene. When he took up his pen again, he continued his pleading in handwriting that grew continually smaller, weaker, and cramped: "You are looking at the affair in a bad light," he argued. He had held to the promises he made her "pretty well." "You ought to be more considerate," he accused, though he was sorry he had told her about another woman and never would again. In the future, if she asked, he would lie to her.

Her letter conveys her decision to return the engagement ring. "I'm sorry you mentioned the ring," he wrote back, but he realized that she loved neither him nor it any longer. "I'm going to try to find something else to live for, work for, strive for. But it won't be another girl."[41]

Long exhortations of love, care, and denial comprise two more letters written that March: "Dear little Girl: Your last letter and the ring came about a week ago," he wrote, but he decided that she didn't mean what she said! They have been "honest-to-God loving each other for a long time" as one another's "True and only Love," he wrote his "little Clairene Girl."[42]

Over and over, he implored her to remember their plans: "The little ring is yours, your own, not mine"; he plans to give her a larger one someday, and he will send this one back "pretty soon, anytime" she says she wants it. His signature, "*Alden* who loves you and forgives you," must have been as disturbing as the letter itself with its implications of his martyrdom in the face of *her* disloyalty, ignoring that he has confessed to having relations with that "Amarillo girl."[43]

His next letter opens, "My Own Darling Little Girl: —You are not my own darling little girl because you won't be." Twelve accusatory pages follow, with no indication that she is not a "Little Girl" at all, but a woman defining herself as independent. Time and again, Clairene struggles to help him understand, and Alden avoids her claims and struggles to convince her that he is right.

The letter, which took him four hours to write, ends with a barrage of guilt-provoking love declarations: "The love I have for you is morning, noon and night, daylight and evening," he signs off, "The same forgotten Alden."[44]

The only letter from Clairene to Alden in the archive is an undated draft on scraps of paper. Apparently she mailed the finished version, and he stopped writing. The next letters in the archive are from Bisbee, Arizona, addressed to Clairene in New York City the following year. Her words finally must have had an effect. In the draft written in her scrawling handwriting, she stops and starts, scratches out, rewrites and frees herself, once and for all, from his clutching embrace: "Yes, you do deserve a letter from me. What is it that you want me to say? I don't dislike you Alden . . . But I can't make any definite promises. . . . I am sure that I don't want to marry for at least three more years and that I want to be absolutely free during that time to do and go wherever I wish and think as I please. . . . I can't remain engaged to you and be as free as I wish."[45]

She realizes that she cannot make him understand her; indeed, she "scarcely understands" herself, "but there is that desire deep down in me that impels me irresistibly [or irrationally] along certain lines and it won't be denied." She closes, "sincerely" wishing he will be "happy, ambitious and a great success."[46]

Perhaps one of the reasons she had such a hard time explaining her motives was that she herself barely understood them. She was, after all, on a journey of self-discovery.

"Gaily Bedight" enacts Sibyl's decision to return the ring and stages it shortly before Christmas 1916, her first away from home, a time when she is feeling in charge of her life. For the first time, she can give "all the gifts she wanted to give. Oh, the joy of not having to ask her father for money!"[47]

The author has reached a point in the novel where she begins to explore the split between instinct and reason, lady and intellect, in ways that firmly establish "Gaily Bedight" as a precursor to *The Unpredictable Adventure*, where the two personae split into separate characters, Tellectina and Femina. Inner conflict frustrates Sibyl, an early version of Tellectina: "I *must* have some one to adore me," she realizes at the height of her stand for independence.[48]

Such ambivalence, Claire explained in the Ring interview, results from an Oedipal pull. "My love of my father affected my life, made me reluctant to marry."[49] According to her interpretation of the Freudian theory, the daughter can be a rival to her mother, causing jealousy on the mother's part and ambivalence toward marriage on the daughter's.

This same ambivalence appears in Sibyl's classification of men: those with whom she would flirt because they would bore her otherwise, and those whom she respected too much to flirt with—men she could have married had they not been psychologically associated with her father.[50] But Sibyl is sure of her platonic relationship with Karl—she can depend on Karl; "*he* won't ever change."

Sibyl's initiation moves between the personal and the political, with bridges connecting the two. Just as she seeks to balance her relationships with men in terms of physical and intellectual love, so she seeks to understand the relationship between her ideals as a social worker and the reality under which the system operates.

A radical social worker opens Sibyl's eyes to the liberal position by introducing her to the *Masses*, the small, avant-garde magazine published in New York between 1911 and 1917.[51] "It being in favor of labor," the girls kept their copies hidden until they could go up in the hills "where they read and smoked to their heart's content. . . . Heated condemnations of all existing orders thrilled Sibyl's young blood, kindling the fire of her own rebellion which needed only a match to set it flaming."[52] Whereas the *Masses* closed down in 1917, shortly before Clairene arrived, its radical, liberal voice echoed throughout the Greenwich Village culture for years to come.

Clairene's friend Robbie McKnight, in her letter of March 1914, had warned her that her idealism would "blind her sight" and her expectations of the real world would cause her pain. Disappointed by the lying hypocrisy of some of her colleagues in the mines, Clairene determines to leave after her year ends, summarized in Sibyl's words: "I can't fight them—I don't even want to."[53]

But the most disturbing intrusion of the real world came with the declaration of American involvement in World War I, which foreshadowed Claire's overwhelming reaction to World War II. Both wars affected her psychological condition long after their end. After reading the announcement of World War I in the newspaper, she cried, remembering her grandmother's stories of the Civil War and the dreadful suffering and depravation left in its wake. In the Ring interview, she recalled condemning “the tragedy that the human race could do this to one another.”[54]

In “Gaily Bedight,” Sibyl’s reactions are equally dramatic, and she is baffled to discover that her coworkers are not affected on the same level. She writes home and finds that even her parents seem detached and unconcerned. Filled with despair, she becomes physically ill, sobs violently. Searching for a sympathetic ear, she writes Karl in Chicago, the “only one” who understands her: “I am utterly alone except for my other inside self to whom I’m always talking [and] except for the beautiful strange voices which speak to me. The wind in the trees . . . the whisperings of the night, and the dear fragrant dancing flowers—these are my only friends.”[55] The equally romantic Karl, delighted, replies that they must correspond more frequently until they meet in the fall in New York City.

Clairene departed from Alabama, disappointed in the work, bored with the project, ready to move from country to city, from South to North. She realized this kind of social work was like “rubbing syrup on a cancer . . . not getting to the root of the problem.” In any case, her goal had always been New York City; Alabama had been merely a “waystation.”[56]

5

Nithking

1917–1919

[Nithking] offers the greatest possible adventure in all life.
—Aunt Sophistica
Claire Myers Spotswood, *The Unpredictable Adventure*

THE GLITTERING CITY, as Clairene called New York in "Gaily Bedight," turned out to be everything she'd dreamed it would be "and more so"—exciting, the best of everything. When she first arrived, she attended Columbia University primarily as an excuse to pacify her parents about her decision to move to the "wicked city." Alas, when she began attending Columbia, she found she had to take cooking again! "I couldn't get away from it!"[1]

Columbia University's College Woman's Association provided a job placement service. Although eventually the two World Wars would open many jobs for women normally filled by men, in the autumn of 1917, jobs for women proved difficult to obtain.

Sibyl's trials in "Gaily Bedight" mirror the situations Clairene and other young, single women of the period encountered. After several weeks of job hunting, Sibyl runs out of money and ends up living in a woman's hotel on lower Fourth Avenue in Greenwich Village, answering ads for everything—"moving picture actresses, mannequins, models, companions, playground leaders, social workers."[2] Sibyl finally secures a job as a tutor but is insulted when asked to "mend the household linen." Claire spoke of the same kinds of frustrations, feeling humiliated and exploited by the jobs open to her. Down to her last fifteen cents, Clairene finally found a job as a social worker at the Children's Clearance Bureau, located at the corner of W. Tremont and Andrews in the Bronx, where she occupied a fourth-floor room.

In fictional accounts, Clairene describes the settlement house as a "glorified orphanage, hospital, school, designed to remedy [children's] physical and mental defects as far as possible," and her charges as "dirty half-witted little devils—pitiful products of the city streets."[3] Clairene came to hate the oppressive environment surrounding the underclass, "the dirt, the odors"; social work in the Bronx did not appeal to her any more than it had in Chicago or in Alabama. During the Ring interview, Claire looked back on her settlement work period and indicated that she was unsuited for the demands and atmosphere and eventually found more satisfaction managing bookstores and pursuing "an artistic life" writing novels and short stories.[4] Obviously, though she learned from the children in Alabama, the lessons did not stick—not yet. Without a clear understanding of class difference, she could not have seen her own life as one of privilege that allowed her to look down on the less fortunate. Besides, no one is wholly privileged; personal struggles focus on the gaps in one's developmental needs. People take for granted the privileges they are born into, whether in terms of wealth, family attitudes toward education, ethnic difference, and myriad values passed from generation to generation as untold stories.[5]

Girls brought up to be southern belles would have a hard time doing work that involves getting their hands dirty or taking orders from "ladies" talking down to them. Unprepared for the "real" world, Clairene needed to find a niche that preserved her self-image even as it allowed her to participate in an authentic career. Clairene, who left Texas determined "to save the world overnight," remained dedicated to that challenge, though the focus of her quest changed drastically during this period. Rather than saving others, she began working toward saving herself.

Whereas Clairene scandalized most of her Texas friends by her unconventional behavior, Robbie McKnight considered Clairene a role model. Robbie's letter dated January 30, 1918, indicating her intention to join her friend in moving east, provides further insight into the times and their effect on women's lives. Apologizing for being such a poor correspondent, she thanks Clairene for sending two hat veils, which make her feel "perfectly Fifth Avenueish." Robbie, then a student at the University of Texas, where she "always longed to be," was happy, busy with her sorority, Zeta, and dating young aviators stationed there. "Clothes?" she jests, "call mine '*clo*'—I haven't enough to be plural. But that is being patriotic these days. . . . Consoling!" The war has changed campus life, leaving a shortage of men, but she doesn't care, for Robbie is "a seeker after wisdom, this time, *strictly*."[6]

Enrolled in stenography and typewriting—a new course adopted as a "sort of war measure"—Robbie "jumped at the chance to take it. . . . Be looking around for me a job in NY, my dear—I'll be there in June." A long newsy letter follows with confessions that her boyfriend, Aubrey, "is mighty *serious*, but I don't think your Roberta can give up the status of single blessedness for some time."

Robbie's use of the term *single blessedness* captures a significant aspect of the pervasive New Woman attitude. "The Cult of Single Blessedness," an early nineteenth century idea, "upheld the single life as both a socially and personally valuable state."[7] Acknowledging the "transitory nature of domestic bliss," the tenet of single blessedness "encouraged the search for eternal happiness through the adoption of a 'higher calling' than marriage": specifically, discovering God's plan for the individual design of one's own life. However, the cult's approval of women remaining single, along with its implicit rebellion against marriage, gained appeal because of many women's desire for autonomy, selfhood, and for expanding their intellectual and personal horizons. Thus, women would develop their talents and use them to serve God and the community rather than just husband and family. To paraphrase Louisa May Alcott, liberty was a better husband than love, to many of her contemporaries.[8]

The desire for the freedom to choose one's life and destiny surfaced in the wake of the European Enlightenment and American Revolution, with the drive for personal autonomy and individual liberty emerging as inalienable rights to America's sons and daughters. With increasing numbers of women educated in colleges and universities—eighty-five thousand by 1900—came the New Woman's insistence on the right to put her studies to use.[9] It is curious, however, to find the term *single blessedness* appearing out of nowhere in Robbie's letter; and yet, given Robbie's regard of Clairene's idealism as both dubious and laudable, perhaps Robbie expected that Clairene was familiar with the term and its significance. As New Women, both women were engaged in the search for autonomy. While there is no evidence that Robbie followed her friend to New York City, both women considered their college education as valuable an asset as their youthful good looks; both determined to define a life beyond marriage and family, "singly blessed."

Clairene had her own new sexual vocabulary. Like many rebels who settled in New York City around World War I, Clairene's definition of freedom included the embrace of free love. While the initial demand for recognition of female sexuality came from free love and women's rights advocates in the nineteenth century, twentieth-century proponents of free love, unlike single blessedness devotees, assumed celibacy was unnatural and dangerous for men and women alike.[10]

The rebels, some known as the Young Intellectuals, congregated in New York's Greenwich Village before World War I, pioneers in a new Bohemianism.[11] To a far greater degree than any of their nineteenth-century predecessors, the pre-war villagers attempted a fusion of the personal and the political, concerned with solving their own conflicts rather than those embedded in world politics. *The Masses*, a magazine of "free expression," opened its pages to "arguments by socialists, anarchists, syndicalists alike," engendering an eclectic profusion of liberal ideologies rather than a cohesive philosophy, which fostered more "conviviality than commitment among its exponents."[12]

Refusing to deny the "demands of the flesh," these rebels came to Greenwich Village from all over the country during the first twenty years of the twentieth century, seeking to satisfy their sexual gratification both through free-love unions and through marriage. Men began to feel responsible for the sexual satisfaction of their mates. Numerous books were published on the subject. Ads appeared in the *Masses*: one page in May 1917 offered five books dealing with the sexual lives of women.[13] Greenwich Village became a symbol of the repudiation of traditional values; many young men and women came to escape community, family, or themselves.[14] Most of the time, between 1917 and 1937, Clairene Myers was part of this milieu and, even during periods when she did not reside in the Village, her life and ideals remained deeply influenced by the values it represented.

Clairene was well primed to enter this atmosphere. She arrived in 1917, torn by conflicting values, aware of the contradictions that troubled her night after sleepless night. Deeply anxious to clarify the notions of sexuality alluded to by her peers, but never fully discussed, she anticipated the excitement and turbulence generated by the atmosphere of change the Village manifested—a rebel in search of a cause.

Her drive to break with the past for the sake of her creative future, her need to shed the shackles of her fundamentalist heritage, left her eager for the new order of Young Intellectual paganism. Groups congregated in teahouses, where they recited verses by candlelight, and in dimly lit cabarets, where they held passionate discussions on politics, literature, and theater. They spouted revolutionary attitudes toward marriage, sexuality, birth control, and free love. Although the *Masses* had shut down by the time Clairene arrived in New York, its writers had led the crusade against America's neo-Puritanism and the genteel tradition. The stage was set. By the early 1920s, the Village had become the capital of America's Bohemian free love, unconventional dress, erratic work schedules, all-night parties, and a sense of living from moment to moment. However, as Leslie Fishbein suggests, "the puritan they tried to exorcise still lurked behind the pagan façade," and the revolt inspired by the *Masses* was for the elite rather than the masses. Nevertheless, the Young Intellectuals popularized Freudian and Nietzschean theories, tailoring them to suit their own, and advocated for women's rights in the areas of suffrage, birth control, and simplified clothing. In addition, they worked toward industrial unionization for working class women along with the establishment of public kindergartens for their preschool-aged children. The paradigms that developed among these so-called elite held sway for the next two decades.[15]

The Greenwich Village portrayed in "Gaily Bedight" captures this spirit of Bohemianism during World War I. While working at a settlement house on Staten Island, Sibyl becomes involved with the chief physician, Dr. Goldstein, "an elderly Jew" with whom she spends "evenings in Greenwich Village, going to costume balls at Webster Hall . . . [and] to the cafes: The Purple Pup, the Vermilion Hound, the Black Cat, Polly's, The Rabbit's Hole," and their favorite, the Turkish Room—typical Village hangouts populated by "Mexican pianists, divorced actors, fifth-rate poets, bobbed-haired designers, cubists and futurists, barefooted gypsies, escaped Russian prisoners, Jewish dentists!" Sibyl loves talking to "those most wonderful and mysterious beings—artists! All her life she had longed to do just this!" Discussions revolve around socialism, theater, art, literature, and the "most popular topic . . . sex—always." Smoking and drinking in public is an act of defiance for Sibyl, as it was for Clairene; her spirit of rebellion delights her as much as the glamour of New York nightlife and the company she keeps.[16]

The relationship between the older doctor and younger woman turns into a deep friendship that nourishes Sibyl's need for intellectual discussions of "modern"—meaning radical—ideas, and "advanced"—meaning unconventional—theories. At a meeting of the Modernists Club, she hears of a colony in California where men and women go bathing nude. Sibyl loves it: "Bring sex into the sunlight and it will become purified of itself!" she tells Dr. Goldstein. "Overly fascinated by sex because she is still curious," Sibyl places a piece of paper and a pencil before him on the table and demands that he draw a picture of the anatomy and physiology of each sex. "*You've—got—to—tell me!*" she insists, because she is "as ignorant as an infant of two."[17]

Although there may not have been a real-life Dr. Goldstein, his presence in Sibyl's journey helps clarify the turmoil seething beneath the surface of many New Women's and Young Intellectuals' carefree social lives at the time. Claire looked back on these years with great enthusiasm, focusing on her social life and the heady experience of financial independence and autonomy, as well as opportunities for rebellion that she acquired living and working in the city. She seems to have become something of an "it girl," the 1920s stereotype of the single girl that falls somewhere between the flapper and the New Woman.[18] Like other "it girls," she socialized and dressed in the latest fashion and discussed political, literary, and artistic trends with genuine concern for the liberating ideals represented by the progressive movement and outspoken writers like those in the *Masses*. She mingled with artists and intellectuals and dated a wide variety of men. "A millionaire one night, a college student the next," she told Kenneth Ring. Despite her parents' disapproval, it was exactly what she had dreamed about: "The best of everything, the best concerts, the best operas, the best books, best conversation; everyone was so alert—so alive. No longer did it matter who your family was or whether you had money or not—it was you that counted."[19]

She was free to be herself, "not my real self, but more than I had ever been before," she explained to Dr. Ring. She found, among the men she knew, that she confronted the same problem she had faced in the South: "I mustn't talk about anything interesting, just . . . gay banter." Although she could not express her true self, at least she was no longer expected to be a lady. But, as she put it, "I still had to be a woman, I couldn't be a person. That bothered me because my intellectual life was very rich; it was a very exciting time."[20]

In "Gaily Bedight," Sibyl observes this developing dichotomy of her personality, the dual self that splits between the feminine, which she sees as frivolous, and the intellectual, which she sees as without gender, describing the two sides of her nature as being "like a piece of rough natural leather lined with soft pink silk." The same dichotomy presents in *The Unpredictable Adventure* as Tellectina rails against socialized hypocrisy and the double standard, wondering: "Why must I be split? Why must I feel one way and act another?" Claire's search for the answers takes place on the pages of her fiction and nonfiction, reflecting the author's high ideals and wild fantasies of life's possibilities. Torn between love (the feminine) and work (the masculine), relationship (the feminine) and independence (the masculine), she lived in search of a balance, recognizing that pursuing both love and career was a problem for women. Men expected women to behave in ways that would make the male feel superior, in charge of women's lives, even as society pretended to be making a place for women in the public realm. Clairene confronted the same conundrum she had faced in college: if she were too intellectual she would be considered unfeminine. Her frustration reflected her disappointment: in the wider world, she believed she would be respected as a thinking woman, a Tellectina. Yet in both Chicago and New York City, intellectual and cultural centers and the hubs of Nithking, she found women marginalized by the same values she had left behind. The double standard was subtler, but there, especially in sexual contexts. Still, during her early years in New York, Clairene embraced her ideals and lived her fantasies. The contradictions inherent in her rebellion became more obvious as the idealism funneled into the utopian life she and Leo Saidla planned to create by forming a communitarian enclave in the Blue Ridge Mountains.

It remains unclear when and where Leo and Clairene reconnected in New York, having first met in Chicago. Clearly, the Sibyl-Karl courtship in "Gaily Bedight," which began in Chicago and continued when Sibyl arrived in New York, is a fictionalized version of the Clairene-Leo courtship. Both were as perplexing as they were avant-garde, or at least presumably avant-garde. The great difference between the public and private nature of their relationship reveals the naïveté and confusion of the two exceedingly idealistic participants.

In the fall of 1917, Leo Saidla entered the New York picture when he arrived to work on his doctorate in theology at Columbia while teaching at a boys' school on Long Island. The couple became romantically involved and shortly thereafter, engaged. The circumstances surrounding their agreement seem unconventional, even for today. After they announced their engagement, Clairene saw Leo one night a week and continued to date an array of men the other six. She and Leo believed in the concept of free love and companionate marriage, though Clairene did not understand the implications of either. If Leo did, then perhaps he had ulterior motives: perhaps he wanted the freedom to substitute the companionate portion for the sexual. During the week between their visits, Leo and Clairene exchanged long letters, literary compositions that masked their self-consciousness, transcribed nearly word for word in the text of "Gaily Bedight."

Three sets of letters document the Myers-Saidla relationship. The first set marks the early days of their courtship in New York City before they agreed to marry; the second set marks their separation after Leo was drafted into the army during World War I; the third follows their activities after Clairene left their utopian haven in the Virginia mountains and fled back to New York. The high emotional content of this same period is further revealed in letters from Clairene's estranged fiancé, Alden Evans, from her concerned mother, and from two mysterious beaux, one from Toronto and another from England (who at times seem to be the same person).[21]

The first set opens with a March 19, 1918, letter from Leo, living in Cheshire, Connecticut, to Clairene at the Children's Clearance Bureau in the Bronx. Written in archaic, flowery language, it captures the romantic idealism the couple shared: "Dear Love and Life, Surely thou art my life Love. . . . You know not how completely you have entered my life and entirely fulfilled the vision of her who might be!" Often Leo would switch to third person, and back again to first: "Leo can just say and act and be love to Clairene. . . . Still my heart craves—it hungers and thirsts for you more and ever more."[22]

He gushes about nature and spring, conjuring visions of a hideaway they will share in the mountains where they can live platonically. The exact nature of their relationship seems confusing even to Leo. In one paragraph, he indicates their love life has already begun: "Our sublime night was a wondrous entrance into the holy mysteries." In others, he carefully plans their first time together. "We naturally will mate in the season of mating—spring—April to June. . . . When we see and hear the birds and watch the growing flowers mating how could we not mate—for surely we are mother nature's children. Oh! you dear Clairene woman. You will almost crush the breath out of your Leo."[23]

Is Leo afraid that Clairene's sexual power will "crush" or overwhelm him? Is that why he calls her "Queenie" and hides behind a veil of language that sounds like a prayer? "O my Love! I know not what thou art or where thou art I only know I love you. In the light of this golden evening sun Leo feels your lips upon his forehead. In the temple let me enter to worship in the spirit of holiness."

Both Leo and Clairene were terrified to actually perform the "great mystery"; comments in the fiction demonstrate their ambivalence. In "Gaily Bedight," even after Karl and Sibyl arrange to live together on weekends, they agree to postpone the consummation of their union. Karl tells Sibyl they will have a "beautiful and original ceremony," when they first see one another nude. "Oh, love, I shall kiss your divine white body from head to foot!" Sibyl replies that she shall kiss his too—that very night. "But," she balks, "Karl, you too want to postpone—the—consummation of our union, don't you, my dear?" Of course he does; it's better to complete their "soul union" before their "bodily union." They decide to wait until they can unite "in the open under the sky on a bed of flowers down in our lovely woods" rather than in an "old ugly room." The narrator interjects, "This young girl's ideas did not seem at all absurd to her, for the woman has never known intimacy, has no particular desire for it, (in fact she dreads it), her desire is merely to be loved and caressed." At twenty, still a romantic child, she believes in fairy tale relationships.[24]

Free union, free love, and companionate marriage beat like a mantra throughout their exchanges, both in the actual letters Leo and Clairene exchanged and in those transcribed between Karl and Sibyl. Leo and Clairene's decision to live together, even part time, without marriage reflects their commitment to the concepts of free love and companionate marriage and to the idea that women should be able to share joys and sorrows with a mate who will not be merely a protector and provider but an all-around companion.

Sexuality was an integral part of the companionate marriage of the 1920s; women were considered sexual beings, and marriage both a sexual and a romantic institution. Nevertheless, social habit prevailed; institutional changes come slowly, and the romantic, passionate, companionate nature of this trend slowly fell back on its traditional roots. Women remained responsible for keeping romance and friendship alive.[25]

Beneath the exterior of change, sexism delegated the domestic sphere to women and the public to men. While the wife would be considered an equal partner, she was in charge of social arrangements that would please her husband; furthermore, she had to be attractive, agreeable, and available. Within the private sphere, women would still be appreciated as beautiful and desirable by those from her husband's public life. In most cases, companionate marriage worked best when the wife had no ambitions and voiced few opinions. Differing from the contemporary sense of women's sexual freedom, the mores of the 1920s liberated women into personhood *within marriage*, but not within the public sphere. Male resistance to working wives prevailed.[26]

Clairene and Leo imagined they could create a situation where, living on a mountain secluded and protected from urban society, they could eliminate the public sphere and live in their own private world. Clairene would have equal say in the fundamental values that would define their community, and she and Leo would share in the domestic chores. Therefore, *companionate* for them would carry, in theory, a connotation of togetherness and shared responsibilities toward their common goal. Furthermore, their sexual theories expressed unique answers to their fears. Leo and Clairene, terrified of the sexual act, devised a complicated system of beliefs, based on Leo's studies of philosophy and religion, which allowed them to sublimate their sexual urges and transport them into a sacred realm. Clairene seemed much more attracted to Leo the philosopher-theologian than to Leo the man. She found his mannerisms effeminate and weak; his hesitancy about sexual matters both comforted and repelled her. He managed to seduce her into his world and keep her there by spouting high-minded theories regarding their remote utopian world, communing with nature and each other.

Letters between them struggle to precisely define their own values, each accusing the other of wanting and not wanting sex, of offering and withdrawing from intimacy. And yet, as young, frightened, and innocent as they were, they were nonetheless daring and rebellious. Letters addressed to Clairene indicate that they used a hyphenated form of her name: Clairene Myers-Saidla. In "Gaily Bedight," Sibyl explains the politics underpinning the form: "I'm still the same person I always was so why change my name? I don't believe in a woman's submerging her identity and her individuality in that of a man. . . . Name the children after either parent or even something entirely different—the silly people get into a rut. . . . I'll do exactly as I see fit. . . . And I want everybody to know we're not married—that we're above men's silly little laws—that we're proud of our free union."[27] Sibyl and Karl agree to tell everybody except those they deem it necessary to deceive.

For Clairene, *everybody* means everybody except her parents. Nothing in the existing letters from Susan Myers to her daughter indicates that she realized there had been no official marriage ceremony or that Leo and Clairene were living most of the time in separate quarters.

Two letters dated April 1918 betray the shock the Myers family felt on learning of their daughter's marriage to Leo. But Mrs. Myers assures her, in their "hearts we feel toward you just as we always have and never let the first thought of anger or unkind feeling toward you or Leo enter our minds. Of course your marriage hurt us as is natural for all parents that give their child into the keeping of another and we were grieved . . . but you will always be our baby and our lovely daughter in whom we find no fault."[28]

The Myerses' shock and disappointment is understandable. Although Clairene had written glowingly of Leo's intelligence and charm, she had been firm in her resolve not to marry, at least for several more years. The Myerses, traditional parents, had not met this man, whom they considered a stranger and a Yankee to boot. Add to this disappointment the fact that not only had they missed their daughter's wedding, there had been no church service to legitimize it on a religious level. They would have been disappointed in being denied the pleasure of hosting, much less attending, their only daughter's wedding.

Mrs. Myers's April 17 letter reiterates that she felt "overcome" by the news, but that she had taken heart in the reactions of Clairene's girlfriends, who all assured her that "Clairene could make no mistake, she is too wise and prudent to act on impulse." A Mrs. Field paid a compliment: "Clairene will fill any sphere wherein she may be placed."

No matter what her husband did along "social, educational or domestic lines," she would be equal to anything.

Public opinion matters in the South, and to southerners like the Myerses it took precedence over their daughter's happiness, but only at first. The next letter apologizes for the first, in case it caused Clairene and Leo "one minute's sorrow," and expresses parental concern for the couple and the life they plan. Adding to the conflict for Clairene is the knowledge that she and Leo are not legally married, even though she took his name in a hyphenated version of her own: Myers-Saidla, which, Mrs. Myers wrote her daughter, she had left out of the newspaper notices, because she "feared some wouldn't quite understand." Though she tries to express support in other ways, her letters testify to her struggles:

> April 29, 1918—
>
> My dear Children:
>
> I realized when I wrote that letter that it didn't have the proper sound, but to save my life I couldn't speak my heart because I was so surprised.

Clairene had described Leo so she could "thank our dear Father in Heaven" that Leo came into her life at this time. In closing, she inquired, "Little girl how are you feeling? Better and stronger and more rested?"[29]

Woven throughout the encouraging words are warnings that women lose their "sweet womanly way . . . when they go up against the hard places out in the world for a long time," and that disappointment is part of life. After all, "It would make us too selfish and too forgetful of the dear Father who is the giver of all good things if our plans worked out altogether."

A third letter urges Clairene to "start Mr. S out on proper foods" to avoid a breakdown from lack of nourishment. Instructions follow on keeping a man happy—"marriage should be 50-50"—and warn her not to insist on having "everything her own way." "The only thing you lack is strength and I want you never to overtax that." But "Mr. S" is athletic and will look after Clairene's "development" in that area. Delegating birth control to the husband, Mrs. Myers assures her that Leo "is wise enough to realize it is best for you not to have children now. One can't hope to raise a healthy strong child if the mother isn't physically fit." Clairene, she believes, was not fit because she had been under the "long constant strain" of living on her own in the "wicked city."[30]

She signs this letter "Devotedly Mother and Daddy" and adds a postscript that Clairene must know each letter is from "both of us," though Mr. Myers is unable to write yet. Evidently, he has not recovered from the blow Mrs. Myers keeps denying affected them so deeply, but, she assures her daughter, "someday the spirit will move him." Undercurrents of denial embedded in her message had to be confusing to Clairene. Perhaps her mother's response was predictable; perhaps Clairene even took pleasure in observing the effects of her rebellion on her parents.

Behind closed doors, Clairene and Leo continued to formulate radical plans for their future home. They pictured themselves settling on a mountain and later allowing their friends to join them, until their plans were interrupted when Leo, a conscientious objector, was drafted to serve as a chaplain, stationed stateside, and later shipped off to France.

With Leo no longer in Connecticut, Clairene moved back to New York City full time and took a job, first in business, later with the telephone company, and resumed her social life. Perhaps that explains the mysterious love letter she received from Toronto, dated July 18, 1918, which opens, "Dear little Lorelei—little 'Clair de Lune' . . . little Moonbeam." The letter, seven-and-a-half nearly illegible pages, filled with dashes, underlines, and exclamations, is lyrical and repetitious. The writer—no name, no surviving envelope—will be coming South sooner than he had anticipated: "Do not *you* be away! we shall play . . . Cheré Lorelei—Let us talk and walk—Let us play." His political discourse rambles for several pages, referring to his childhood in Europe, mentioning Scottish ways. He closes with a gentle, "good night Little Lorelei" and a parenthetical admonition: "(Do not make the provoking disappearance of your namesake!)."[31]

During this period, Clairene fell madly in love with a British sculptor she met at a cocktail party. She attempted to hide his identity in her autobiographical writings, referring to him sometimes as Barton and in her fiction as Chester, though his real name is Carton Moore-Park. He signs his nearly illegible letters *C*, or simply *Carton*. Most likely, Carton *is* the mysterious, anonymous letter writer from Toronto—his handwriting is similar and equally as illegible. Apparently, he moved between Toronto and New York. *The Unpredictable Adventure* characterizes him as Elam Domitann, or dominant male, and casts him as a science professor—though this character seems a composite of Carton and George Wanders, Claire's second husband. *Awakening to the Good* confirms that he was a sculptor, like Chester in "Gaily Bedight." In each version of her fiction and nonfiction, he appears to be the great love of her life. As she told Ken Ring: "I did fall in love with an English sculptor. I was very glad I did. I thought he had great nobility and the only person at the time I thought had a touch of nobility had been my father, and I thought this man had it because he was much older than I, he was married, he was a Catholic and couldn't get a divorce, so we didn't get married."[32]

She didn't mention that when she met Carton she was, if not married, at least committed to Leo, by then in the army. In fact, she didn't mention Leo at all during the Ring interview, nor in *Awakening to the Good*, where she insists she didn't want to marry anyone—"not now, not yet. Not even the gayest and noblest, the wisest, and most quixotic man I ever had known . . . a British sculptor whose small exquisite bronzes were in the Metropolitan Museum."[33] Whereas in *Awakening to the Good*, she describes how the sculptor awakened in her a reverence for Swinburne's poetry, especially "Hertha"—which dramatically altered her understanding of God—in "Gaily Bedight" she describes the way the British sculptor awakened her sexually, comparing the puny Leo/Karl to the manly Carton/Chester. Indeed, in the novel, after she and Karl finally make love—which they call "the main mystery"—before he leaves for France, Sibyl dreams that a "great primitive brute dragged her off the bed by her hair," crushing her bones. She smiles at him adoringly and murmurs that she loves him for it.

When the primitive man changes into a "pale thin counterpart" of Karl, she cries, "Go away" and runs to hide under the rocks in her cave.[34] When she awakens, she realizes that she has felt only contempt for Karl, that he was "too—too gentle" and that she needed a manly man like Chester. She compares her experience of the "main mystery" with each man, exclaiming after making love with Chester, "Thank God, [she has] actually done it at last."[35]

In her "Autobiography," referring to Carton, C, or Barton, taking great care to obscure his true identity, she reveals that he was the man who "deflowered" her and that, since she and Leo claimed to be in a companionate marriage, she was ashamed to admit to Carton that she was a virgin. It might have scared him off. Carton Moore-Park, however, would not have scared off quite that easily. Since Clairene claims Carton "deflowered" her, perhaps Leo did not quite perform in a "manly" enough way as to penetrate young Clairene. Perhaps, if not impotent, Leo may have been inadequate in his ability to satisfy a woman.

Despite Carton's betrayal of his wife and family, Clairene considered him a man of noble character, "chivalrous to the point of being quixotic," she wrote in the "Autobiography." "One night a streetwalker solicited him. He gave her some money and told her to be on her way." A policeman happened to see the encounter and tried to arrest her. Carton came to her defense, claiming they had a dinner engagement he was unable to keep; the money was for her dinner. The policeman didn't believe "a word of the story," and he arrested the prostitute. Carton went along to the jail and saw to her release.[36]

Another time Carton passed an elaborate Italian funeral procession. He noticed that onc of the horses had a deep cut on one haunch, and the harness went into it with every step. He accosted the driver and forbade him to drive the injured horse another step. A melee broke out when several irate Italians piled on top of him. Carton "might have been killed" had the police not intervened. Claire defined such incidents as heroic, a sign of his courage and compassion. In fact, his exile in America was the result of his integrity. It seems he offended a duchess at a party at her house in the country when he praised and defended two condemned labor leaders. The duchess "invited" him to take the next train back to London; his reputation ruined in England, he left home and family to come to the United States, but with "absolutely no money."[37]

Because she did not value his marriage as a happy one, because she had such conflicted feelings about marriage period, Clairene did not consider Carton's infidelity a betrayal of anything worthy of his loyalty. His first loyalty, she hoped, would be to their relationship. He was her lover and he was her teacher. During this period, Carton introduced Clairene to Edward Carpenter's *Love's Coming of Age*, and she began to understand the high idealism of the notions she had shared with Leo.

In "Gaily Bedight," Clairene demonstrates the passages she found important to her own growing sophistication, paralleling the roles Carpenter and Carton played as sexual mentors to both herself and to her fictional alter ego: "Let every woman constitute herself—a free woman. . . . Every woman should be free to work out the problem of her sex relations hampered as little as possible by legal, conventional or economic considerations." Carpenter's ideas, exactly what Sybil needs to hear, put her in the "love mood." Like Sybil, Clairene needed permission from a voice of authority to allow herself to awaken to the physical experience of love and sex. Carton's mentoring, along with the physical relationship that evolved between them, filled that need.[38]

With Leo in Europe, Clairene freely engaged in this affair. She wasn't officially married anyway, and she was as confused about her marital obligations as she was smitten with Carton. She refers to their year of bliss in her "Autobiography" and captures its passion in "Gaily Bedight." This year as a whole was the happiest of the fictional Sibyl's life, and of Clairene's, as well:

> She had no cares or worries and all the admiration, all the beaux, (men clamored for engagements with her). . . . At one o'clock every Saturday she went to Chester's studio. They locked the doors, disconnected the telephone, cut out the entire world . . . oblivious of everything except each other . . . they created a world of their own:

> a world of books and cheerful open fires, of candles and incense and flowers—a world of loving playfulness [where] they romped about. . . . She danced bare-footed in her blue chiffon costume, or in her pink filmy under-things, or nude—with flowers in her long black hair—bubbling over with gaiety.[39]

Chester calls Sibyl "Daphne" and wonders if she might turn into a tree if he embraced her. They talk of many things, disagreeing "amicably": prohibition, war, suffrage, marriage, and ultimately sex. The subject always returned to sex, her obsession. He introduces her to artists, writers, painters, sculptors—she begins to feel less accomplished than others and wishes she had already written something of value. She is confused by new feelings of ambivalence that arise out of the nature of this relationship that she, in theory, found ideal. Torn because she knows he does not love her, she realizes that she had wanted a lover she could worship without being worshipped. Finding such a love, ironically, she feels hurt because he *does not* worship her.[40]

Still, with Karl away, she considers Chester a delightful interlude, and she can remain committed to Karl and their now "irksome" plans. Marie Stopes's *Married Love*, an avant-garde book published in the early 1900s "to increase the joys of marriage," provides her with theories on companionate marriage that refurbish her understanding of gender roles and give Sibyl new hope that things will work out with Karl.[41]

Leo's letters from overseas indicate that he sensed he was losing Clairene. His letter dated January 4, 1919, indicates that he kept a numerical count of their exchanges. His letters #V, #VII, and #VIII survive in the archive. His letter #V, written just after he received her #VIII, reports that he has read and reread all her letters until they were "almost worn out."[42] Then his tone shifts—gone are the flights of adoration, replaced by practical logistics detailing their move to the mountains and the life he envisions, idealistic as ever. "Joy and happiness to you Dear Queenie," Leo ends, providing a glimpse of his controlling manner. "Please take good care of my Lady Claire and teach her to be a free but symmetrically developed person." He closes ironically, "I love you entirely your own lover."

Letter #VII, written to "Dearest Lady Claire," compliments her on the "increasing depths of her feelings and gradual maturing of thought." Now nearly twenty-three, Leo wonders if they can put off the "holy responsibility" of having children until her "25th to 26th years." Most of the letter expresses his ardor:

> Each night I kiss your eyes and put you to sleep. Then I hold you close and our lips are pressed. You are so wonderful a Love. Your lover longs for you and his heart aches for you dear Love—my Lotus Love. I caress you and love you into the boundless universe. Joy and peace be to you Dear Babby [*sic*].
>
> I love———you
>
> —*Liams*[43]

Meanwhile, Clairene had myriad concerns during Leo's absence. On February 1, 1919, Susan Myers wrote her daughter a letter that indicates the rift between them still had not healed. The letter, contrary to Claire's remarks in later years concerning her mother's feelings toward her, conveys tenderness and caring. Clairene had written that she was ready to come to Temple if her parents wanted her "bad enough to send for" her. They sent her money, but she didn't come home after all. "Now daughter," the mother pled, "let's be real sensible and not allow any imaginary things to come between us. Honestly in our hearts we feel toward you just as we always have and never let the first thought of anger or unkind feeling toward you or Leo enter our minds. . . . You will always be our baby and our lovely daughter in whom we find no fault." They welcome her anytime "to stay 4, 5, 6 months or even a year—until Leo gets back" from the war.[44]

Despite such polite disclaimers, Clairene believed that her parents disapproved of her lifestyle and choices. She was a rebel with a cause, aware that if her parents knew she and Leo were not legally married, they would genuinely disapprove. Susan tried to reconnect with her prodigal daughter and found it impossible to understand Clairene's rejection of her and Coren's lifestyle and traditions.

Leo's January 28, 1919 letter implies that Clairene was anxious to get pregnant on his return. However, Susan Myers's comments suggest otherwise and offer insight into the level of discussion regarding sex and reproductive matters Susan was willing or able to reach: "Clairene I can't express myself as to Birth-Control as I've given it no special thought but I have always been an advocate of it but knew nothing of it scientifically." Abruptly, she changed the subject.[45]

Obviously, neither Susan nor Coren Myers had any idea that their daughter was not legally married. Surely they would have been even more shocked by their daughter's affair with Carton Moore-Park, married with three children. In this same letter, Susan inquires after Clairene's "artist friend," never suspecting that Clairene had been sleeping with him regularly while Leo was away.

Clearly, Clairene needed some instruction concerning birth control. Despite the efforts of activists like Margaret Sanger, who delivered pamphlets to women living in the tenements, reliable information available for middle-class women in Clairene's position was scant. At the time, feminists like Sanger were concerned with women's rights to control their own bodies, educating them through the dissemination of birth control information, teaching them to prevent abuse of wives by their husbands, and empowering them to end the double sexual standards of the time. Clairene, in effect a married woman, should have had access to preventive instructions. But feminists were not organized in the same way they have been since the 1960s. In the 1920s, "modern women" were less likely to speak of such matters in any candid way.

During this same period, Alden Evans began to pursue Clairene again. Before Alden knew about Clairene's involvement with Leo, he sent a letter addressed to her at the Children's Bureau from Bisbee, Arizona.[46] Hoping for reconciliation, he speculates on the distance between them and proclaims he would "walk that far" to "bring things between us back as they once were." A letter dated December 6, 1918, addressed to Clairene Myers-Saidla at the Breevort Hotel, indicates he has been advised of her marriage.[47] Writing at two o'clock in the morning, Alden maps his activities since Bisbee. Still single but engaged, he "absolutely can't" love anyone but Clairene, "(but am not going to talk about that now)" he writes, because the girl he loves is "already married": "Sweetheart, my Sweetheart, if I thought you were happy with that fellow you married I wouldn't be writing you. I'd never say a word to disturb your mind or to make you think of me. I know that you are not happy. I know you wouldn't marry him over again if you had it to do. You know we still love each other. . . . I'd go to hell for you."

He urges her to come to Texas while her husband is in France, to "get away" from her "associates and surroundings," to come home where she can "be sensible once again": "If you love me, I want you to say so . . . if you don't answer . . . I'll consider you lost—temporarily. This isn't a love letter my darling. It is just facts. We can be happy again. . . . Do you want to do you? the same, Alden."

The same indeed. Alden had not changed a bit. His characteristic denial of purpose—"this isn't a love letter"—and his persistence indicate that he would wait forever. Four months later, on April 18, 1919, the invitation to his wedding arrived announcing his forthcoming marriage on April 26 to Bess McChesney of Fort Worth, daughter of Mr. and Mrs. Floyd McChesney, at three o'clock in the afternoon. The envelope is addressed, once again, to Mrs. Clairene Myers-Saidla at the Breevort Hotel.[48] There is no indication that Clairene felt any regrets whatsoever; she made no mention of Alden in any autobiographical writings covering this period. In short, she was happily free of him, thoroughly entrenched in a new set of love interests and intellectual pursuits.

6

New Chimera

1919–1920

> One of the problems which we ought to face in a new way it would seem is that of our sex relations.
>
> —Leo Saidla

LOVE LETTERS, suitors, dates, and affairs notwithstanding, upon Leo's return during the summer of 1919, he and Clairene moved forward with their plans to establish a utopian community. "Our Cooperative Colony" tells the story of the time she spent at age twenty-two in the Blue Ridge Mountains of Virginia with Leo Saidla, whom she calls her husband Earl.[1]

"The Big Three, Philippe, Earl, and Claire" formed an ideal community, a cooperative colony, "that would put Thoreau and Emerson's Brook Farm and the Oneida Community and Plato's Republic right in the shade!"[2] They started with five members—four men and Clairene. With assets that totaled "$300.00, unlimited self-confidence, unbounded zest and about a thousand books," Earl and Clairene set out for Virginia on July 1, 1919, to select a suitable site. In this version, she writes that she and Earl, twenty-six, a college professor and PhD candidate in philosophy at Columbia, had been married two weeks. Philippe, a scientist educated at Yale, planned to join them and bring along his "two charges," one of whom was a seventeen-year-old millionaire and the other a fourteen-year-old orphan.[3]

Life in their colony would be "perpetually bathed in sweetness and light" with twenty or thirty of them in one large house, built of logs by their own hands, with a patio in the center.[4] There would be no envy, jealousy, or competition. A tight schedule would guide their lives, with mornings devoted to "intellectual pursuits," afternoons to "manual work," and evenings to "wit and wisdom," with brilliant discussions of the "eternal verities."[5] Clairene would write stories all morning while Earl finished his PhD thesis.

After Earl and Clairene tramped "hundreds of miles" in the Blue Ridge Mountains, they settled on a location about eight miles from Waynesboro and three miles from the village of Lyndhurst. "Standing on the side of our mountain we were encircled on two sides by rolling hills, friendly, and yet with an ever-blue haze which with their eternal silence lent them an impenetrable and melancholy mystery."[6] From this spot they could gaze across the Shenandoah Valley to the Allegheny Mountains in the west.

They agreed to buy fifty acres, paying fifty dollars down. "It was virgin land," she wrote, jesting, "not only because it was cheaper but [the idiom] sounded so much better [to] nature's children." Cooperation was their motto, with everyone sharing—no private ownership of anything.[7] They would "commune with nature as with a great and loving mother—knowing nothing as yet of the cruelty of icy blasts, torrential rains, and havoc-playing storms." Under their care, the land "would grow and flourish till its beauty astounded the world."[8]

Clairene seemed perfectly formed for at least one of her assigned roles: to prance around wearing her "long hair down in a wild free fashion with a wreath of red berries in it and colorful gypsy clothes." In reality, she wore Earl's khaki trousers.[9] With the barest necessities, including Earl's cot and Clairene's large mattress with springs—obtained at her mother's insistence since "ladies" must sleep on comfortable beds even in the woods—they hired a farmer with a wagon to drive them to the "temporary" log cabin Earl had constructed while Clairene waited in Waynesboro. Thirty feet long, and exactly the width of the mattress, the "one room house made of tar paper nailed to the outside of a frame-work constructed of logs" had a "nice clean dirt" floor which was only a nuisance if they dropped their bread and butter on it "butter-side down," or in the winter when it was too cold to wash the laundry or bathe outside.

When the driver "beheld their abode" he exclaimed to Earl, "Gemminy [*sic*] crickets, Mister, you don't mean you're goin' to bring this kind o' lady into that kind o' hut!" Clairene protested, calling herself a "real woodsman" realizing only later how miscast she must have appeared, tall and slender, wearing "a large straw picture-hat with hand-made French flowers."[10]

Susan Myers, "ante-bellum to the marrow in the old tide-water Virginia tradition," expressed her outrage in a letter: "To think that you should attempt to live in such primitive fashion in the very state where your ancestors lived on broad rich plantations with hundreds of slaves! Why it's a sacrilege, an insult to their very memory!"[11]

Totally unaware of her own deep ties to her privileged southern heritage, and therefore of the irony in ridiculing her mother, Clairene must have delighted in this latest provocation of her parents. She claimed that she and her companions had "evolved the theory that slavery was anti-social (despite Plato's contention)." Furthermore, she had "eloped with a Yankee," which she knew her parents considered a disgrace.[12]

With furniture made from pine packing boxes, they arranged their tables, cupboards, benches, and bookcases, designating the bedroom at one end, the dining room and "library" in the middle, and the kitchen at the other end, where the door and fireplace would be installed. All within thirty feet! The first night it rained; the roof leaked and turned the dirt floors to mud. Their Plymouth Rock chickens failed to lay the eggs they planned to eat and sell. They had to walk back and forth three miles for mail and bread—eight for other supplies—and to haul water uphill from the springs. Optimistic, they planned to dance "barefoot under the trees singing songs. . . . Lie on beds of wild violets in the very arms of Mother nature herself." Once they tried it, they discovered that leaves have a way of tickling "in the wrong places," and flower stems stick with "surprising pertinacity."[13]

When the money ran out, Earl went to find a job. "Although we both disliked seeing a man who should have been writing his thesis on philosophy spend his days picking apples."[14] Clairene, "like a true pioneer, stayed in bed all day, consuming one book after another" warding off the "fear of nameless terrors" of being alone in the forest "without a human being for miles around."[15]

When Philippe and his two charges arrived, "the millionaire's son brought a racing car with him, which helped in getting supplies from Waynesboro though he could not do much racing" on the primitive dirt roads. Life improved. When the "glory of the autumn burst," Clairene neglected her chores, "to stand at the window gazing speechless on the riot of colors [as] young maples . . . blushed faintly like young maidens and then deepened into scarlet, the sumac flamed forth in abandoned splendor. . . . Then to see all that riotous color turn into the uncanny still whiteness of a winter landscape."[16]

But the beauty did not compensate for the harsh reality and backbreaking labor it took to survive: chopping wood and dragging it down the hill for the "perpetual fire" necessary in winter; carrying countless pails of water from the spring; preparing three meals a day; caring for the barren chickens. Little time was left for intellectualizing or for writing. Earl "never once took his thesis out of his trunk."[17] By the time winter set in, though Earl and Clairene together had managed to build a stone fireplace that drew well, they were freezing, starving, and penniless. The snow grew deeper and the roads grew icier. Clairene developed chilblains on her feet so bad she "could scarcely walk," which had a "peculiar effect" on her eyes: she began to awaken from her beautiful dream and "saw the folly" of their ways.[18] In this version of their story, the group agrees to call it quits, and the colony "dies a quiet death." In reality, the ending is not so simple nor so congenial.[19]

The futuristic essay "Wherein Two Can Live More Cheaply Than One and the Only Bill Is the Grocery Bill" portrays this same experience with less humor and even less honesty.[20] Apparently, the author's goal in writing both pieces was to earn badly-needed money after she left Leo and the boys in Virginia. Set in the twenty-first century, perhaps to project the idea of utopia, in a style that merges how-to with philosophical musings, this essay offers encouragement to like-minded couples with idealistic leanings toward communitarian living.

Here, a couple goes "a-pioneering." The details, straightforward and dry, cover practical matters, lists of expenses and earnings, the latter of which imply a profit nowhere else described. It seems to have been written closer in time to the actual experience, when it had not begun to seem funny yet; nor does the tone reflect bitter defeat but rather a sense of accomplishment. This rendition has the "man and wife" resettle together in the city, though that part is pure fiction.

The novels *The Unpredictable Adventure* and "Gaily Bedight" recount delightful renditions of this escapade. Indeed, in the former, the events obtain mythological proportions, which prefigure current feminist interest in matriarchal spirituality. Chapter 5, "How the Young Explorer was captured by Cannibals in the Jungle, Swam Against the Current of the Sacred River, Publi Copinion; and Founded the Colony of New Chimera," announces its satirical humor.[21] Tellectina learns to connect female power with female sexuality through rituals attached to goddess worship.

The chapter opens with Tellectina captured by a band of rebel cannibals, Noequists (questions), the leader of whom is Woqu (the woman question). Pygmies, armed with spears shaped as question marks, guard the sacred river, Publi Copinion—the banks of which are "white with the skeletons of those who go against its current." The Noequists tie Tellectina to a stake, but she is saved by a procession led by their high priestess, Freelo (free love) and their goddess Frewo (free woman). They take Tina to a crude temple made of Ophe (hope) bamboo.

Taken allegorically, the pygmies correspond to the traditionalists—small-minded worshippers of public opinion—such as Clairene encountered during her travels and those she left behind in Texas, including her parents—people she found intellectually starved. The band of women Noequists corresponds to the Young Rebels, Young Intellectuals, Bohemians of Greenwich Village, and friends who planned to join her and Leo at their mountain utopia. The ensuing ceremony represents Clairene's initiation, the values she has adopted and learned to articulate since embarking on her adventure into the outside world, the "jungle."[22]

The religious ceremony begins with a procession of worshippers whose names represent the philosophical: Equi and Vomo (equal rights and voluntary motherhood[23]), Eco and Sub (economic independence and sublimation of sexual gratification), Sin and Cooco (single standard and cooperative community), and the particularly beautiful twins, Sexu and Sexu (sexual union and sexual purity). After imbibing several cups of wine from the Semsianic (messianic) Vineyards, Tellectina assumes the role of spiritual leader and urges the band of rebels to bring along their idols and swim with her upstream, against the current of Publi Copinion, until they reach an appropriate spot for their colony, New Chimera.

When the rebels arrive at an appropriate site, they build their huts of Norancegi (ignorance) bamboo and zest leaves, and sleep on shiw-mats (wish mats). Ignorance and zest comprise a dangerous combination, but are surely the stuff of youthful dreams. Here in New Chimera, Tina meets Ray Nivisio (visionary), whom she calls Olev (love) the second, the first having been portrayed in earlier chapters. This Olev, a version of Leo depicted in explicitly sexual terms, is satirized as the idealist who turns out to be a wimp. In terms of the metaphorical concept of creating a religion of love, the two romantics express their ideals in concrete terms by building a temple, employing both the "Gothic and Pelvic arches seen everywhere in nature." Olev, who designs the center column modeled on the "Early Phallic" period, "experienced great difficulty in its erection," a matter which would have been interpreted as an "evil omen" by anyone but a novice like Tellectina. Above the altar, they place a statue of the Goddess Seva-Doxnel, whose name, according to the two "who know nothing of either," stands for love and sex.[24] Indeed, Olev, who has never even kissed a woman, saving his "initiation" for the woman he would love, vacillates between desire and restraint. When Tina's sister Femina runs her hand through his long blond hair and whispers, "Kiss me," he kisses her perfunctorily and says, "No, not yet, we are not spiritual enough."[25]

The "climax" between Olev and Tellectina/Femina at New Chimera occurs when the three of them perform the "great event." The temple is thrown open for the special ceremony; the "bowed head of the priest" is anointed with oil, and he rises slowly and prepares to make his entrance. While Olev manages to pour his libations over the altar and withdraw, he is unable to "stand entirely erect during the ceremony"; thus, the secret initiation leaves Tina disgusted and Femina disappointed.[26]

This version of Leo and Clairene's sex life differs slightly from the one depicted in "Gaily Bedight," where the woman, repulsed by her lover's feminine ways, discourages sex. However, when Tina in *The Unpredictable Adventure* discovers her mate in a flirtatious pose with an older man, the colony falls apart. Shocked into realizing her "terrible mistake," she remains uncertain what his "deviant" behavior means. In life, young and vulnerable, Clairene impulsively went along with the couple's prewar plans for their community in the mountains, despite her misgivings about Leo's femininity, as compared to Carton's more masculine sexuality.

In "Gaily Bedight," the details of subsistence living closely parallel those in "Our Cooperative Colony"; gender roles, class stereotypes, and sexuality issues move to the center of the narrative. Immediate changes in Leo/Karl's personality become apparent after a romantic first evening in their log house, cooking their meal over a "fragrant wood fire." When it rains and the roof leaks, the gentle, tender Karl becomes verbally abusive. "Had he struck her in the face Sibyl would have been hurt no less."[27] Each day his temper grows worse, until one day Sibyl simply walks away, accusing him of speaking to her as if she were a "nigger" or worse; he wouldn't even speak to a "nigger" as crossly as he speaks to her. The author would not have flinched at using such language to convey the humiliation women feel when men exert their power and treat them as inferior. The parallels between sexism and racism, obvious to the contemporary reader, escape the characters in the novel, despite their liberal attitudes toward women and children's rights. They are products of the author's pre–human rights mentality and southern heritage. Unaware that his behavior is abusive and her reaction racist, Karl doesn't apologize, but makes excuses: he is only trying to repair the house before winter sets in.

The couple argues about everything, from Sibyl's refusal to socialize with the neighboring farmers' wives she finds crude and stupid, to her refusal to perform chores she had been brought up to see as unfit for a lady.[28]

Evenings, they attempt to recapture the intimacy they feel slipping away. Although their caresses "mend the rent," Sibyl insists Karl return to his cot to sleep. She finds most things about him repulsive: his "wet kisses," his finicky eating habits, the way he chews his food, his effeminate mannerisms, and his condescending instructions when they converse.[29]

When did the lover turn into a husband? How did her prince become a frog? Sibyl is incensed when Karl refers to her as his wife: "We're not married—and I do wish people wouldn't call me your 'wife.' I loathe the word more and more every day."[30] It takes many months and nearly one hundred pages in the narrative for her to realize that when two people live together with or without a marriage ceremony, they become as husband and wife.[31]

Because she feels guilty about her attitude toward his sexuality and his burden of the labor, she agrees to plant a vegetable garden, but the activity reminds her of the women back home who "gardened and knitted and read the 'Ladies' Home Journal!' Her very soul rose in hot rebellion against the groceries to be cooked, fires to be built, dishes to be washed, clothes to be washed—beds to be made, wood to be cut, water to be brought," and more work than either had imagined possible.[32] Sibyl finds little satisfaction in domestic labor: "I'd far rather do the kind of things you're doing than housework," she tells Karl. "Whatever you do is constructive—it's permanent. If you spend a day building a hen-house—it stays there—it isn't torn down tomorrow so that you have to rebuild it the next day. . . . But what pleasure can there possibly be in doing only temporary things . . . I cook a meal—for what? Only to be eaten at once! I wash dishes—for what?—only that they may be soiled again in a few hours! Beds must be made daily; clothes repeatedly washed. Oh I loathe it all from the depths of my soul!"[33]

Here, the author expresses a fundamental feminist perception, expounded nearly fifty years later by feminist authors like Adrienne Rich: women's labor is repetitious, monotonous, and undervalued in a world where the lasting achievements produced in the male domain are considered heroic and worthy of pay.[34]

When their friends appear, both Sibyl and Karl are grateful for the extra help. Yet, with three more men around, competition and jealousy add to the strain. Jeffrey (Philippe) dotes on Sibyl, addresses her as "the lady," assists with her chores—bringing logs up, lighting the fire, carrying water. Naturally, Karl doesn't like it; naturally, Sibyl does, using Jeffrey's obvious attraction to her as an opportunity to flirt.

"The tradition of the old South," which put women on a pedestal, was so "deeply rooted in her that it was a part of her very being." Once, when Jeffrey draws her bath, she invites him to watch her bathe: "Jeffie—Jeff . . . would you like t'see Sibylla all white and shiny and naked?" He would. She has him close his eyes as she undresses, because she looks "unromantic in all those old woolie undies," but she chatters and flirts, using her store of southern idioms and charm. She justifies her nudity by recalling their original ideals: "People are always talking about things and never doing them" she says, recalling their talks in New York about how "silly clothes were—and how much better in mind and body people would be if they went nude. 'Lookie—Jeffie—lookie here's me!' and he with surprised and adoring eyes responds, 'Oh! Oh!'"[35]

Sibyl pretends not to notice the affect her nudity has on the young man who brings her bath powder, helps her dress, ties her boots, and changes the sheets. While she cooks dinner, making an extra portion of creamed onions for him and his charges, she shows him pictures from Jean Christophe's books of marble and tile Egyptian baths and of "nymphs dancing under the trees in the moonlight," representing the ideals she dreamed would come true here in the woods.[36]

Karl's face belies the jealousy he does not verbalize when intimate letters and books with loving inscriptions arrive regularly from Chester (Carton) to his "Dear Daphne who leads THE INTELLECTUAL LIFE."

Sibyl dreams of walks with Chester along her favorite paths.[37] Periodically, either Sibyl or Karl suggests games that will reinstate their love and happiness, but each time the attempt ends in disappointment: "Our sex life is hopeless—hopeless—hopeless," Sibyl concludes.[38] When winter sets in with snow and ice, and the larger, permanent house is not ready, life becomes too hard for the lady to endure. Confiding in Jeffrey, she plans her escape by writing the "silliest stories I can think of" for women's magazines! Hoping to earn enough money to get herself back to New York, she writes compulsively day and night, eventually sending the manuscript of her first story to Chester to help get it published.

The climax comes when she decides to spend several days in town putting the finishing touches on her story. Sibyl is disappointed when Karl comes to take her back to the cabin. As they walk along the frozen road in the gathering dusk, Sibyl slips on the "glassy surface" and falls. "It would be a blessing to die now," she thinks. Tears roll down her cheeks as she "stumbled on in semi-consciousness no longer trying to hold the coat whose ends the winds whipped about her legs."[39] By the time they reach the cabin her feet are frozen numb with chilblains, but she is determined to leave. To soften the blow for Karl, she explains that she must go to New York for a while, her feet are sore, it's too cold, and she wants to write to make money for them both. Karl, weeping ceaselessly day and night, blames himself as a failure, and begs her to promise to return.[40]

In New York, Sibyl receives letters daily, written "as though absolutely nothing had happened—promising all the same beautiful things . . . not one of which—ever—came true!" His entreaties force Sibyl to recognize that Karl has not faced the end of their relationship. Sibyl's thoughts reveal the depths of her suffering: "O God will the misery of it never—never leave me? Will I ever feel normal and vivacious and happy again!"[41]

So much for utopia. So much for companionate marriage. After all, *chimera* means monster, and companionate marriage worked best when women "lacked individual goals and forceful opinions."[42] Certainly, Clairene never lacked forceful opinions, not even as a child.

Now she had life experience she could draw on for her writing and the freedom to pursue her destiny once more. Clairene's goal to become a writer grew more intense on her return to the city; Carton Moore-Park came to her rescue.

The story Clairene tells in "Gaily Bedight" most closely resembles Leo and Clairene's actual experience in the mountains. Although the endings of each version of their New Chimera are tragic, sad, or poignant, the fictions are narrated with a keen sense of irony and humor. Clairene's ability to laugh at herself apparently was not shared by Leo. Like his predecessor Alden, he finds nothing humorous in Clairene's assertion of freedom or in her escape to New York. Indeed, he is devastated. The series of letters from Leo beg her to return to Virginia, to their "marriage" and to their land of idealism. The tone of the letters shifts midway through from profusions of love to derogative, accusatory harangues.

The question emerges, did Clairene attract abusive, controlling men? They seemed nice, gentlemanly enough in the beginning. Perhaps the mores of the culture that put men in charge of relationships left both Alden and Leo in a quandary: what to do with a difficult woman, *difficult* being a synonym for independent—New. The fist-shaking tone appears in the pleadings from both men. Ultimately, Leo attacks Clairene's intellectual and educational training, the core of her strength.

These letters following the breakup of their companionate marriage mark the third set of letters from Leo. They document Clairene's life after she fled utopia. At this time she was residing at the Greenwich Club at 26 West Ninth Street in the Village. One of Leo's letters contained a pressed flower from their mountain home. Fifteen pages front and back—thirty pages of writing—comprise the letter dated Monday evening, February 23, 1920: "My very Dear Clairene," Leo begins, with his life "hanging suspended." Despite the "ugly things" between them, his words reflect his spirit of love; he holds no ill feelings, though his "entire insides are completely shaken," and he fears that their letters create more misunderstandings than resolutions: "If we were together we could make things clear," he suggests.[43]

Ensuing letters indicate that he continues to prepare for their life together. Refusing to believe she has left him for good, he describes practical matters regarding their farm, his plans for a vegetable garden, his claims that the chickens now have laid eggs and that he has sold enough of them to buy supplies in Lyndhurst. He even bakes his own bread. In his usual style, Leo switches from the secular to the sacred: "Hold thy faith firm, my heart, the day will dawn. The seed of promise is deep in the soil, it will sprout. Sleep like a bud will open its heart to the light and the silence will find its voice."[44]

Most significantly, he addresses the issues surrounding their sex life, reporting completely different perceptions of their problems than those realized by Clairene.

"One of the problems which we ought to face . . . is that of our sex relations." He thinks they never had much difficulty, but that she was not "well satisfied" nor has he always been. "Then we must come to a clear understanding of the matter of kissing. I do not like to give up that fine custom with which we started, of kissing each other goodnight and again welcoming the new day with a warm expression of our affection."[45]

His next letter indicates she answered in ways that Leo had not expected, and his letters hereafter mark a shift. Terms of endearment disappear, replaced by reprimands: "Concerning the marriage question, I think that you are inclined to exaggerate it very much. You have guessed at my ideas of many things but frankly I must say that you have not gotten to them . . . I am much concerned about our union." He decides they need a divorce ceremony in order to allay a "certain fear." Legal advisers have warned him that he is "subject to prosecution under the Mann Act."[46]

While no letters directly from Clairene to Leo survive, the letter from Sibyl to Karl in "Gaily Bedight" could well be a copy of the real thing. Taking responsibility for her share of the problems, she offers that she was too young and ignorant to unite her life with anyone, too "absurdly romantic, impossibly idealistic and impractical," and essentially "undomestic" and selfish. However, *he* had betrayed their ideal, that *he* "would have preferred to marry—to have had a legal or religious ceremony" and did not regard her as a "love-lady—a beloved—but as a mere wife—a mere *haus frau.*" Graciously, she leaves unsaid how his kisses, his dainty gestures, chewing, and his generally effeminate ways repelled her.[47]

By this time, Clairene had moved on, deciding to leave social work and try business for a while. A life of excitement in the big city was far more appealing to her than returning to life on the "utopian" farm or working at tenement houses. When Wall Street and the telephone company, like social work, proved less than satisfactory, she decided to surround herself with what she loved best in the world, books.

As she explained her change of vocation to Kenneth Ring, she loved books and figured she had two options: publishing or selling them. In a statement of self-diminution rarely found in her rhetoric, she recalled: "I didn't think I was smart enough to work as an editor. I figured no publishing house would be willing to hire me." But she was certain she could sell something she loved, so she got a job managing a bookstore. Over the years she worked at several bookstores, both uptown and in Greenwich Village, the most famous one being Dauber and Pine on lower Fifth Avenue. It proved a perfect environment for the vivacious young woman, "glamorous," she recalled.[48]

"[I] met fabulous people . . . lots of interesting men come into a bookshop—I had a dinner date every night of my life for all those years. I loved all the arts. . . . And that's what you talked about: the new books, the new plays, the new concerts."

Finding work took several months, along with weeks between temporary part-time jobs before Clairene restabilized her income. For the first time in her life, she was doing exactly what she wanted: "I was financially independent. I had an infinitesimal apartment, books, a piano (rented), and a place to write my own novels on Sundays."[49]

Obvious also was her family's relief at the termination of her "marriage" to Leo. Clairene often insisted that her family had disinherited her in 1916, ignoring or forgetting the love and financial support she received from home, documented in letters from her father, one in May and one in July of 1920.

"My dear Clairene: I doubt if any Southern girl with fine sensibilities could be happy with a German Yankee." He advises her to "lay aside" her pen until she feels "normal" again—"You cannot be yourself in literature now"—and to resume writing when her ambition can be realized. "Lean on me and keep with your noble courage . . . depend on us for whatever you need—we understand." He enclosed a money order for forty dollars, no small sum in 1920, and offered to send more if work did not "come easily," signing off with "A thousand kisses for my Clairene, Your loving Father, CL Myers."[50] On July 12, he sent another twenty-five dollars to help her through the "rough places" and kindly encouraged: "Whatever you do, smile, smile, smile, and hope and be joyous and keep everything out of your consciousness that would rob you of happiness, sentiment and joyousness. I miss you more than ever this summer. Take my love and encircle it about you."[51]

Papa's support was crucial at this time. Although no existing letters document Susan Myers's insensitivity, throughout her life Claire writes of being deeply hurt by her mother's judgmental attitude.[52] Claire claims that Mrs. Myers regarded divorce as a disgrace and asked her not to come home for visits anymore, suggesting instead that they meet in New Orleans.

Additional letters from Leo arrived, complicating her healing, begging her to return, promising to make her "the happiest little girl in the world." His heart "crieth after her."[53] The letter that calls the question regarding their "marriage" contains attacks reminiscent of those from Alden. Leo rejects her offer of friendship "for the sake of the woman who may love me." Desperate to save face, he launches an attack on her intellect, her education, and her sexuality: "You are greatly handicapped because you have not the acute training you should have had. . . . You think that I am not physically fit to be a father. My last physical examination did not show such evidence nor has any past one ever shown organic troubles."[54]

The last letter from Leo, dated August 8, 1920, sent to Mrs. Myers-Saidla at the Junior League Hotel, her second address after leaving Virginia, expresses considerable pain as he finally faces her rejection and the end of any hope that she would return. He does not feel anger or bitterness, just a challenge to his "self-respect." He signs off, wishing her better than she is "willing to believe."[55]

A letter from Philippe (a.k.a. Jeffrey in "Gaily Bedight"), dated August 26, 1920, surely brought comfort in the wake of Leo's animosity. Philippe, like Leo at times, addresses her as "Dear Queenie Girl" and reports that he is having trouble getting his money, which grieves him because "it may mean [Clairene] is going in want." He offers words of encouragement: "I somehow feel the strength of you and know in my heart you will conquer life and win." He promises they "shall both be happier when he comes to New York"—anything he has is hers—and sends "a goodnight kiss."[56]

Evidently Clairene's life in the city contributed to her healing; part of her happiness attained from her renewed social life—dinner, theater, opera, symphonies, art—and part from her work at the bookstore. But her greatest joy came from writing. During the next decade the young Clairene matured into the more adult Claire and began to define herself primarily as a writer—determined, focused, productive.

Love was not enough, she realized. Work was the source of true happiness. Love and work. Between 1921 and 1931, writing became a source of joy through which to transform the effects of a greater sorrow than those she now sought to escape.

7

Rivers of Light

1921–1931

> As she sat at the typewriter, gradually a mysterious river of light seemed to flow from somewhere out in space, pour into her mind, through her arm and come out as words on the typewriter. . . . It was like something supernatural. Like a revelation. It was exciting—frightening—this whole incredible process of creation.
>
> —Claire Myers Spotswood, "Belle Randolph"

COMING TO WRITING as a way of supporting herself financially, Clairene threw herself into a busy schedule, searching for a day job, writing at night and on weekends. During this period, she began to record her adventures in college, Chicago, New York, and the Blue Ridge Mountains in a variety of fictional and nonfictional stories, submitting some of the shorter pieces to magazines and newspapers in hopes of earning a living. She recorded her writing experiences a decade later, describing the process as "something supernatural" when the words seemed to flow like a "mysterious river of light." The process of writing seemed "like a revelation" because the process of creating fiction out of her real-life experiences revealed the deep-down core of the self.

Creative nonfiction or autography, as feminist critic Jeanne Perreault calls the process of writing the self through a lens of autobiography and feminist thought, excavates the self.[1] Although Perreault published her book on autography two years after Claire Myers

Owens's death, and Owens never associated herself with the formal feminist or women's rights movements, Claire wrote a new self out of her experiences and recognized that her struggles arose, in part, from being a woman living in a man's world. Thus, most of her fiction resembles memoir, which as Don DeLillo once claimed, "starts with lived experience and then derives meaning out of it."[2]

By adhering to a disciplined schedule, she practiced the art of writing while earning a living at mundane tasks, driven by the hope that her girlhood dream to become a writer would be realized. Although she had tried to write from her mountain cabin, the need for an income seemed to justify her efforts, which until recently had seemed trifling. "Money," as Virginia Woolf contended in 1929, "dignifies what is frivolous if unpaid for."[3]

Clairene used her life as a resource for telling adventures, and writing developed into a source of gratification, a tool of survival and self-insight, growing, as Mary Karr puts it, "organically out of lived experience."[4] Words, she would write years later, "are neglected diamonds. Wash them in your own warm emotion and they sparkle like scintillating jewels." Phrases cry out like "dangerous sirens"; sentences swing like "trapeze performers" between disaster and safety; paragraphs build "like large blocks of beautifully poised marble" waiting to be shaped into art.[5] Her need for solitude, a theme that resurfaced throughout her life, expanded from the romantic musings of late adolescence into a practical asset to the writing life. By age twenty-five, Clairene seemed grounded in her role as a New Woman and a New Yorker, though she was still naive, vulnerable, and very much a belle.

Her characterization of Sibyl in the final chapters of "Gaily Bedight" provides a glimpse of the sense of self a young belle might have achieved as a result of the significant years of early adulthood, within the context of her generation's coming of age in the years just before and after World War I: "Although Sibyl considered herself original and unique in both thought and action—a decided individualist—she was but the product of her age, an instrument of that unseen power which affects the changes in the human race. She was borne irresistibly onward by an invisible tide, for all over the world there was a simultaneous movement on the part of women to aspire toward what they considered freedom."[6]

And of course, freedom begins with the self and moves to changes in the law. Jeannette Rankin of Montana, suffragist and peace activist, was the first woman elected to Congress in 1916, the same year Clairene graduated college. Four years later, women won the right to vote nationally, with the ratification of the Nineteenth Amendment in 1920.[7] At the same time, Clairene explored these new freedoms and learned to weave her life into the fabric of a wider world. Women were birthing themselves, and as Clairene/Sibyl was learning, birth does not come without pain.

While Sibyl's radical ideas proved impractical, she had yet to be "disillusioned and pained" before she admitted that "life was hard and unjust and ugly; and even after admitting it intellectually, that little spark of hope which keeps the idealist alive continued to glimmer fitfully in her heart."[8] Writing these words a few years after the events, Clairene pins down the strengths and weaknesses of her earlier self, as cast in the character of Sibyl. Clairene seems to understand that unconsciously she relished the joy of struggle, realizing later in life that her own youthful idealism had provided some of life's richest sensations.

Through the process of autography, as she writes the story of her younger years, she reaches a new level of self-awareness, "wrenching" at her insides to arrive at her core. From this new state of resolution, she can move on to the next phase of her life.[9] For Clairene has moved from her dubious commitment to Leo into a full-blown affair with Carton Moore-Park.

On New Year's Eve of 1920, a telegram arrived at eleven o'clock at night from Toronto: "In Faith, in Hope, with Love—Carton."[10] Clairene had reclaimed her single status, despite Leo's insistence on a legal divorce; unsigned letters in a variety of handwritings testify to the numerous men Clairene dangled at arm's length during this period.[11] That summer she received a formal photograph of a handsome man with a mustache, dressed in a coat, tie, and debonair hat, inscribed, "*Toujours a vous*, Pierette, 1921," and signed, "Pierrot, In

8. Mystery man. Verso inscription: "Toujours a vous Pirette, 1921. In gentle memory of July 9—1921—also that late afternoon of August third with its clouds and foreboding; its shadows and valley and sunlit mountain top might not be forgotten." Photograph courtesy of the TWU Woman's Collection.

gentle memory of July 9—1921—also that late afternoon of August third with its clouds and foreboding; its shadows and valley and sunlit mountain top might not be forgotten."[12]

With the resumption of an active social life, she recognized her need to sit "in the blessed solitude" of her apartment and feel herself expand like "those incredible Japanese flowers" (origami) she had as a child: "You dropped a crinkled little bit of colored nothing into water. And lo and behold, it uncurled into a full-blown flower."[13]

Thus, during the second half of her twenties, healing from the trials of the first half, she blossomed into a woman with a comfortable understanding of her sexuality and a deep regard for her needs as a writer. However, the "Autobiography" indicates her transition was anything but smooth. She returned to New York in a state of shock, walking the streets of the city she loved, not knowing "where to go, what to do, what to think. The golden glow had disappeared from life." Why did it happen? she asked herself. Who was to blame? Our puritanical culture that keeps girls ignorant of sex and its perversities? Her family who had protected her from life's unpleasant aspects? Herself for being so naive and trusting? But was not trust a virtue? Must she cultivate skepticism about everyone she met? With "utter irrationality," she blamed her parents for allowing her to marry an unsuitable man, whom they had never even met! And whom she had not actually *married.* She began to question her definitions of freedom, wondering if it would have been wiser to conform to the old custom of allowing parents to pass judgment on prospective spouses. Guidance, she could have accepted, but not dictatorial directions.

Clare Ousley contributed a level of worldly insight to the failure of her doomed relationship. "I'm not as dreamy eyed as you," she said. "As I see it Leo knew all the time that he was impotent. He used you to try to cure himself; it was grossly unfair."[14] Impotent at most, inadequate in the least. Clare Ousley's observations likely released Clairene from some of her guilt and confusion. Ultimately, Clairene realized, "Not till one suffers a great deal can one arrive at that inhuman god-like carelessness and aloofness of the artist—of the really free person."[15]

Several accounts indicate that Clairene's relationship with Carton Moore-Park lasted three more years and, for all the pain it caused, it brought her great joy as well.

Carton failed to meet Clairene at Grand Central Station when she arrived from the mountain commune, having been "grounded" by his irate wife, who discovered their letters. Subsequently, he advised Clairene to move uptown lest his wife find and kill her. Clairene left Greenwich House in the Village and moved to the Junior League Hotel at 541 East Seventy-Eighth Street at East River, her first uptown address.[16]

The incident, detailed in the "Autobiography," seethes with drama. Clairene was having breakfast when Carton called, frantic. "You are in great danger. My wife has found out about us. She is now on her way to your house. Under no circumstances are you to confront her. She threw acid at one woman and pulled out nearly all the hair of another. Hide and protect yourself quick now. I'll call you tomorrow, dearest one."

Oblivious to the implications that her philandering married lover has been through these things before, Clairene rushed upstairs and locked herself in a third-floor bathroom. Carton's wife told the landlady that her husband was using money on Clairene that belonged to her and her children, and that Clairene had taken her husband away. Clairene tried to explain that the couple had been separated for years, and that she had loaned the husband five hundred dollars, though it is unclear where she would have gotten that much money. Unconvinced, the landlady ordered the "tainted woman" out. Clairene moved to a woman's hotel, "a dreary place filled with dreary women but . . . inexpensive." The affair continued off and on despite myriad obstacles.

Meanwhile, life for Clairene settled down to a satisfying routine once she landed a job at a bookstore and moved back down to the Village. She reserved one full weeknight and every Sunday for writing and had dates every other night but was home by eight for more writing. This was the life she had dreamed about back home in Texas, this life her family considered "infra dig."[17] In addition, she spent time pondering the dichotomy between organized religion and spirituality—her individual journey of soul—a conflict that pursued her daily "like a hound of heaven" and would throughout most of her life.[18] Her inner thoughts began to expand from a narrow focus on self to larger universal questions, a harbinger of things to come.

How was it possible, she mused, to worship any deity that allowed evil to exist in the world? "Disease. Weakness. Ignorance. Ugliness. War. Poverty. Stupidity. Misery. Floods. Earthquakes. And . . . man's inhumanity to man. . . . Either God was not omnipotent or he was not benevolent—in which case, could he be a God? There was no answer."[19]

In *The Unpredictable Adventure*, these questions become part of the allegory of the heroine's quest to reach Mount Certitude and discover Truth. The truth she seeks would explain world religions and verify the definitions of *Godidea* and *Onegod* she'd been taught to believe through the Baptist religion of her childhood.

In the "Autobiography," she recalls feeling guilty at abandoning Christianity: "Whenever I passed a church and heard the congregation singing hymns, I wanted to take to my heels and run." She even wondered if she had lost her faith in traditional religion in an effort to hurt her mother. Her thoughts in a "terrible tangle," she had no one to consult, not even a book.[20]

In each work, she poses the same questions in a variety of contexts. But she has no way to fully explore the answers until years later, in her 1958 autobiographical account, *Awakening to the Good.* Reflecting in this book and its 1963 sequel, *Discovery of the Self,* she recognized that her moments of rebirth resulted from reading two volumes during this earlier period of her life: Swinburne's poem "Hertha," which provoked insights into the nature of God, and Emerson's "Self-Reliance," which provided a key to the nature of self.[21] "It was like plunging into a swift icy river. The shock of it was painful at first then warm and stimulating."[22]

One Sunday night, after a long day of writing, she picked up "Hertha"; the words affected her profoundly:

> I am that which began;
>   Out of me the years roll;
> Out of me God and man;
>   I am equal and whole

The line that stopped her cold, "Before God was, I am," seemed like blasphemy because of her fundamentalist background. "The meaning pierced like an icicle—alternately cold and burning." Stricken, she could see the "whole world, and all that's in it being born, issuing from the vast womb of time." She had not considered the idea of "Unity! Oneness out of many." Now, moved to a rapturous height, she saw, "diversity . . . the separateness of everything" as confusing, misleading.

Reading "Hertha" she realized "everything came from one source—the grass, the sea, everything we did, everything we failed to do, wars and peace, disease and death, joy and grief—good and evil—and even perhaps man's conception of God!"[23] Her body, mind, and spirit suddenly felt as if they had attained perfect harmony for this one glowing instant. "There was an unseen order in the universe. I did not understand it intellectually but I *felt* it. . . . There was an impersonal spirit, energy, cosmic force in the universe. It changed my life."[24]

The "Autobiography" adds a second level of insight, one that becomes significant years later when, through her research into Carl Jung's theories, she understood these "small ecstasies" in a larger context. In this account, that same night, a vision of a man in a long white robe appeared before her. "Was it Jesus come to reprove me for ceasing to believe he was a god?" Rather than reprimand, the figure smiled indulgently with approval. As the figure faded away and the light vanished, she thought it beautiful but frightening. "What did it mean?" she wondered, vowing not to reveal this mysterious incident to anyone, not even to Carton, who "understood everything."

Shortly after this spiritual realization came an equally profound moment of self-realization. As a reward for having sold a millionaire British architect a large order of books for his yacht, he and Clairene's employer arranged a party in her honor. Friends of the architect, a writer and his wife, agreed to host the party at their apartment. Customarily Clairene and her escort would have attended in formal attire—a long gown for her, a tuxedo for him. However, because the hostess assured Clairene that it would not be necessary for her to dress for dinner, she wore a short, simple dinner dress, instead of her "new long yellow evening gown," and Carton wore a "sack suit."[25] "When we arrived our hostess and all the other women were decked out in . . . gold evening gowns and half the crown jewels. The architect's face fell perceptibly as he stared at my short dress. Was that a gleam of triumph in my hostess' eyes?"[26]

But the small-minded betrayal catalyzed deep insights. "I was I, no matter what I wore," she realized, even as she knew she had "violated [the] sacred rites" of the English whose "god" was "good form."

The dinner consisted of the rarest delicacies—caviar, truffles, grouse, vintage champagne. But the conversation, "dominated by the hostess—not the artists . . . was personal, trivial and dull." Clairene longed to go home and write. Carton told Clairene that the hostess remarked, "That Miss Myers thinks she is so young and beautiful she can outshine us in our best gowns and jewels; that's why she wore that simple little street dress."[27]

"Poor woman," Clairene answered. "I feel sorry for her. She cannot face losing her youth." Carton clasped her in his arms: "That's what I like to hear! Not one woman in a thousand would feel such compassion."[28]

Later, alone in her room, she felt "odd" and sat on her bed for hours "thinking—thinking—thinking" about the significance of the evening's events.[29] As a result of the ecstatic experience that followed—"the night of the storm, the lightning, and the glory!"—Clairene's epiphany at age twenty-five brought a life-changing resolve. "For twenty-four years I had been a dutiful slave to all the conventions imposed on weak willed women. But the whole last year marked a continuous revolt against all the conventions." Of course, Clairene had been rebellious against gender and religious restrictions far longer than just the previous year; she had been rebellious all her life. But this night was different: "Originally I had believed that when I freed myself from the restrictions of home and school and church I would be blissfully free . . . to act, think, speak, and dress exactly as I saw fit. I wasn't."[30] Later she became convinced that being self-supporting would bring freedom. It did not, because she could feel the invisible power of social custom dictating her opinions, behavior, manners, and fashion choices. Fashion, she realized was "tyranny." Who had the "right to tell us we must wear dresses touching the ground after dark or be considered an inferior species? Who says we must wear dresses above our knees in the daytime? Who . . . are these people who decide my fate, every woman's fate, so arbitrarily? Who gives them the power? Is it women ourselves?"[31]

Throughout the night she questioned each fashion mode until suddenly she felt shaken inside as if by a "mighty earthquake" and became possessed by an indescribable elation that carried her, metaphorically, to the site of a great mountain. "Eons" seemed to pass, the "constrictions of society dropped away like an outworn cloak"; she lay "naked, naked on the mountain top with nothing to cover me but my own confidence."[32]

In a flash she began to perceive truths "which logic and reason had long sought in vain." She came to understand the nature of laws as words written by "a few men as stupid and ignorant as I"; ideas as "opinions of people no wiser than you and I"; "Conventions, Clothes, Styles, Fine houses, Jewels"—all meaningless. Even God was not "a great omnipotent man" but the "blinding light! This dazzling source of truth." These realizations set her "free, at last, free of the whole world," of other peoples' opinions; she felt herself capable of being "her own master henceforth."[33]

As the "glorious afflatus" gradually ebbed away, the bed, the room, became realities again, and she thought perhaps she had experienced the "kind of light, the kind of ecstasy the men who wrote the Bible felt."[34] Unconsciously she reached for a volume of Emerson's essays.[35] The words leapt out at her as if for the first time, and she was stunned to find the guidance she needed. "To believe your own thought, to believe that what is true in your private heart is true for all men—that is genius." "Trust the instinct . . . it shall ripen into truth." "A man should learn to detect that gleam of light which flashes from within, more than the luster of the firmament."[36]

Clairene came to recognize these lights, "flashing from within," which began with her dance in the wind when she was ten years old, as temporary insights into an ultimate reality—overwhelmingly powerful when they happened, yet transitory in effect when compared with the Great Awakening that she would experience in her fifty-fourth year.[37] But these early lessons in the nature of the universe, "small ecstasies," precursors to the great one, provided insights that nurtured the strength of character necessary for surviving alone in the world. Inevitably, all of these realizations came later, not while in New York. These experiences happened when Clairene was in her mid-twenties and early thirties, but she did not fully realize their significance until she was in her fifties and sixties. When they happened, it was impossible to make sense of them. The adventure unreeling before her eyes was too fleeting, too unpredictable to leave time for analysis. Yet, clearly, such moments set her on a new path.

The light of new understanding into which she emerged at age twenty-five was not purely rational, but a result of these moments of ecstatic, blissful eruptions of intuitive insights stimulated through her reading and her self-exploratory writing. Like Bernini's portrayal of the ecstasy of Santa Teresa,[38] where spirituality and sexuality merge into a moment of bliss, Clairene's spiritual ecstasies took on a sexual component she describes in her third novel, "Belle Randolph,"[39] which captures this period of her writing life. During a particularly dazzling ecstatic event, having experienced the phenomenon of being penetrated by a "river of light," the writer-protagonist is "filled with a cold white shining ecstasy." She falls limp across the bed, "wrung out like an old rag, strangely exhausted. Waves of desire surge within. Writing, she observes, is an aphrodisiac."[40]

However, sexual highs that resulted from her writing, paradoxically, interfered with her work. She would walk quickly around the block to discharge the erotic energy, something society had taught her to believe women were not inclined to enjoy.[41]

And what, at this point, was she writing?

Stories. Essays. A first novel and a second. During the years between 1920 and 1935, Clairene wrote "Gaily Bedight," *The Unpredictable Adventure*, and numerous short stories and articles contrived to appeal to slick women's magazines. The themes of these short stories and essays—creative nonfiction, autographies in today's vernacular—fall into four general categories: her experiences in Utopia, her experiences in the Alabama Mining Company, satirical anecdotes that capture the atmosphere and clientele of popular bookstores in the Manhattan of the 1920s and 1930s; and life in a woman's hotel. In 1930 or 1931, after "Gaily Bedight" was rejected as too biographical, she began a new autobiographical novel based on the same material but allegorical, fantastical, and influenced by another southern writer, James Branch Cabell. She spent four years writing *The Unpredictable*

Adventure, and several weeks revising it after its acceptance by Burton Rascoe at Doubleday Doran, in 1935.[42]

For Clairene, writing was nourishment—vitally important to her psychological, physical, and spiritual well-being. While she wrote, she forgot every ache and pain, every worry and doubt, men, love, and sex—"her ego flew out the window." She felt called to the task, as if she were doing "something important."[43] Throughout her writing life, Claire experienced moments of transcendence. The "rivers of light" depicted in "Belle Randolph," written in the early 1940s, describes an event that occurred while writing *The Unpredictable Adventure* in the early 1930s, the same event described in *Awakening to the Good*, written in the 1950s, and at the mountain cabin. In the "Autobiography," she recalls that when she began to write her first book, a whole new world opened up, "in which I had the power of a creator, a god."

And while her fictions during the 1920s and 1930s depicted lessons gleaned from her own life, during this period she wrote one seemingly antifeminist essay directed at a commercial, female audience. "Concerning Woman's Soft Dominion," whose title was taken from a line in the Lord Byron poem she used as an epigraph argues that "*all* men," like the persona of the poem, are attracted to women not only by their looks—"eyes of blue or lips carnation"—but by their "ANIMATION," which makes them "queens of all creation."[44]

In other words, energy and vitality attract men to women because they seek woman's society for one reason: "recreation." For men, work comes first. Women are always second. Man stands alone while woman only thinks she does, until she falls in love. The tone of the essay, though upbeat, expresses the inevitability of this double standard as if it were a fact of nature. Such an essentialist view is confirmed by the research of the day, the author assures, though she admits none of us like it. "Woman rebels, she votes, she holds offices, she supports herself; while Man looks on, applauds, and then calls at the stage door after the performance, as if to 'take her out on a party.'" Even after a trying day, whether a housewife or a "Tired Business Girl" who seeks "relaxation, pleasure, laughter," woman must rise to the occasion and pretend to be animated and vivacious. Pretense has its own rewards since "vivacity tends to carry itself along of its own momentum—she feels happy before she realizes what has happened to her! The man, in turn, responds . . . and they achieve a beautiful evening . . . [discovering they] actually out-sparkled the Sparkling Burgundy!" Fake it until you make it, and the payoff for the girl who learns to play by such rules is a marriage proposal, for "animation is a charm . . . which often works The One Great Wonder that every woman desires—that of causing Man to fall in love." The ironic undercurrent of the essay reflects Clairene's ongoing struggle to resolve the conflict between the feminine and the intellectual.[45]

The cover and rejection letters tell the story behind the essay. On June 6, 1920, "Mrs. C. M. Saidla" submitted this editorial to Miss Frances L. Scher, editor of Fashionable Dress Publishing Company on Fourth Avenue, with a letter indicating that Miss Scher suggested she write on this subject at their recent interview. Clairene tried to write what she believed the editor wanted to print—she was writing for a living, after all. But the piece was rejected, Miss Scher deciding that while the subject was "good," the writing was not "forceful enough."[46] Perhaps the lack of force indicates the betrayal of Clairene's true feelings. For surely the woman writing feminist novels such as "Gaily Bedight" and later *The Unpredictable Adventure*, would not have believed women should resort to such pretension to seduce a man into loving, much less marrying, her. In fact, Clairene had ended Sibyl's story with a strong resolve against marriage and a determination to write the "silliest" stories imaginable to sell to women's magazines.

Likely, this was one of those "silly" stories. Ambivalence and contradiction seethed beneath the surface: "Ideas of equality seem not at all impossible—until love, or time, awakens the slumbering Female—who, alas, sleeps lightly."[47] Tellectina resolves autonomy and Femina laughs, flirts, and makes men fall in love.[48] Seduction is the survival tool of the southern belle and the source of entrapment. As Claire explains in her "Autobiography," the men she met during this period seemed to know so much; she longed to ask them questions. But men did not care to engage in serious conversations with women, so she made them fall in love with her first, "then they would tolerate an intellectual impersonal discussion," briefly. To transcend the conundrum, Clairene wrote novels that focused on the dilemma of women, especially southern women, in a sexist society.

In rebuttal to derogatory newspaper and magazine articles, she wrote feminist-inspired defenses of women. An essay responding to an antifeminist article by Christopher Morley in the *Saturday Review* defends women's intellectual capacity. Morley's "A Letter to Leonora," which appeared in his weekly column, "The Bowling Green," on November 10, 1928, insists that ladies were not smart or sophisticated enough to be true intellectuals and settled for popular fluff.

His condescending attitude infuriated Clairene; she took his insults personally and wrote a rebuttal, hoping it would be published in the prestigious periodical. "Such accusations should not be allowed to pass into history unchallenged," she wrote.[49] Speaking from her own experience as a voracious reader of books and as a salesperson in a bookstore, she could attest that American women have "mental awakenings aided by books." Just as Melville claimed that Hawthorne's book inspired his rebirth at twenty-five, she wrote of her own experience of being "born" at age twenty-five, after an ecstatic night of reading.

Evidently Morley wrote a "hand picked letter" in response to her article that both "pleased and piqued" her. Clairene sent a revised and expanded essay with a cover letter contrived to reconcile their differences and reiterate her points. Tongue-in-cheek, she agreed that "females should not ratiocinate too much—for who . . . could love a reasoning woman!" She added a jab, which must have offended Mr. Morley for it set up a dialogue that ensued for another round of correspondence. Though her essay was not printed in the *Review*, she claimed several of her letters were. Morley, as an accepted authority, would have found it impossible to bend to this impudent woman's questioning. As a white man he was doubly privileged, having been born with what Peggy McIntosh terms "an invisible package of unearned assets" he could cash in on each day while remaining oblivious to the source of his sense of self.[50] Nor would Clairene have understood from whence his attitude came. The exchange becomes yet another example of what Betty Friedan called "the problem that has no name."[51]

As her affair with Carton Moore-Park continued, Clairene's love for him grew deeper. Painful though their long separations were, she realized that she was truly in love for the first time. Once, when he left for Toronto on business, she felt as if her heart were being torn from her body, a metaphor she employed in the characterization of Carton as Elam Domitann (dominant male) in *The Unpredictable Adventure*. Carton's love had an incredibly powerful influence on Clairene. His presence in her life, his admiration for her every virtue, caused her to blossom. Perhaps part of his appeal was his unavailability, which allowed her to remain independent. Another part sprang from his own spirit of rebellion: taking her away for weekends in secluded hide-aways; tramping ten miles along the Hudson on the New Jersey side to avoid being recognized; reading poetry to one another while cooking lunch over an open fire; walking through the woods of private estates in Connecticut, ignoring the No Trespassing signs. His cavalier attitude toward all social decorum satisfied Clairene's sense of adventure and romance. "Was there anything on earth so wonderful as loving and being loved with complete acceptance?" She felt she was "floating in a warm sea of love." Despite the concomitant pain, those three years turned out to be the happiest in her life; she came to see Carton as her one true love, her soul mate.[52]

But there were other loves, if not necessarily lovers. In February of 1922, Miss Claire Allen—as she at times signed her name following her separation from Leo—received two letters at her 129 East Fifty-Ninth Street address from someone at the *Sun*: "Dream-lover, I float with you in the magic current of your life until I pass beyond the borders of reality. New worlds of beauty, timeless, spaceless, open out before me until my hungry heart is swept with all the anguish of fulfillment. From your lips I drink the wine that binds the fragments of my soul into a being whole and complete."[53] The unsigned passionate letter ends with a poem peppered with images of "hot throbbing" lips and hearts, "chasms of solitude" and wind.

Clairene had a penchant for attracting ardent lovers, inclined to profuse outpourings of sentiment. But her heart belonged to Carton. While Carton was in Toronto, she felt restless, disoriented, unable to concentrate, eat, or sleep.[54] Carton wrote her love letters daily, describing his longing to speak with and touch her. Once he went down to the depot and boarded the train to New York, thinking he could be with her in thirteen hours. But he came to his senses in Buffalo and turned around to go back to Toronto to finish his work there. The handwritten letters are nearly illegible, but one long typed letter opens, "Dear dear most dear—lovely—Your most wonderful and delightfully long yet too short—and wholesome as always and 'understanding' letter [arrived] today." This letter attests to the intellectual content of their communications: discussions of books, authors, religion, morality, and current events.

"STUPIDITY is the Father of all Evil. It is ridiculous for the 'people' to visualize the Devil as a Brainy creature. . . . He should be shown as a Clod—a Dull Thing—INCAPABLE of creative thought. . . . Why should not Lilith be a quite desirable Mother or 'foster' mother . . . What IS 'im-moral' and 'un-moral'?"

Two pages of stream-of-consciousness rambling comprise another typed letter that mixes declarations of love with responses to her last three letters. He tells her he is "still ill"; his brain is becoming "almost paralyzed." He asks that she read his letters and then return them when she writes next, then switches subjects, asking about her "poor little feet" and her work. Parts of his many letters continue discussions on human nature, morality, Cabell, Dreiser, Shaw, Yeats, and other authors, on books they plan to read together, and allusions to their work.[55]

Clairene either kept copies of the letters she wrote to Carton or he gave them back to her when he returned from Toronto to keep them out of his wife's hands. None address him directly by name but use "my love" or other endearments. None are signed and often they seem to be letters to herself as much as to him. A typed note placed in with this unsigned batch suggests she meant them as diary entries rather than mailed correspondence: "Do you KNOW how interesting and useful . . . you will find your diary letters in years to come?" They meander through a wide range of subjects and introspections.

"My very, very dear Beloved" she writes in letter #2. "Why must so fine, so unselfish a person suffer so much and continually?"[56]

In the "Autobiography," she describes their unhappy ending. In the past whenever Clairene confronted Carton about the hopelessness of their situation, suggesting that they should stop seeing one another, he would "grasp" her arms and in an "anguished voice" implore her to stay. "You are my life. I would go through hell fires to keep you."

Eventually, in the absence of his "warm loving presence" she achieved a new perspective on their situation, resentful of the undignified quality of her life dodging an irate wife, living "a hole and corner" existence in a game of "cat and mouse." She began to prefer a "normal marriage to a nice normal man with a beautiful home and children" after all. Her pride and self-esteem shattered, she sought the advice of a friend in a similarly difficult relationship. Over dinner at the Russian Tea Room, Clairene's friend pointed out she was "blind" to Carton's faults. "Like all men," Carton was thinking of his own pleasure, not hers. "He knew when he met you that you were an innocent, inexperienced girl. Your fine Mr. Carton can swear a thousand times he'd go through hell fires to keep you but the brutal truth is he won't even go through a divorce to marry you."

She began to weigh the advantages against the disadvantages of staying involved. Suddenly, she redefined her commitment as "foolishness": what if she got pregnant? Her family would not come to her rescue—they would be disgraced. Noting the inherent unfairness of a woman's lot—"the burden of sex"—she decided to end the affair. Soon after his return to New York, Carton received a call back to England for an undesignated length of time, and Clairene made the break that she never would have had the courage to make while he was in town. Sobbing, in a blind daze, she telegraphed her parents that she was not well and was coming home for a long visit.[57]

At this point, Leo, on friendly terms with Clairene through some resolution of their differences once the divorce was secured, came to see her in the bookshop. When she told him she was going home for a rest, he offered to take over her apartment. Planning to stay three weeks, she ended up spending "three wasted interminable years" between 1923 and 1926 in Temple, where she felt estranged from her own roots, like an "alien."[58] Her parents were patient, kind, and generous, but after seven years of separation from their prodigal daughter, their "lives ran like parallel rivers never merging." Her grandmother and her grandmother's circle of friends considered Clairene's loyalty to New York City a crime: "'You love the city more than your own home town,' they said. 'You love all the wild free life of that wicked New York better than the wholesome normal life of the provinces. You love the theater and opera more than . . . church, other books more than the Bible, the arts more than God.'"[59]

During this time she did not write a single letter to Carton, and she arranged for Leo to forward her mail but to divulge her address to no one. Collapsing in bed, existing like a "vegetable rather than a person," she wallowed in solitude, grateful that all her old friends had married and moved away. Unable to eat or sleep, she became ill with a serious though undefined condition. Talking exhausted her; reading "nauseated" her; she became too weak to write thank you notes for books and magazines sent by friends, forwarded by Leo. Her only pleasure was to lie in bed and stroke her purring kitten.

"Soon letters of great distress and small gifts" from Carton arrived; she never answered them, which caused her mother to "raise her knowing eyebrows," though she asked no questions. Clairene engaged in endless daydreams of becoming a famous novelist, of Carton's wife dying so they could marry, of being carried off by a "prince charming" in a powerful automobile. Her fantasy heroes were writers, painters, college professors, kings, dukes. "Nothing was too fantastic," she wrote years later.[60]

Three letters survive this period, all written in 1925, all addressed to her at her parents' house at 204 West French Avenue in Temple: Two were from her mysterious lover, "Pierrot,"—with whom she had sustained steady contact—written from New York, though there is evidence he lived in Toronto. The other, from Leo, dated June 25, 1925, on the letterhead of the Department of French at New York University, Washington Square, indicates a congenial dialogue had developed between him and Clairene.

Leo had received two letters from her instructing him how to dispose of their jointly owned properties—books, dishes, and such. He was moving, packing their things, cleaning rugs and curtains, sending her remaining books. He offered advice and kind encouragement: "You should not worry and spend your energy in rebellion. It only makes things worse. . . . You may never have a religion in the sense that most people understand it. You must have a philosophy, an attitude toward life and the world." To escape despair, she should build a new world of ideas and stop thinking dark thoughts. "Be of good courage and anticipate a new day. Sometimes the struggle may not seem worth-while, but when you are stronger you will find your spirits rising. . . . May a new light shine in your eyes."[61]

Pierrot's letters that same year express his deep longing: "Dearest Darling Child" he wrote, frequently calling her "Pierette." "Never before have I experienced loss or absence of anything, or any person, in such a complete overpowering way. . . . At times I feel that there is nothing in life that is not pointless, aimless, futile." He attributes the intensity of his feelings to the frequency of their encounters. "In fact, there have been times when for several days you were the only person I met and conversed with. And I thought of you always, always Pierette, that means unceasingly . . . and of nothing else in the world. . . . And in the heart of every thought of you were kisses and a desire to say 'I love you', 'I adore you', 'I worship you.'"

The nine-page letter, with script that grows larger and looser as it continues, responds to the "wonderful" news that she had gained "eight good Texas pounds" from consuming country milk, and he wonders what "black art" her good mother employed to get her to "take raw eggs." There are so many things he wants to know—he intends to attach a list of questions so she can just write yes or no at the end of each and send it back.[62]

As is true of all of Clairene's suitors, Pierrot's meanderings indicate they share a rich cultural and intellectual connection. He has already sent her the *Times* and *Post* book reviews. He also assesses several books: *On the Margin*, a collection of essays by Aldous Huxley that he finds "well bound and printed" but the "merest drivel," and J. K. Huysman's *Against the Grain*, the best thing he has read since Butler's *The Way of All Flesh*. "What a mind!" he exclaims, referring to

Huysman's work, though noting it is marred by "inexpert proofreading and careless typography." He notified the publishers, who thanked him and took his name for their mailing list.

In a lighter vein, he writes: "A steak for 3 is 25¢. 1 big cantaloupe is 15¢. A lovely apartment is 35.00 a month. Where? Where?? In Temple? Call a cop and bring a marriage license at once." He closes with effusions of love: "Know my Sweet, that you are loved . . . as a darling priceless jewel . . . life is eased only by the thought that some day I shall hold you in my arms—Always Pierrot." His letter dated December 25, 1925, reiterates his love for her and his hurt that she has chosen to break off their relationship. "Love me for a while longer any how," he implores.

Interestingly, even during this period of healing from her love affair with Carton, Clairene continued to play the coy belle with her beaux, as evinced in the cruel game she seemed to play with the mystery man, Pierrot. What did Pierrot mean to her? How long did this relationship last? Did they meet again when she returned to New York the following year? There is no evidence in letters of further contact, nor does she mention Pierrot in her autobiographical writings or in her fiction. Is Pierrot a pseudonym Carton uses; are Pierrot and Pierette just pet names they have for one another? Perhaps. However, Clairene is careful to note she has broken off completely from Carton, the cause of her illness. The similarity between Pierrot and Carton's writing style and illegible handwriting creates suspicion that they are the same person, though no document survives to conclude they were. Nevertheless, such intensity of feelings, such effusions of passion, seems to be routine with every man during this period. Years later, after she became familiar with Freud's theories and sought therapy, she attributed her behavior to never feeling accepted and loved for her true self by her parents.

As she writes of this period in the "Autobiography," her father was sympathetic in a remote way; her mother disgruntled: "All of your ailments are imaginary," Susan told her daughter. Clairene longed to unburden her heart to her father, but dared not. Years later it occurred to her that Carton, nineteen years her senior, might be a surrogate father, that her devastation at his inaccessibility might be unconsciously linked to her father's unavailability. She called their relationship Oedipal.

As she grew weaker, an unspecified operation became necessary. Her parents' attitude changed from judgmental to solicitous when they realized the breakdown might be caused by a physical dysfunction rather than a mental one.

But the voices of her grandmother's friends chanted in her head as she lay in bed, stroking her cat, day after day. "'We could not bear to live in the city,' the grandmothers opined. 'It has no birds or flowers, no sunshine or fresh air. There are no friendly neighbors, no good fresh food, nor quiet. And worst of all, no trees.'" A silent dialogue "shaped itself between the eternal provincials and the converts to the city," like herself: no birds, she thinks, but "*ideas* flock to the city," the only safe place for new species to breed. Flowers may not bloom, but people do: "Freedom replaces sunshine; privacy replaces neighbors; an atmosphere of success replaces fresh air; the feast of the arts replaces fresh food; a forest of stone and steel—skyscrapers—replaces natural forests."[63]

In New York, "the world is knocking at your door." Shops on Fifth Avenue and people from all over the globe: beautiful women, young and old women as slim and vivacious as girls, men radiating success and sophistication. Her grandmother did not hear her praise the city, but Clairene's silent affirmations convinced her she would go back to the only place she had ever felt completely at home in her adult life.[64]

Finally, her brother Coren Douglas, two years her senior, came to visit from Dallas where he had moved for business reasons. Though most of their lives they were not close, this time Coren made a difference. He stood before the fireplace and said, "Snap out of it Sis. You don't have to be so weak and helpless. Will power, that's the thing. Exert a little power and you'll be well again." To "snap out of it" was exactly what she longed to do. She "refused to be defeated by life."[65]

One day she and her mother had a slight altercation concerning some trivial matter. Suddenly, for the first time in her life, Susan slapped Clairene. "And automatically, involuntarily" Clairene kicked her back. Mortified that she could behave in such a "disrespectful and unladylike" manner, she marched out of the room, packed her bags, and arranged to return to New York.

"That slap was the kindest thing my mother ever did for me." She took a train to Galveston and a boat from there to New York. If she were going to die, she reasoned, at least it would be in her "beloved City."

Clairene's return to New York after her long absence was like a reunion between estranged lovers. A handsome Irish actor met her boat and took her to lunch at the Plaza and then to a woman's hotel on East Fifty-Seventh Street. Dreary though Clairene found these accommodations, she had learned from experience that "an apartment could be a trap. Men would bring up a bottle of Scotch, expect the girl to cook" him dinner; then after "plying her with liquor, attempt to maneuver her into bed." Men were not allowed into the rooms of woman's hotels. The anecdotes she collected while there made great material for short stories about other women and their lovers, allowing Clairene a temporary "vacation" from her own.

That following morning, what she wanted to do more than anything else was walk down Fifth Avenue and savor its flavor to the fullest. The great canyon formed by the "wall of stone" skyscrapers lifted her heart, filled her with hope and renewed ambition. As she strolled southward from Central Park, she observed the finest objects from all over the earth—Chinese porcelains, Tiffany and Cartier jewels, great masterpieces of art at the Duveen Galleries, linens at Jensen's "so exquisite some were in the Metropolitan Art Museum's permanent collection." Furs—chinchillas, sable, minks. Books—first editions, hand-tooled, leather-bound volumes: "useful items transformed into art." All the treasures of the world lay at the feet of New Yorkers: Carnegie Hall, the Metropolitan Opera House—the best in music, the best in human creativity, and the most fascinating people. "I loved the rush, the crowds, the noise, even the dirt of this fabulous city."[66]

As she settled in, she perceived subtle changes in attitudes regarding women's sexual freedom. "World War I had liberated women from Victorianism, Puritanism, and the restrictions of being a lady. Women worked during the war because they were needed. After 1918, they

9. Clairene Myers, c 1920s. Claire was known for her taste in hats all of her life. Photograph courtesy of the TWU Woman's Collection.

refused to relinquish their new freedoms." For the first time in American history, Clairene observed, young self-supporting women lived in their own apartments, separate from their families, which allowed them to have love affairs. And yet, when she returned to New York in 1926, she knew of only one friend involved in an affair; "old traditional taboos did not break down easily or quickly."[67] Perhaps the Roaring Twenties were quieting from their original roar to a stable hum.

She found a job at the Dauber and Pine bookstore as the manager of their New Books Department on the street level; used books and first editions were in the basement.[68] She began to write articles for *Publishers Weekly.* Her short stories, gleaned from her daily experiences, capture the tenor of intellectual life in Manhattan between 1926 and 1931, the period before and during the stock market crash of October 1929, and the onset of the Great Depression.

Clairene was comfortable in the intellectual milieu drawn to this fine shop and to the glamour lent by its patrons—famous writers, actors, architects, and many of the elite inhabitants of the city. She moved to a small apartment at 38 West Twelfth Street in the Village, from which she could quickly walk the few blocks to Dauber and Pine, located at 66 Fifth Avenue between Twelfth and Thirteenth Streets. "Now began five rich glorious years full of everything—excitement, happiness, fulfillment, dinners, dances, plays, concerts," and inevitably, marriage proposals. But even "at age thirty, I was reluctant to marry." She concentrated on her intellectual development. During this "fecund period" in American literature, she focused her energy on reading, writing, and socializing with her heroes of the art community.[69]

Many famous people came into the bookshop. She had "friendly talks" with Sinclair Lewis, who once purchased twenty new novels and carried them "in his arms" to his hotel apartment on Tenth Street. Once a woman accompanying Lewis asked Clairene to order a book. When Clairene asked for her address, she answered, angry, arrogant, "The same as his, of course." Clairene did not recognize Dorothy Thompson, whose columns in the *Herald Tribune* she later came to admire, and who became the subject of one of her essays. When Lewis received the Nobel Prize in 1930, he phoned, frantic to find a Swedish-English dictionary "at once" to take with him on the boat. He planned to learn enough Swedish to accept the prize in the language of its presenters. Clairene sent her assistants out to scour New York until they found one and rushed it to his apartment.[70]

She had long talks with Bertrand Russell on companionate marriages, of which she had first-hand knowledge. With Walter Lippmann she discussed the philosophy expressed in his recent book, most likely

10. Dauber and Pine bookstore. Photograph courtesy of the TWU Woman's Collection.

Men of Destiny. When *The Bridge of San Luis Rey* was published, she went to Thornton Wilder's cocktail party, where "he went around and introduced himself to each guest." She noticed a man peering so intently at the books, she feared he planned to steal them; the man turned out to be John Dos Passos. George Jones, an editor at McBride who became her friend and suitor, offered to introduce her to James Branch Cabell, whose novels had such a deep personal influence on her own writing and spiritual quest. She declined: "I don't want him to meet me in a bookshop. Wait until my book becomes a best seller."[71]

Aline Bernstein introduced her lover Thomas Wolfe to Clairene after his *Look Homeward Angel* "made such a splash" with critics in the popular press. Wolfe visited Clairene at her apartment shortly after the publication of her own novel in 1935, and became the subject of several of Claire's short stories. Poet Elinor Wilder passed through the shop "like a cool breeze." Everyone was quoting Dorothy Parker's "men never make passes at girls who wear glasses." Clairene put her own away, though she was "very nearsighted."

Edna St. Vincent Millay's poems were "already becoming collector's items." People who had never read her quoted her poems, especially lines from "Figs from Thistles: First Fig."

> My candle burns at both ends;
> It will not last the night;
> But ah, my foes, and oh, my friends—
> It gives a lovely light![72]

Millay was an icon for the dramatic decade of change, the poem its mantra. Margaret Mead and her Barnard classmates took the subway from their uptown dorms down to the Village to serenade beneath Millay's apartment in Waverly Place. Once, Millay came to the window and the young women threw flowers up to her. All the Barnard girls were in love with her.[73]

The first edition of Millay's *Renascence* was "snapped up" in bookstores. At the time, *Renascence* was praised for its themes of social consciousness. "No critic of the time referred to it as an account of her spiritual death and rebirth," which Claire came to consider as its central significance, though she "understood nothing of it at the time."[74] However, she embraced the explosion of energy that Millay and her poetry represented. She moved among intelligentsia, participating fully as a member of the "generation that expressed themselves by breaking down old habits, old restrictions, old ways of being" and making a real "push toward freedom." More than a decade of sexual liberation, the 1920s represented a time of possibility; its participants possessed that "yes" spark, the attitude that the "doors have not closed."[75] Clairene liberated herself into that atmosphere of change; she took advantage of the moment and assumed, what Carroll Smith-Rosenberg called the "power of a liberated person who was working in concert with other liberated people."[76]

The boom on Wall Street, everyone was sure, would last forever. Conversations spun around the concerts at Carnegie Hall, the operas at the Metropolitan, and "suddenly" the French Impressionists. "New York was flooded with excellent German prints of Degas, Renoir, Manet, Monet. In our shop we sold every print of Van Gogh's *Sunflowers* we could lay our hands on."[77] Clairene saw all the latest plays running on Broadway—Eugene O'Neil, George Bernard Shaw. "[O'Neil's] *Emperor Jones* with Paul Robeson was considered very daring because for the first time a Negro had a leading role. Many women seemed afraid to go; I went and found it deeply moving. [His] *Strange Interlude* delighted me with the idea that to be complete, a woman must have a husband, lover, and son."

Though Shaw's iconoclasm delighted her, his *Arms and the Man* and *Mrs. Warren's Profession* disturbed her deeply. "I imagined how I would feel if I had been that daughter whose income derived from her mother's brothels." Havelock Ellis's *Dance of Life* "caused many people to attempt to live as freely as he advocated." Clairene liked his ideas on "sexual freedom for women," which reinforced gender difference in ways that seemed to confirm her own paradoxical drives for sexual and financial liberation while still appearing soft, feminine, and alluring.

She distributed Dr. Marie Stopes's *Married Love* to friends "who might need it." Novels of the day, she devoured to nourish her own writing ambitions. Faulkner repelled her, though she admired his talent: "Never in the South had [she] encountered the sick abnormal people" he portrayed, naturally unaware of her own classism. She respected Hemingway's genius for narrative and characterization, but "deplored his emphasis on killing, his attitude toward sex as a purely physical act." Aldous Huxley's *Point Counter Point* delighted her for its erudition and satire. She admired his essays on mysticism, which, along with his friendship and support, became central to her own work in later years, though she did not understand them at the time. She loved John Galsworthy's novels with a "wild passion," though critics disparaged them for his celebration of the rich, propertied class. For Clairene, his characters came alive because he wrote "convincingly of love between man and woman, father and son, and father and daughter," and she often used them as models for her own characterizations.[78]

By the end of the 1920s and the beginning of the 1930s, the world was once again in flux. A decade earlier, Prohibition had given birth to gangsters, illegal liquor, and speakeasies. "All the people I knew felt prohibition was a crime against freedom of choice, which justified their breaking the law. In speakeasies, I always ordered the same drink as my escort and when he wasn't looking, I poured half my cocktail into his. Who needed cocktails? Life itself was intoxicating enough."[79]

8

If It's Predictable . . .

1928–1935

> Demand everything from life and you shall receive much; ask nothing and you shall receive even less. When life stabs you in the back . . . laugh in her face; wrestle with the old bitch, fight to the finish, show her she has chosen a worthy opponent.
>
> —Aunt Sophistica
>
> Claire Myers Spotswood, *The Unpredictable Adventure*

IF IT IS PREDICTABLE, it is not an adventure—and adventure was Clairene's first priority. With typical spontaneity, and "because everyone she knew was going," Clairene decided to take her first trip to Europe, in the summer of 1928. On her passport, she changed her date of birth to February 11, 1900, making herself twenty-eight instead of her actual age, thirty-two. "I met Frances [Crane], a social worker who had married a successful business man in advertising and moved to London and her rich aunt in Paris and was taken to many of the finest French restaurants. In London, Sir Thomas [Glen-Coats] came up from the [regatta] races at Cowes and took me to Oxford to see his room as a student and to night clubs."[1]

In London and Oxford, he "dined and wined" her in grand fashion; former Prime Minister David Lloyd George sat in a box opposite them one evening at the theater.[2] "But I was not ready for Europe; the trip was wasted on me."[3] Nevertheless, the excitement of her return, which she described to her parents, was no waste: "Dear Mother and Daddy," she began, less formal as always with her father. "Did I tell you . . . about [the] catch in my throat that the first sight of the Statue of Liberty gave me? I saw it quite suddenly an enormous black figure it looked against a flaming crimson sky. . . . And the lower end of Manhattan was softened by a blue haze of mist as it was just dusk. The buildings piled up so close they looked like one gigantic palace twinkling with thousands of lights that looked like jewels. Nothing Europe could offer could equal that—it's peculiarly American, for skyscrapers have existed in no history till today."[4]

Enchanted with her New York life, Clairene was unable to appreciate Europe's charm. That would change in the 1940s and 1950s when she and her husband, H. Thurston Owens, made frequent trips abroad. At this point, she thought the *Paris Follies* could not compare with the "N.Y. Follies & Ziegfield." She found French food much better than English cooking—"an abomination unto the Lord!"—but was impressed with "perfectly trained" English servants who only cost "4 & 5 [£] a week." The typical tourist sites, "stodgy dark plain," left her cold.

When Sir Thomas introduced her to his friends in London, she would claim to be from New York; but Sir Thomas would explain she was actually southern. The English thought southerners were "by far the nicest people in America," she wrote her parents, because so many colonists were English and "of good family." English life reminded her of the South she knew as a girl, "slow & easy going & courteous & kind—only they appear more cold & reserved."

The Myerses must have had a mixed response to Clairene's assessment of Europe—her claiming to be from New York might have offended them, while her compliments about southerners would have delighted them. Still, they would hardly have shared Clairene's enthusiasm about her return to New York, and likely, wondered at her wonder. There is no evidence that Coren Lee and Susan ever visited their daughter in New York, though Clairene's brother, Coren Douglas, would in 1931. Travel was not as swift as today, and perhaps neither parent was physically up for the trip, even in the 1920s. However, more likely Clairene's parents were not interested in confronting their prodigal daughter's lifestyle head on.

When she returned to New York from Europe, Clairene submitted a trio of essays to the *New Yorker*, having been encouraged by rejection letters that invited her to keep trying.[5] On October 12, 1928, she submitted "A Dangerous Thing" to a Katherine Angell, "a little sketch in the same tone as 'Audition' by Arthur Kober, which the *New Yorker* published on October 6.[6] On October 18, 1928, Wolcott Gibbs, Mrs. Angell's assistant, wrote that "A Dangerous Thing," which satirizes a bookshop encounter between an obviously uneducated customer looking for a book by "Nitsky" (meaning Nietzsche) and a clerk who helps politely, "just misses": it didn't hold his interest, he wrote. "An idea like this is very hard to make plausible . . . perhaps the dialogue is a little too tough."[7] They hoped she would send something else, soon. Clairene quickly submitted "Evening Dress in a Bus," only to be turned down again. Her "pleasant and amusing" story had the "right tone," but seemed a bit pretentious.[8] However, this story of a girl in formal attire who cannot get a cab and must take a bus captures this period of glitzy styles, formal attire, culture, charm, and breeding as symbols of worldly success.

Not easily discouraged, Clairene tried again, searching for tone and subject matter that would please a popular audience. "Latest Styles in Crime" was rejected on November 10, as "too familiar," but again the editors invited her to send something else. If she did, no other rejections survive, and she was never published in the *New Yorker*. Perhaps her effort to contrive a popular story resulted in observations that were more fluff than substance—too superficial even for an audience that enjoyed gossip about the latest fads and fashions of the rich, famous, and scandalous.

A close look indicates Clairene's stories were not so different from those the *New Yorker* published in 1928. Set in a chorus line, the callous and insensitive narrator of "Audition" uses sexist and racist language in a thick New York dialect: "Yeah, she's aw'right, kinder fat. . . . Now get the colored girls in line."[9] Clairene's "A Dangerous Thing" affects the same tone as "Audition," characterizing a customer in a bookstore who asks to see "Nitsky's *Zarathusala*" and misquotes Shakespeare. Holding up inequities to a snickering audience denotes the *New Yorker*'s willingness to publish articles driven by elitism. The same issue in which "Audition" appeared contains a cartoon parody of a stylish matron telling a young bookseller, "I don't want anything too exhausting."[10]

Clairene's series of anecdotes entitled Bookshop Brevities portrays a satirical look at the daily activities in bookstores.[11] Several incorporate images of either the flapper or the highly paid prostitute as measured against the intellectual New Woman and reflect popular attitudes toward celebrities, contrasted with the struggles of a working girl in the 1920s and 1930s. Satirical portraits of flappers as empty-headed flirts reflect the author's bias against nonintellectual women. Ironically, the author herself flirts expertly, though she considers herself an intellectual. These stories often demonstrate the Tellectina/Femina conundrum. Women who like men must flirt to capture their hearts; flirting creates an image of a helpless, though lovely, female who worships strong, brilliant men. But the author's deprecation of the flapper represents the dichotomy that developed among New Women of Claire's generation.[12]

The flapper became the celebrated "babe" of popular culture, an icon of female sexual autonomy that divorced women's rights from their political and economic underpinnings and reinforced society's stigma: that fun and exciting women cannot have minds. There was no way out. If a woman could think, she could not be normal. Only "unnatural" women struggled with men for economic independence. A dichotomy emerged with New Women considered inverts or lesbians—celibates or sexual deviants—while the flapper became the icon of sexuality, and both images carried negative implications.[13]

Conservative thinkers created a divide-and-conquer strategy in much the same way that the backlash of the 1980s and 1990s created a rift between homemakers and "liberated" women, professionals, and activists.[14] Ultraconservatives resisted issues enabling women's autonomy. The assumption was that liberated women—feminists—marginalized as sexual deviants or "dykes," become autonomous because they are repulsive to men; femmes fatales, bimbos, need men for support, but do not deserve their respect. Respectable women are married women—housewives and mothers. Clairene's short stories reflect those same stereotypes and portray women who concentrate on getting a man through good looks rather than good ideas—the seductive power of the flapper or prostitute as opposed to the attractive appeal of the intellectual.

Thus, her stories betray the progressive movement that won women the right to a college education and to vote. Just as the author depicted her literary forebears like George Sand and Madame de Staël in the City of Women as role models manqué in *The Unpredictable Adventure*,[15] so with the flapper stories, she confused the purpose of sexual freedom, which then and now, means the freedom to choose on all levels in every arena of life, with the freedom to dress and act a certain way in public.

Though flappers were girls who wanted to have fun, in fact, by day they contributed to the workforce in significant ways as clerks, fashion retailers, phone operators, and other new roles that arose with their new freedom as full citizens.[16] Clairene sought to resolve the dilemma of her own struggle toward sexual, intellectual, and financial liberation by writing satire as a means of confronting her inner conflicts. At times she found herself on the side of her longtime opposition.

Jabs at materialism and lack of intellectual finesse flourished among popular columnists of the day: Christopher Morley, and his discourse on Leonora—a moniker used derogatively against women—in the *Saturday Review of Books*, Harry Hansen on browsers of bookstores in the *New York World*, and H. L. Mencken, endlessly satirizing the middle class "booboisie" to mention only a few of Clairene's models. And yet, such stereotypes are disconcerting when drawn by an author who endorses sexual freedom for women; who, returning to New York in 1926, was disappointed that none of her friends were involved in affairs; and who found the folks in her Texas hometown to be judgmental.

Ironically, this same Clairene Myers who wrote these short stories maligning flappers not only maintained a correspondence with Morley in defense of modern Leonoras, she also wrote a letter to Harry Hansen at the *New York World* in behalf of "poor browsers" of bookstores, whom he maligned in an article.[17] She defends a new type of browser who comprises "a fast-growing class who know as much about books as any bookseller, who know exactly what they like and dislike," and who browse leisurely but leave with books under their arms. With such "increasing book-knowledge," she asserted, browsing has not gone out of fashion, but rather is evolving into a kind of self-service method. "Long live the browser!" she enthused, her letter reflecting her affection for books themselves and the industry as a whole.

Clearly, she loved her job, enjoyed her customers, respected the people who wrote books, and longed to become a famous writer herself. Several stories in the Bookstore Brevities series depict the pastime many New Yorkers love: celebrity spotting. In these stories, the narrator regularly attends activities where celebrities congregate, or at times, the celebrities themselves come to buy books by other celebrities. In either case, the first-person narrator is dazzled by the presence of the rich and famous, especially writers like Carl Sandburg, Edgar Lee Masters, Carl Van Doren, Sinclair Lewis, James Branch Cabell, Bertrand Russell, Thornton Wilder, Upton Sinclair, and Walter Lippmann; publishing stars like William Rudge and the Boni Brothers; and the wives of famous men, such as Mrs. Stanford White and Mrs. Marshall Field. "For the parade of notables is endless." Most of the time, the author's name-dropping anecdotes provide glimpses of the celebrities that humanize even as they mythologize them.

One of Clairene's favorite anecdotes included in this series narrates Carton Moore-Park's altercation with the police when he defended the horse's rights at an Italian funeral. Moore-Park himself tells this story on the occasion of the publication of his limited edition book of etchings, *Polo: Six Drypoint Impressions of a Chukker*, brought out by William Rudge for one hundred dollars a copy.[18] Moore-Park comes alive as a public persona in ways that are not apparent in his fictional persona in "Gaily Bedight" or *The Unpredictable Adventure* as the protagonist's forbidden lover. Here, the "tall slender Englishman with his tie awry, his hair disheveled, and his eyes blazing . . . a born *raconteur*" spins amusing stories about his life in London and his adventures with King Edward VII, Lady Diana Manners, the Rothschilds, Rodin, the Rossettis, and his childhood visits with the British poet, Algernon Charles Swinburne.[19]

But Clairene's favorite story, the one she most often included in submissions for publication, involves the following anecdote, in which the joke is on her:

> A modestly dressed woman of exceeding politeness came in and after selecting several books and Christmas papers said, "How much does it come to, please?"
>
> "$4.35," I replied.
>
> Opening her purse, she responded, "Oh, I'm sorry, but I don't believe I have that much with me.
>
> "Poor woman," I thought. "Imagine not even being able to afford to spend $4.35 at Christmas time! What a pity!"
>
> "But," she continued, "I used to have a charge account here. Maybe I could just charge it."
>
> "There goes my sale," I thought, "she probably hasn't any account at all." Aloud I said, "Well, I'll see." I took out my paper and pencil and asked wearily, "What is the name, please?"
>
> And the polite lady answered modestly, "Mrs. John D. Rockefeller, Jr."[20]

Such star-gazing should have been highly marketable in the 1920s and 1930s. Surprisingly, none of this series saw print, as evinced by several rejection letters. Still, Clairene's essays and fiction as a rule addressed serious issues regarding class, race, sexuality, and the progression of her spiritual journey.

Her "Alabama" series discloses the essentialist racism prominent among southerners of the day and among certain northerners as well.[21] Ironically, the patronizing tone of "Among the Alabama Hill Folk" suggests a pride in the narrator's southern roots, which give her special insights into the ways of the "Negro."[22] In a sense, the narrator functions as interpreter for the northern educated classes who just do not "get it" when it comes to southern black customs, and who were far more frightened by blacks than their southern coworkers. In the mining camps, whites were the minority, two to one, with "3000 Negroes and only 1500 whites," including the poor white mining families and their middle-class supervisors—a ratio that startled the northern girls who worked as professionals with the miners' families.

Conditions in the camp appear far more primitive than "Gaily Bedight" indicates; indeed, only one miner's cabin has a bath tub, and it is filled with coal. The white supervisors live in marginally better accommodations, but the permanent plumbing has not been connected, and the young women use an outhouse.

Clairene describes the miners' wives as "mothers of twelve" with swollen ankles who ask questions about birth control. These poor women knew only to continue nursing their babies for three or four years as a means of contraception.[23]

The author separates the customs and problems of the black miners from those of the white ones. Payday nights among the black miners included "liberal drinking," which inevitably led to shootings, about which the "white boys" would remark, "'Nother nigger dade." As a rule, the narrator explains, "the lower the white the more unkind he is to the black," though she does not elaborate on the rationale.[24]

"The Magic Kindergarten" tells the story of Clairene's moments of ecstasy evoked by the magical awakening experiences on the hillside while blowing bubbles with the miner's children, described also in "Gaily Bedight."[25] The focus of this version addresses class, as the spiritual encounter with universal oneness breaks down the narrator's aversion to the children's ignorance and filth. In the spring sunshine, as the children awaken to the delightful discovery of bursting bubbles in the air, their supervisor awakens to a cosmic awareness of the "very essence of childhood—the sweetness, the purity and innocence emanating from them like a fragrance made visible."

These creative nonfictions in the light of today's perceptions of racism and classism, and with contemporary sensitivity to politically correct language, reveal the author's intolerance, but her goal was honorable even if her perspective by today's standards seems naive.

As a New Yorker, Clairene saw herself living at the center of the universe, with the boom on Wall Street in full flourish and everyone buying books. She approached her job and her writing with equal commitment, even working extra in the bookstore during the Christmas season without expecting, or receiving, extra pay.

Then came that "black day in October 1929—the day of the catastrophic" stock market crash. "Many people lost every cent they possessed. Some men in Wall Street committed suicide by jumping out the windows of their offices. Banks closed. Thousands of men and women lost their jobs."[26] Even the crash did not dampen Clairene's enthusiasm nor dull her mood. Perhaps because of what she called her "abysmal ignorance of economics" or perhaps because she possessed "a blind faith that she was born under a lucky star," her lifestyle continued—dining with male and female friends, even taking an unmarried acquaintance who was expecting a child into her tiny apartment and nurturing her through a secret pregnancy. And still she found the time to write and submit short stories of her own adventures to popular magazines with stunning regularity, stoically absorbing the pain of rejection.

According to the "Autobiography," about this time she began to notice two trends she found deeply disturbing. "All the popular nonfiction books were concerned with physical adventure"—safaris in Africa, climbing Mount Everest, or swimming the Hellespont. "Physical adventure was considered life's supreme adventure. I felt outraged. Surely the supreme goal in life was the intellectual search for certitude, for ultimate truth embodied in a work of art, preferably literature."[27] In addition, she noticed, adventure books were written by and about men with male heroes. Where were the female adventurers? Where were the stories of women like herself? Waiting to be written, or discovered, by women like her!

Goaded by popular trends in what she considered the "wrong direction," Clairene took matters into her own hands and began to work on a "different kind of book." In the late twenties, she had written one book about her adventures as a young woman out in the world—which, in her "Autobiography," she pronounced that it "wasn't any good."[28] Editors criticized and rejected "Gaily Bedight" for being too like the "biography of a real person, not like a novel or story!" The material and the humor were good, one editor determined, but the method was bad. "You've skimmed the cream of [Sibyl's] mental and emotional life but omitted the solid foundation of fact and material environment on which it must of necessity stand."

On the contrary, "Gaily Bedight" sets a strong sense of place. The South comes alive with its rigid rules concerning gender roles that confine women to the domestic sphere, the stereotype of the archetypal Lady as the appropriate image of woman, the stigma associated with the disease metaphor the protagonist faces on leaving home in search of a different life. A classic coming of age novel, a bildungsroman with a female heroine on a journey of self-discovery, "Gaily Bedight" takes its title from Edgar Allan Poe's poem "Eldorado," used as an epigraph to the novel:

> Gaily bedight,
> A gallant knight
> In sunshine and in shadow,
> Had journeyed long,
> Singing a song
> In Search of Eldorado.[29]

The title refers to an exterior image: the heroine—a female knight gaily "decked out" for her entry into the world. Much of the book concerns itself with outward appearance, how people and places look to the heroine, and how she looks to the world, the juxtaposition of appearance and reality, the war between idealism and materialism, the "sunshine and shadow" of the journey, and the maleness and femaleness of the sexes.

With *The Unpredictable Adventure*, the focus shifts to the adventure itself, the obstacles rather than the reward. The heroine sets out in search of the highest mountain in the world, Mount Certitude, where she will climb to the top and discover the ultimate Truth. Sibyl's dream of finding contentment in a city of gold—the Glittering City, New York—is replaced by Tellectina's dream for an affirmation of her inner convictions. Self-realization is sought through the acquisition of Knowledge, the adventure of learning, of mastering rationality by mastering the language, Reasonese.

The Unpredictable Adventure draws on the same autobiographical experiences as "Gaily Bedight." Written several years later, the former expands to include incidents that occurred after the latter ends. "Gaily Bedight" laid the foundations on which *The Unpredictable Adventure* stands. Indeed Clairene uses the metaphor of architectural construction to describe the writing process as she recalled it years later: "Creating a novel is an architectural process. The writer pushes and pulls, inserts and removes, rejects and rearranges. Words, phrases, sentences, paragraphs become like blocks of marble. Unlike marble, however, they acquire a will of their own. One polishes the exterior and hopes it will become a thing of beauty. . . . Gradually one erects an enormous edifice, its inner framework concealed from the eyes of others."[30]

Writing consumed the author, who described it as more satisfying than dating or even than eating. Still, at times she found the process controlled her as much as she controlled the process. *The Unpredictable Adventure* seemed to arise out of the author's unconscious, of its own accord, in ways that reveal the social construction of "Woman": Tellectina, the intellectual woman determined to achieve financial independence and worldly success as a writer; her psychological twin sister Femina who cares only for love, romance, men, and marriage. Femina functions as a foil, the "great deterrent," to Tellectina's quest for intellectual advancement. This characterization of a double protagonist, "natural sisters," personifies the struggle within the author between her feminine nature and her masculine drives. The dichotomy pulls her in two directions at once and represents the split between the male-modeled and the female-molded aspects of woman also explored in "Gaily Bedight" through Sibyl's painful self-disquisition, and in several of the stories featuring flappers. Here, the spirit of rebellion merges with the journey of self-discovery and the drive to achieve wholeness.

The Unpredictable Adventure can be read as a prototype for a female adventure myth that follows the archetypal patterns defined by Joseph

Campbell in his 1949 landmark study of mythic journeys, *The Hero with a Thousand Faces*.[31] When Tellectina leaves Smug Harbor to explore the land of Nithking, she answers the "call to adventure" into the unknown. The inspiring send-off Aunt Sophistica provides, to "be wise and rush in where fools fear to tread," establishes the tone of the novel and identifies the heroine's task as a rebellion against standard definitions of wisdom. Aunt Sophie, who in Campbellian terms, represents the first encounter of the hero journey, "a protective figure (often a little old crone or old man) who provides the adventurer with amulets against the dragon forces she is about to pass."[32]

A familiar feature of European fairy lore, the crone or fairy godmother appears in Christian saints' legends in the role of the virgin. In a reversal that fits the novel's satire of Christianity and of the cult of womanhood, Sophie is no virgin. To the disapproval of the Errorians of Smug Harbor, and to Tellectina's delight, she flaunts her unconventional past. As mentor, role model, and inspiration in this autobiographical novel, Sophistica appears as a surprise. Where did she come from?

While writing this novel, the author explained, "a third woman [in addition to Tellectina and Femina] mysteriously emerged from nowhere, unplanned, uninvited, unwelcome. Aunt Sophistica. She pranced through the pages full of laughter and cynicism."[33] Perhaps the author found the delightful Aunt Sophie unwelcome and intrusive because in life she didn't exist and Claire often complained about the lack of female role models or encouragement extended by older women. Perhaps, in the context of autobiography, Aunt Sophie represents the older heroine speaking back through time to the younger one, teaching her to live her life in a pattern of self-discovery that will lead to self-realization.

As an archetypal figure whose name stands for wisdom, Sophistica represents the "benign, protecting power of destiny."[34] Through the irreverent Sophistica, the heroine's send-off provides an opportunity to satirize both cultural and religious injunctions against freedom and reverses the axioms entrenched in Tellectina's—and Clairene's—fundamentalist Baptist background, called Puritan in the novel.

Thus, Sophie assaults not only the double standard, which she covers in her prejourney lectures to Tina—guide archetypes love to lecture—she also directly attacks the values of Southern Baptist decorum. Aunt Sophie, "drunk on her own words," admonishes the adventurer to remember her commandments and keep them "wholly." "Demand everything from life and you shall receive much; ask nothing and you shall receive even less. When life stabs you in the back . . . laugh in her face; wrestle with the old bitch, fight to the finish, show her she has chosen a worthy opponent."[35]

The amulets come later. As a parting gift Aunt Sophie shows Tina her latest book, *The Chastity Myth Exposed.* Thus, the protector charges her protégée to obtain two kinds of knowledge: The intellectual kind she will acquire when she leaves the Land of Err, where the only language spoken is Halfish, and wanders in the Land of Nithking, where Reasonese is spoken. The second kind of knowledge, carnal knowledge—both physical and emotional—clearly forbidden in the land of her birth, she will acquire when she allows herself to experience the passion of learning and the passion of loving. For it is the passion for living that has been denied the Puritans of Smug Harbor. Sophie should know; a New Woman herself, she had lived there and had escaped into the land of Nithking. Thus, like most guides, she is a product of a similar kind of journey: a heroine-survivor of the unknown.

The send-off carries another important metaphor, that of androgyny. When Tina comes to bid her aunt farewell, she has cut her hair short and donned rough trousers. With a pack on her back, ready to roam, she proclaims, "I have no destination as yet, but I shall travel 'everywhither.'" Unhampered by outer accouterments or inner restraints, she is a woman behaving like a man. Yet, Aunt Sophie compares her to a delicate flower, tender, fragile, and erect."[36] According to Carroll Smith-Rosenberg, "women writers of the 1920s and 1930s deliberately transposed the male sexual metaphors into a feminist language."[37] By imitating one of her role models, George Sand, the author intuits an understanding of feminist literary politics. Liberation equals imitation: dress like a man and go where destiny leads. Plus, George Sand never forgot her womanly attributes—feminine and deeply alluring.

The author employed this same precedent in marketing "Gaily Bedight" by assuming the pseudonym Clarence Myers, though it seems unlikely that the book, clearly by and about Woman, could have been written by even a sensitive male feminist. To further mask her identity, she listed the return address of her Twelfth Street apartment in care of Chester Queensbury, a highly suggestive name in itself.[38] With Chester as the name she often assigns Carton Moore-Park and Queensbury as an appellation that summons Leo's effeminate qualities, the pseudonym seems ironically contrived, especially since one of Leo's nicknames for Clairene was Queenie.

So, dressed in trousers, pack on her back, Tina, obscuring her femininity in the light of gender inequality, crosses over the Great Wall of Err and enters a shadowy world Joseph Campbell describes as the "first threshold," where the hero moves in "a dream landscape of curiously fluid, ambiguous forms, where he may survive a succession of trials."[39] The fuzzy descriptions of place common to fantasy settings also situate the novel in a tradition established by other feminist modernists of the 1920s and 1930s "who often set their novels in 'unnatural' worlds and unstructured situations, beyond the threshold of conventional order."[40]

Landing first in the deep sand of the vast Desert of Dotbu (doubt) the heroine is greeted—and harassed—by the band of outlaw Noequists (questions), led by Woqu (the woman question). Mythologically, these characters represent "threshold guardians" who guard the boundaries of the world and limit the hero's sphere; the fear Tina confronts reflects the fear and turmoil any hero faces when leaving familiar territory, home. Tellectina, however, overcomes her fears, quickly grasps their alien language, Reasonese, converts to the religious worship of their idols, Frelo and Frewo (free love and free woman), and takes over as leader of the group.

A succession of trials comprise the initiation stage of the journey and the main body of the novel—a phase in the tradition of myth-adventure that has "produced a world literature of miraculous tests and ordeals."[41] *The Unpredictable Adventure* is no exception: Tina gets lost in the Jungle of Otherpeoplesideas, is pursued by three White

Hounds of religious dogma—Godsson, Onegod, and Godidea—and gets tangled in Sillidinous Vines whose deadly poison creates a rash of "disillusionment," which she cures with the magical healing powers of the drug, Cianite Vitigrew (creative writing). As Tellectina preaches a philosophy of free love and communal living, Femina ensnares men with her feminine charms. Tina struggles to hold their interest without sacrificing her autonomy by use of her powers of reason and idealism. And, as behooves a model guide and protector, Aunt Sophistica magically appears and disappears, by post or in person, dispensing amulets in the form of books that help Tellectina discover answers to her questions or focus on her next task.

Since the power struggle between Tellectina and Femina forms the central tension of the novel, the double heroine must pass the pivotal test and discover a way for a woman to love a man without sacrificing her independence or fundamental identity. On Cape Coverture—named to denote women's legal status during marriage—a "tropical fever" strikes Tellectina when she meets Olev the Third, Elam Domitann (dominant male). He finds Tina a delightful mystery with whom he can engage in high-level discussions, but he loves Femina. Throughout their tempestuous affair and brief marriage, Tina and Elam argue in diatribes that explore issues of female dependency: "As long as a woman permits a man to support her," Tina rages, "it's in the very nature of the bargain she must pay in return . . . by subservience."[42] Femina paces impatiently during their verbal battles and responds with deep sexual and emotional passion during their intimate moments. Elam considers himself a "lucky devil" to have found a woman with attributes that combine the intellectual and the feminine—claiming such women to be as "rare as snowstorms—on the equator."[43]

Their marriage, a compromise on Tellectina's part, dramatizes the effects the double standard has on women's lives. They must marry to preserve Tina's reputation—Elam's is *not* in jeopardy. As husband and wife, all aspects of the relationship, both positive and negative, intensify as Tellectina/Femina watches Elam change from a lover into a husband "who won't have his wife going out to work every day." Elam decrees that she needs "some children" to satisfy her drive for financial independence. That would "stop all this nonsense about 'freedom.'"[44]

The author's observations concerning this marital dilemma seem prophetic in light of recent theories concerning the cycle of violence identified in domestic relationships: "Tellectina never ceased to be amazed at the way in which marriage moved forward in cycles of happiness and misery."[45] Elam's moods move between violent rages, which Femina euphemistically calls "nocturnal attacks," and ardent lovemaking. The morning after one particularly fervent episode, Tina wakes up with her hat still on and their dinner untouched on the table.

Elam, a composite character, merges the charisma, charm, and benevolence of Clairene's "noble" artist-lover, Carton Moore-Park with the passionate, volatile nature of her second husband, George Wanders. Taken together, they embody the best and the worst aspects of male-female relationships and serve as a masculine counterpart to the Tellectina/Femina psychic split. Femina, attracted to Elam's strength, tells her sister he is the first man she could not "twist around [her] little finger." But Tina chides, "there's such a thing as carrying male dominance too far."[46]

As the marriage wears on, his rage ignites her rage—violence breeds violence—and Femina confesses, "When a woman is hurt . . . the impulse to strike back is stronger than any other impulse in the world—it is primitive and irresistible. . . . At moments I hate the man I love with a sort of exquisite agony." The level of emotional violence frightens Tina: what is this "deep dark uncontrollable antagonism that arises between a man and woman who are married," they wonder.[47] Elam's fortuitous death—he is killed in action during a war—precludes a resolution. But "in love, there is no death," Tellectina discovers when she notices "a red mark resembling a small face on the under-side of her left breast: a stigma she will carry with her throughout her life."[48] Though she finds loneliness and desolation unbearable, she resumes her search for Certitude with relief and leaves Femina behind to grieve.

The mourning period, which in biographical terms can be seen as a merging of the pain that followed the end of Clairene's relationship with Carton Moore-Park in 1923, and with George Wanders in 1932, functions on an archetypal level as a moment of rebirth. "A woman whose life seems destroyed by the end of a marriage and whose basic sense of herself is radically shaken cannot pass simply to a new life and a new identity," writes Kim Chernin in her study of women's archetypal journeys of self-discovery.[49] The crisis evokes questions of personal identity resolved through the creation of a new self.

In this case, Tellectina applies the drug Cianite Vitigrew to her wounds and resumes her adventures in Nithking. This heroine's sword is a pencil, "a cylindrical yellow container" filled with "gray powder."[50] Wielding it wisely, she can conquer the world—her own world, the world of woman liberated into herself, seeking her destiny and her place in the universe and a source of self-knowledge. In Campbellian terms, this phase of the journey parallels the hero's reentry to battle after a period of defeat, for all journeys are cyclical. As the heroine matures, the obstacles she faces rehash old conflicts in new guises.

On her way to Mount Certitude, Tellectina gets lost in the Jungle of Otherpeoplesideas; as she approaches the top of Mount Certitude, she collapses under a signpost marked To Manu-Mission, a place signifying the release from slavery, a place for the disenfranchised to experience freedom. Though she held "no belief in the supernatural," an uncanny splendor pervades her being; a blinding light overcomes her senses, recalling those "rivers of light" the author described in her "Autobiography" and in *Awakening to the Good*, which hit her like a bolt of lightning with insights into the "mystery of the universe itself." Closing her eyes, "she fainted with a bliss that transcended consciousness." When she awakens, she knows that she is in the "throes of a strange process . . . of rebirth" which, again, resemble St. Theresa's ecstatic bliss, except that Tina's "revelations were not religious but intellectual." For Tina, universal knowledge is an aspect of self-realization and part of her spiritual quest. Psychological and religious drama coalesce to ignite powerful revelations of truth, and she comes to understand that: "God is not a great omnipotent man. . . . He is this—this blinding light—this revelation of truth! THERE IS NO GOD!

GOD IS DEAD! LONG LIVE GOD! . . . For one long divine moment she was an audacious young god."[51]

At age twenty-five, Tellectina declares herself free! But she is not finished with herself yet, for she has left Femina behind. In keeping with the author's struggles with sexuality, her heroines must battle for sexual identity wherein the masculine and the feminine principles can function as allies. In a society that divides woman against herself, the struggle within demands a victory without. As Chernin explains, "when a woman divided within herself seeks for wholeness and authentic power . . . the mother goddess speaks. From dreams, from nature, from memory, she leads our development forward by guiding us into the past." Rather than a regression in the Freudian context, however, the crisis takes the heroine back to the "fundamental roots of female being," to the source of female power, a step in the heroic quest for self-knowledge.[52]

When the heroine meets the great goddess, reversals in the archetypal quest appear strikingly clear. In male hero myths, a final battle defeats the temptress, protectress, or other evil goddess figure and represents the hero's mastery of life itself, for woman is the primal life source. The glory of man lies in his defeat of the powers of woman.[53]

In contrast, when a female hero confronts the goddess, she faces a reflection of the deepest regions of her own soul, her own drop into memory and unconscious desire, marked by archetypal symbols of the ocean, the feminine symbol of fluid timelessness.[54] Thus, in the novel, Tellectina abandons herself to the natural currents of the ocean, which carry her to the next site of adventure.

The Seven Siren Islands set the stage for what Joseph Campbell defines as the apotheosis of the hero's journey and form the centerpiece of this novel, both in structure and significance. Tellectina's encounter with the great mother goddess, Yeta Bu (Beauty), provides the author an opportunity for stunning descriptions and hilarious satire that fully express her understanding of female sexuality in her unpredictable adventure.

The Siren Islands present a world of mythical proportions designed in an elaborate metaphorical and anagrammatical scheme. The first island is Forta Feli (art of life), the last, Forta Velo (art of love). In between sit five islands representing the cultural arts: Tni-Pa (painting), Cumsi (music), Tru-Sce-Plu (sculpture), Blidu (architecture), and O-We-Tri (literature or O write). Sirens inhabiting the islands represent the various senses: Ese (see), Reha (hear), Mllse (smell), Astte (taste), and Ceve-peri (perceive), all priestesses who serve Yeta-Bu. They lead Tellectina on an educational tour of the first six islands, which awakens her to the beauty and sensuality of life and functions as foreplay to her initiation into the Mystery of Mysteries awaiting her on the seventh island, Forta Velo (art of love). Tina's sensual awakening, enhanced by large doses of wine, bathes her in paroxysms of joy, delight, and wonder. Although there are moments of intellectual discussion, the emphasis here is on the sensual—the Siren Islands are the one place in Nithking where Reasonese is not vital. As a woman who has been preoccupied with developing her rational side, Tellectina has resisted the call of the feminine and idealized the male model of achievement. To pry her away from her allegiance to rationality and logic, she is seduced into the world of the intuitive, the sensual, the erotic. Experience replaces explanations.[55]

When the young priest Chotu, whose "touch" all women love, joins Tina in the waters off Forta Velo, he primes her to visit the main temple, which lies "buried in the very heart of the jungle, in a perfect state of preservation," a monument to female anatomy: "Two beautifully molded columns of white marble lay recumbent in the deep grass—like the thighs of some fallen goddess—while beyond them rose a low white dome with a strange Gothic doorway stained a dull red. Above this, the temple was ornamented with small twin domes . . . the tip of each dyed with red."[56]

Thirty pages of ritual, filled with puns and innuendoes, create a sexual mythology that celebrates women and instructs men in the art of loving, a virtual sex manual delineating fourteen preliminary rituals the priest must perform before he can enter the temple. Only a connoisseur of the erotic can serve the god Ecstaci and perform the Mystery of Mysteries in a manner suitable to honor the great goddess

Yeta Bu. Erotic symbols reverse our expectations and describe rites of passage designed to satisfy woman's deepest fantasies.

The ceremonies open with Femina and Passino performing a tribute to the male idol, "composed of some plastic red material . . . which, when sufficiently heated"—by Femina of course—"was capable of expanding till the god stood erect like a divine athlete; so lifelike, so strong and muscular, so full-blooded that the turgid veins were actually visible beneath their delicate covering."[57] Though unmoved, Tina admits this is the "finest representation of a member of the male sex she has ever seen." Femina warns Tina, the first Puritan ever initiated into the Mystery of Mysteries, "If you interfere in any way, you'll regret it!"[58]

Tina stands to one side and watches the "native orgies," a spectacle involving all the youths and maidens of the island. They form two lines facing each other; the girls bear wine jars with a pear-shaped base and narrow elongated neck. The boys flourish "small blunt spears"; a maiden's head is severed and the cessation of blood is "regarded as a propitious omen." The dance begins: when the youths, holding their weapons erect, advance, the girls retreat; when the girls advance, the youths retreat. "The drums beat louder and louder, faster and faster like the throb of a gigantic heart. Finally, in a frenzy of ecstasy the youths plunged their spears into the jars until the red wine spilled like blood over the floor."[59] Couples disappear into the shadows.

And that's only the beginning. The main mystery, a moniker borrowed from Leo Saidla's own euphemistic lexicon, involves Tellectina herself, and she needs further preparation. "The ordeal is a deepening of the problem of the first threshold," which for Tellectina embodied her meeting with the band of Noequists.[60] The "woman question" still hangs in the balance. Tina notes that although convinced that religion in their utopian New Chimera turned out to be "ridiculous," she remains "irresistibly attracted and yet unaccountably afraid of even the external manifestation of such cults."[61] It is high time she came to terms with her fears, and that's what the ultimate ceremony accomplishes. The activity of worship in the flesh replaces the worship of idols representing female issues of freedom during the first phase of the journey. The presence of Yeta Bu transforms intellectual knowledge into carnal knowledge. Puritans have no business here, as Femina explains to Tina. The concept of sin dies as the wholeness of womanhood is born. Tellectina and Femina must merge; the mastery of the feminine is a mastery of life itself, just as for the hero. But the heroine who owns her sexuality and her intellectual and creative capacities, reigns as mistress of her own life and self.

Femina takes charge of Tina's instructions, chanting the "Vaginae, a Woman's Song of Ecstasy": "I am a flower full blown—heavy with amorous perfume; a luscious tropical fruit lain long under the Southern sun. I am a bed of lotus blossoms opening wide voluptuous petals under the strong sun of his passion. . . . I am the earth—the parched and hungry earth . . . wherein all the rivers of all the world fill and rise and rush headlong to the primal sea, when ecstasy moves within me."

Man is lover and child—"with my milk, my blood, my flesh," she comforts him. She is woman giving; she is woman taking. Radiant, her proud head lifted, Femina sings: "I am fearless and unafraid! I am proud of my passion. I exult in it. My blood leaps and laughs in my veins. I sing a song of the happy woman, the free, the natural woman. I sing of fulfillment and radiant bloom."[62]

The Mystery of Mysteries culminates in a celebration of sexual unification with Femina's impassioned voice as background music to Tina's final submission: "At last in this moment of white heat we become one, my senses no longer able to distinguish my limbs from his limbs, my body from his body, my self from himself—united, irrevocably and forever. The twain shall be one flesh—godlike—hermaphroditic like the original gods . . . a divine dual oneness . . . perfect and whole."[63]

In the presence of Yeta Bu, with the assistance of the High Priest Passino, Femina and Tellectina miraculously merge into one being, for the healing of the split psyche is a healing of all oppositionals.[64] Splendid and divine, the moment, in art as in life, is temporary. All obstacles are cyclical. To be a "Tellectina," to be taken seriously as a person, she had to squash the feminine principle, Femina. But to be whole, balanced, and self-realized, she would need to honor both parts of herself no matter how society chose to define them. This paradox comprises the source of her pain and frustration, the root of the urgency that propels her quest. Unused to the intensity of such emotional rigors, Tina escapes on the frigate the *Esse McMoonn* (common sense). Femina, by now a fanatic devotee of Ecstaci, remains on Forta Velo chanting of "fulfillment and radiant bloom."

Armed with a new trust in her sexuality and in her autonomy, Tellectina launches the next phase of her quest, which takes her back into the world. *The World's World*, a cross between the morality play and vaudeville, provides a forum for Tellectina to expound the lessons of her initiation in a public sphere. On an archetypal level, Tina becomes the messenger for the great goddess of the ancient world seizing a historic moment that can balance the masculine with the feminine, the self with history, the spirit with politics.

The play portrays the virtues of mankind, but the players are anything but virtuous off stage. Tellectina exposes the hypocrisy of the actors and of contemporary values—religion, war, economics, family relations, and the treatment of women and prostitutes—in lengthy diatribes; the audience shouts her down, throws missiles at her. Femina materializes during one of Tina's confrontations on the issue of sexual morality and tries to save her sister: "You can't make the world over," she tells her, "you nor all the rest of the intellectual women."[65]

The rest of the book demonstrates the trials that follow the sexual initiation rites. Tellectina and Femina are fully women now, but they must learn their place as human beings in the world. Thus, Tellectina must continue her search for Mount Certitude—a path she alone can define. Only through the lessons of the ordeals the heroine has survived can she emerge as a "superior" person, qualified to bear the "ultimate boon," the reward of her quest back to the land of her birth. And she isn't quite there yet.

According to Joseph Campbell, the boon is a "symbol of life energy stepped down to the requirements of a specific case."[66] In this case, Tellectina must discover the nature of certitude. Resumption of her quest takes her through a new round of obstacles, but the reward is a sumptuous tour of the houses that occupy the highest peaks of Mount Certitude. Dorothy Parker, Ellen Glasgow, Edna St. Vincent Millay, Edith Wharton, and Jane Austin, each have remarkably fine views. Visits with H. L. Mencken, Burton Rascoe, and James Branch Cabell reveal that there is no place called certitude after all. The highest peak in Nithking turns out to be Mount Ghaulot (to laugh), for not certainty, but laughter is the source of all truth. To laugh at human foibles places one at the height of wisdom—satire and humility, apparent opposites, become two sides of the same coin.

An important key to understanding the bridge between the human world and the divine, the hero's birth home and the fantasy landscape of adventure, lies in the significance of myth and symbol: the two kingdoms are actually one. Indeed, when Tellectina looks out from the top of Mount Ghaulot, she can see Smug Harbor right below. Though her journey has taken her but a short distance from her point of departure, she has traveled uncountable miles within her alternate universe. Now, to be a true hero, she must find her way back home to share the lessons of her journey with the uninformed society she left behind. She must find a balance between the "wisdom brought forth" from the adventure and the prudence required to live in the world of reality.

Often, crossing the return threshold requires assistance from outside the supernatural realm in what seems like a "magical flight." Tellectina's return from Nithking to the Land of Err occurs abruptly: unexpected and unpredictable, ironically just after she vows never to return. Cold, hungry, and exhausted, she falls to the bottom of the mountain where she meets T. A. Riley (reality) and "clambers" aboard his carriage. His price for delivering her to warm shelter? "Sec Sept Fler" (self-respect). Resigned that her adventure has come to an end, she notes that in the ten years of her travels, nothing has changed on Expiedway Ten, the highway back to the Land of Err.

But magic follows her home when Aunt Sophistica appears out of nowhere—as is her custom—anxious to debrief her weary protégée. This time their dialogue establishes them as peers, colleagues in their mastery of Reasonese, the mistresses of two lands. Tellectina is clearly on her way to becoming a grande amoureuse.

"It is time that someone wrote a new plot," a character says in Virginia Woolf's *Between the Acts.* Written in 1938–39, Woolf may have been calling for "a new plot for marriage," for Woolf wrote a new plot with her life, but not in her fiction. Nor did many other innovative writers of the time.[67] But, in 1935, Claire Myers "Spotswood" already had. For the end of the novel, the reconciliation phase of the adventure, becomes a parody of the marriage plot. Passion is essential but love is not enough, Tellectina proclaims: "Having lovers and writing books is much more satisfactory than marriage . . . Love is but one of many passions—an inexplicable fever that makes the heart tremble with joy one minute and cruelly lacerates it the next. [Not love but] Passion—that is the secret of life!"[68]

In Tellectina/Femina and Sophistica, the author created new kinds of exemplary women with full and meaningful identities; in so doing she redefined *exemplary.*[69] Not surprisingly, the novel received rave reviews throughout the country when published in the fall of 1935. Nor is it surprising that it was banned. For many critics, these are not the kind of exemplars they had come to expect.

When Burton Rascoe, her editor at Doubleday Doran, first read the manuscript, before it was cut and revised, he prepared her for the paradoxical response the book would receive. "You must resign yourself to being misunderstood and you must do so without bitterness or exasperation or sadness. . . . I expect much of you as a writer." He expected it to cause a stir, and called it a "fine piece of work. . . . the sort of book no women have had the courage to write."[70]

"Get an unlisted phone number," Rascoe warned as the September 20 publication date approached. "Be prepared—the world will hate you for this critique." And of course he was right. "When a woman seriously asks herself what it means to be a woman she is pulling at a thread that can unravel an entire culture," Kim Chernin observes.[71] Or, as Muriel Rukyser famously put it, if a woman told the truth about her life "the world would split open."[72] But Claire Myers Spotswood was accustomed to having her world "split open" as she lived her own story. As it turned out, more critics loved it than hated it.

As early as June 8, before publication, "Miss Spotswood" mailed Rascoe an outline for the next seven books of the series Doubleday agreed to publish and began another book. Her old friends Sir Thomas and Lady Glen-Coats invited her to their castle in Scotland and offered to send her a steamer ticket. She would live in their tower and write her next book. She told them that she was already working too hard on her second book to leave, and that if she went dashing off to Scotland this summer she was afraid Mr. Rascoe would "spank" her.[73] But she promised to take them up on their offer the following summer, and Marian Murray published the news in a story about Miss Claire Myers Spotswood in the *Hartford Daily Times* on May 18.[74] Meanwhile, Rascoe arranged for Doubleday to send her weekly checks so she could devote full time to writing, to contacting publishers for permission to quote, and to sending advance notices to reviewers.[75]

Claire corresponded tirelessly with reviewers at major New York newspapers to assure ample publicity. Randolph Bartlett, reviewer for the *New York Sun* began a letter to the author, "Dear Lady (if I may still so call you after reading the first few pages of your charming book)." He considers her book a relief from "the present stream" of murky fiction.[76]

The New York Times, on October 20, 1935, called the heroine a "seeker of truth, an intellectual wayfarer and a 'grande amoureuse of life.'" They praised the author's rendering of this feminine Jurgen's adventures: "Miss Spotswood, in short, has tried something genuinely ambitious and should be praised accordingly," the reviewer concludes. The *Los Angeles Times*, on October 27, 1935, hailed it as reminiscent of *Pilgrim's Progress* with "double meanings, anagrams. . . . Lightly amusing, intelligent, mildly wicked, enough to shock the rigid-pious . . . [and] more instructive than most manuals about what a young girl ought to know." Murat Williams claimed in the *Richmond News-Leader*, a Virginia newspaper, on October 21, that *The Unpredictable Adventure*, which sought "to tell the literary world about woman's search for happiness" showed prospects for financial success until it was banned by the New York Public Library because "it was too risqué for its shelves. The author . . . said too much about the strange affairs of Tellectina in the Land of Nithking." The Romeike Press Clipping Bureau sent reviews from all over the county: New Haven; Hartford; Philadelphia; Washington, DC; Toledo, Marietta, and Dayton, Ohio; Reno, Nevada; Newark, New Jersey. Even the Breckenridge, Texas *American* printed a tiny notice. All the major New York papers, including the *Brooklyn Daily Eagle*, the *Herald Tribune*, the *World-Telegram*, and the *Post*, carried reviews and notices. Rascoe reviewed it for *Esquire* on November 15, and he listed it as a favorite in a Books I Have Liked column in the December 1 issue of the *Herald Tribune*.[77]

On October 8, 1935, Claire wrote a letter to Paul de Kruiff, author of *Our Medicine Men*, whom she had met years earlier. Most reviewers, she complained, saw *The Unpredictable Adventure* "primarily as an erotic book—perhaps they don't read anything but Chapter 10," set in the Siren Islands. She thought the book "merely honest on [female sexuality] and everything else."[78] Many authors quoted in the novel received advance copies. Cabell wrote that he considered the book a "fine masterpiece of true discernment," though, as a star character in it, he admitted he was not unbiased. Robert Briffault wrote from France: "It is too intellectual to ever be very popular." H. L. Mencken wrote from Baltimore to report he had read it "with great pleasure. . . . It doesn't surprise me to hear that the pious object to it. Let them howl."[79]

Richard Aldington "appointed himself champion" of her book in England. Before Aldington read the book, based on her comments regarding critics' negative responses, he responded with words relevant even in these early years of the twenty-first century: "I have a deep faith in the possibility of women playing a great and decisive part in the world of the future. Men have made such a disgraceful mess of human life that only women can bring back sanity. Only, it can't be done in the old silly terms of 'woman on a pedestal' and 'woman in the home.' They've got to face the realties, and this you seem to have done."[80]

He invited her to visit him and his wife and drop in for lunch. If she came by train he would pick her up in his Buick. She accepted his invitation and spent a most enjoyable visit in their "charming home." After he read the book and solicited British publishers, he advised her that unfortunately her book had come out just as England was passing through a puritanical period and books were being suppressed. Publishers are "afraid of being prosecuted because of what [Aldington] terms 'that admirable Chap 10—which is the clue and center of the book,'" she reported to Rascoe.[81]

Publishing in America was nearly as restrictive as in Britain at the time. As Claire confided to Aldington, she was dealt a terrific blow by Doubleday:

> [They] refused to use favorable comments from Robert Briffault, Aldous Huxley, Carl Van Doren, James Harvey Robinson, etc. because certain wealthy and powerful members of the firm were very religious and Puritanical and though willing for the book to sell quietly, forbade any publicity. . . . Yet a score of their publications contain passages equally as frank—written by men authors. Is it because I am a woman that they discriminate or because the others are famous or what? To me it is inconsistent and unjust beyond words but what, in heavens name can an author do?[82]

She considered trying to publish an expurgated edition in London hoping later it might be published in its proper form, though no evidence exists she pursued this tactic.

Even in the 1960s, Britain reacted in similar ways to avant-garde women who broke the rules of social decorum. When Angela Carter revisioned fairy tales such as "Beauty and the Beast" and "Little Red Riding Hood," she imagined female agency as sexual power, echoing Spotswood's mythology of female sexuality in the Siren Island segments, thirty years earlier. Because both authors created strong female protagonists who approach, seduce, and at times triumph over their male partners during conflict, they scandalized readers and were demonized by critics. "Because Carter took on fairy tales, she was sometimes pigeonholed as a 'white witch,' the sort of person who reads Tarot cards,"[83] just as Spotswood was derided for being too risqué.

Progressive readers, including the famous ones, lauded her accomplishment. Aldous Huxley called the novel a "remarkable achievement" and said she was "wise to use allegory" because it was easier to "get everything in." The problem with telling a straight story lies in covering "all the ground," as he was bitterly realizing while writing his own novel *Eyeless in Gaza*, which would be published the following year. Flattered by what she had written about him, he confirmed he was on his "own unpredictable adventure leading toward . . . 'religious pacifism'" and invited her to visit if ever in London in winter.[84]

Huxley's comments on allegory address an important aspect of the feminist use of the genre. Allegory "attempts to evoke a dual interest, one in the events, characters, and setting . . . and the other in the ideas they are intended to convey."[85] The genre, thus, provides a suitable vehicle for feminists to explore political, religious, and moral structures, as they affect women, without resorting to didactic lectures. Allegory functions as a veil for otherwise terse criticism and allows a writer, as Huxley put it, to "get everything in." Even veiled, Spotswood's ideas provoked controversy. Unveiled, the book would not have been published and would have incited the kind of criticism "Belle Randolph" provoked a few years later. Claire's search for certitude and women's liberation ultimately parallels the utopian quest for alternative possibilities. Like Charlotte Perkins Gilman's *Herland*, this book posits a process with the focus on the heroine's goals.[86] The idea of a comic adventure suggested by the subtitle, *A Comedy of Woman's Independence*, reinforces this focus. Although portions of the novel fall into long lectures that sound pompous and even stiff, for the most part Spotswood's combination of satire and anagrams makes this radical critique of social structures seem like a game, which held a unique appeal for her diverse reading public.

Fan letters arrived regularly offering enthusiastic support of "Miss Spotswood," a "gifted artist, a visionary, one who recognized the fun and games of life and learning." "You are the first who has been able to write a book *like Jurgen* without writing an *imitation* of it—and this includes Jurgen's creator," wrote one man. A woman thanked her for her "great contribution to the struggle of woman's enlightenment" and predicted that her book would open a "way to many women for that free expression suppressed by every known superstition, creed, and property law in every country in every age." She looked forward to future adventures. Emily Vanderhaven called it a "literary masterpiece" and predicted that some "intelligent men who can take it from the shoulder" would welcome this "clever portrayal of their foibles." Many asked for help translating some of the more difficult anagrams, usually Gatherulic Iron (ironic laughter) and Cianite Vitigrew (creative writing). Critic Carl Van Doren of the Book of the Month Club, wrote that he had figured out all of the anagrams except the latter and deemed the book "beautiful, one of [his] favorites." Fans called her frantically on the phone for help. A notary from Trinidad wrote nearly a year later to ask for the meaning of Cianite Vitigrew. In July 1937, a man from Decatur, Illinois, sent a list of ten words with their page numbers asking for translation. He urged her to hurry and write another: "I want it as soon as the ink is dry."[87]

Dauber and Pine displayed entire windows of her books accompanied by letters from literary dignitaries. Doubleday gave a luncheon in her honor in their private dining room—"twelve men, I was the only woman—the ideal arrangement," she quipped in the "Autobiography," suggesting that despite the applause for her intellectual performance, Femina lurked quietly in the wings.[88] She found herself sitting next to one of the more important officials who asked for her autograph, which was "unheard of," Rascoe told her later. The "tall handsome" publicity manager took her to dine and dance at an "expensive rooftop restaurant," probably the Rainbow Grill above Rockefeller Center.

"Then [the novel] died a quiet death." Claire moved back to the Breevort Hotel on lower Fifth Avenue and began to "write like mad. I felt justified as I could not get a job."[89] Ultimately, of the 2,700 copies printed, all but five hundred sold at the regular price; by April 1939, only seventy-five copies were left on hand at Doubleday.[90]

9

Parallel Letters/Parallel Lives

1930–1935

Freedom was a delusion.

—Claire Myers Owens, *Awakening to the Good*

DURING THE PERIOD WHEN *The Unpredictable Adventure* was conceived and the early drafts written, Claire's personal life was in turmoil. She married, divorced, and moved several times. She changed from an energetic, devoted young writer and bookseller to a depressed, even suicidal, wife and back again. The parallel journey of her personal life and her professional goals collided on several occasions between 1930 and 1935; she became disenchanted with her life and many of her choices. But this time she stuck it out. She did not return to Texas. Unsettled to the point of being nomadic, she moved around a lot: from New York to Hartford, Connecticut, from Fort Wayne, Indiana, to Washington, DC, in search of privacy to write and of a steady income. Life was unpredictable and the adventure, rigorous.

A brief affair with a married editor at Robert McBride Publishers ended in a flurry of letters in January and February of 1930 when he, after a period of "armistice," returned to his wife and children. Although Claire saved his letters, she never mentioned this affair in her writings, nor did she keep copies of her letters to him. But perhaps this relationship contributed to her change of attitude about her lifestyle.[1]

As she put it, her "mad gay pace" ended in 1931—the glamour of the city "palled," fading in disillusionment. "I'd had enough of men and dinners and theater and enough of selling books. What a stupid occupation. All you do is hand out books and take in money. They might as well be groceries or hammers and nails. No wonder my grandmother's generation in the South looked down on the trades."[2]

During this brief interlude, considered "burnout" in today's vernacular, she began to look closely at her preoccupation with men and her "insatiable hunger for love." In some ways, writing *The Unpredictable Adventure* was an attempt to transform her hunger for love into a spiritual quest. The writing delineated the search and often replaced her desire for men.[3]

"I was not aware then that all the love of all the men in the world does not compensate for a lack of parental love."[4] Later she came to understand that men became "Don Juans, seducing every attractive woman they met in an effort to compensate for lack of mother love." Perhaps her relationship with Carton had been an "effort to compensate" for her feelings of loss when her father seemed to withdraw his devotion because of her refusal to conform to his definition of the ideal southern woman. This glimpse into the mysteries of her own psyche foreshadow the deep levels of self-insight, fraught with pain, she would attain in the future. She failed to recognize the enormous satisfaction she got from writing as balance to her social life or the support she received from her parents during her three years recovering from her bouts of melancholy in Temple. Rather, she decided to "get off the treadmill," which in this case meant her social life, and settle into a marriage to a man who would treat her "not only as a woman, but as a human being."[5]

Seven years after her breakup with Carton Moore-Park, Claire met such a man, one who respected her for her intellect as well as for her beauty. After a "whirlwind romance" she married—really married—George Wanders in a ceremony sanctioned by the state of New York at the municipal building, city hall. Once again Claire deprived the Myerses of presenting their daughter in a traditional church wedding, but correspondence indicates they supported Claire's choice in a spouse and cooperated in helping her set up housekeeping in a mode befitting a middle-class bride in 1931.

Despite the Depression, those lucky enough to remain employed managed to maintain the appearance of refinement. Hems dropped and heels lowered, but the fashions were as elegant as ever: sumptuous fabrics, long flowing gowns, close-fitting hats. Home fashions were as important as street fashions to those who could afford them. Claire threw herself into the role of housewife with the same enthusiasm with which she approached any other task. After years of avoiding domesticity, she became the epitome of domestic finesse.

When it comes to the story of Claire's relationship with George Wanders, the truth is in the fiction, and the fiction is in the letters she wrote home to her parents. Her letters sanitize the struggles the relationship encountered even before the marriage, as evinced in her autobiographical writings. Her novels seem to follow more closely the details covered in the "Autobiography" and in her memoir, *Awakening to the Good.* The novel "Belle Randolph" dramatizes this period of Claire's life, with several drafts of this novel under several titles. By the time Claire wrote her "Autobiography," late in her life, even she could not have distinguished fact from fiction. Most of the events that transpired between Claire and George can be pieced together by examining all the genres of her writing to reveal the emotional impact this important phase of her life had on her psychological journey as a whole.

Claire's letters to her mother reflect her need to protect her parents from the harsh reality of her life with George. Face to face, Claire and Susan Myers could not communicate with the same consideration they achieved in their correspondence. During visits home, Susan Myers's pretenses left Claire feeling ostracized and often confused. True to her southern breeding, Mrs. Myers's impeccable manners belied her embarrassment of Claire's lifestyle: how could she explain to her neighbors the ways of this prodigal daughter who left home and went out to earn her own way, married then unmarried but without church weddings, lived in Alabama, Virginia, New York, and rushed about the country without regard to her reputation? Time and again,

Claire would be hurt by her mother's emotional distance and the disdain she expressed for Claire's break with tradition. But by mail they could speak Halfish and skim the truth.

The pattern developed early in Claire's life, beginning with the letter she wrote in January 1911 to her mother who was visiting her grandmother.[6] Claire claimed to love cooking, housekeeping, and sewing, though in her heart she was already an intellectual with plans to become a writer. In "Gaily Bedight," she portrays Sibyl's rebellious attitude concerning the limits imposed on women's lives in her comment to her best friend. "How did they know we weren't going to live down to the slogan: 'Future wives and mothers of [Texas]!'"[7] Was Claire "living down to the slogan" now in New York? Had she become the wife she had dreaded becoming in college? The answer is yes and no.

George Wanders seemed like the ideal man when Claire first met him at Dauber and Pine Bookshop in May 1931. Tall, nice looking, he came up to her desk and inquired about having his copy of *Lady Chatterley's Lover* bound in leather:

> "Have you read it?" he asked.
>
> "Oh, I glanced at it," I said casually, switching the subject: "What kind of leather do you want?" She had learned that it was fatal to discuss sex with men; they interpreted it as an "open invitation."[8]

George Wanders would have appealed to many women. He wrote a financial column for the *Herald Tribune* with his own byline. Intellectual, articulate, with a nice sense of humor, he was just her age, thirty-five, and recently divorced. He invited her to dinner several times. Often they went to the theater or returned to his "very attractive bachelor apartment in a new high rise. We looked over his books, many of which were the same as mine, discussed the plays and music we liked best."[9] They seemed well suited for one another.

However, Claire had plans to leave New York, temporarily. She had submitted a three-chapter outline to Jonathan Cape & Harrison Smith Publishers of the novel that would become *The Unpredictable Adventure*, and they had expressed interest.[10] Shortly after meeting George, she quit her job at the bookshop in order to devote herself to

11. Claire Myers Wanders. Verso inscription: "To my life love Hartford, Conn., 1931." Photograph courtesy of the TWU Woman's Collection.

writing full time. "Evidently I had a blind faith that I was born under a lucky star. I felt immune to disaster."[11] She went to live with her cousin Laura Lee in Indiana, where she thought she could write. But while she enjoyed their literary and musical evenings, Laura Lee and her husband, both pianists, had a new baby, and the household proved too noisy for Claire to concentrate.

George's letters were charming—conversational, pleasant, absent of the dramatic sweeping statements of love she had received from Alden, Leo, "Pierrot," and even Carton. They came addressed to "Miss Claire T-F Myers," referring to her characters Tellectina and Femina, and inquired as to their nature: "Look here, now. Are you Tellectina and Femina *and* Claire, or are you Claire, split into Tellectina and Femina or how does it work? Are you twins or triplets, that's the point?" Detailing his job as "oceans of fun," if dry, he enclosed a reprint of an article he had written for the *Herald Tribune*. He urged her to hurry back as he had "a lot of tales to tell of doings around town."[12]

Such lighthearted repartee betrays no indication of the dark side of his personality, nor of his deep familial attachments. "Drat family reunions," he wrote on May 15, for they interfere with a "day in the woods."[13] By June 10, Claire was back at her West Twelfth Street apartment in New York, where she received a letter of apology from George, asking her to forgive his "ignorance or lack of taste and let's see where we are?" Within the next ten days, he had asked her to marry him, after he felt certain she was "intellectual enough" for him. "Here was a man who actually wanted to marry me because of my mind and because of my writing. It was almost too good to be true."

Two incidents during their brief engagement might have served as warnings of the troubled times ahead. The first indicates a difference in their class and educational backgrounds that would prove calamitous later. Claire was surprised to learn that George had not gone to college. Self-educated, like many newspaper reporters in those days, "he seemed the best educated man" she had ever met. Only later did he reveal his deep resentment of her privileged upbringing. Her stories about her southern grandmother's pride in their aristocratic ancestors incited him to rage. In fact, he had told her early in their relationship that his parents were lower middle class, born in Germany but "the salt of the earth." Claire thought little of it. Then, on July 6, George took Claire to meet his family. On the way out to Long Island, they passed "rows and rows of small houses" and Claire commented, "I wonder who on earth lives in funny little houses like that." George stiffened and answered: "My parents do. They are not funny."[14]

Claire described George's family as "plain simple people"; all twelve she met that day seemed unpretentious, honorable. "At the dinner table there were no serving spoons . . . everyone rose up in his chair and stabbed the potatoes or meat . . . with his fork. I had never seen such a performance before but I wasn't rigid about etiquette."[15]

Dressed in a fashionable red suit and hat and wearing high heels, Claire's sophistication must have set Mrs. Wanders against her from the first. After using the upstairs bathroom to freshen up before dinner, Claire descended the staircase to find Mrs. Wanders gazing up at her, cold and unflinching.

His mother dominated the conversation and everyone present. When she took George down to the cellar for a private conference, George's sister-in-law Flora warned Claire: "Never, never let George come out here alone. She will do everything she can to break up your marriage as she has mine. . . . She is a selfish dominating tyrant. So beware." Claire did not "believe a word" at the time. But Flora's counsel proved prophetic. She became Claire's "dear and trusted friend," the only daughter-in-law with the courage to risk displeasing Mrs. Wanders; none of the women in the family openly took a stand against her.[16]

The novel "Belle Randolph," titled "Sons and Husbands," and "Love Is Not Enough" in its two earlier drafts, supports Claire's autobiographical claims: after a lengthy tour of the farm, during which Emma Schiller, Hans's mother, complained about her daily chores, Belle, turning on her southern charm, smiled broadly at Emma and said: "'You know, after we start housekeeping I'll probably wear out your telephone asking your advice about things. I hope you won't mind.' No answer. No change of expression on that stony face." Belle's attempts to connect all fail, with Hans ignoring her, leaving her feeling "punished for a crime she didn't know she'd committed."[17]

The second painful incident provided another warning regarding George's destructive temperament. In mid-July, George called in a rage because Claire had stayed out too late with an old boyfriend, whom she wanted to tell in person about her forthcoming marriage. Around eleven that night, George phoned: "I have called you three times. Where on earth have you been? We are getting married tomorrow. I don't want to run the risk of losing you."[18]

Claire was not ready for marriage. She wanted time to collect a trousseau. She argued that they had only known each other around six weeks, been engaged only three. "Clothes are not important," he snapped. "Tomorrow morning. I'll call for you in a taxi at ten. Be ready."[19]

Like Femina in *The Unpredictable Adventure*, Claire liked "masterful" men; his words made her tingle with pleasure. Later in bed, her

Tellectina voice turned her "happiness to fear and doubt as a strange turmoil boiled up from deep within." She feared losing her personal identity, her "precious freedom." But she was sick of living for herself alone.[20]

The next morning at the courthouse when the "clerk with the bulbous nose" asked if she would nourish George in sickness and in health, the word sickness "undid" her. The thought of his being ill was too much, and she could only answer in a whisper. They spent their wedding day moving furniture from his small apartment to a larger one "at a dizzying height on the twentieth floor." She could see the Empire State Building uptown and Wall Street to the south. At five that evening, she stood at the door of "the first home of my own I had ever had—and fell hopelessly in love with our new apartment." Ambivalence about the marriage dissolved into the romance surrounding life with this seemingly strong, decisive man.

She who had always "loathed cooking above everything else except mopping and cleaning," felt a warm pleasure cooking breakfast. George decreed that since they had not had a honeymoon, they could eat dinners out during this hot part of the summer. When she did prepare dinner, however, she strained every nerve to get it perfect, setting the table with candles and flowers and creating menus she knew he liked.

Their erotic life was gratifying. Indeed, though she had been reluctant to have sex with him before marriage, and though he respected her too much to suggest it, after their engagement he asked if they could be sure they were sexually compatible since that had been a problem with his first marriage. Given Claire's experience with Leo, she welcomed a test run. Their first time together proved ecstatic. Now the erotic aspect of their relationship grew even more intense.

> Every morning I rose first, showered and slipped on silk house pajamas—nothing else except gay red slippers. As I stood at the kitchen counter squeezing the orange juice George would come up behind me in his pajamas and press his warm body against my back and cup my breasts gently in his hands. Such waves of love, desire and

> sweetness would flow through my body I would have to hold the counter to prevent swooning to the floor. Somehow those moments seemed the embodiment of the relation of a husband and wife, of marriage, of love and desire. It was sweeter than the ecstasy of passion in bed.[21]

Such intimacy, perhaps, was particularly important to Claire because, though she had been involved with other men, and had experienced erotic satisfaction with Carton, the level of intimacy she and George shared was entirely new. One night he asked her to sit at the table without her clothes on because he enjoyed just looking at her. In theory, she believed in nudity, she wrote in her "Autobiography," but she agreed to comply only if he would do the same. He found he could not eat: "That little black cloud no bigger than a man's hand draws me like a magnet," he told her.

There was nothing about a man's body that drew her in, other than his "broad shoulders and well-shaped calves," which gave her a thrill. She liked a "strong man" and felt "privileged to study his private fireworks," which looked "unaesthetic": pale, wrinkled, useless, "except of course when it was loaded and aimed and ready to fire—that was exciting."

> And oh those nights in that wide double marriage bed. Passion, when intense and prolonged is like a primeval storm that subsides when it climaxes. It calms a woman's nerves, sweetens her disposition, solves her problems, eliminates conflicts, induces laughter and encourages confidence. . . . Passion satisfied is a magic elixir of life. At the height of ecstasy, the face beside me was no longer the face of the man I loved. Somehow it seemed the face of—of God. . . . [For a woman] with both his tongues in both her mouths satisfies a hunger that is more than physical, more than sexual. . . . this union with a man and through him union with the mystery of the universe.[22]

Linking love to spirituality, Claire sees the erotic as an entrée into the realm of a higher sensibility she will investigate in her later years. But for the first time in her life, she believes this relationship answers all her needs, merging the dichotomies between emotion and intellect, love and instability.

Letters home during their engagement period told the "truth" about her "darlin' man," but she chose her words carefully in regard to his family. On July 2, she wrote her parents describing her fiancé, "a writer on high finance—both domestic and foreign not only having that daily column in the *Tribune* but [he] also writes editorials for a weekly *Financial Journal and Chronicle*," which she sent her father. He made seven thousand a year, she told them, but could make more. "Well known in the banking and financial world," he had many other offers but did not want to give up so much time to writing. He was also writing "some very serious and scholarly books on world sociology which will take years." Furthermore, George made his own hours, generally going to the office at noon every day.[23]

She described him as almost six feet tall with a wonderful physique and amazing broad shoulders. His name, Wanders, like Myers, was of German origin. With a face as "strong and noble as a Roman senator," he was the "gentlest and tenderest man" she ever knew, the "soul of honor and honesty," the hero of his family whom she would meet that Sunday. She did not think he was wonderful because she loved him, but she loved him because he was so wonderful.

The letter goes on for eleven typed pages, reiterating her past mistakes, claiming that she has found a man who possesses all the qualities she desired in a husband. "Having been brought up in such a happy home" made her "discontent with the way most people lived. And his Father and Mother have been very happy too and adored each other"—so they both wanted the same things in a marriage, she wrote, knowing how this statement in no way described George's family. She asked her parents to write and tell her how happy it has made them to hear her good news.

The next letter answers theirs and bubbles on for three more typed pages about their marriage plans and his career as a financial writer. She reports on their first trip to Long Island: George's mother and father were "so dear and sweet—they were all very fine people . . .

pure gold. . . . They seemed to like me and the whole atmosphere in the Wanders family is perfect, beautiful. You seldom see a family . . . so harmonious and loving," she wrote, skipping the part about Flora's warning, the family's manners at dinner, and George's cold, silent mother. She ends by assuring them that "he is simple and honest to the point of bluntness." Naturally, she does not mention the negative side of that honesty—though she had discovered it earlier.

In "Belle Randolph," the morning after their engagement, Belle receives a letter from Hans, warning her about a "vicious" side to his nature, desiring to be "absolutely honest," declaring his love.[24]

Though no such letter appears in the archives, chances are during his lucid moments, George warned Claire to expect episodes of irrational rage. To her parents, Claire reported that she always knew where she stood with George because of his honesty. In pencil she scribbled an offer to come home to be married; by her next letter home, she had been married a week with everything lovelier than she had dreamed.

"The ceremony was utterly beautiful and as sacred. . . . as if it had been in a hundred churches. The real holiness of marriage lies in the mind and hearts of the two people."[25] Subsequent letters glow with delight and center around practical things they need for their apartment, answering questions regarding gifts from friends and family and the Myerses themselves.

They could use "more big sheets and extra-large pretty colored bath towels and small nice guest towels for hands and more good dish towels and pillow cases for regular size pillows." Claire, the happiest homemaker, details color schemes for the apartment and appropriate serving paraphernalia that would have made her college professors of domestic science beam with pride. But her personality reversal masked the reality of her perplexing situation.

Between August and December of 1931, the newlyweds were anything but blissful. Letters that passed between the couple parallel situations in the novel, the "Autobiography," memoirs, and short stories: all indicate an immediate and profound shift in George's attitude. A summary letter written to a lawyer during the summer of 1932 further indicates that Claire's year with George descended into a new kind of hell.[26] Yet, as far as her parents knew, life with George was pure bliss; their unconventional daughter had met her prince at last, and he had carried her off to a sheltered life in the kingdom of Cape Coverture, as she called their marital home in *The Unpredictable Adventure*—a term indicating her lack of autonomy, her rights as a woman subsumed under the domination of her husband.

On August 3, 1931, Claire wrote her parents asking them to write George "real often for a while for he is so used to being close to his family that I think he can't quite understand why you and I don't write every other day!!!" She explained that he called his mother, sister, and sister-in-law, every other day—"they all live separately too." She did not write her parents in this or subsequent letters of George's overattachment to his family, especially his mother. However, the fictional version of life with George captures the tenor of their relationship.

In "Belle Randolph," on their wedding night, the couple drives straight from a champagne and caviar celebration with Hans's cousins Winnie and Jack, to Hans's farm for dinner. Belle imagined Emma Schiller preparing an elaborate wedding dinner, judging by what her own mother would have done. When they arrived at the farm, Belle embraced Emma, murmuring ecstatically, "Oh I'm so happy . . . it makes me positively light-headed!" There was no reply; the family had eaten their supper at six, as usual; Emma set out a few cold leftovers for their wedding supper.[27]

The novel portrays their honeymoon drive through New England, with Hans narrating like a tour guide the historical sites and beautiful scenery and Belle listening with rapt attention. The first discordant note occurs when Belle asks Hans to drive them to Provincetown, home of the small theater made famous by Eugene O'Neill and Edna St. Vincent Millay—Villagers like Belle herself.[28] Hans "clamped his lips together in a hard line and refused to speak for the extra thirty miles of the drive." Belle felt "slightly sick at the chill hostile air emanating from this silent man beside her."[29] As time passed, she would become all too familiar with his icy blue stare, tightly clamped lips, and cold silence.

A second unsettling incident occurs in Newport when Hans points out the "great palatial summer homes of the Vanderbilts, Astors, and other members of America's former Four Hundred."

> "Aren't they magnificent!" Belle exclaimed.
>
> "Unforgivable extravagance when thousands of people in America are starving and jobless in this Depression," Hans answered.[30]

Belle claimed she admired their "architectural beauty."

"But how can anyone fail to hate the symbols of a system which causes such uneven distribution of wealth?" Hans counters. Belle wonders if that was an "actual sneer on his lips or just her imagination. A passion for justice was admirable. But wasn't class hatred as deplorable as hatred of all kinds?"[31]

Belle dismisses the incident, determined to allow nothing to mar their honeymoon. Unlike the "Autobiography," the fictional version portrays Belle refusing to have sex with Hans before marriage to avoid beginning "their marriage with a cloud on it."[32] Their erotic relations begin with unsatisfying intercourse first occurring on their wedding night. "Men are like chimpanzees trying to play a violin," she reflects, regarding his clumsiness and insensitivity. But gradually Hans understands her subtle suggestions and "not many more nights passed before her husband, as the Bible phrases it, gave his beloved sleep." More than just peaceful, their lovemaking becomes passionate, satisfying to them both, and establishes the erotic tie that binds them together throughout the relationship.[33]

In the novel, Hans drives them to his mother's farm on their way back from their honeymoon and they again receive "a supper of Emma's cold leftovers—and cold looks."[34] On neither occasion was the bride consulted by her groom as to their destination.

The following week, while Belle luxuriates in spending their first quiet Sunday together since their marriage, Hans stands up at noon and announces he is going to his mother's farm. Belle expresses her disappointment, and he coldly answers that Belle can come with him, or not, as she wishes. But she must be ready to leave by the time he brings the car around; he will not wait. Hurriedly she dresses and meets him downstairs only to endure a silent drive and the usual cold reception from Emma.

Claire's letters home sanitize the story. Her August 3 letter recounts their wedding day and describes the lovely rings George bought her: a gold wedding ring, hand carved with violets to go with her "very old rare" gold and star sapphire engagement ring, carved with lotus blossoms. Wedding presents continued to arrive as a result of the announcements Claire had sent, which George had suggested she purchase, then scowled at as too pretentious. She describes the gifts and again lists things she still needs in scrupulous detail.

She also describes the new furniture she has been buying: a beautiful old French bedroom set of three pieces—a table trimmed in gilt with a marble top; a tall chest of drawers, also with a marble top and mahogany trim with inlaid rosewood. "George never buys anything but the best. . . . He is not the least bit pretentious but solid and fine and genuine and likes everything and everybody to be that way too."

She fails to mention his belligerence over every purchase, his sulking in silence for hours, even days. When she bought new ashtrays to replace the old brass ones he received as a gift from family, but claimed to dislike, he refused to use the new ones, and carried the brass ones around with him. She reports this anecdote to her parents, endearingly claiming that George hated the ashtrays, but did not throw them away in order to avoid hurting his family's feelings. This same letter suggests the whole family go in together for their Christmas gift, rather than sending "a lot of little trinkets." She needs some dessert spoons to complete their silver set, which the Myerses had given as a wedding present. And yet, George reacted with acerbity toward the extravagance of silver, refused to touch serving pieces placed on their dinner table, and would not discuss items he considered luxury.[35] Another letter thanked them for sending myriad things, but asked they stop since "these NY apartments have so little room. . . . Oh, my dears, I can't tell you how wonderful it is to have my very own home. Since I left . . . as a girl I've never really had a home. And to have somebody that you care about coming home . . . somebody to do things for is such a joy." Descriptions of their social life skimmed the surface. "George is too generous and lavish—gradually I want us to live more economically. I feel so funny having a checking account with no questions asked. . . . And a savings account too. We live very well."

Claire took special delight in the opportunity to set up housekeeping, which allowed her to express her proclivity for fine things and her talent to arrange them artistically. Money was not a problem for Claire and George since she had a small savings and George earned a good salary. Indeed the longer the Depression continued, the more in demand were his wise and astute analyses. Claire's taste in clothing matched her taste in fine housewares. Although some accounts indicate she had no time to buy a trousseau, others indicate she spent one day shopping with her new friend, George's cousin Winnie. Her letter home of August 18 takes several pages to describe her trousseau, beginning with her marriage outfit: "I wore one of those new Empress Eugenie hats all turned up on the side you know—to marry in and what color do you suppose it was—bright *red*!!! And my purse was red and red beads and a flowered print silk suit with red flowers on it. Never heard of any body being married in red but I was so happy I thought it the only appropriate color!!! and black patent kid pumps. The dress cost $95 but I got it for $85 . . . it's of very fine imported silk."[36]

Thin and willowy most of her life, she was delighted to weigh 136 pounds and "for the first time" she had "a figure," which George thought wonderful but "I think I have too much tummy." Gertrude Dauber saw her recently and said she looked radiant: "'Well Claire all you needed to do to cure all your troubles and ills was just get happily married' . . . and she said happily married—not merely married—because that I could have done a dozen times over." Ten typed pages describe her complete wardrobe, including her lingerie, "a wicked black chiffon . . . I've discovered that it is dangerous to wear around a *he-man* like my George!" The less she had on the better he liked it. "Well, after all that's the proper spirit for a bridegroom, [not only] a fine husband but a marvelous lover which after my first ghastly experience I realize is the basis of a happy marriage." Of course, that part was true, though surprising to find in a letter to her parents.

Housekeeping details follow—the maid "does all my silk underwear and I have a laundry for the household things . . . which has been five and six dollars a week."

According to the "Autobiography," the subject of the maid was a source of bitter quarrels, rooted in classism and sexism. George had a part-time maid while he was single, whom Claire arranged to keep after they married. But George figured any man with a wife did not need a maid. Besides, his mother never had a maid, he argued: "I do not believe in personal service." Claire asked if he believed in waitresses and cooks, but he merely turned away and immersed himself in a magazine.

In "Belle Randolph," Belle's mere suggestion of a maid sends Hans into a spin. The incident occurs as they approach New York City at the end of their honeymoon. A bitter argument follows but this time, Belle wins.[37] However, by the time the couple gives their first party, Belle had let her maid go. Together she and Flora work all day cleaning and dusting, hanging pictures, preparing hors d'oeuvres.

But the party proves most embarrassing. Hans, caught off guard with his lack of social graces, becomes sullen and despondent, then suddenly shifts and holds the floor with dogmatic lectures on economics. Now her friends knew the truth about her marriage. After the party, he refuses to speak to Belle. Exhausted, she goes to bed, only to be awakened by his hammering as he hung the pictures she had decided to store and hang together at a later date. His anger and silence last all day Sunday.[38] That evening, after a long day at his parents' farm, Belle sits him down and asks what is wrong. "Nothing," he answers with a frightened glance over the top of his magazine. She presses him for more information: "We've only been in our lovely new home two weeks but already I—I feel something's wrong with our marriage. I grope and grope for a reason. But it's like trying to see in a dense fog. We're so marvelously happy for a few days. Then suddenly we're unhappy. And I never know why." Hans answers that it helps him to know how she feels; then he withdraws into his shell.[39]

And yet, when Claire wrote her parents about their first party, she sounds happy and excited. Needless to say, few brides would be eager to confess the negative aspects of a new marriage. And most brides would be anxious to protect their parents from the worry that their daughter had made a mistake in choosing a spouse, especially a second spouse. What seems extraordinary about this period of Claire's life and her connection to her parents is her preference for long chatty letters glamorizing their life. Yet, if the events portrayed in the fiction and autobiography were good in real life, why fictionalize them in negative scenarios?

Perhaps because there *were* good times, and bad; life moved in a cycle comprised of ecstatic happiness interrupted by violent displays of temper, followed by a period of withdrawal and stony silence, followed by contrition, reconciliation, and then the cycle repeated. As Claire describes these same cycles in "Belle Randolph," she compares them to "Ferris wheels at a carnival. First you were up then you were down. Always you went round and round. The speed and frequency of the changes left you dizzy." By the time the couple had been married a month, Belle had come to dread the long periods of "cold silence."[40]

Claire's descriptions of her unsettling relationship with George have come to be known as the "cycle of violence," first explained in the late 1970s and early 1980s by social scientists Lenore Walker in *The Battered Woman* and Del Martin in *Battered Wives*.[41] Although these early theories and observations have been fully and richly developed over time, with a vernacular common in popular culture of the late twentieth and early twenty-first centuries, the cycle remains the same: periods of happiness dissolve into periods of sullen withdrawal and tension, ending in an explosion, physical or emotional, followed by contrition, apologies, vows it will never happen again, beginning renewed periods of happiness called the "honeymoon period." As relationships evolve, the violent phase intensifies and the periods between incidents shorten. According to C. J. Newton, "Domestic or partner violence isn't just hitting, or fighting, or an occasional mean argument. It's a chronic abuse of power. The abuser tortures and controls the victim by calculated threats, intimidation," which at times escalate to a physical level.[42] No wonder Claire felt she was trying to see in a "dense fog." George's erratic behavior blindsided her time and again. Thus the image of the Ferris wheel in "Belle Randolph," leaving her "dizzy."[43]

Incidents in the "Autobiography" follow the ups and downs with grueling regularity. One particular scene portrays an evening that became routine in their relationship: one night they were having an early dinner at home so as to get to the theater on time.

> As we ate our soup, I said, "You know, George, with my thin southern blood, I have never become acclimated to these cold northern winters. I have always had a fur coat. Not expensive but warm. I gave last winter's away and now the summer sales are on and I can get one cheap . . ."
>
> He stopped eating and glared at me angrily. "You don't need a fur coat. The majority of women in New York never had a fur coat in their lives. My mother never had a fur coat. You don't need one either."
>
> We argued back and forth more loudly and more angrily. I offered to pay half the cost. "I can support my own wife! Better save your little bit of money for a rainy day."[44]

He was unreasonable concerning all extras—maids, furs, evening clothes, serving spoons, he would not listen. "It was like striking my head on a stone wall." That night suddenly she took the crackers from the plate, crushed them in her hands and flung them all over the room. Then she rushed into the kitchen; he followed to taunt her further:

> I caught up the long bread knife lying on the counter and brought the point down on his white shirt. I could see every thread in it as if magnified a hundred times. He did not move or resist or speak. His courage under danger filled me with pride. Suddenly aware of what I was doing I dropped the knife to the floor in utter mortification. I would have fallen had he not caught me in his arms. Ashamed I said, "Forgive me."
>
> "Why dearest Claire, you were magnificent. You leapt like a tiger. I could gladly have died at your hands. But hurry up now and get dressed or we'll be late to the theater."

> He stood in the door of the bedroom and watched me dress. The very air was vibrant with desire. I fumbled with my long dinner dress and small hat scarcely knowing what I was doing. He came up behind me and lifted me onto the bed . . . and the next thing I knew it was morning and I still had my hat on.[45]

For her parents, Claire would only highlight the good parts. An August 31 letter idealized her role as loving wife: "You know Mother dear, I used to wonder why you always gave Daddy the largest and best piece of everything at the table but now I know for I find myself doing the same thing for my husband without even stopping to think." Her domestic science classes seemed to come back in ways she ridiculed while in college.[46]

Claire invited George's parents and siblings to a cold dinner on a Sunday. Her letter home on September 10 gives a glowing report to her parents that everything had "come off fine. George was wonderful at helping me." She claimed to have used the blue vase Coren and his wife Ruby had sent her and the "pretty green one . . . as they all brought me beautiful roses," a statement that seems highly uncharacteristic of George's family.[47]

In "Belle Randolph," Claire dramatizes this disastrous Sunday dinner: The children are rambunctious and ill-behaved, while the adults sit "stiffly on the edges of their chairs" ill at ease. Belle's hospitality meets with her mother-in-law's hatred and rudeness. No one offers to help serve or clean up. "Emma sat in the living room holding court with her four sons grouped about her." Without warning, Hans dashes out and returns with an "enormous mound of cold roast beef," which he places on the table next to the large baked ham Belle had lovingly prepared. No one touches the ham—though Belle remembered seeing Hans eat ham innumerable times. Hans makes a point of not speaking to or looking at Belle during the entire meal.

Alone she washes the dishes hour after hour, on the brink of exhaustion, her feet aching. Finally one sister-in-law "surreptitiously" slips in and begins drying dishes without a word. Belle bites her lips to restrain her tears. The family stays late in the afternoon, waiting to be invited for leftovers, but Belle, at last showing some grit, pretends not to notice. Not one person thanks her when they depart, certainly not Hans, who leaves with them to lead them out of the city traffic, returning at one o'clock in the morning. Neither of them ever mentions the dinner, and Hans does not speak to Belle for an entire week.[48]

In *Awakening to the Good*, the chapter "Sea and Sand" provides a lovely description of a beachside reunion with her husband following a bitter fight.[49] The ecstasy of their passion precedes their ecstatic dancing, swimming, and frolicking nude together in the wind and sunlight on the beach, which for Claire swells into an intoxicating moment of universal oneness. This particular incident emphasizes a theme foreshadowed in her earlier descriptions of mystical events: death. "A fathomless blackness was drawing me into itself as mysteriously as a magnet. Toward what? Dissolution? Disintegration? Was it a foretaste of death?"[50]

The idea of "fearful bliss" appears in an earlier incident, described in both the "Autobiography" and in "Belle Randolph," where ecstasy and bliss coalesce with love and death. Late one afternoon shortly after their engagement, Hans and Belle stroll up Fifth Avenue from Washington Square.

> Hans took short steps to match Belle's. He put her arm through his, then he intertwined their fingers and held her right hand so tight her fingers grew completely numb. She loved it.
>
> "This is the way we're going to do everything in life, dearest," he murmured. "Together. Forever and ever!" Belle gave his arm an answering hug. He did not tell her where they were going. There was something infinitely sweet in permitting him to take her wherever he wished.[51]

Eventually they arrive at Thirty-Fourth Street—a mile and a half from Washington Square. Belle, wearing thin sandals, remains unaware of the two huge blisters on her heels until she undressed that night. Along with the crowds of sightseers swarming into the Empire

State Building, the tallest building in the world, Hans pilots Belle through the mob into an elevator and up to the eighty-sixth floor.

> It was exhilarating, intoxicating, to be up so high! The violent force of the wind blew the words out of their mouths. Conversation was impossible. . . . Hans's arm pressed against her soft breast, against her pounding heart! Death, now, together, at this instant, she thought. . . . They'd reached the greatest height of human happiness. . . . Only the supreme act of life—which was death—could adequately express it, seal it, make it eternal and irrevocable! . . . If only she could die for him. This instant! She'd die with a song on her lips. . . . like the dying Isolde standing beside Tristan's dead body. Belle stood motionless . . . transfigured, in a veritable ecstasy of love![52]

This episode atop the Empire State Building, like the blissful romp on the beach and the knife incident in the apartment expresses Claire's fascination with love, self-immolation, and death. As Freud observed in his controversial 1920 book, *Beyond the Pleasure Principal*, "the goal of all life is death," tying Eros, or basic sexual and life instincts, to the death instinct, or Thanatos, which leads to destruction, violence, and self-immolation.[53] These themes foreshadow the tragic ending of their relationship.

The couple married on July 20, and all of these incidents took place before their first Christmas—a miserable time beyond belief according to the novel and the "Autobiography"—a time during which George/Hans stopped coming home for dinner without warning his conscientious wife. However, one would never suspect a moment's discord from the letters to and from home, excited exchanges over what to buy whom for Christmas. Starting in September, the Myerses began sending special southern delicacies, like chow-chow, along with a five-pound can of Mr. Myers's favorite cotton blossom honey, which George refused to taste. Claire wrote her father: "Oh, Daddy, you don't know how much we enjoy that honey . . . we eat it every morning for breakfast." Thanksgiving and Christmas boxes contained more delicacies, along with a special gift for George's December 3 birthday.[54]

A letter from George's cousin Winnie, who had been busy moving to a new apartment on Madison Avenue, reveals the time and care Claire spent choosing gifts for the entire Wanders family. Winnie gave exact sizes for the various children and made practical suggestions, warning that George's parents do not want to receive gifts because they do not give them to the "grown-ups," only the children. But traditionally Winnie gave them small things like woolen stockings, handkerchiefs, and a tie, and she recommends that Claire do the same.[55]

After Christmas, Claire wrote a long letter thanking her parents for their generous gifts, especially the homemade fruitcake her mother made, the "hit of the Wanders Xmas dinner! You'll be horrified when I tell you that we ate it all at one sitting! It was the first homemade fruit cake they had ever tasted."[56] She also mentions packing the fruitcake in a huge basket she "fixed up," with pecans, jams, jellies, and candies, tied with a big red ribbon. A subsequent thank you letter indicates the Myerses immediately sent another cake, so gratified were they by the Wanderses' response to the first, and they sent George more honey, since Claire had written how much he liked the first batch. But the fiction and memoirs reveal that no one ate the fruitcake and George never touched the honey.

In "Belle Randolph," the pre-Christmas stress throws Hans into a state of deep depression and, filled with contrition, he tells Belle she is living with a "dangerously sick man."[57] Naturally, she tries hard to help him. By Christmas day he is back to his old self—mean and stingy. Belle gives Hans a book he mentioned wanting; she received nothing from him or his family. To Belle's surprise, Hans's mother offers to give them fifty dollars to buy a radio for their Christmas present, but Hans retorts angrily, "You keep your money . . . I wouldn't be caught dead with a radio." Belle is even more surprised when Emma suggests that perhaps Belle would like one, though she politely declines the offer in deference to her husband's hostility. New Year's Eve and Belle's birthday pass with funereal dinners—and no gifts from Hans. Life becomes increasingly unbearable.

In life as in art, the marriage is doomed; by the end of six months, George/Hans has begun to withhold both money and sex. Yet, Claire/

Belle never breathes a word of her plight to her parents. In the novel, when Winnie asks if she has told her parents, Belle answers, "Oh, no, it would break their hearts!"[58] Throughout her marriage, the only thing that saves her sanity is her writing. When her husband is in the apartment, she can only edit manuscripts, but when he leaves each day at noon she loses herself in writing.

It is difficult to tell exactly when their marriage ended. A letter from George written to Claire on February 24, 1932, indicates that by that time she had moved to a woman's hotel, was searching for a job, and desperately needed money. A May 4 letter to George from Claire's attorney offering to act as a mediator toward reconciliation indicates that their separation continued without change in George's attitude. Pages and pages of undated letters—one marked "unsent" from Claire to George—testify to her misery, her determination to understand the mystery of his "sickness," and to find a way to "cure" George and mend their differences.

Needless to say, Claire did not have the advantage of a background in psychology, nor would she have had access to current understandings of the causes and effects of domestic violence, emotional abuse, or pathological mother-son relationships. Her relationship to George, however, laid the groundwork for her to become an expert.

To a trained eye, the signs were all there from the beginning. George and his mother and the overall Wanders family dynamic exhibited classic pathological symptoms: the son who remains stuck in adolescence, exhibiting highs and lows of angry, petulant behavior, followed by sullen bouts of depression, often the result of being raised by an overbearing mother and an absent, meek, or passive father. Controlling mothers do not allow the son to develop proper independence, which injures his masculine identity. To overcompensate, he becomes distrustful and controlling of all other women, veiled by a "smoldering rage."[59]

What in Claire's background, upbringing, or adult life experience made her vulnerable to such an unpredictable, controlling, hostile man? What attractions, beyond sexual, bound her? Perhaps her lifelong feelings of insecurity regarding her parents' expectations doomed her to accept George's unreasonable demands. Perhaps her financial dependence on George fed her fear of breaking free.[60]

By early May, Claire had no choice but to end the charade and tell her parents the truth: "Dearest One in all the world," she began, and thanked her mother for her "wonderfully kind sweet letter. It makes me sick that I have to hurt you this way . . . but I postponed it as long as I could. I can't come home tho' it was wonderful of you to ask me and want me—I sometimes feel that no human being in the world loves me but my own Mother. A mother's love goes on through good and bad . . . I've nearly walked my legs off looking for a job but I might as well be asking for a million dollars."[61] Such ironic sentiments regarding her mother's love given her past claims of parental disapproval have resolved due to the deceptive letters that inspired trust between the two women.

Writing about it all made her "sick": "In a nut shell, I feel now that the real hidden root of the whole trouble is what the modern psychologists call an inferiority complex. The fact that he has no real cause to feel that way . . . does not prevent . . . these complexes."

Eight typed pages attempt to fill in the details of their turbulent year. But the last two pages instruct her mother to write George and tell him the following: "that I told you he was [the] best educated man I ever knew"; "how proud I said I was of him"; "you are worried about me because I have tried so hard to get a job." A postscript reminds her to "be sure and say all the things I have told you and also that you are writing him of your own accord but intend to tell me afterward because he is sure to think I have put you up to it," which she, of course, had.

Claire seems unaware that building one deceit on top of another will only deepen her dilemma. On May 7 George wrote the following:

> My dear Mother-in-law:—
>
> I am at a loss to know how to answer to your satisfaction the very kind letter. . . . I can assure you the distress I feel in regard to the whole affair is rendered even keener by your heart-ache. . . . After several months of rather easy-going life together, I attempted one evening in mid-September to discuss with Clairene some things

> which were making me most uneasy . . . to make her realize some of the responsibilities . . . marriage entailed for a woman. . . . While I was gone the next day, and without a word, Clairene left *my* home. I found a note . . . that it would be useless for me to try to get in touch with her [emphasis mine].[62]

Clearly George believed *their* home was *his* alone. He left Susan Myers to picture the anguish he suffered then pulled out his hidden weapon, a vengeful letter Claire had written during one of their separations. He retyped it word for word and offered profound apologies for the "sorrowful mix-up," for he had "no consciousness of having wronged you or yours."

Imagine the frustration that letter caused Claire's parents. They must have realized the marriage could not be reconciled. Claire's letter home on May 24 indicates she may need an operation if her stomach problems did not subside—an illness caused by the strained relationship she had with George and his mother. Now, for the first time of record, she details George's "mother complex" and her own hopes for reconciliation.[63] George did not share those hopes; on February 24, George stated his position. He forgave her, but what happened between them was not to be remedied by forgiveness. "Beyond that lies the very grave difficulty of our mutual loss of respect."[64]

Respect? Forgiveness? Who owes what to whom? In the chapter "Winter" in *Awakening to the Good*, Claire describes an evening she spent alone during a storm, waiting for her husband to come home for dinner. "I lighted the candles, arranged the flowers for the tenth time, straightened the silver again, returned to the kitchen, lighted the broiler, and admired the thick beautiful steak once more—and waited." Briefly, she summarizes the misery that had become part of this marriage, the "mysterious grief . . . consuming [George] like a cancer." Pacing from room to room, "hope and joy lay heavy as an unborn child dead within"; she glanced listlessly out the window to discover "an astounding spectacle! The whole white world had gone mad."[65]

The imagery used to describe the storm outside reflects her turbulence within: "The snowflakes were waging a fierce battle against each other. Like avenging furies . . . like slanting white spears . . . they swirled upward in angry spirals flinging themselves against the low white sky." Expecting the city to be "devastated by the violence," she faces her own devastation: "He was not coming home . . . I sat on and on numb with grief."[66]

But Claire, gifted with an innate ability to connect to some cosmic force beyond the corporeal world, finds herself suddenly transported by the beauty and turbulence of the "celestial battle . . . the witchery of the winter night." As "white bullets of sleet struck viciously at the window pane," she waits for the "climax that might reveal some final secret"—one that gives her a glimpse of the immutable nature of the human spirit: "The vulnerable human heart might be deadened but the senses, the mind, the spirit—they were alive even against their own volition." Like a "white bird of winter, [her] battered spirit burst to freedom and flew not away from the storm but straight into the heart of it." Transcendence awakens her irrepressible strength and fortifies her with the courage to persevere. Ultimately the question that saves her that night, the same one that saved her in past crises, emerges: "Did our final happiness lie in attaching ourselves to something larger, more enduring than mutable human beings? . . . like art, or nature, or . . . the Unknown—for want of a better name?"[67]

In July, shortly before their first wedding anniversary, George wrote Claire a letter that pretended to be sympathetic but, in fact, hurled an insult. This was a time of "bittersweet memories," he agreed, but her "characteristic" remembrance of the "delicious dream" they shared carried significance only because "it was a dream." He dismisses her advances though somehow they maintained a correspondence that lasted two more years. Evidently Claire had asked if George would "someday explain" his social ideas "at length," and he was only too glad to oblige. His letters from that July 1932 through September 1934, contain exhaustive, impersonal discourses on his economic and sociological theories, at times scattered with chatty items regarding mutual friends. Perhaps this pleasant—if not pompous—connection eased the transition for Claire as she pieced her life back together. Perhaps she had loved him so desperately she still hoped to "cure" him of his mysterious sickness. Or perhaps she was simply determined not to fail in another relationship.[68]

Whatever her motives, on September 26, 1934, George wrote an answer to Claire regarding methods of obtaining a divorce in Reno, though she did not proceed until 1936. Throughout this time, Claire maintained a friendly correspondence with her mother, whose loving support through long handwritten letters should have reconciled their differences once and for all. There seemed to be a level of truth between them at last—truth, but certainly not the whole truth.[69]

For the novel, Claire dramatizes a far more violent denouement to this bitter tale than the letters document. A "love letter" Belle sends Hans backfires. "Evidently you don't understand men at all," he awakened her in bed to say. "Your display of emotion disgusted me." Belle can hear in his voice suffering that reveals self-torture. But her intuition does not cushion the blow of the lengthy sadomasochistic assault that follows.[70]

At the end of this sleepless night—around January 15—Belle leaves the apartment she has come to love and walks out into the street. This time she leaves no note and takes only a small suitcase of essentials. She goes to the bank and withdraws two hundred dollars, leaving Hans with fifty—"so he'd know—she didn't know what."[71] Dazed and confused, she takes a taxi to a woman's hotel uptown near Columbia University. Here in a room "so small, so bare it looked like a prison cell" she began the next phase of her life.

Several short stories, told with the benefit of hindsight and often humor, relate incidents that occurred during Claire's stay at The Altora and other woman's hotels during the Depression years. Some use first-person narrators; others create characters. The chapters in the novel concerned with this period relate days and months of suffering and fear that mark the end of Belle's marriage and her fruitless search for a job. The novel sets the time as the winter of 1933; the events it fictionalizes occurred in 1932, and both years represent a time of frequent company layoffs. Even college graduates could not find jobs.

In the novel, other women in the hotel, in similar situations and often disillusioned with the male sex, advise Belle to get a lawyer and make her estranged husband "pay through the nose . . . attach his salary."[72] With a large measure of pride and a small measure of hope, Belle refuses to beg Hans for money. They have a few uncomfortable dinners together. During one, Hans claims he asked her out because he felt "a sense of responsibility," obligated to buy her a good meal.[73]

The novel's climax centers around Alfred Adler's theories on the Oedipus and inferiority complexes, which Belle hears discussed on a radio show. Excited to find possible help for Hans, she dashes into Adler's office and gains audience—they had met once before. She spends two hours discussing the crises of her marriage and Hans's symptoms. Adler posits exciting explanations and renews her hope. Exhausted and ill, she visits Hans's cousin Winnie and then Virginia, Frances in real life, to tell them her news: "*Now I know!* Everything . . . that mystified me!" She explains, in "modern psychological terms," Adler's theory that Hans was suffering from "an *acute* mother complex and . . . a social inferiority complex that's so advanced it's developed into a neurosis." Seventy percent of all people in the world have complexes of some sort; neurosis makes the complex worse; Freud's theory explains that these complexes have to do with sex, but Adler disagrees. Millions of men suffered from inferiority complexes, especially talented ones from poor families—like D. H. Lawrence and Chekhov. Some became alcoholics; others became aggressive dictators like "that new German leader, Adolph Hitler. The inferiority complex was the curse of the modern world."[74]

Winnie seems shocked, but Adler has helped Belle fit all the pieces of their life together, determining that her and Hans's contrasting backgrounds led to their battles. Hans interpreted everything she and her friends did as criticism of him and his mother. Belle, ever optimistic, armed with her understanding of the psychology behind their problems, takes a cab home to Hans. He meets her enthusiastic "news" and her attempt at reconciliation with "eyes like blue ice."

"How dare you come into my apartment unannounced? How did you know I didn't have some woman here?"[75] He disappears into the bedroom and does not emerge for several hours. Belle cooks a beautiful breakfast and plans a way to bring up Adler's theories. When Hans emerges, nothing Belle says can break through his glacial distance—he refuses to believe she is ill, needs surgery, or has looked unsuccessfully for a job. He will not use his connections to help her find a job, nor will he "loan" her money: "NO Belle . . . I have my own family to think of." Ignoring that legally she is still his wife, he turns his back on her and leaves the apartment without touching the breakfast.

This time his cruelty defeats her. "Something inside Belle snapped like a spring that had been wound too tight. The whole world went black. . . . She turned on the oven spigot . . . held her head over the top of the stove and inhaled the fumes." Stifling her impulse for self-preservation, she laughs to herself that people would think she did it because of her love for Hans. "No one would ever know she had done it . . . because love had failed her, because she refused to be ill, penniless, alone and miserable. . . . To decide your own fate, this was the one last defiant gesture a human being could make against life." The novel ends with Belle awakening to voices trying to revive her—a policeman, an ambulance, and a measure of melodrama: some day she "would be filled with rebellion . . . and laughter again, too, as she walked about this strange, exciting, cruel beautiful place called Earth."

Using her pseudonym on this novel in each of its versions, Claire Myers Spotswood explored the deeper truths about her marriage to George Wanders. But again, not the whole truth.

Whereas the novel ends with a suicide attempt, this chapter of her life continues: A nineteen-page letter Claire wrote to her lawyer indicates that the fictional episode was based on fact. What might serve as an epilogue to the novel appears in the fourteen surviving pages of that letter.[76]

The suicide attempt described in the novel and in the letter followed many agonizing nights when, unable to sleep, she would walk along the Hudson River, contemplating suicide. The ambulance that came for Claire was obliged to take all suicide attempts to the psychopathic ward of the hospital for observation. "Imagine my horror when I realized that I was confined with a lot of poor raving crazy women some of them violent. It was only by the greatest effort I ever exerted in my life that I held on to my own sanity."

Certain that George would "break his neck to get his wife out of such a hideous place no matter what," she waited for him to come for her. She "gave George credit for that much humanness." That night, Claire lived through a hell she could never have imagined: "I shall never forget [the] poor toothless drunken lunatic raving in the bed next to me all night and dead bodies being carried out from the violent ward right through our ward. It's too terrible even now I can't go into detail I get sick all over." But the next morning, "some young squirt of a doctor" told her that her husband had been there the night before and had left without even trying to see her or ask for her release.

"I went icy cold all over—I knew I was in for something more terrible than anything I had ever experienced in my life . . . his terrible inherent brutality" dawned on her at last. Knowing that he had the power to have her committed, wisely, she called her long-time friend Frances Fox, whom she calls Virginia in the novel, and urged her to come with George on Sunday. Her intuition, accurate as usual, saved her. George "strolled nonchalantly in" with Frances who had "a look of real concern on her face." Without speaking to Claire, George acted angry, as if she had injured him. He laughed and talked to Frances while the hospital went through the "red tape" of getting her street clothes and processing the release documents.

"The man I had thought I was marrying never existed" she wrote her lawyer. "I imagined him." When he left to speak to a doctor, Claire instructed Frances to claim to be her cousin and not to leave her side a minute while George was present and to interfere if he began to say "the wrong thing." Again, Claire's intuition saved her; Frances told her that George thought it best to leave her in the hospital a while. Frances, horrified, argued: "My God, no, George, if you leave her here any longer she might really go insane—anybody would." When the doctor asked him if it was all right for Claire to leave, George hesitated and said, "Well she was very nervous." The doctor, on the verge of signing the dismissal, stopped abruptly: "Oh, so you aren't sure of it?" Prepared for George's tricks, Frances and Claire both intervened—"because in that kind of place everything you say and do and even the expression on your face is used against you."

The letter to the lawyer recounts her struggles to get her half of their money and claims that she had looked for jobs every day, even with her "crippled feet," and would supply the lawyer with a list of some twenty applications she had made and the agencies she had solicited during her job search.

In some respects, Claire's suicide attempt can be seen as predictable. Claire's associations with love and death foreshadow the morbidity that accompanied the intensity of passion she and George shared. This, combined with the level of despair resulting from the Depression, complicated by George's financial success and her own inability to get a job, along with her highly emotional nature, make suicide seem almost inevitable. But Claire's innate sense of self-preservation saved her; she seemed to realize that to conquer despair, she must fully engage it.[77]

Like the "white bird of winter [who] . . . flew not away from the storm but straight into the heart of it," Claire discovered a way to "go into" her despair by giving up her search for a job, leaving the city and the seedy environment of woman's hotels, and going to stay with various friends.[78] This solution bought her time for a solitary, creative healing period. As Penelope Washbourn indicates in *Becoming Woman*, "A woman whose life seems destroyed by the end of a marriage and whose basic sense of herself is radically shaken cannot pass simply to a new life and a new identity."[79] Rather, she must confront the question of personal identity and the meaning of her own life. She must reinvent herself and create a new normal existence. For Claire to recover her sense of independence would mean more than just having an independent income. Claire seemed to realize that to emerge gracefully from her sense of failure would involve rediscovering her center of creativity.[80]

When *The Unpredictable Adventure* went to press in 1935, she had already begun her next book. Writing would be her salvation, a renewal of her life, identity, and energy. Telling the story of Belle Randolph functioned autographically as catharsis of her wounded soul—a purification that prepared her for her next series of adventures.

10

The "Wolfe" at the Door

1935–1937

All honest fiction must be from the stuff of human life.
—Thomas Wolfe

THE AUTHOR'S NOTE to "Belle Randolph: A Story of Democracy and Ecstacies," [*sic*] reads: "When democracy fails to function in people's personal lives, intense suffering ensues no less than in international and national life." Drawing on themes that explore parallels between democracy and feminism, the author argues that "if there had been equality of the classes in America and equality of the sexes, tragedies like Belle Randolph's and Hans Schiller's might never have happened." The synopsis accompanying an early draft, "Sons and Husbands," highlights its parallels with D. H. Lawrence's *Sons and Lovers*, and explores "what might have happened to a gifted man like Lawrence if he had married his Baroness before his mother died," and what happens to marriages when "the Oedipus-social-inferiority complex is the strongest force in a man's life."[1]

Claire's assessment of George's inferiority complex and attachment to his mother relies on Alfred Adler's popular theories. Adler, "the first one to coin the term" *inferiority complex*, believed that children feel inferior because they are "surrounded by stronger and more capable adults." To overcome these feelings of inferiority, a healthy individual learns to "compensate" and achieve success.[2] To apply Alder's theories, George may have developed a need to show his mother, and by extension Claire, his strength and importance, with an unhealthy "superiority complex" to cover his feelings of inadequacy.[3] Whereas early drafts of this novel struggled to understand the personal relationship between Claire and George, later drafts moved away from the personal to universal, politically oriented themes.

The unique quality of this novel, as in her earlier ones, lies in her portrayal of the modern woman's dual personality: "No matter how developed a woman may become mentally, underneath she is still primitive emotionally—especially in her relation with men. This sets up conflict between her feminine and intellectual natures."[4] Thus, this novel continues to explore the Tellectina/Femina conundrum.

What made Claire strong and independent, susceptible to this mercurial man's anger, control, and abuse? Perhaps the lack of stability she felt in her relationship to her parents and her need to please them created an equally strong need to please him, to make things right. If she could just love him enough, make him love her enough, all their problems would resolve.

The draft entitled "Love Is Not Enough" argues in its foreword that Belle exemplifies the highly civilized woman who makes "marriage more difficult but life more interesting. . . . The passion for a career is only second to her passionate desire for a happy marriage."[5] Modern woman's dilemma, she argues, lies in the choice between career and marriage, which places her in the situation of having to face that "love is not enough" for a happy marriage; yet, life without love would be "unbearably bleak and brutal." Until women, like men, relegate love to a "secondary place," women will continue to live troubled lives.

Claire had high hopes for this novel, expecting both critical and commercial acclaim. "'Sons and Husbands' would make a good motion picture" she suggested in the foreword, if only the "framework of the story" were used.[6] "'Violent triumphs have violent ends,' as Monk says in Romeo and Juliet. Such ecstatic and passionate love affairs generally explode," she wrote in all three synopses, shrewdly implying the melodrama and the passion would attract a wider audience. Unfortunately, every editor who read the novel, no matter which draft, had a violent reaction to it. Burton Rascoe, who had appreciated the feminist themes of *The Unpredictable Adventure*, was incensed by the presentation of Belle as a heroine. He voiced his harsh concerns: Belle was "too consciously superior to everybody else, both men and women"; she lacked "humility" and felt sorry for herself. He told Claire to demonstrate charm by having Belle "do and say charming things." He offered to get the reaction of others to see if their response differed from his.[7]

Claire sent Rascoe a telegram in defense of her heroine. He replied, "You should not be so touchy; for it is not my business to flatter authors or to encourage them in their faults [but] rather to offer them helpful criticism." He called her first chapter "very bad art."[8]

Subsequently, Harrison Smith at Doubleday Doran sent an equally caustic assessment. He told her "frankly" they did not like the novel, that it lacked the vitality, intelligence, and charm of *The Unpredictable Adventure*. What puzzled Harrison Smith—in life as in literature—was how a girl like Belle could fall in love with a man with a mother complex. When Belle "falls in love and marries Hans, the reader loses a good deal of his sympathy for her." What the author sees as "high tragedy" he defined as the "story of a woman who made a fool of herself"; therefore her difficulties are "not tragedy and not comedy but an uninspiring recital of minor calamities." He realized "eager young women" fall in love and marry men like Hans. But their reasons escaped him, unless it was "because there was nobody else on the horizon at the psychological moment."[9]

The reasons that escaped Smith have to do with the structure of society, which the novel exposes as sexist and classist. Without realizing it, Smith had identified precisely what made the story unique: Claire Myers Spotswood portrayed gender and social inequality—themes au courant; but, as in her earlier novel, to explore these themes, she wrote a new plot, an "unmarriage plot." Rather than building toward marriage, both *The Unpredictable Adventure* and "Belle Randolph"/"Sons and Husbands" build toward unmarriage. The heroics in Spotswood's novels involve a series of obstacles from which the protagonist must untangle herself. Resolution requires freedom from male authority and oppression: solitude and autonomy replace love and dependence; writing and career replace Elam Domitann, dominant men.

"Belle Randolph" offended male editors in ways that *The Unpredictable Adventure* did not because the earlier novel used fantasy and satire, rather than a realistic story. Smith had expressed interest in *The Unpredictable Adventure* in its first draft, declining it only as a matter of financial necessity as a result of the Depression. Burton Rascoe championed it and saw it through to publication; Richard Aldington promoted it in England. Harrison Smith and Donald MacCampbell, three years later, both suggested that if "Belle Randolph"/"Sons and Husbands" used satire, the heroine would be more sympathetic, more entertaining, and less "painfully real." Smith found Belle unstable. MacCampbell deemed it unacceptable to build a novel around a woman who had the "unenviable record for attracting pansies and mama's boys—simply because she wants to be *more than a woman can normally be*" (emphasis mine).[10]

Clearly MacCampbell missed the point of the novel; Belle is a protagonist ahead of her time. Smith reasoned, "A novel could be written about a woman like Belle," provided it revealed "her as a weak woman and [showed] what havoc her emotional unbalance can cause in her own and in other people's lives. It would have to be a pretty savage book." Smith believed that as a "brilliant" writer who "understands the emotional lives of women," Claire could have written such a book, but had failed. Rather, she wrote as if she thought Belle were "admirable and her story . . . worth telling." He only wished he had known "what [she] was up to" so he could have warned her earlier.[11] The irony embedded in these comments seem antiquated to most modern readers and MacCampbell's inherent sexism, abhorrent.

For Donald MacCampbell knew exactly what was wrong; he wrote Claire instructing her how to correct it:

> Show your pathetic intellectual in her equally pathetic search for an honest-to-God man who will be proud of her novel writing, who will laud her for her intellectual accomplishments and at the same time be her dream lover. Put her through a few preliminary affairs

> with the type of men this type of woman would attract. Then have her come up against a *real man who, against her will at first, subjugates her: makes her fit into her proper niche.* Then show how she finds herself, marries the man, has a baby, and behaves like *any normal woman* (emphasis mine).[12]

MacCampbell believes a heroic woman is a subjugated woman; he further points to a scene in which Belle thinks of German composer Richard Wagner while she is "*being made love to*" and calls it an "extreme instance of decadent idealism" (emphasis mine). "What man would be flattered to know that his wife was thinking of music-drama at such a moment?" Even though Belle imagines herself the object of this act of love, MacCampbell still finds the protagonist "decadent," implying that women should not be moved to ecstasy, even with the husband they loved.[13]

For a model heroine, he suggests Aldous Huxley's "masterpiece," *Brief Candles*, "about the intellectual woman who needed a man but didn't know it. That's what I have in mind. You could bring out clearly—so stupid people like myself could understand and enjoy—Belle's tragic misconception of her sex, and once and for all you could *slay the intellectual female in fiction.* Then, at the end you could have her subjected to a thorough physical experience: but, please God, NOT by a mama's boy but by *a man who understands a woman's true place in the world*" (emphasis mine).[14]

A man like Donald MacCampbell himself, no doubt! Funny, no one but Claire seemed to find in George/Hans the "he-man" she wrote about to her mother. Both editors condemned Belle's "stupid judgment of men" and emotional instability rather than condemning Hans's cruelty, insensitivity, and abuse. Neither editor conceived the abusive quality of Hans's treatment of Belle; neither mentioned or realized how men like Hans destroy other people's lives, nor how domineering women like Emma Schiller harm the men, and ultimately the marriages, they try to control.

Claire Myers Spotswood had hit on characterizations and themes that men of her day found not only offensive but incomprehensible.

Men just didn't get it: the dominant male could be hostile to women because he was masking hostility toward his mother and such a man was effeminate, a "sissy." Sadly, Miss Spotswood's book might have saved other young Belles from misery had it been published. If published today, it would take its place on the shelf with novels that dramatize the effects of domestic violence on families and celebrate strong female protagonists.

Was "Belle Randolph" a novel ahead of its time? Contrary to her male editors, Claire knew exactly what she was doing—and why. The portrait of a "normal" woman was precisely the kind of novel Claire did not want to write. Nor would she have thought of Belle as passively "being made love to." In a 1940 letter to Burton Rascoe, Claire compared her book to Willa Cather's reissued *Song of the Lark*, which she thought "profoundly moving with beautiful phrases and ideas studded like jewels on a *very* drab background." The novel's protagonist, Thea, represents a most "convincing portrayal of an artist." But Thea "loves beauty only in art and nature" and not in her personal life; she has "no life on the human side, I mean men and love."[15]

Claire had tried to portray Belle, as "the woman artist who strives for a balanced way of living" with beauty affecting every aspect of life. Her revisions, she assured Rascoe, strove for a universal story of one man and one woman whose love and marriage were "symbolic" of all relationships between intellectual, artistic men and women. She had tried to show that some of the most important and dramatic battlefields are located in the human heart and brain and "how a woman's erotic life may be full of the most varied and exquisite poetry." Thousands of marriages are plagued by evil, she believed, especially in America where materialism blinds men to women's need for intimacy.[16] Claire had not only written a domestic novel, she had portrayed the cycle of violence in domestic relationships defined by feminist activists in the 1970s. Even the progressive editor Burton Rascoe could not recognize the attributes of a strong, independent female character unless she was veiled in satire and fantasy.

Two years later, Claire submitted "Belle Randolph" as an entry for the 1942 Thomas Jefferson Southern Award sponsored by Dutton, highlighting its "timely" theme dealing with the "basic differences between Americans and Germans." While Germans were not popular in 1942 America, women were. With many men away at war, women filled their jobs as part of their patriotic duty. Claire contended that this "story of democracy and ecstasy" explores the creative possibilities for establishing equality in male-female relationships: "Although millions of books have been written about love and marriage" most failed to have lasting impact. "'Belle Randolph' might be alternately titled 'The Flowering of the American Woman,'" she suggested.[17]

But no matter what she wrote about Belle, nor how she worded the title, no editor "got it." Not in 1936 when it was completed; not in 1940 when she asked Rascoe to reread it before she sent it to Maxwell Perkins at Scribner; and not in 1942 when it did *not* win the Jefferson Award. Indeed, Rascoe had turned her down, despite her offer to pay "a *substantial* reader's fee [because] I can afford it now."[18]

Claire's prosperity was not a result of her writing, but of her marriage to H. Thurston Owens. The years between 1932, when her marriage to George Wanders ended, and 1937, when she married Owens, were decidedly lean. But lean years provide good source material. "The life of a successful artist in the full tide of achievement," Willa Cather once observed, "is never as interesting as the story of the struggle it takes to achieve success—the story of the artist's victory over adversity."[19]

The stories writers tell reenact the struggles they survive, and art imitates life. Often women's stories of the 1920s–1940s were set in woman's hotels. Cheap but respectable with their tiny rooms and seedy accommodations, they provided a safe haven from men eager to exploit women's vulnerabilities.

The Woman's Hotel Series Claire M. Wanders wrote reflect her experiences during the Depression in the aftermath of her marriage to George and create a picture of women as community, kind or cruel, nurturing or competitive. Whether between husbands, lovers, or jobs, women found solace in one another and the stories they shared. With few material assets, women gave from their hearts and their minds the wisdom gleaned from their experiences, in a 1930s version of the "consciousness raising" groups that would emerge in the 1970s. They passed on the wisdom awakened from living and thinking passionately to achieve love *and* independence. However, for Claire and her contemporaries, the price for attaining independence often meant sacrificing love and living a solitary existence.

This cluster of stories captures a unique slice of women's history. During the nineteenth and early twentieth century, woman's hotels were the only option outside of family where a single woman could take refuge between jobs or husbands. Respectable hotels, too expensive for her meager assets, would not rent to a woman alone.[20]

In 1934, a friend recommended Claire for a job in Washington, DC, managing the bookstore in the large, glamorous Shoreham Hotel. Leaving the woman's hotel scene, with its tragic stories and meager provisions, Claire moved to Washington, where she expected to meet interesting men and women who worked in government. She was appalled to discover the people who governed America were "straight from the cornfields of the middle west."[21] Since they never came into the bookshop, she assumed, they did not read. Equally disappointing was her visit to Congress, where she witnessed the inane activity of the Senate in session. Still, she loved DC—loved visiting the Lincoln Memorial, which she approached reverently. "The majesty of this homely man sitting motionless in a marble chair awed" her into silence. In Lincoln's expression of sorrow and nobility, strength and suffering, she believed she would have recognized greatness even if she had not known his identity. She visited the White House and noted that as elegant as it was, as beautifully furnished, it seemed "small and modest for the home of the President of the United States compared to the enormous palaces in which the kings of Europe lived. Perhaps this was more suitable for a democracy." Still, deeply impressed, she loved visiting museums, furthering her education.

But soon she confronted "a new fact of life." Being a "Mrs." was a decided handicap. Men assumed any previously married woman, whether widowed, divorced, or separated, was "frothing at the mouth . . . to hop into bed." She tired of their obvious schemes to get her drunk and seduce her; she tried to avoid a life of liquor and sex—without conversation, affection, or friendship. She wondered if at thirty-eight she should call herself "Miss." "Oh why did women's sex condition have to be publicized to the world by their labels? All men were simply 'Mr.' whether married, single, divorced, virgins or otherwise," she moaned and integrated this theme into her fiction.[22]

One morning a gentleman in his fifties strolled into the bookshop and purchased two books. He was "small, homely, beautifully tailored with old world manners." They had a lengthy discussion of favorite authors, including Shaw and Balzac, Maugham and Galsworthy. They talked of the various plays they had seen in New York. Finally he presented her with his engraved calling card, "H. Thurston Owens." He invited her to have dinner with him on Saturday evening: "Shall we dress?" he asked. "Oh, yes, I'd love that," she answered. When she arrived home that afternoon a large bouquet of pink roses from him awaited her. He called for her in a Packard, and they went to a "posh" hotel restaurant. He was the first man she had ever met who did not seem to enjoy talking about himself. But she questioned him, and they told one another their life stories. The next morning, they visited the National Gallery and spent the afternoon at Mount Vernon. He was keenly interested in art; she was deeply moved to walk in Washington's footsteps. She told him that Martha Washington was one of her mother's ancestors. He told her about his Dutch ancestry and the family farm on land that became Madison and Thirty-Fourth Street. They shared a common pride in their privileged genealogies.[23]

But later that afternoon, he suggested that she come up to his room at the Mayflower so they could "go to bed together." Claire was furious and burst into tears. "Sex! Sex! Sex! . . . You men think it's the most important thing in life. . . . There was promise of a pleasant friendship between us. Now you've ruined everything." He told her he did not understand women. She agreed. "What makes a man think that if they give a woman dinner, wine and flowers, she should automatically go to bed with him?" she asked. She was not attracted to Thurston. "For a woman sex grows out of affection, not out of lust. My lecture is finished; will you take me home, Mr. Owens!" At the door he told her good-bye and that he was leaving for New York, cutting his time in Washington short. She kissed him lightly and thought, "That is the beginning and the end of the briefest romance I ever had."[24]

The next day, the contract for her book *The Unpredictable Adventure* arrived, along with instructions to "cut the manuscript by 50,000 words." She locked herself in her room, lined up a row of milk bottles and crackers, and spent the entire day reworking the text—cutting a word here, a phrase there, and occasionally a paragraph. "It was torture." But she mailed it back to Doubleday the following morning.[25]

Men, love, marriage; nothing mattered to her except that her first book was going to be published. In the autumn, she moved back to the Breevort Hotel in Greenwich Village and waited for publication day—September 20, 1935. "When the bell boy brought up the package of complimentary copies, I held the book against my breast and wept tears of joy, as if it was my baby. It had a delightful dust jacket with a drawing of a centaur with a lovely nude lady on his back—against a pink background."[26]

Between 1934 and 1937, Claire moved around both within the city and without, from the Breevort Hotel, to East Ninth, to Perry Street, to the Hotel Albert. During this time, she maintained an active correspondence with her mother and renewed exchanges with Carton Moore-Park.

Chances are Claire initiated contact with Carton, writing to let him know that her book had been published. "I wonder if even you with all your great understanding of me realize quite what this means to me." She had kept her longing for recognition private even from friends.[27]

His response to her first note was sent from "On Board Cunard White Star 'Laconia'": "Dear Little Lorelli—Certainly I remember—I have elephants in my family—I never forget!"[28] In handwriting as illegible as ever, he filled her in on his "extraordinary adventures and meanderings." Indeed, his permanent address in England was c/o The Zoological Society, London. In return, she answered that he could always locate her through her publisher, Doubleday Doran. Catching him up on her career, she wrote that she had written "very dull" magazine articles, "purely commercial," and had begun writing the first of a series of seven literary novels.

She expected to come to the British Isles the following summer. Havelock Ellis had invited her to visit him, and her friends Sir Thomas and Lady Glen-Coats had insisted she come to Scotland and stay long enough to write, though she wondered if the invitation would hold once they read her book, written to appeal to "liberals not conservatives." Nevertheless, she wrote Carton, "It's a damned fine book" and she thought he would like it whether or not he agreed with it. "I have tried to give a wholly honest picture of life, love, marriage, sex, men, religion, the seven arts, the business world . . . as seen from a woman's point of view which differs radically from that of a man's in many ways—unfortunately."[29]

If she meant to renew their friendship, this time she was careful. She noticed his family was still listed in the New York phone book on East Thirty-Seventh Street and reminded him of the "ghastly mess" he had caused allowing his wife to discover her love letters. She asked that he return these letters after he read them. "The spirit of a woman who has suffered much and deeply has not the strength to undergo another such unpleasantness—once burned thrice cautious."

She wanted him to write her publishers the minute he read her book, mention his one-hundred-dollars-a-copy edition that William Rudge did of the "Chuckers," and then write her separately to extol her talent as a writer. In her usual way, she closed with a philosophical postscript: "I find that the chief trouble with human beings is that if they have fine minds they don't have fine characters—and . . . and I desire both—as do you!" In his experience, he wrote back, "a fine Mind goes generally with a fine 'character' but words are dangerous. . . . Further I find that women more than men are apt to be wrong in quick judgment—they base on intuition—a man on experience. . . . [A] woman is apt to let emotional considerations warp or blind her first judgment. . . . But I may be . . . wrong."[30]

Certainly he was not wrong, for Claire's intuition, otherwise sharp and accurate, was not reliable for screening interesting men. Even if she used her intellect to gain their attention at first, her feminine charms would sabotage her better judgment when she was physically attracted. But by now, she was safe from Carton. With distance as a cushion, she seemed comfortable reviving their friendship, and wrote: "So after twelve years here we are again—just as you predicted. Yes, you were more than right [when] you said to me once that never again in my life would I be able to talk to anyone else as I talked to you. And in all these years I doubt if one single month has passed . . . I have not thought of you. . . . In the interim I have been married and unmarried and now the dream of my life has come true and I am at long last having my book published."[31]

Letters back and forth brought them up to date concerning one another's lives. On August 26, 1936, Carton asked Claire to meet him at four o'clock on Thursday at the Waldorf Astoria Hotel in the lounge at the head of the stairs on the Park Avenue side. He warned her that he had changed in appearance, his hair now "nearly white," and gently reminded her that he would be leaving New York soon after; "officially" he was "*not* here—you understand?"[32] If that meeting took place, no written recollection of it exists.

The warm letters exchanged over a period of a year and a half brought Claire joy and comfort. Painful though her love affair with Carton had been, it had given her long leisurely hours of joy and sensuality, plus intellectual and artistic companionship with a man who was a tender, considerate lover, mentor, and friend, despite his tendency to philander. With Carton, she gained maturity, knowledge, and a higher level of self-confidence. George, on the other hand, had drained Claire of all energy and self-esteem. Despite their passionate erotic life, he inflicted volatile pain on Claire. Reconnecting with Carton, from whom she had healed during her three-year stay in Temple, brought back good memories.

During this same period, disturbing letters from her mother arrived regularly. Circumstances in the once prosperous Myers family had taken a downward turn. Although Susan wanted to spare her daughter unnecessary anxiety, she was compelled to keep her apprised of Claire's father's deteriorating health. As sole caretaker of her husband, as well as of her aging mother, Susan found herself in the precarious position of breadwinner and nurse; her exhausting life left few moments of relief.

In April 1935, Susan wrote that she wanted Claire to have all her handwork and silver because she "would appreciate it." There was "not much sterling but some useful pieces." And she wanted to give Claire her "best china and glassware" since Coren and Ruby had some of their own. "You've never seen it," she wrote, "it's in the white gold decoration both china and glasses. I have water and sherbet plates except 2 broken to match. The table is very pretty indeed with the silver and china on white linen. . . . It's not *fine*, but looks fine." She also had some new quilts she made that Grandma Allen had bound, which she wanted Claire to have as keepsakes, and another from an aunt. "Now Coren would appreciate these too but Ruby wouldn't and would not take care of them—I know."[33]

Susan Myers decided to pack them in Claire's old trunk and "freight it . . . when the time comes," hoping that someday Claire would have her own home and could keep these things for herself. Claire would have to decide whether or not to make a trip home. She feared it would "wreck" her to see the house "broken up and see Daddy not himself," so for her own good, Susan thought Claire should not come. "But if you feel you must why you know I'd be more than glad to have you."

Whereas Susan Myers's letters seem congenial and loving, Claire was often offended by things her mother wrote or said to her. For example, to spare Claire the long trip back to Texas, the sight of her now invalid father, and the house and business in disrepair, Susan suggested a "common meeting ground," like New Orleans, where they could "have a visit together for awhile." Claire interpreted this suggestion to mean Susan felt ashamed for her daughter to come home after her second failed marriage. Polite as ever, Susan wrote that Claire need not worry about the "Geo. business" but added, Grandma would "have to know all about him and your affairs. . . . That's the reason I say we'd meet somewhere."[34]

Claire, unconvinced, remained hurt for many years. Meanwhile, the letters grew ever more pessimistic. "Daddy said Sunday, 'I don't mind so much going on except leaving you to carry on all this worry alone.' Poor fellow he doesn't realize that my greatest anxiety is for him, his comfort. . . . Poor Grandma just hangs on [without] hearing, eyesight or smell and can't get around to do any good."

"When the time comes," that is to say, when her husband died, Susan thought she might get an apartment. She knew her daughter-in-law, Ruby, would not want her to live with them. She would not want to live in New York with Claire—it would be such a different life for her and "might handicap" Claire's plans. She was trying to put things in order so it would not be so hard on her children when her own time came. Claire had asked her parents and grandmother to move east with her, but, though Susan appreciated the offer, she declined: "If you were able and had a nice home out of the city we could come to you maybe but it would not be the same as you've always known." It is, however, doubtful that Susan would have ever left Texas, no matter what her daughter's circumstances had been.

On June 1, 1935, Susan wrote that "Daddy is gradually growing more helpless. I can't just come out cold and tell him he won't ever be any better."[35] Humoring him was not easy; he wanted to go back to his office, though he could barely get around at home. Susan drew strength from the things in her life that were still good. She had her son and his family close at hand. Granddaughter Sue, Ruby and Coren's daughter, would have her tenth birthday on June 23, and grandmother would be ninety on June 16, which was also Father's Day. She urged that Claire send only cards, no gifts, as they needed "nothing." She had been to Sue's ballet recital and had commented to friends that her granddaughter "reminded me of Clairene on the stage," she was "so beautiful." Detailed descriptions of each of her costumes followed. Cordial though this letter sounds, it has a curious ending: "Hope I have a letter from you soon. What keeps you so busy?" She signed with "Lots of Love."[36]

For one thing, Claire stayed busy writing and publishing. In addition to the novels and short stories she wrote and revised, she made endless attempts to publish in magazines and periodicals. The November 17, 1934, issue of *Publishers Weekly* carried her article profiling the Dauber and Pine bookstore on lower Fifth Avenue.[37] The July 27, 1935, issue carried her profile of Schulte's Book Store on lower Fourth Avenue.[38] Each article, with her byline "Claire Myers Wanders," describes the store's physical accommodation, its specialties, unique features of the clientele, and a history of both store and owner.

For another thing, Claire stayed busy constantly moving from city to city, apartment to apartment—New York in the spring, Hartford by June, when she received a letter from Grandmother Allen. Written in shaky, large-lettered script, two days before her ninetieth birthday, the letter read, "The world is so *big* and full of people, each one must do their part, otherwise some poor discouraged or condemned may be left to grope in dark despair. God has work laid out for each of his creatures, work that no one else can do. If we fail to accomplish it, we let *one star fall from our Crown—don't fail Him.*"[39]

Her report on Claire's father was as foreboding as those from Susan. He was "so weak." She worried that with both Grandmother Allen and Coren "almost helpless," the burden was too much, though she knew she brought comfort to her daughter while Coren was so ill. Then, she shifted her emphasis: "Excuse me!! I should have thanked you first for the card and hdk [handkerchief]. I will keep it to spread over my poor disfigured face when laid in my coffin so the curious can't make remarks. . . . Farewell my dear one. Let us strive to meet each other in an unbroken family reunion. My prayer is to this effect. Your Grandmother Allen." She added a PS: "Do you remember the Honeysuckle on the porch at the old house where you were born?"[40]

Grandmother Allen adored her granddaughter, despite being baffled by her way of life. And, by all indications, she had a loving relationship with her own daughters as well. Susan Myers was as devoted to her aging mother as her sister Laura, Mrs. H. B. Griffin, who lived in Brawley, California. Laura wrote the most poignant letter in the entire collection, to her "dear Sweet Mother" in honor of Mother's Day 1932: "I love you because of all the sweet relations of mother and daughter and your years of loving kindness; in your character are found the highest and noblest human principles, and your life has been lived according to them. Though not blest with riches, you have possessed great wealth of soul and mind [inspiring others to] 'Follow the

Gleam.' How far your light has shone . . . Tennyson said it thus: 'Our echoes roll from soul to soul, and grow forever and forever.'"[41]

Such loving words from a daughter are surely to be cherished; but Braxton, Laura's husband, wrote an equally beautiful letter to his mother-in-law: "I send greetings to the loveliest mother in all the world. I owe you much for what you have been to me." He wishes that this beautiful Mother's Day will find her "comfortable in body, and of serene mind, and joyous in soul." With reverence equal to that expressed by his wife, his most poignant tribute invokes his prayer that her "memories of the dim past bring sweet gifts," and that the future "still charm[s] and invite[s] you to live on and love on until your beautiful soul returns to God who lent you awhile to bless the world with virtuous womanhood and sweet motherhood."[42]

Laura Smith Allen's passionate soul echoed in her granddaughter's, "from soul to soul." Perhaps Clairene inherited Grandmother Allen's proclivity for passionate spiritual experiences. Whatever the motivation, her grandmother's conversion to the Baptist faith was a precursor to Claire's embrace of the spiritual. By leaving Texas, Claire broke the boundaries set by Laura Allen and Susan Myers, her maternal forebears, and discovered her own sense of the universal, which she found missing in the narrowness of Southern Baptist mores. But the bonds established early in her life were never broken. "Follow the Gleam," Grandmother Allen fondly told her children and grandchildren, words Claire must have appreciated all the more as an adult since that was her raison d'être, the basis for her choices, and the rewards she received through her ecstatic moments connecting with the universe.

A July 1935 letter between extended family members praised Grandmother Allen: "She is a wonderful woman. Her mind is as active and alert as anyone's. She is keenly interested in all her kin, friends and acquaintances and in all current events. . . . She has many friends in Temple. . . . Some friend brought her a birthday cake with 90 candles on it and she didn't know anyone was coming and had on her gown. So they had the party with the honoree in her nightie"![43]

During the winter of 1936, Susan continued to write Claire long letters filled with small-town news and the vicissitudes of nursing her mother and husband. Dressing "Mama & Dad" took up her mornings; a frozen pipe complicated her difficult routine. Dad was unable to tell her when his kidneys "want to act," which required her washing and cleaning continually. Her hands rough and chapped, she was tied down with no time or space for herself. She could not read at night since the light kept her husband awake. She spent afternoons at the office waiting for renters to bring their checks. So far from home, it must have been difficult for Claire to read about such interminable problems, powerless to help relieve her mother's burden.[44]

As luck would have it, Claire found support from an unlikely source. No records document when Claire and her "briefest romance," Thurston Owens, reunited in New York. However, sometime after she moved back to the city, Owens reentered Claire's life and became a good friend, visiting her on weekends while staying at his club uptown. Though he did not understand *The Unpredictable Adventure*, he bought extra copies on its release and sent them to friends—the only person to show such enthusiastic support. His generosity extended to Claire in other ways. She was living in a small apartment on Ninth Street, "beside Mark Twain's old house on Fifth Avenue." The man in the apartment directly above her tramped back and forth for hours in the middle of the night on the bare wooden floor, making it hard for her to concentrate on writing or to get a decent night's sleep. Thurston gave Claire a small radio to help mask the sound. One day in 1936, she heard a fanatical voice speaking German that made her "blood run cold." It turned out to be Hitler, haranguing the German people. It was not so much the man himself, but the "frenzy of the mob" that Claire found terrifying.[45]

On March 29, 1936, Claire received the devastating news that her father had died that day. Thurston bought her train ticket, accompanied her to the station, and met her when she returned. Contrary to the tone of their letters, Claire's version of her trip home for her father's funeral describes her mother as distant, aloof, and not pleased to encounter her prodigal daughter in person.[46]

A note dated April 1, 1936, written by Susan, possibly while Claire was on her way back to New York, apologized for her failure to wire her daughter in time for her to get home for the funeral.[47] She claimed she and her friend Miss Rolia "decided to not wire you because you weren't well & I said alone so it might upset you too much. Everybody so lonely. Coren Douglas at home. I am all right but feel quite nervous yet. Hope you understand we were trying to spare you the sudden shock. Grandma quite nervous too."

Claire did not understand. She wrote in her "Autobiography" that she had so longed to see her father alive one more time, but she felt her mother had deliberately prevented it. The train trip to Texas required two full days and nights. She arrived at the family home just in time for the 3:30 p.m. funeral service. R. L. McKnight, Robbie's father, served as one of the pallbearers. Standing at the graveside at the Bruceville-Moore Cemetery, just as his body was lowered into the ground, Claire turned around and saw her father's cousin, who looked so much like him that she burst into tears, ran over and "flung her arms around his neck." Susan Myers did not approve of such emotional displays, nor did she approve of this cousin. She had told friends that Claire would be unable to come to the funeral because she was ill. Claire believed that her mother had not wanted her to come because she was "the twice divorced daughter and an embarrassment," and that Susan was distressed when Claire showed up at the last minute. "I felt immediately too sick at heart even to think. Some vital part of me had been in that grave with my father."[48]

Back in New York, she tried to forget her "double sorrow"—her mother's coldness and her father's death—by "concentrating fiercely" on writing her second novel. One evening that April, Thomas Wolfe rang her apartment bell around nine o'clock and announced himself over her speaking tube. Claire, soaking in the bathtub, swallowed her excitement and invited him in: "Two flights up. Apartment A. Right at the head of the stairs."[49]

"Can't stay but *five* minutes," he warned.

"That's quite all right," she said, amused at his caution. She didn't blame him. After all, they had never met. Apparently she forgot that they had been introduced at Dauber and Pine by his then paramour, Aline Bernstein, shortly after he published *Look Homeward Angel.*

Thomas Wolfe came to call now because on December 2, Claire had sent him a copy of her novel with a four-page letter praising him as a writer: His books had "profoundly moved" her, especially *Of Time and the River.* The experience of reading them was like "listening to a great symphony. The mighty rush and force of sensations and ideas . . . sweep one away—like Beethoven's Fifth. . . . .The warm flood of words pours over one in such torrents that . . . one loses the sense of them." She compares him to Swinburne and "certain passages of the Bible," and that's only the first page! The rest of the letter discusses his philosophy of writing and characterizations, along with her own. She directs him to specific passages of her own book to "support [her] contention about women." She mentions a discussion she had with Burton Rascoe a week *before* Rascoe's review of *Of Time and the River* appeared in the *Tribune*; they had discussed a certain "curious quality" regarding Wolfe's portrayal of women. She closes with an invitation; she will bring out her "most ancient and honorable Scotch" should he care to come down for a highball. No wonder, four months later, she found him standing on her doorstep the day after he returned from an extended trip.[50]

She dried hurriedly, "flung on an evening dress," and opened the door to find "a perfect giant of a man with a large pale unsmiling face and no hat on his dark, disorderly hair." He stepped into her living room and began to walk around: "Did you decorate this yourself?" he asked.

"Yes."

"I have a new apartment but I haven't any curtains in it. I don't know how to do things like that." He stood still, looking at her expectantly. She did not answer. So he walked into her dining room and kitchen, turned, and asked, "Can you cook?" She knew what was coming; they were both from the South.

"I should be able to," she answered. "My father saw to it that I majored in domestic science in college."

"I'm looking everywhere for someone who can cook me some beans the southern way."

"You mean with salt pork instead of butter?" she asked.

"That's it!" Again he waited expectantly. Again Claire said nothing.

She recalled how he had portrayed his treatment of Aline Bernstein in his autobiographical novel, *Look Homeward Angel.* "She slept with him and cooked for him and he abused her and her husband dreadfully. I would not let any man abuse me as a woman, not even a genius," Claire observed in stories portraying this encounter, ignoring having had such a relationship with George Wanders.

He sat down in the living room and asked to use her phone. Claire recounts that evening and the one that followed with great humor in several short stories, creative nonfictions verified in her "Autobiography."[51] Though each account differs slightly, the high points remain consistent.

Every fifteen minutes, Thomas Wolfe picked up the phone, dialed a number, and said, "I'm detained. I'll be home in a few minutes." Then he would hang up. Three times that first night, he said: "I'm thirty-six years old and a hardworking man and I want to get married." Each time Claire laughed and responded. "Don't look at me Mister, I've been married and never again!" She told him she admired his book. He told her that he had not read hers yet, as he had just gotten back in town.

During one of his many phone calls, she studied him carefully. He did not look well—his face was pasty white, his grooming unkempt; she observed food on his coat, his frayed shirt cuffs, and his dirty fingernails. She could not imagine allowing him to touch her. At midnight, he made another call, this time instructing the person on the other end to "find the clean sheets in the closet and the Scotch on the floor." When he hung up, he announced, "That's Maxwell Perkins, my editor at Scribner. No matter how happily married a man is, there are always times when he does not want to go home. Will you have dinner with me tomorrow night?"

Claire was shocked; she felt no chemistry between them, thought that the evening had been a failure. But she accepted, thinking it would be an opportunity to spend a long evening talking about literature, like one she had spent with Richard Aldington a few years earlier. Wolfe asked her to meet him in the Chatham Hotel cocktail room at seven, explaining that he would not be able to pick her up because every day at six o'clock he met Max Perkins at the Waldorf for a drink. Since it was a man's bar, he could not invite her to join them. He had to see Maxwell Perkins every day for encouragement.

"Thomas Wolfe!" she said. "Do you mean to tell me with all your talent, your genius, your critical acclaim, you still need encouragement?"

He glowered at her and thrust out his lower lip: "I couldn't write a word without his encouragement," he replied.

The following evening would have been funny if Wolfe were not so pitiful and sad. As they walked into the Chatham bar, the hat check girl, bartender, and waiter profusely greeted Wolfe by name. He "seemed to purr like a cat at all this attention." Claire wrote that she "didn't blame him in the least. I should have been delighted if they'd recognized me at one of New York's most fashionable bars." After cocktails they went to a small French restaurant in the East Fifties. "He ate every crumb of his dinner very quickly and then, with hungry eyes, sat watching my every mouthful. Pretending I couldn't eat all of mine, I offered him half. He accepted."

After dinner he asked her if she would rather go over to see his "beautiful apartment with its fine view of the East River," or go call on Mr. and Mrs. Maxwell Perkins. Claire said, "Both." They went first to Wolfe's apartment, on First Avenue, in a tall new building surrounded by slums. They entered a large dining room, empty except for a large packing box overflowing with books. Then he showed her into the kitchen, where she admired the view of the river and the unused appliances. "Very nice, very modern," she said. He looked at her expectantly, but she said nothing more.

Bare floors and undraped windows. "The living room was large with a narrow cot, two tables and two straight chairs with cane bottoms. The bottom had been sat out of one of them. 'My mother came to visit me so I had to get this for her,' he said, nodding toward the cot." He pointed to the ceiling where he had written "Merry Christmas" with a pencil to prove to friends he could reach the ceiling and write on it; then he led her to the bedroom to show her his wonderful seven-foot bed. "Some friends of mine had it made especially for me. I thought they meant to give it to me, but *I* had to pay for it." The large bedroom contained an oversized double bed, one straight chair, and one small table on which rested a telephone and Claire's novel, *The Unpredictable Adventure.*

He fixed them each a Scotch, then sat on the one good chair, leaving Claire the chair with the hole in the bottom. Instead, she perched on the edge of the cot. His conversation jumped from one subject to another "without the slightest transition." He brought up the line about marriage again, thrusting out his lower lip. "I'm thirty-six years old and a hardworking man and I want to get married."

"Well, who's stopping you, for heaven's sake?" Claire replied. "There must be a score of women who'd break their necks to marry a famous man like you."

"Everyone can get married but me," he repeated several times. Even his publishers did not want him to get married because they thought he would make a woman unhappy. What could "Miss Spotswood" say to that? she wondered aloud. Wolfe changed the subject again.

"Nobody invites me to parties anymore. When I had a dress suit three times too small for me, everybody invited me to parties. And lots of society women wanted to sleep with me just because I was famous. Then I had an expensive dress suit made by a tailor and now nobody invites me to parties." Claire, stumped, said nothing; he continued: "I've read some of your book, Miss Spotswood. But the human race would have to be born over again to be the way you want them to be. No man on earth could learn all those things you suggest in that chapter about the Siren Islands."

He wonders "why all this talk about sex . . . an animal function," then condemns women's obsession with "romance" all of which sends Claire into a spin. "There's nothing to know about women. God made women just for one purpose—man's pleasure," he concludes.

He then goes to sit beside her on the cot, hugging her, "suffocating, like a bear. I did not care for it. I rose: 'I think I should go home, Mr. Wolfe.'"

When they said good night at her door, Claire knew she would never see Thomas Wolfe again. It was as if they were "fundamentally antagonistic to each other—not as writers but as man and woman." But the following day, he called. "This is Thomas Wolfe. I just wanted to tell you what a pleasant evening I had. And I hope you'll go around to the Brevoort with me some time soon for a drink."

Now that her anger had cooled, she felt sorry for him. Thomas Wolfe died of a brain tumor in 1938. Claire admired the writer tremendously but, as a man, he did not appeal to her. Years later when she read his last novel, *You Can't Go Home Again*, she wrote in her journal that she was delighted to see how much he had developed as a writer and a person; he had learned to think of someone other than himself.

In May, Claire left for Reno to file for her divorce from George Wanders. Thurston Owens, divorced himself, had encouraged her to take the legal steps necessary to set herself free and prepared her for what she would find in Reno. Once again, she boarded the train for a long trip west. In Reno she stayed at the Riverside Hotel, where she found "a collection of bitter humiliated men and . . . women who cried into their drinks . . . before dinner and then spent the evenings gambling at the innumerable casinos."[52] Neither liquor nor gambling worked well for Claire, so she stayed in her room, trying to write. She found the whole Reno scene pathetic, with men hovering about hoping to score with a rich divorcée or widow or a lonely, willing bed partner. Everyone in Reno felt guilty for his or her part in the failed marriage. It was a harsh experience. The six-week waiting period seemed interminable. On June 4, after four weeks had passed, she wrote George that she needed another $50 for her expenses and $150 for her lawyer's fee; he agreed to pay. Once her case was called, the proceedings were simple. She left glad to have Thurston waiting for her return.

Through the fall and winter months, letters from her mother arrived, sounding as if nothing unusual had passed between them. She continued to apprise Claire of her grandmother's failing condition; she continued to send boxes of heirlooms and loving, caring messages. She took great pride in Sue's straight A report card, "the highest grade made by anyone in 6th grade." Grandmother Allen was not "at all well . . . her going would be a sweet relief to her from all her terrible suffering."[53] She signed the letter, "Much love for my darling child from Mother," but for whatever reasons, Claire never believed her mother loved her—not the way she needed to be loved.

Laura Smith Allen died on July 4, 1937, at age ninety-two at her daughter's home at 618 South Seventh Street in Temple, where funeral services were held at seven o'clock that evening.[54] She was buried beside her husband the next morning at ten o'clock in the Rockdale cemetery. Chances are Claire did not return home for the funeral. But they had shared a few beautiful hours together in April 1936 during Claire's visit for her father's funeral when together they wrote, one last time, the family genealogy, reciting the myth of their aristocratic heritage and ties to the Old South.[55] Claire had found closure; she was free to affirm her new ties—to the North, to realign her loyalties, and revise her definition of family.

11

Expiedway Ten

1937–1949

> "How would you like to buy a house in the country and live there all year around?" I laughed. This was his idea of humor of course. For we were both incorrigible New Yorkers.
>
> —Claire Myers Owens, *Awakening to the Good*

FOR HER FORTY-FIRST BIRTHDAY, Thurston took Claire to the Waldorf Astoria. Naturally, they "dressed" for the occasion. He told her his mother had brought him there at age sixteen when he wore his first tuxedo, one she had tailor-made. She taught him how to order in French, then took him to Europe as her escort. He had been back five times since and felt a deep rapport with European traditions and cuisine. But during his adolescence, his mother lived six months of the year in Europe, leaving him to fend for himself in the city.

Born in New York City on October 23, 1879, Harry Thurston Owens was the only child of Edwin Owens and Mary Thurston Horn.[1] A fourth-generation American of Dutch ancestry, Thurston was a descendant of the Hudson Valley Van Hornes on his mother's side. The family traced their earliest American forefather to Jacob Horne who sailed from New York City in 1696 as a member of the crew of the *Adventure* under the notorious Captain Kidd.[2] Owens's great-grandfather, James Horn, had his summer farm at Madison Square in New York City. His grandfather, Henry J. Horn, spent many years in Europe as an amateur painter, devoted to the works of Titian; he was well known to New York artists. Thurston inherited his grandfather's gift and painted as a hobby.[3]

Thurston Owens never knew his Welsh father, Edwin Owens, who died a young man; he identified only with his mother's side of the family.[4] According to Charles Lockwood, the family lawyer who became a judge, Mary Horn Owens was the "best dressed woman in New York. She cared more about clothes, food, music—or rather sitting in a box at the Metropolitan Opera"—than about her only child. But Lockwood doubted if she had ever read a book.[5] Even in his fifties, Thurston nursed the scars of her abandonment.

Spoiled and imprudent, Owens's extended family took their inheritance for granted. He was the only member who worked for a living; all the others tried to live off old New York property and investments. His eccentric family was like a page out of an Edith Wharton novel. His Aunt Mary's living room walls were lined with original French Impressionist paintings: Renoirs, Cézannes, Seurats. Thurston had hoped she might leave him at least one picture, but when she died, she willed them to a museum.

Eventually, Claire took Thurston to meet her friend Frances Fox. The following morning Frances called: "He certainly is a gentleman," she told her. "But too desiccated—all his juices have dried up."

"That's not true," Claire responded, protectively. "He puts his worst foot forward always. He never makes the slightest effort to make people like him. He is a strange man, but very good to me and I am sorely in need of that right now."

"Well, I hope you don't marry him," Frances replied.

"I don't intend to marry anybody," Claire assured.[6] After her ordeal with George Wanders, and Frances's intervening hand, perhaps Claire thought it wise to get a second opinion, and perhaps Frances felt blunt honesty would save her friend more heartache. But that did not mean Claire would listen to Frances's advice, nor was she completely honest with Frances. She did intend to marry again—someone, someday. The years of depression, years of "stark terror [standing] at the foot of her bed like a burglar," caused her to feel lonely and vulnerable. Rather than feeling bitterness, the legacy of her marriage to George Wanders left her convinced that "without love, life is not worth living. Without a husband, a woman feels only half a woman. Once a woman tastes the potential joys of marriage, its companionship, its warmth and enrichment, she longs for the real thing permanently. Freedom was a delusion." Southern belle to the quick, she enjoyed having a "strong man to lean on."[7]

Surely Thurston Owens was a man she could lean on. But was he the "real thing"? Was he a man she could love? He was a successful business representative for the Northern Engraving and Manufacturing Company based in La Crosse, Wisconsin. Owens went to work for the Gelatt family–owned company in 1910, at age thirty-one. "Until I was 40, I knew little about life, love and literature. By life, I mean business."[8] He credited Philo Gelatt, president of the company, as his mentor: "He was only three years older but like a father to me." Thurston served the company well for fifty-two years; the Gelatts, in turn, remained loyal to him long past his death.

Thurston earned a handsome income, excellent benefits, and the lifelong love and respect of the entire Gelatt family, including three generations of company presidents. When he wanted to put his "best foot forward," he knew how. He set his own schedule, but the job required that he travel most weekdays; on weekends, he came into the city and stayed at his club uptown. Frequently, Claire and Thurston dined together on weekends. As much as she disliked cooking, she often cooked dinner for him. He had the worst case of ulcers she had ever encountered, and she was determined to cure them through her expert knowledge of nutritional balance: "His breath was unspeakable. I felt dreadfully sorry for him. He seemed so terribly lonely, so in need of affection, so in need of sex." Their first time together, Claire wrote in her "Autobiography," "I turned my head aside so he would not see the tears flow down my cheeks. Afterwards, he said, 'No woman knows how grateful a man is. Even though he may realize that she does it primarily out of kindness.'"[9]

Why did Claire, with her history of attracting exciting, desirable men, become involved with Thurston Owens? Was she looking for money? Security? Prestige? Companionship? "To be first in somebody's life—that knowledge sustains us through all vicissitudes. And we tire of living only for ourselves. We long to live for someone else. So I remarried."[10]

Claire Myers Wanders married H. Thurston Owens on the morning of June 12, 1937, at the original Gotham Hotel in New York City. Marian Murray, the book and art editor for the *Hartford Times*, was her matron of honor; they had been friends since Marian had given her book, *The Unpredictable Adventure*, an "intelligent" review two years earlier.[11]

The night before the wedding, the two women were so busy talking and packing Claire "had no time to think." Only moments before the ceremony, she remembered to instruct Thurston on the procedures she had planned. In his own prenuptial excitement, he did not listen to a word she said. Judge Charles Lockwood performed the ceremony; Thurston responded to his cues by repeating: "I love you, I love you" which "touched" Claire's heart. An elegant wedding brunch for twenty followed the ceremony. But on her wedding night, she turned her head away again and cried bitterly. "I should not marry, or even sleep with a man unless I love him. It was an affront to the best in me," she wrote years later.[12]

The following day, the couple sailed for Bermuda for a two-week honeymoon. The first afternoon on deck, Thurston ordered two champagne cocktails. "No bitters in mine, please," Claire told the steward. When he left, Thurston frowned, "Why didn't you let me do that? I want you to depend on me for everything but breathing." So began a thirty-two year alliance—difficult yet rewarding, traditional yet eccentric, demanding yet privileged, as steeped in paradox as all her prior relationships, but with rewards beyond her expectations.

And what were Claire Myers Owens's expectations of Thurston, this man for whom she felt so little physical attraction? He was seventeen years older; she was around four inches taller. She was vivacious, expressive; he was quiet, introverted. She was beautiful, glamorous; he was homely. And yet he was dignified, well bred, respectable, an impeccably tailored man of excellent taste. They had more in common than appeared on first glance.

They shared a passion for music, literature, philosophy, and art; they relished attending theater, ballet, opera, symphony, and museums. He knew a great deal about paintings, and she was eager to learn. They shared the same taste in theater, responded in the same manner to nuances of humor, methods of acting. And that was the ground on which they met—art, the passion they shared.[13]

They enjoyed one another's company; but they were cautious, distrustful, still healing from the failure of their prior marriages, determined not to fail again. Thurston's previous marriage, painful albeit brief, had proven "a frightful mistake."[14]

Had Claire, in marrying Thurston, compromised her values? Her feminist spirit? With Thurston, life was no longer an adventure. It was predictable, safe. In choosing Thurston, had she chosen the path of least resistance? Had she, like Tellectina, found Expiedway Ten—the expedient way home? Certainly, with Owens, she could anticipate what she referred to as "the good life," a life of privilege and ease. She found his generosity, good taste, and breeding, his knowledge of the arts, his eagerness to please, and his genuine love for her irresistible. Like Carton Moore-Park, Thurston Owens was a father figure, but without the erotic connection of either Moore-Park or George Wanders. This time her marriage, though not based on passion, would be based on wisdom, the wisdom of her Grandmother Allen's childhood admonitions to never marry beneath her own heritage and to "choose good stock." Quality of mind and character "stand the test. The ability to meet emergencies was the mark of an aristocrat . . . The bloodline is everything," Grandma Allen preached.[15] Harry Thurston Owens had the "right" bloodline.

After their honeymoon, Thurston rented a house at Pine Orchard, New York, off Long Island Sound. Claire engaged a cook and took charge of planning menus based on her determination to cure his ulcers.[16] His gratitude for everything she did for him was touching, endearing. "I guess we were both difficult people," she told Kenneth Ring, ten years after Owens's death. "But we were determined to make a success of it . . . and it was very rewarding."[17]

Mrs. Owens was well suited to the upper-class life she assumed in 1937 when she and her "Thursty" moved into one of the famous mansions on Livingston Street in New Haven, Connecticut. However, Thurston's wish to leave New York came as a complete surprise.

"You don't know," Thurston said when she objected, "you might like to live in the country." That meant he preferred to live in the country, which to Claire conjured memories of Texas farms, a throwback to stagnant ponds and stagnant minds. Besides, she and Thurston considered themselves "incorrigible New Yorkers."[18] But like a dutiful wife, she inspected the houses he chose when he surprised her with an outing one fine summer day.

When they got to New Haven, something changed. For one thing, New Haven was not exactly the country; the population was 250,000. It was a quiet town, provincial compared to New York, but a cultural center with the impressive Gothic buildings of Yale University at its heart.

The East Rock neighborhood, prestigious from its inception, marked a seductive turning point for Claire. The majesty of the East Rock Cliff and park below served as a powerful regional resource. The neighborhood, developed by Eli Whitney, attracted Connecticut's wealthiest, most educated people: doctors, lawyers, university professors. Livingston Street, considered by locals as the "most beautiful" in New Haven, was surrounded by other beautiful streets: Whitney, Edwards, Prospect, and Everit. Today, these streets are lined on both sides with stately three-story homes, manicured lawns, well-kept gardens, as elegant now as they were a century ago.[19]

When Thurston spotted the house at 280 Livingston Street and accompanied the real estate agent to the office to pick up the key, Claire sat on the white stone bench in the old deserted garden behind the house and "cast a prejudicial eye" about her. The surroundings looked like the country because they faced a "park with trees, a river, and a minor mountain with red rock palisades thrusting themselves upward like those along the Hudson." She thought the garden lovely with "some kind of red flowers blooming" near the white lattice fence, but certainly not comparable to the "glorious florist shops in New York."[20] Then suddenly she experienced a deeper level of awareness.

A "large audacious blue bird" swished by and perched on the edge of the round marble birdbath. "This bird, an exhibitionist. . . . spreading his wings wide to display his beauty." When a squirrel flowed down the trunk of a tree, a flood of yellow warmth poured over her. Her hungry body absorbed the sunshine like a "baba au rhum soaking up its sweet rum sauce." Someone had gone to a lot of trouble to design the bird, the squirrel, the wonders of "sly old lady nature," she mused. But how could they compare with discussions of the latest books, politics, or of the war; would not she die of loneliness here? Still it was lovely, quiet, a place of "unutterable peace."

The longer she looked at one particular tree, the more difficult it became to tear her eyes away; its "alive-ness" drew her into the "non-human" world. "A new perception opened within." The tree appeared to vibrate like "heat waves in the distance," emanating a power that was "almost palpable." Her feet, resting on the solid earth, felt heavy, as if they were taking root. Breathing deeply, she noticed the earth at dusk "smelled of elemental strength and permanence," eternity. "Suddenly I was struck motionless as though laid under a magic spell." The physical world vanished; "some dark uncanny force flowed" between her and the earth, leaving her feeling fecund, wise, loving, and strong, "prepared to face life in the country, marriage—war and even death—with a warm smiling serenity."[21]

When she walked around to the front of the house, the beauty of its facade struck Claire "like a blow in the chest." Built in 1914 by the architect Aymar Embury, II, 280 Livingston was an "etching come to life." She felt utterly undone. A majestic oak threw the shadow of its leaves across its white face. "The portico with its white columns and Ionic capitals, the well-proportioned fan light above the wide door, and the Palladian windows above seemed to be a part of me long submerged."[22] Modeled on the Deming House built in 1793, this white colonial had its roots in Litchfield, Virginia, the state of Claire's maternal forebears.[23] Entering the front door, one was "greeted by a wide hospitality hall that ran from front to back of the house. The living room was well proportioned—I was coming to realize that to sit in an ill-proportioned room actually hurt. There was a gracious fireplace with hand-carved mantle, opposite a long wall of continuous empty bookshelves. In the glassed-in sun room beyond, overlooking the garden with its birdbath, one could be near the trees and shrubs. One could commune with nature."[24]

"It's more expensive than I planned," Thurston told the agent, "but if my beautiful bride wants it I am willing to rent for a year, then we'll see." They stayed at this home for around three years. In 1941, the house next door at 286 Livingston, built in 1916, came available, and they purchased it. It was not so fine architecturally as the one at 280, but the interior better suited their habits. The large white, pillared mansion she had believed as a child was her "birthright" would now be her own. Whenever she wrote of her houses on Livingston, she wrote as if she had lived in the same one for all thirty-two years of her marriage. The houses were inextricably linked in her mind, and if number 280 had a more prestigious architect, number 286 had an impressive history as the one-time residence of Supreme Court Justice William O. Douglas. Time and again she described the Adam-green paneling of the dining room, the graceful sweep of the staircase between the first and second floors. Fortunately, Claire and Thurston shared the same taste in period and style, declaring eighteenth-century England Hepplewhite and Sheraton the most elegant, delicate, and graceful:

> I fell in love with the silky luster, the simplicity and graceful lines of the Hepplewhite sideboard with its inlay of satinwood. The chairs, delicate and feminine yet soundly constructed. Many times, I would sit alone in the living room and watch the red in the oriental carpet leap into new life where a random ray of sunlight touched it. My eyes would caress the graceful curves of the great blue barrel back chairs [and] pass quickly over the rather homely chair that Thursty said fit his behind exactly. On winter nights we always sat before a wood fire listening to Beethoven, Brahms, operas, musicals, or read our books; but we rarely talked. When the maid drew the vast sweeping red draperies, I loved to see the way the firelight lit up the damask

figures here and there. It was all so warm and secure and private—and to my eyes, so beautiful.[25]

From her third-story study window Claire could look out across the trees in the College Square section of East Rock Park, thrill to the drama of the changing seasons, the sunset flashing auburn across the red rock cliff, crowned at its summit with the Soldiers and Sailors Monument, a memorial dedicated in 1887 to New Haven's Civil War Veterans. English Drive wound to the top amid dense forests, ending with a view of the entire city and its harbor off Long Island Sound.[26] The Mill River snaked along the back roads and through the park, connecting the sound to the east with Lake Whitney.

Thurston Owens, who kept his membership in the New York Athletic Club, joined the New Haven Lawn Club founded in 1890, the Scarsdale Golf Club, the New Haven Country Club, and The Quinnipiack Club (the "Q"). The membership list of the Lawn Club read like a who's who of Yale University and New Haven.[27] The "Q" was chartered with twenty members as the "OURS" Club in 1871, and subsequently renamed after the Indian tribe to first settle in the New Haven area. From its inception, and for as long as Thurston Owens was a member, the club was for men only. But Claire probably did not mind; she had her own clubs, her own circle of peers, who often met at the Lawn or the country club. And the "Q" had certain dining rooms women could reserve for special luncheons.[28]

Claire joined the League of Women Voters, the American Association of University Women (AAUW), and several writers' clubs; she remained a member of most of these organizations for the rest of her life, joining others as her interests expanded. Although early in her career she joined the Author's Guild to protect her interests as a writer, she had avoided women's clubs while living in New York. Now in a smaller city, she felt pressured to acquire women's club affiliations. To refuse was to be considered unpatriotic, peculiar; to be different from the majority was considered unthinkable: "You were branded a queer."[29] No longer swimming against the river of public opinion, Claire turned a seeming obligation into an outlet of creative expression.

12. Claire with AAUW members. Photograph courtesy of the TWU Woman's Collection.

During the mid-1940s, as chair of the League of Women Voters Radio Committee, Claire wrote six radio "playlets." These "skits," an early version of today's "political infomercials," focused on civic issues and city politics surrounding the need for a new charter.[30] One sought to raise women's consciousness about their individual right to different political choices from their husbands'; others addressed policies of city government. Although intended to provoke change, they also evoked light humor. Claire did not realize how amusing they were until she heard them read aloud at an AAUW meeting, at which Edith Cook, who had run for mayor, laughed out loud. A minister's wife told her, "Claire you are a bird of paradise in a nest of little brown wrens." With affected modesty, she laughed and replied, "I never thought of myself that way."[31]

Serving on committees in small organizations, she found, not only revealed human nature but also gave insights into the way governments ran: power politics controlled decisions, based more on personalities than on principles. She learned from her affiliations, just as she learned from everything she did. The vestiges of her Bohemian days disappeared with her new, comfortable lifestyle. Now her peers were primarily white, upper- and middle-class, educated women.

The Owenses employed four servants: a gardener, a cook, a chambermaid, and a maid who lived in the room on the third floor, next to Claire's study. Claire had become a "lady": she could administer her domestic responsibilities without having to "lift a finger." Each week she planned the menus, ordered the groceries, and supervised the help. On the cook's day off, she prepared Sunday night supper, which pleased Thurston immensely. He would "gambol about like a happy puppy" while she worked in the kitchen: "You cook everything just the way I like it and yet I feel guilty to have my Southern Lady soil her lily-white hands." She enjoyed his pampering and bringing him pleasure in return. She felt guilty that she did not cook for him more often, but "every atom of her body rebelled against cooking and housework."[32]

Although as a couple they were considerate of one another, and discreet in front of their servants—it was an unwritten law not to disagree in their presence—in the early years they quarreled, usually about trivial matters. One source of their arguments turned out to be Claire's writing: Thurston reacted as a jealous lover. He resented anything that diverted her attention from him. Another source involved Claire's friendship with certain women, especially Marian Murray, the Hartford journalist.[33] But Claire learned to negotiate between her friends and her attentions to her husband. Claire would arrange for Marian Murray and Margaret Daniels, a psychoanalyst from New York City, to visit while Thurston was away on business, offering to pay their train fare and purchase theater or symphony tickets, welcoming her old friends to share her privileged life. They cherished their time together, which Marian called "talk fests."[34]

On March 9, 1938, Coren wrote his "Dear Sister" to inform her, "Mama is looking and feeling much better." She had been staying with him and Ruby in Dallas during a delicate time, but he would drive her back to Temple, to stay with Miss Rolia. He would get her a "Negro woman" until she could get around by herself. Their mother was "his last tie to the old home life" he loved so well. Clearly, Susan Myers was declining; she could no longer grip a pencil to write letters. As for their financial problems, "their affairs," he could work out his own, but not their mother's. If Claire's husband wanted "to help you help Mama," Mama would appreciate it. If not, he understood; he had in-laws himself. Appreciating Owens's kindness toward his sister, Coren did not want to encourage anything that might "impair" her relationship with her new husband.[35]

Claire was not impressed by the way Coren handled their mother's business affairs. In July, she wrote to let him know she was "upset" by his failure to answer her list of questions. Her mother was sick with worry about money. Claire wrote that she and Thurston were "hard pressed," that they had cut down on their expenses and had not gone away for the summer. Thurston had been burned once when Coren lied to them about a bank loan: since Coren could not get credit in Temple, he had his mother sign for him, which meant that if he died suddenly, Susan Myers would have to pay it, and she could not. Obviously, Claire resented his implied assumption that if Coren defaulted, she and Thurston would rescue him. Until he clarified "this situation," the Owenses would not be willing to help Mother, she wrote.[36]

Her letter to her mother indicated that they did take a "little anniversary trip," but they were enduring cutbacks, and she was annoyed with Coren for failing to answer her questions. Mr. Owens would help only after he understood their business affairs sufficiently. As things stood, he was "not willing to pour money into a bucket with a hole in it." Though she surely would never let her starve, she asked her mother to understand they did not see Coren the way she did. "I've lain awake at nights too because I did not feel free to write and ask you to come and live in my home and never to worry again. But of course, no wife's home is entirely her own—if it were things would be different.[37]

Claire understood that, as Adrienne Rich puts it, "for women all privilege is relative."[38] She was free to help, but only in a limited way. "Mr. Owens," as she referred to Thurston in letters, was in charge of the money. Ironically, though living in upper-middle-class ease and elegance, financial autonomy eluded Claire Owens, just as it had eluded Susan Myers.

In October 1938, her mother suffered a third stroke and was not expected to live. Claire was sick with the flu and high fever but insisted on going to Temple. She wanted to fly, but Thurston and her doctor, Paul Vestal, forbade it, so she took the train ride west again, two days and two nights. It would have been easier on her physically to fly, but in the late 1930s, the advantages of air travel were not fully appreciated. During the long trip to Temple, she wondered why she felt so compelled to see her mother one more time alive. "To ask forgiveness for not loving her? To receive her dying blessing? To hear her [mother] ask forgiveness for never having loved her?" It seemed of "vital importance."[39]

Once again, Claire arrived just in time for the funeral. Susan Allen Myers died at 4:50 p.m. Thursday, October 7, 1938, five weeks short of her sixty-ninth birthday. Worn out from nursing her husband and her mother and from trying to manage the declining family funds, exacerbated by the heartache of her son's business problems, she could not hold on to see her daughter one last time. Services were held the following Saturday at three o'clock at the home of her lifelong friend, Mrs. J. K. Campbell, "Miss Rolia," who lived on the Temple-Belton highway. A member of the First Baptist Church since childhood, Susan Myers was honored in an obituary that listed her many accomplishments in civic work in the small Texas community. She was buried beside her husband in the Bruceville-Moore Cemetery on Highway I-35, in a double plot surrounded by a white cement curb. With its gray granite double headstone, the grave resembles a marriage bed, quilted with grass and stones.[40]

"Her death seemed to cut the ground right from under my feet, to sever all ties to the past; I was grateful to have a loving husband and beautiful home to return to. My mother, however, was still alive to me after her death."[41] Like an apparition she appeared in Claire's bedroom every night, a "frightening" period. To her dismay she found herself calling on all the elderly ladies in the neighborhood, as if trying to connect with her mother through establishing bonds with women of that generation. But this brought little comfort, for it "seemed unnatural and unhealthy" though her efforts "lasted a whole year."[42]

Claire kept track of the family estate from a distance, while Coren took control of the holdings. In January 1939, Miss Rolia wrote a letter bringing Claire up to date on the status of several properties and debts owned by the Myers estate, payments on rental properties or on bank notes Mr. Myers had carried. Most of the renters and debtors were black, longtime residents of the small-town community. When banks would not give them credit, Coren Lee Myers would. One by one, Rolia investigated each business matter and reported its status. She refused the Owenses' generous invitation to visit them in Connecticut despite her loneliness: "Oh Clairene I feel now I stand alone," she wrote in one of her letters.[43]

In March, Claire's Aunt Laura Griffin expressed her grief over Susan's death; whenever she tried to write, her efforts "dissolved in tears."[44] She expressed joy that Claire had such a fine husband and thanked Claire for sending mementoes of Susan's life.

Thurston indeed loved and cared for Claire. He willingly lent his business acumen regarding the remnants of the family estate. In later years, Coren and Claire corresponded about the status of Grandmother Allen's property, the old farm.[45] Based on comparable property in the area, Coren estimated it to be worth about ten dollars an acre. "Because there is no road to it—and not fit for anything but to run a few cows. . . . I am quite sure that there will never be oil on it in your life time or mine." He suggested that she could get out of paying taxes if they joined in a deed to his daughter, Sue Allen. Claire was "glad to give Sue Allen my share of the land Grandmother Allen left me . . . if you will keep up the taxes. If she ever gets rich from this land then she can make me a little present."[46] Claire could afford to be generous when she chose.

Although her life seemed perfect to observers on the outside, many sources of conflict lay behind closed doors. For one thing, Claire had an immediate and profound reaction to rumblings preceding the Second World War. For another, she spent years agonizing about her failure to attain success with publishers; and finally, she seemed predisposed to frequent vexing, if not serious, illnesses.

In early September 1939, as the Owenses returned from the seashore hotel north of Boston where they had spent the summer "swimming, eating elaborate food, dressing for dinner every night except Sunday," Claire turned on the car radio just as the newscaster announced that "England had declared war on Germany because Hitler had invaded Belgium [*sic*]."[47] She became so agitated and sick at heart that Thurston turned off the radio. At home, she hung on to every word, closing the bedroom door so as not to disturb her sleeping husband. When Paris fell to the Germans in 1940, she "took to her bed, ill," horrified that all she had loved about Paris—symbol of Western civilization, the arts capital of the world—could be destroyed.[48]

Similarly, Claire reacted on a personal level when the Nazis began to bomb Britain in the summer of 1940. "I felt as though my mother and father and all my ancestors were being attacked. England was our mother country; all of America's culture, literature, derived from Britain." Reading war accounts in the morning papers, she would choke back tears, responding to this war in much the same way she had responded to the First World War while living in Alabama. Many of her friends overseas, "guiltless and helpless, showed stamina, good humor, courage, a fundamental nobility." She felt the least she could do was send them bundles of clothing and food.[49]

Unlike many women of her generation, Claire struggled to maintain a balance between love and work. In her 1940 letter to Burton Rascoe, she alluded to the restrictive nature of her marriage, asking him not to phone or wire her but to write her. "My family prefers to ignore all my writing activities."[50] Since her only family was Thurston, she made sure her writing did not intrude on their time together. She kept her discomfort about such limits to herself. Once Thurston told her,

"I don't like for you to write. It takes you away from me. But if you don't write you aren't happy and if you aren't happy you are not so good to me so I have to allow you to write."

"Allow," I thought, but said nothing.[51]

Pushing her feminist compulsions for freedom aside, she opted to preserve her marriage; it gave her leisure and intellectual freedom to write without worrying about finances. But privilege often has its price; as Roxanne Gay has put it, "privilege is relative and contextual."[52]

Nevertheless, with her study on the third floor and four servants minding the house, Claire could easily coordinate her writing time with Thurston's travel time, and their life was fairly harmonious. But she missed New York. Although happily married with a "beautiful home" she wrote Rascoe, "I sometimes feel that I'm drowning in a provincial sea of church-goers and bridge players and country clubbers. And alas, most of the University men here who're interested in the things I care about are Oscar Wildes—without the wit," implying they were effeminate, if not gay.[53]

Determined to get "Belle Randolph"/"Sons and Husbands" published, she had reconnected with her old editor in hopes of finding a new one. Without using the word menopause, she claimed that for the last five years she had been waging a battle royal with "old lady nature." In the last year, she had gotten the "upper hand." Despite her physical concerns, Claire wrote daily from nine to one. She had written five complete, separate drafts of "Sons and Husbands," she told Rascoe, "hardly living for anything but this book these last five years."[54]

She wrote endless fan letters to writers she admired: Pearl S. Buck, to offer comfort after an attack by critics of *This Proud Heart*, and Van Wyck Brooks, praising his *Oliver Allston*. To Buck, she opined, critics of *This Proud Heart* had missed two points she illustrated so well: "how most men, particularly husbands, do everything in their power to discourage a woman's creative work," and her convincing portrayal of the "passion and joy the woman artist feels while under the hypnotic spell of her work."[55]

Writing to successful writers made Claire feel a part of the writing community while she struggled to "make it" herself. Usually she included descriptions of her own projects, offers to send copies of *The Unpredictable Adventure*, queries for advice. She asked Van Wyck Brooks "in strictest confidence" if he thought Dutton wanted "merely good commercial best-sellers" for their Jefferson Prize contest or something with "literary pretensions," as she prepared to enter her "Belle Randolph" manuscript.[56]

That same year she typed a journal entry reflecting on the state of literature, worried that it had become too political. Many popular writers, it seemed to her, had aligned with communism as a way of standing against Hitler's fascism, naming Ernest Hemingway, John Dos Passos, John Steinbeck, Clifford Odets, and Dorothy Thompson. "Even Thomas Wolfe had gone political-minded and cast literature, individualism and beauty to the winds." Thomas Mann, in a speech at Yale, argued that "writers and intellectuals must enter politics." Claire worried about this trend; everything in her "rose up against" it. She had not "lost interest in social problems," but felt "too ignorant" of social movements and political corruption to use them as material.[57]

And she did not want to learn! She wanted to stay focused on the political aspects of male-female relationships, foreshadowing the feminist mantra of the 1970s, "the personal *is* the political." "Sons and Husbands" was a novel of sexual politics no matter how she defined it. But she feared that she was too old and that her writing would seem "1920s-ish." She tried to reassure herself, saying "that if you write anything good enough, vital enough, interesting enough, the subject doesn't matter a damn. People will read it. I believe this intellectually but emotionally where despair resides, I felt I was to be a double failure in my writing and the dream of my whole life would be a mockery."[58]

She compared her literary inventory to offering flowers on the market only to discover there was no market for flowers; that "people wanted to buy bombs and guns—politics." Still, preparing "Sons and Husbands" for submission to Max Perkins at Scribner must have boosted her energy, for she wrote Rascoe that she felt "that old exultation and joy" of writing.[59] Perkins evidently did not like the book; two years later she pulled out the manuscript to revise it. This time for inspiration, she turned to her one published book.

On September 4, 1942, Claire recorded in her journal that she had just reread the first seventy-five pages of her *Unpredictable Adventure.* "It's wonderful! Full of wisdom, wit, and poetry. . . . Sophistica—is superb! Audacious—wise—witty—kind." It seemed as much a classic as Samuel Butler's *Erewhon*, which she had been reading that week. She agreed with the criticism that it lacked direct description of people or places but, she thought, "Doesn't the reader accept the author's way of doing it like we accept Conrad's way of writing *Lord Jim*?" In short, she was proud of the book, pleased with her effort: "I wrote this book out of my inner self—it's what I really think without regard for what anyone in the whole world might think or say! It's so much better than I thought . . . Surely I can't be wrong this time."[60]

"God, it makes me sick to despair that I must live among people who are incapable of appreciating such a book." Not only the people in New Haven, but all communities outside New York City. Of course, she realized that there were isolated people all over the United States who would and could appreciate it if they knew it existed—"but I can't find them and they can't find my book. All I can do is possess my soul in impatience and hope and pray and wait for the day when someone like a Reader's Club will revive it."[61]

In the last year or two, in the face of numerous rejections, she hit rock bottom and had given up her lifelong dream of being not only a successful writer—meaning recognized by the "good critics"—but a "genuinely fine dignified important writer." Doubting herself, she doubted her book, even "doubted Burton Rascoe's judgment and Doubleday's in publishing it." But rereading *The Unpredictable Adventure* reminded her that she was "a writer and a damned good one." For forty-five years she had been "surer than sure" of her destiny; now at forty-six, she would take up her third novel, which she renamed "Belle Jefferson," and start to revise it for Dutton's Thomas Jefferson contest.[62]

At this time, she also began a fourth novel centered around her domestic life—integrating descriptions of decorating and furnishing her home—which seemed to develop a "personality of its own, it came alive like a child." Like the persona in Anne Sexton's poem "Housewife," Claire became like the women who "marry houses" and wear them like "another kind of skin."[63] She often referred to this house as the first she could call her own, reflecting the lack of ownership she had felt in the home she tried to create with George Wanders. But why did she become so obsessed with material things? What was she trying to accomplish by throwing herself into the role of "housewife?" Had she forgotten the bitter attitude she expressed while writing "Gaily Bedight" regarding the unearned privileges of the fashionable New York housewives riding the Fifth Avenue bus?

Perhaps her motives were unconscious. With the death of her father, grandmother, and mother, Claire felt cut off from her roots. Her sense of rebellion became entangled in her struggle with grief; her lifelong quest for parental approval, unfinished—and unfinishable. She sought resolution through an unconscious drive to recreate the state of grace she had abandoned in her youthful flight from home. Becoming obsessed with the house displaced her need for parental approval because she was essentially living in a way that her parents would have found admirable. In the end, as Sexton's poem concludes, "The woman is her mother,/ That's the main thing." Her new life might have been the "good life" but it was not necessarily good for her fiction.

The protagonist of "Mrs. Oppidan" is a composite of Claire and her mother, an archetypal housewife fashioned like an icon for the popular women's magazines of the 1940s. While this novel of manners does not employ anagrams, "Oppidan" functions as a satirical anagram of the expression *p' in a pod*.[64] Mrs. Oppidan, who never receives a first name, mirrors every upper-class housewife at the time, nestled in the protective "pod" of home, servants, and affluent husbands. The material is straight out of the Owenses' life together. This time Cape Coverture is located in New Haven.

How like Claire to embrace the life of a typical housewife, and then write a book making fun of that lifestyle. One editor wrote that the "title was too sarcastic for so sincere a book." Whereas few readers would think to unscramble the name, given that it is the only anagram used, the author's sincere tone implies approval of Mrs. Oppidan's perfectionist approach to maintaining the home and garden, her intense preoccupation with decorating the house, entertaining guests, and managing servants. This woman's enemies are sunlight, which fades expensive rugs and upholstery, vacuum cleaners run by careless maids who chip polished table legs, tarnish on silver, parasites on plants, dust, dirt, and more efficient housewives.

While such musings may be mildly interesting provided they do not take up too many pages, a novel that centers on such mundane themes lacks tension and significance without a sense of larger purpose. Set in 1941–42 in New Haven, this novel attempts to capture the effect of World War II on patriotic, educated, affluent Americans. What little tension exists derives from the war.

The author's special talent to observe male-female relationships and the politics of domesticity emerges amid the tangled banalities of everyday life. Brought up in the southern tradition, Mrs. Oppidan knows how to listen to men admiringly, but secretly wonders "why women considered everything about men's professions interesting while men considered everything about women's (domestic) professions dull—unless it was humorous." At dinner parties, men laugh at women's comments "in that indulgent masculine tone—the peculiar gift of all husbands." "Apparently all husbands preferred for their wives to turn to *them* for information. It must be a great burden."[65] Secretly she was amused at the human undercurrents that ran beneath the smooth surface of polite social intercourse.

LeBaron R. Barker Jr., editor-in-chief at Doubleday, called to say he liked the book. "It has all the promise of a best seller," but when he described the required revisions, Claire's intuition told her "they will never publish it." He turned the manuscript over to a "brilliant young editor," whom Claire described as "just out of Vassar and hot on left wing politics."[66]

She thought that Owens's "sketch of a happy, adjusted married woman" showed potential popularity, inviting women to say, "Why, Mrs. Oppidan is just like me!" But she advised her to tone down the raptures and "tighten the narrative."[67]

"Like an idiot," Claire tried and "ruined the manuscript forever."[68] Apparently, she was right, for the novel never saw print, nor did she make further attempts to publish it.

As the war continued, news reports concerning Hitler's treatment of Jews, rumors of his efforts toward a "final solution," grew increasingly terrifying for Claire. She became obsessed with the growing sense that something evil had been released, and she had no control over its spread. She felt her "heart bleed for all Jews on earth." One day an acquaintance, a talented painter, invited her to lunch. The artist confessed in a whisper that she considered Hitler to represent the second coming of Christ. "I felt I had entered a demented realm; I fled from the place in terror."[69]

When the war ended, she reflected that she never doubted that America, with all its influence and technology, would win; but the war for men's minds frightened her. The theater of war, of governments, seemed like a farce. In Claire's opinion, Hitler died a coward in the arms of his mistress; Mussolini died a coward as well. Claire's passionate reaction to the evil unleashed by Nazism and Fascism, perpetrated by two grand-scale bullies, on the one hand, and the bombing of Hiroshima and Nagasaki by America on the other, shook the foundations of her life. "Is this what you call civilization?" she raged, appalled by "the baseness to which [mankind] could descend." She believed that the male sex—those who run the world and make the wars—had let her down.[70]

In truth, despite rationing and minor inconveniences, life went on as usual, a paradox. The war years for the Owenses were prosperous. The best thing about wealth, Claire noted, was that it made it possible to lift the mundane in daily life to the level of art. Thurston gave her a generous allowance, enough to live graciously and still make contributions to her college and other organizations. "Never tell me what you pay for your dresses; I might think it too much," Thurston insisted. But he could tell. Once Claire bought a dinner dress for three hundred dollars, "extremely simple, but the wool was a beautiful, unusual weave." Feeling guilty, she bought another one for fifty dollars. When she wore the expensive dinner dress Thurston said, "Well you must have paid a pretty penny for that." When she put on the fifty-dollar one, he said, "Where did you get that thing, at the five and dime store?"[71]

They found equal pleasure in purchasing items of quality. Both enjoyed handling the swatches of fine wool Thurston's tailor sent from New York. While she had never cared for jewelry, considering it "silly and expensive," she often found herself turning her "diamond engagement ring in the light, watching it reflect all the colors of the rainbow. Perhaps I was wrong; perhaps there was a secret about jewels that caused the world to love and be fascinated by them." Many years later she learned that in religious meditation, seekers often beheld jeweled objects to stimulate their transcendence to a higher realm. Aldous Huxley considered the reason "precious stones are precious" is because jewels are the "objects in the natural world which most nearly resemble things which are seen with the inner eye by those who have the gift of vision. And even those who don't consciously have the gift of vision, seem to have an unconscious inkling of it."[72]

At the time, however, Claire felt a "little guilty" spending so much time, money, and effort on clothes and grooming, but she excused herself by saying she did it to please her husband who loved for her to dress well. She came to realize clothes could create drama and beauty. To simplify the hassle of shopping, she purchased all her clothes in New York, primarily at Jay Thorpe's, where their stylist seemed to design "dresses just for [her] figure—tall and slender with small breasts." Each trip, she would purchase four or five dresses after trying on thirty. For years she had the "same pleasant clerk" who doted on her, saying, "Now Mrs. Owens, you look tired. Sit down and put up your feet; I'll take off your shoes and bring you a cup of tea."[73] Fashion was queen in post-war New York; many of the women who walked along Fifth Avenue were "works of art. Beautifully dressed, perfectly groomed," vibrating with vitality, health, and confidence. And for Claire, hats, especially red or pink ones, were special works of art. All of her formal portraits, and many informal snapshots, show Claire in a favorite, elegant hat. Often, a man would approach her and say, "May

I just have a closer look at your hat; I've never seen anything like it." Whenever she wore red, both men and women stopped to tell her how lovely she looked.[74]

Life with Thurston was filled with luxury; but there were problems between them, sources of tension. The eternal power struggle between man and woman Claire believed arose as a result of their differences in temperament. "Whenever we approached an intersection where there was no traffic light and each driver had equal right-of-way, Thurston would slow down; the other driver assumed this was a courteous signal to go ahead. Then instantly Thurston would dash ahead and cross in front of the other car."[75] Claire used a subtle, psychological approach to resolve her irritation at his habit. She asked him to tell her more about his childhood. He admitted to always being the smallest boy in the group, feeling powerless. Claire determined that his dangerous driving evinced psychological compensation for his "deprived" childhood as the "poor little rich boy." A large car substituted for his small person. She used her perceptions with utmost discretion, disciplined herself never to mention her insights, but realized truth in the old cliché: to understand all was to forgive all. She felt sympathy instead of anger.[76]

Thus, Claire developed a strategy for making their marriage work: listening, understanding, and probing for their source led Thurston to deal with his shortcomings himself. Thurston, "his own worst enemy," hid his virtues beneath cool indifferent silence or perverse sarcasm. He was generous at finding positions for young men but only if they "sat at his feet." Otherwise he was rude. A baffling combination of refinement and coarseness, his faults detracted from his virtues. While he had the fine gift of artistic discrimination in the arts, which made him an interesting person, he only seemed relaxed with their good friends, Ina and Paul Vestal, Lucy and Torval Hammer, Peggy and Gideon Florian. And, of course, the Gelatt family. Otherwise, the very presence of others aroused his hostility.

Thurston's attitude was paradoxical, for while he did not seem to care for people, he loved to entertain. Uncomfortably shy at small dinner parties, he would sit mute until Claire helped get him started:

"'Thursty did you tell so and so about that funny incident last week?' And he'd be off and running. He loved to relate stories of his grandfather who filled his country home every summer with musicians and artists he had met in Europe."[77] Giving a dinner party was like staging a play, Claire believed. The props—flowers, food, service, conversation—must be perfect, the scenery beautiful; the hostess, a director skillful at making each guest appear at their best. When the guests left she was always ready to collapse with fatigue but filled with the "great sweetness" of giving.

Her marriage to Owens brought privilege, grace, and comfort, the "good life" she had dreamed about, but not without consequences. Although Claire found herself enmeshed in the trappings of privilege she had fled in her youth, she never fully embraced this new life. Rather, she held herself apart and questioned society's tyrannical hold over women using the allure of material values. "Why did I need three closets full of clothes? I was sick to death of straining every nerve to wear the latest fashion . . . the competition and rivalry among women was idiotic. Why in the name of common sense did we allow this invisible monster—society—to tyrannize our lives? Material things determined our social status, not our characters, brains, talents. How ridiculous; how false."[78]

She chastised herself for allowing her husband to heap expensive clothes, jewels, and furs on her, to praise her female attributes extravagantly, and to tell her she was beautiful and good in bed. "He praises you as a sex object. Yet he never reads your books or articles, never reads your fan letters, resents you going up to your study to write, . . . prevents you from developing into a whole human being—keeping you in a luxurious cage where you cannot try your wings. He even sings you the old song about the bird in the gilded cage."[79]

Was it his fault or hers, she wondered? Or was it the fault of this patriarchal society that objectifies women? Reflections in her "Autobiography" suggest that, angry with herself, she projected anger toward all women who, whether as a result of biology or custom, place too high a value on love. "Byron the poet was right: 'To men, love is a thing apart; it is woman's whole existence.'"[80]

13. Claire and Thurston Owens in London. Photograph courtesy of the TWU Woman's Collection.

In the spring of 1946, Thurston and Claire went to Europe—the second overseas trip of their marriage. They traveled to Germany, Holland, France, Italy, and England, sensitive to the ways post-war Europeans perceived Americans. Italians and Germans were "defensive at first," the French "indifferent," the English "insolent and condemning" but would "walk a block to show us where we wanted to go." In short, they felt "startled" to be hated for being Americans.[81]

Claire enjoyed moderate success writing short "featurettes" for *Today's Woman* magazine, first as Claire Myers Alexander and later substituting Owens for the surname.[82] The short articles, household-management tips grounded in current psychological theories, offered such advice as ways to keep tabs on guests' food preferences and special interests, and how to take criticism from spouses. She frequently contributed to the *New Ocean House Daily News*, the newsletter for a large "swank" hotel in the resort town of Swampscott, Massachusetts, where the Owenses often summered.[83] Her letters to the editor periodically appeared in the *Saturday Review of Literature*, though never the articles she tirelessly submitted. *Publishers Weekly* printed another piece, this one featuring the Channel Bookshop of New Haven and its print library.[84]

As a couple, the Owenses appeared on the Society page of the *New Haven Register* in announcements of parties, both as guests and as hosts. Their impressive guests included New Haven's most influential residents, such as Dr. Louise Ames, a child psychologist, and Dr. Paul Vestal, their physician, and his wife, Ina, all dear friends. In December 1946, the Owenses hosted a cocktail party at the Biltmore Hotel in New York City for Claire's longtime friend Lady Glen-Coats of Scotland, who returned to New Haven as a guest in their home; Mrs. Owens hosted a luncheon in her honor at the "Q" club.[85] A December 30 article in the *New Haven Evening Register* carried the headline, "Politics in Scotland Draw Women Workers. Lady Glen-Coats, Liberal Leader, Gives Her Views." The article stressed politics affecting middle- and upper-class women in Scotland regarding equal pay and post-war rationing.

Friends duly feted the Owenses as well. A Washington Society page announced an "after six" in their honor, hosted by Major General and Mrs. H. K. Rutherford and their "beauteous" daughter, Dorothy Anne. "The attractive authoress and her husband" would soon return to Connecticut, adding, "the lovely 'Claire' admits to having at least five *noms des plumes*."[86]

Claire did not take her social connections lightly, nor did she relate superficially with her acquaintances. A long letter to Dorothy Anne Rutherford following their visit prompted the eligible socialite on marital expectations. For a woman living such a conventional life, the advice to her would-be protégée proved highly unconventional and self-revealing.[87] Assuming the role of an Aunt Sophistica, Claire instructed Dorothy Anne on the differences between a lover and a husband: "Look around you and study the marriages of the women you admire [and] you will observe that . . . superior intellectual women seldom marry men who correspond in type to themselves." Nature was not interested in happy marriages, and was, in fact, against them. Children who are too brilliant and too sensitive to adapt to their environments result when a couple is alike in their strengths and weaknesses. She advised Dorothy not to expect too much of men or marriage lest she be "hurt—deeply" and to marry a man who is not an "improved edition" of herself. Men can love women who are their inferiors; women must learn to do the same. Choosing a mate was different from choosing a lover. A lover can be a soul mate; but a husband may not be. The grand passions must be experienced outside marriage—as she had experienced with her "German"—but will not necessarily make for a good marriage. She must have trusted this young woman to expose herself so openly, but her philosophical advice seems narrow, cynical. And where did her relationship to Thurston fit in her letter of advice?

With Yale University nearby, the Owenses frequented lectures and performances; Claire took courses "coming and going!" in the graduate school "not for an advanced degree because I didn't want to get into the academic style of writing."[88] Her quest for knowledge was insatiable, especially self-knowledge. On September 22, 1948, Claire took a Rorschach test. The psychogram, or analysis of her responses, profiled her as extremely intelligent, equally introverted and extroverted, with a tendency toward perfectionism. Her inner creative drives, at the time of the test, were being suppressed in order to adapt to her current living situation. The psychogram, like the palmist's report when Claire was fifteen, uncovered a "bundle of contradictions." As an adult she was still adaptable, yet reactive and emotional; she held a strong interest in herself, yet was not egocentric; and her sexual reactions were subtle.[89] She seemed to have sublimated her sexuality to her middle-class values. Betraying her youthful spirit, had she begun to value the seen more than the unseen?

Newspaper articles, often accompanied by pictures, described Claire's widely varied community activities. In April 1949, Claire hosted the literature and art department's meeting of the AAUW and moderated a Quiz the Experts program.[90] In November 1949, Lady Glen-Coats returned to New Haven and spoke to the local AAUW, addressing the aesthetic and the political life of women in Scotland.[91]

Claire often noticed that attractive young women took an instant dislike to her, especially those she met in her work with women's clubs. She longed to meet a woman who was "younger, prettier, wealthier and wittier"—then there would be no cause for animosity or jealousy. Thus, when Ina Vestal rang her doorbell one day during Claire's first few years in New Haven, she was charmed to meet "another Southern woman," who like herself had lost her southern accent. Ina, an omnivorous reader and collector of first and limited editions, was from Kentucky. An aristocrat and intellectual, she had read and loved Claire's first novel and other publications. She was the first person who came to their home, walked around and looked at their books. Claire felt she had met a kindred spirit. "After all, our books were the most important thing in our house and most people did not see them."[92]

They spent many wonderful days at Ina's house looking at books—a larger collection than her own. "Fortunately, Ina had flirted with Thursty and he admired her greatly." Their husbands met and became close friends; the foursome spent many happy hours dining and traveling together. Whenever the Owenses went away for the summer, they invited the Vestals to visit; Paul became their physician as well as their friend.

But trouble gradually developed between them as Ina's actions betrayed her jealousy of Claire's writing career. During a lunch visit, Ina "belittled" her in a way that had become habitual, placing Claire in a dilemma. "I could not live with myself if I retorted in anger, but could not allow her to insult me. I didn't know how to handle the situation with dignity and wisdom."[93] That particular day, she fled the restaurant and walked home.

In the fall of 1949, their unacknowledged feud would escalate to a treacherous level with Ina's overt act of betrayal intended to jeopardize Claire's professional writing career. This personal altercation with a trusted friend, in conjunction with Claire's deeply troubled response to World War II, erupted into a conflict that would, ultimately, have a profound effect on Claire, her life, her unresolved mother issues, and the focus of her writing.

12

Awakening—Discovery of the Self

1949–1963

For what is despair but a living death?

—Claire Myers Owens, *Awakening to the Good*

ON CHRISTMAS MORNING OF 1949, Claire came down to breakfast feeling depressed and hopeless. Four years after the victory of the allied forces, her incredulity over the savagery of World War II lingered. For several months she had been confined to her bed with a mysterious illness that wracked her body with pain and plagued her with insomnia, but which doctors were unable to diagnose or cure. The impact of the betrayal by her friend Ina Vestal exacerbated her desolation and despondency.

In October, Ina and Paul Vestal invited Claire and Thurston to their home for dinner in honor of Thurston's seventieth birthday. During the party, Ina confided that she had written a letter to the editors of *Today's Woman* magazine attacking Claire's credibility as a columnist. The evening celebration ruined, the Owenses left in a state of disbelief.

Subsequently, Ina gave Claire a copy of the letter: "It's the act of an enemy," Thurston said as he read it. "If you had to depend on the money you make from your writing . . . this sort of attack might be a real tragedy." Ina's unmitigated cruelty seemed impossible to understand because Claire felt she had been a loyal friend to Ina for over ten years.[1]

"I wish with all my heart that I could help you to realize your own unusual virtues and attractiveness,"[2] Claire wrote Ina on December 2, 1949, suggesting that her treacherous act was motivated by jealousy. Or perhaps the source of Ina's animosity lay more on the surface: Ina confessed that she found Claire's conflicted attitude toward the Jewish people offensive. After years of friendship, Ina admitted to Claire that she had kept hidden her Jewish heritage. Claire wrote Ina: "Let me hasten to say . . . if you had told me years ago that you were a full blooded Jewess or half or one quarter Jewish, it would not lessen my affection . . . one iota. . . . Perhaps I have taken the wrong attitude [about Jews]." But, she assured, Ina's heritage could never alter the Owenses' affection; only her actions, "unworthy of so fine a character," lowered their esteem.[3]

Somehow, over the next twenty years the Vestals and the Owenses reconciled their differences. Despite their elitism, neither Claire nor Thurston could be considered bigots. Both had been profoundly outraged by the Nazi's mass murder of the Jewish people. Claire had reacted viscerally when she heard Hitler's ranting on the radio in the 1930s. If Claire had any anti-Semitic feelings, they were vestiges of her childhood and reflected her belief in stereotypes owing to cultural differences. Indeed, Claire formerly left a lunch outing with an artist friend because the woman made an anti-Semitic remark. Perhaps Ina's slander attempted to retaliate against remarks Ina considered prejudicial toward the Jewish people. Or perhaps Ina's duplicity erupted as jealousy, as Claire believed. Somehow Claire found a way to mitigate her sense of betrayal, but the breach of trust between them at this time left her ravished with grief.[4]

For Claire, the state of humanity and the state of this personal friendship pointed to the moral and ethical deterioration of society. She tried to solve these "two very serious problems" with her rational mind, as science prescribed. But neither science nor reason, nor any sophisticated theory, could help her find a way to overcome her sense of hopelessness. She did not want to live in an "innately evil" world.

Claire could find no way to deal with her suffering; but eventually "an act of nature" lifted her from the depths of despair and catapulted her into a new sense of values, a new way of living, and ultimately a new way of writing that allowed her to own herself as a woman and claim her stories as truth rather than fiction.[5]

To camouflage her depressed state on Christmas morning 1949, she showered, put on lipstick, a red-and-gold housecoat, tied a red ribbon around her hair, and slowly descended the staircase. When Thurston saw her approach, he rose from the dining room table, gallantly drew out her chair; even after twelve years of marriage, she noted, he behaved with decorum. They kissed good morning and wished one another Merry Christmas. She intentionally averted her eyes from the New York paper the maid had placed beside her husband's plate; Thurston invariably urged her not to read it until after breakfast. Headlines turned food into a "hard cold lump, made her heart race." Her reactions to world events upset her digestion and his concentration on the day's business. She took every world issue as a personal responsibility.[6]

She rang for the cook and second maid. Thurston distributed the envelopes of Christmas money and the gifts lying under the small tree. Joy and laughter prevailed. The maid brought in hot cakes, which Claire smothered with "good ole Texas molasses." She tasted them; they had no flavor. The syrup, like life itself, had lost its sweetness. When Thurston passed her the morning paper, he felt safe from worry for this one day, at least. "No world catastrophes this morning to devastate you," he said.[7]

She smiled at him, but stared "incredulously" at the banner headline: "'Peace on earth, good will toward men.' How dare they?" she thought. Such hypocrisy struck her as tragic, ironic. "There was no peace anywhere and even less good will. Hatred filled the air of half the nations of the globe like poison gas."[8] Grief stricken, she could feel her body go limp. She had reached her breaking point. She wanted privacy so she would not collapse and disgrace herself in front of her husband and servants.

Feeling a "thousand years old," she held on to the banisters and pulled herself up the stairs to her "little sanctuary" on the third floor, with the window that overlooked East Rock and the park. Fumbling with the lock, she entered and "fell like a dead weight onto the old blue couch where in happier days" she had lain to correct her typed manuscripts. Today she lay "face down," drowning in "waves of desolation." Deeper and deeper she sank through the fathomless black waters of defeat, on the verge of losing consciousness. "Now I knew I was dying! I did not care." Unable to resist the "horrible cessation of sweet life. . . . [the] terrifying nothingness. . . . Minutes, hours, a thousand years passed. . . . Time became timeless."[9]

Claire was right in assuming that she was dying. Although she had no language to describe the phenomenon at the time, after years of reading and searching she would come to understand that what died was not her entire personality, but her conscious, rational faculty. The "death of the ego"—as Carl Gustav Jung called it—a process essential to spiritual rebirth or psychological awakening, stills the conscious mind so that the soul can speak.

That Christmas day, the reverberations of Claire's plunge into a "living death" would resonate in her lifelong quest for self. But in that moment, her journey of self-discovery, begun at age twenty or even before, shifted in scope, quality, and focus.

Claire had not yet read Carl Jung's description of the ego drowning in the collective unconscious. Nevertheless, the metaphors she employed to describe the occurrence—her Great Awakening—echoed Jung's theories:

> Suddenly I lost all awareness of my body, the room, the time and place. I beheld before me a realistic image of the ocean. I could see myself . . . sinking down, down into the dark waters until I struck bottom . . . I was too ignorant to know that the ocean was a psychological symbol of the unconscious. . . . Finally without effort on my part, I was floated back up to the surface . . . from the deep sea of oblivion. The waves seemed to fling me back physically onto the shores of consciousness. It was so real, so violent that I examined my body for black and blue bruises, surprised that none were visible.[10]

In future writings, whenever Claire related this event, she stressed the inherent violence she had felt. Unlike dreams or fantasies, these moments felt real on a physical level.[11] But how to describe in concrete language that which is ineffable, indescribable? This would become her task, her obsession, and her salvation, defining a project that would shape her future life and work.

Realizing the catalyst for the event was despair and suffering over evil—personal in Ina's betrayal and political in world events—she began to search for "the good in the universe—if any" in humankind's inner nature. Were there such things as a "deathless hierarchy of ethical values," an infallible inner guide to right and wrong, a universal sense of morality, an Ultimate Reality?[12] The search without led to a deeper search within. To discover the innate good in the human spirit, she would learn to search within herself for "intrinsic good—if any."[13]

After years of study, she came to understand that when her conscious mind "surrendered its tyranny," her deepest unconscious released, unhampered. The resolutions she sought answered questions of spirit rather than mind. Penetrating the difference between the two realms became part of her lifelong quest, one that began that day just six weeks prior to her fifty-fourth birthday and continued for the next thirty-three years.

Religious and psychological, this quest would test the limits of her intellect—of all human knowledge—and bring her face to face with some of the greatest psychological, spiritual, and ethical seekers of the twentieth century. That Christmas morning marked the end of her former self and foreshadowed the beginning of a new Claire—Claire Myers Owens. From that day forward, she stopped experimenting with her name and identity and began experiencing the nature of the human soul.

Every morning for the next four months she lay on the blue couch in her study and relived all the most beautiful inner experiences of her life: some twenty incidents she called "small ecstasies," beginning with her Sufi-like dance in the wind at age ten, and including the locust tree on the college campus, the soap bubbles on the hillside in Alabama, the white bird flying over the New York skyline in the blizzard, the sun and sand on the Long Island beach, and the rivers of light.

This was a time of intense, joyous inward reflection, which she shared with no one lest she be thought insane. She could not make sense of the phenomena; rather than discovering her own innate good, or even good in the universe, she came to believe that her altered states "intimated the existence of some transcendent power."[14]

Finally one morning in May, shortly before leaving on vacation, Claire sat at her desk, oblivious to everything—the study, her body, the furniture, the white rain slanting across the windows:

> Suddenly the entire room was filled with a great golden light, the whole world was filled with nothing but light. . . . and my own small kernel of the self. The ordinary "I" ceased to exist. Nothing of me remained but a mere nugget of consciousness. It felt as if some vast transcendent force was invading me without my volition, as if all the immanent good lying latent within me began to pour forth in a stream, to form a moving circle with the universal principle. . . . It was a mystical moment of union with the mysterious infinite, with all things, all people. It was a confrontation with Ultimate Reality, an overwhelming indescribable experience, the ecstasy so intense it was unbearable, the rapture so sweet it was ineffable.[15]

She was reborn, "washed clean and pure like a sea shell by the mighty tides of the sea" as her "ego drowned in boundless being" and all fear vanished. She could not say how long her blissful state lasted; suddenly she returned to consciousness, disoriented, as if she'd traveled to a strange distant country.

Years later in descriptions of this same event, she recalled a sense of resisting the force or pull of the golden light, which she fought "because no one wants to lose their identity." She stressed the experience as being at once transcendent and immanent, simultaneously merging with and being penetrated by the light, resulting in ecstasy unlike any other—"love, romance, marriage, art": a confrontation with Ultimate Reality. This "mystical moment of union with the cosmic principle" created oneness with the "mysterious infinite, with all things, all people." The encounter left her with "no choice but to believe in a supreme impersonal power." She had experienced it.

Intuitive insights into the nature of things flashed before her. She felt like an "all-seeing god penetrating the secrets of the universe": The cosmic scheme of the universe was good; all people possess the potential for innate goodness. She understood the meaning of the unity of all things. Time and space ceased to exist. She could see back through the centuries, the human race struggling to find light, truth. She saw into the future, mankind gradually awakening to the good, creating a "utopia in some sweet tomorrow." Waves of compassion and love for humanity regardless of race, sex, age, or status flooded her heart with the sense of complete oneness with every person and everything on earth.

"Never could I be lonely again. I was now an integral part of the universe, flowing with the universal rhythm. I was filled with unshakable assurance of immortality. There was no death. I would live forever. Fear of life, death, old age, sickness, disaster, and public opinion all fell away. A strange new strength . . . imbued my whole being."

Had the vivid reliving of all the "small ecstasies" of her life precipitated this mysterious rebirth, she wondered? Or was she "queer—or worse—losing [her] mind?" Was this the natural sequence that followed psychological death of the ego, which had occurred in December? If so, then the Awakening had come in two parts: the death in December followed five months later by an equally powerful experience of rebirth. But how was she to understand the phenomena?

"At that time I never had heard of William James's psychological explanation of 'dying to be truly born.' I knew nothing of Carl Jung's . . . 'dissolution of the ego in the collective unconscious' nor of Jean Houston's integral level of the unconscious where religious and mystical experiences occur. I had heard repeatedly as a child that Jesus said, 'unless you (die and) are born again you cannot see the kingdom of heaven.' I had never met anyone who had the faintest conception of its meaning—nor had I—until now."

For eight years, she told no one of this "transforming inner drama," not even her husband. Yet, that day in May, she discovered her own transformation had a transformative effect on others. When she came downstairs after her Awakening, without a word, Thurston, "that taciturn man," went to his desk and wrote kind letters to his two worst enemies in business. The charismatic effect of her Awakening awakened his "true self" as well. "I must have looked extraordinary. They say your face shines like the morning sun. I'd love to have seen what I looked like. I wish I'd gone and looked at myself in a mirror. I didn't have sense enough, but I must have been something."

Claire often claimed, in writings, speeches, and conversations, "Our marriage was revolutionized." Their cook at the time, who was a fine but "exceedingly difficult person became angelic—for one whole month—without a word from me." The love she felt for this "noble Negro cook" and for a "scholarly Jewess in New York" left her "cleansed of racial prejudice forever."

She could feel a physical power flowing through her head, heart, and muscles from somewhere "out there." Some form of energy, not her ego, directed every thought, emotion, and action. It was as if she had been invaded, inhabited by an alien force of goodness. "Christians call it God; scientists call it cosmic energy. I don't think it matters what you call it. What happens is that suddenly to your own amazement, you find yourself selfless."

Her thoughts were for her husband, not for herself. The summer before they had "motored around England." Claire had not enjoyed the trip, but to her surprise, she offered to do it again, since Thurston had enjoyed it so much. Awakening to the good of the universe, she awakened the good within her self, a self she had sought to discover all of her life. "The unenlightened are naturally skeptical of the incredible results of activating the deepest levels of the unconscious. . . . It is above and beyond intellectual comprehension. The actualization of human potentials means becoming what one already is. It is a discovery of one's true self."

Doubt followed certainty. "Why me?" she asked herself. "I felt so unworthy, so humble yet so grateful." Since her early years, Owens compulsively sought intellectual explanations for everything she encountered. Once the shock wore off, she confronted an inexplicable change in herself: her "rational mind rebelled," refusing to accept a spiritual awakening unless verified or validated by reason. So began revitalized research into world religion, philosophy, literature, art, music. She sought explanations in Santayana, Alfred North Whitehead, Bertrand Russell. She reread Whitman, St. Vincent Millay, Dante, Goethe, and Blake. She took comfort in discovering that each had experienced an event of spontaneous self-realization through a mystical moment of higher consciousness. Beethoven documented his awakening in journals and translated it into his symphony *Eroica*. Millay recorded her mystical death and rebirth in her poem "Renascence," which Claire "understood for the first time." The religious literature of the world contained accounts of spontaneous events of cosmic consciousness by their founders: Buddhism, Hinduism, Sufism, Taoism, Christian mysticism, and Hasidic Judaism and all Eastern religions based their beliefs in the intuitive rather than the rational capacities of human spirituality.

Claire's studies of the scientific analysis of mysticism propounded by psychologists brought her to the brink of a new career, a new genre of writing, and into the fold of a community of avant-garde scholars: Carl G. Jung, Abraham Maslow, Aldous Huxley, William Sheldon, Evelyn Underhill, Jean Houston—men and women inventing a language and system of knowledge that ultimately came to be called the New Age.

The painfully slow process, driven by her intellectual impulse to understand in scientific terms this life-altering experience, emerged piece by piece, one clue leading to another, one book at a time. Books seemed to fall into her hands at the precise moment she needed them. Of course, in the 1950s, publications on mysticism, Eastern religions, and spirituality were rare. Transpersonal psychology did not exist as a field; indeed psychic research even in the mid-1970s, twenty-five years after her awakening, was still controversial.[16] Claire Myers Owens was on her own.

Outwardly, Claire did not reveal the nature of this inward journey. As far as her husband and friends were concerned, life continued as usual. Meanwhile, she focused on a separate project that paralleled her search for self-realization, though it would be many years before the two projects could intersect. In October of 1949, just months before her Great Awakening, Claire had begun consulting Dr. Burness E. Moore, a New York psychiatrist who took appointments in New Haven on Mondays. Even he was unaware of her interest in these paranormal experiences. Journal entries record Dr. Moore's unsympathetic regard for Claire's theories on mysticism. Whenever she mentioned the word he seemed "scornful." But she trusted her research; the writings of Carl Jung, William Sheldon, and William James recognized mysticism as a "normal experience of normal people—though not common to all." Even Freud and his followers considered mystical pursuit "normal unless carried too far." Rereading Bertrand Russell, Huxley, Spinoza, and Pascal further validated her perceptions of mysticism as a legitimate field of study and mystical experiences as normal, if rare, psychological phenomena.[17]

Meanwhile, she was going through a period of intense mourning for her parents, especially her mother. Her nerves were on edge; she complained in her journal of the "staggering" effect the unconscious can have on one's body, making it physically ill. Frequent bouts with pain in her urethra and bladder she called "cystitis"; intestinal cramps, twitching legs, vomiting. Rashes on her nose and chin, "disgusting like shingles," lasted from August through December, disappearing around Christmas. Letters passed between her and Dr. Moore. She accused him of overreacting to her symptoms, misdiagnosing her mild neuroses as an extreme mental disorder. She instructed him how to react when he doubted the truth of what she said: to make a note to speak about it later when she felt better, or to check the validity of her claims before disbelieving her.

Dr. Moore prescribed some "little blue pills," sodium amatyl, which let her sleep, but induced bizarre dreams, especially of her mother. Her journal entries following these dreams uncovered buried hostilities. While sitting in a dentist's office, she felt "an extraordinary wave of hatred" when a three-year-old boy climbed up on his mother's lap and caressed her. "I suddenly realized that I HATED MY BROTHER! I had always hated him because I was . . . so jealous when we were babies." She remembered a time when they were playing croquet, and she struggled desperately to win, but at the last moment, Coren defeated her by cheating. "I raised my mallet above his head and felt such hatred I could cheerfully have murdered him." The greatest relief came from realizing that her hostility toward him had nothing to do with his winning the game but with her jealousy of Coren's relationship to their mother. She was able to tie these buried feelings to her eating disorders, frequently vomiting her food as a small child, and as an adult, experiencing stomach ailments during times of stress. Her insights allowed an understanding of her problems with the cooks she hired—she never had problems with her other servants—linking this puzzling source of tension to her childhood eating disorders.

In January, shortly after her mystical event, which she now called the "death of the ego," she attended a stimulating lecture at Yale by Thornton Wilder, "the best speaker" she had ever heard. That night she had a sex dream about her psychiatrist, Dr. Moore; he suggested she might be the "kind of person who has to be released intellectually before sexually." She wondered if intellectual release could prompt relief from nervous disorders as well. During a February session she suffered a "terrific emotional upheaval" and felt like a knife had stabbed her in the heart. She spent most of this session reminiscing about her relationship with her parents. Afterward, she felt "tired and infinitely sad, as if someone had died." Two weeks later, she told the doctor the story of Ina's hostility. Claire concluded that Ina projected feelings against her own "awful mother" onto Claire, which gave Ina the motive to hurt Claire. This realization led Claire to begin to explore the parallels between her mother's power and Ina's power to hurt her. The doctor refused to commit himself to an opinion; however, therapy led Claire to explore mother-daughter relationships on an archetypal level, through dreams and free associations.

A year later, she wrote the doctor that although she had discontinued her treatment, she needed to see him again. Whereas her relationships with Thurston and Ina were better, she was still having problems with her cook. One major insight came with a dream of trying to escape her mother's watchful eye. "I felt her intrusion into my privacy, her jerking at the leash as far back as I can remember. I hid under my bed to read fairy stories and to daydream. Later I hid from her out in the coal bin to write stories so she would not . . . mock my literary efforts." Claire faced her mother's intrusiveness by allowing for the ways it affected patterns in her present life; the third-floor study paralleled her safe spaces under the bed or in the coal bin.

Journal entries covering this period contradict her many published articles claiming that the eight years immediately following her Great Awakening comprised a time of intense happiness when she was "in communion with the life force" and that love, marriage, and sex offered moments of "infinite sweetness." In fact, she fluctuated between extreme psychological highs and lows, periods when she experienced sensations of levitating and saw images of herself floating in a "universal stream," followed by periods of intense self-scrutiny and anxiety she called the "dark night of the soul." Nevertheless, her accounts of the days immediately following that moment of ultimate ecstasy focused on the creativity inspired by the event.

During the summer of 1950, instead of going to the New Ocean House at Swampscott, Massachusetts, or on a tour of Europe, Thurston suggested they go somewhere less pretentious. They rented a "small simple cottage" on Cape Cod that turned out to be rather shabby: "beds with springs 30 years old, blankets full of spots and frayed ends, tired old couches, wicker chairs which squeaked like mice." No telephones, neighbors, servants; no dressing for dinner. Claire prepared to suffer for three months "like a silent martyr." But it turned out to be the "*most glorious summer*" of their lives, the summer when Claire began to write *Awakening to the Good: Psychological or Religious?*[18]

Much later in life, Claire would discuss with Ken Ring the distinctions between the effect of the "small ecstasies" and that of the grand overpowering one. The small ecstasies, often called "altered states of consciousness," do not transform character or behavior. "They are quite beautiful but they are transient"; there is little lasting effect. In contrast, reaching a highest state, a Great Awakening, is transformative. "It alters your character, your behavior, your hierarchical values, your lifestyle and attitude."[19] Rather than living by one's conscious mind or ego, the unconscious mind—feelings and intuition—takes over as a guide. In the aftermath of transformation, old struggles reappear; territories of self-ownership must be redrawn in spiritual battle. And to win, the creative force of the soul must discover a new outlet born from the union of the old and new psyche. Writing helped her make sense of her emerging self by "locating patterns in the life" she had lived up to this point. Claire's sanity depended on her keeping track of these past events, her small ecstasies, in order to explore the larger one.

The act of "retrospection" endows memories with a "premonitory sense," allowing the writer to make "connections across time" and to see the "design in life and text," the true purpose of autobiography.[20] Looking back to her first remembered experience, that dance in the wind at age ten, and chronologically tracing these mystical events of transcendence, put them in perspective and, in some ways, made her Great Awakening at age fifty-four seem almost inevitable. Memories resemble "scraps of life snatched from the void, pages blown in the wind, without order, full of incongruities and inconsistencies." The discipline of writing transforms those fragments into a cohesive, rational theory born of a series of irrational experiences. "Once thoughts are on paper, one can regard them with detachment and review them from a new perspective that can lead to new insights."[21] To paraphrase Carolyn Heilbrun, "nothing really happens until we write it down"—which allows the writer to repossess her life.[22]

Even as Claire wrote, however, the stages of the cycle continued. As the author reflected on the past, the present and future impinged on her reflections. Her sense of despair and loss of faith in humanity's inherent good connected with the loss of her parents as structures of stability and left her in a state of spiritual vacuity. The journey toward self-understanding through writing and reflecting embattles the spirit, "wrenches" the soul, as the seeker struggles toward a "neat analysis."[23]

The painful disillusionment in human morality brought on Claire's period of spiritual death and rebirth and merged in her mind with the weekly sessions with her analyst, which opened the wounds of her childhood. Both periods began in the fall and ended in the spring when she left New Haven for the cottage by the sea. The combination of pain and joy tossed her emotions willy-nilly between despair and delight. Writing this autobiography brought her "obsessively present memories" to a place of rest on the page.[24] *Awakening to the Good: Psychological or Religious?* reflects the author's determination to bring order to the chaos of her emotional life and, as literature, contributes to the ongoing scientific study of human consciousness.

The quest for resolution of such turmoil often involves a confrontation with the mother figure, first as human and then as divine.[25] The root of Claire's disappointment in her mother lies in the mythical past—the idealized primal mother who nurtures, nourishes, and protects her daughter from infancy through young childhood. This ideal, recalled with nostalgia in her novels, separates her from the human mother, the one whose expectations and lifestyle choices differed so radically from her own. In order to reconcile myth with reality, Claire must reject the goddess mother archetype that represents pure bliss and allow herself to love her real mother, Susan Allen Myers, who like her, suffered the inequities extant in a patriarchal world. From this reunification emerges compassion, the compassion Sibyl expresses in "Gaily Bedight" when she realizes her mother has no power or authority in her father's house.[26] For the adult Claire, this moment came through a hallucination: "Along the street . . . an image of my mother appeared. It receded gradually into the distance and disappeared forever as a troubling problem. I felt intense compassion for her, no longer bitter resentment." Claire attributes this breakthrough to the process of individuation, when the "center of gravity shifts from the ego to the self."[27] In Jungian terms, ego is the center of consciousness while self is the center of the unconscious. Reaching the true self involves a return to one's source, a fundamental identification with humankind and the universal principle. Individuation allows separation of self from a preoccupation with parental control or influence. According to Jung, neurosis cannot be cured without a mystical or religious experience involving epiphanies of self. "As a child . . . I could never decide whether [Mother] waited on me hand and foot . . . to cover up her lack of love or to lure me into loving her. It was very confusing. . . . Now I feel intense compassion for her. How she must have suffered. I blamed her for everything."[28]

In the Allen-Myers family there was an infallible maxim embraced by mother and grandmother: "As the twig is bent so grows the tree." Assuming the validity of their belief, Claire questioned her rebellion against her parents' values and wondered if she might cure her self-doubt by finding the freedom to be herself. These questions of identity prompted her to write her autobiographies, "to discover what forces produced a person who longed to be herself."[29] Carl Jung taught that "artists and writers often embody the coming changes of the race." To understand the capacity of the human mind to reach such levels of spirituality as Claire ultimately achieved, she would have to understand her own mind as a model of human behavior. As a writer, she could explore her gift to access the ineffable regions of mysticism and transcendence of material reality. Typically, her search within resonated with her outward life, even if no one knew the personal motivations behind her actions.

In 1952, as state arts chair for the Connecticut division of the AAUW, Claire suggested that the members write essays describing the most beautiful experience they ever had with one of the arts.[30] Most of the women had no idea what she was talking about.[31] But Claire insisted, producing a questionnaire and supervising chairs from eighteen towns in Connecticut. Entrants wrote "charming little essays" describing how the arts had "altered their states of consciousness," though few understood the significance of that term. Claire, in the early stages of her own research, used the project to explore the implications of altered states stimulated by art, then sold the chapbooks as fundraisers. Winners, whose names were announced at an annual luncheon held on May 10, 1952, at the Lyman Allyn Museum in New London, received awards of prized prints, records, and art books, donated by H. Thurston Owens, unbeknownst to him.

In 1954, after four years of research and writing, Claire sent a letter to Carl Jung in Zürich, Switzerland, and asked for an interview.[32] His books, she told him, particularly *Modern Man in Search of a Soul* and *The Practice of Psychotherapy* "virtually saved [her] life." However, because of her recent spontaneous "individuation" and "enantiodromia"—Jung's terms for the identification of a true self and for the resolution of opposites—she had urgent questions only he could answer. "Surely Carl Jung is the greatest and wisest man living today," she wrote, and complimented him on his generosity to other scholars. She explained that her book-in-progress, then titled "The Inevitable Search: The Psychological Autobiography of a Woman's Relation to the Universe," examined her Awakening by applying a psychological framework to a literary task.

Jung granted the interview, which took place on July 24, 1954, at his summer residence, 228 Seestrasse in Küsnacht-Zürich. Claire's description of their meeting, published in the *New York Herald Tribune*, Paris edition, describes the large old-fashioned house on the beautiful Lake of Zürich, with the "snow-topped Alps in the dim distance and a vegetable garden in front."[33] Jung, "a tall man with very pink cheeks and an appearance that belied his 80 years" spoke with her for an hour and a half on his theories of analytical psychology, Freud, his early struggles, religion and the role of evil, politics, and the psychological origin of the "isms." They further discussed the maternal woman and the grande amoureuse, his collected works, the cause and cure of neuroses, and how to find the meaning of life—a lot to cover in a mere ninety minutes.

She told him about the book she was writing, that it contained a chapter on him, and asked, if the book was not accepted for publication, how would she "endure"? He advised her to "write the truth and expect to be misunderstood, and take the consequences." People feared the truth, he explained, but he had pursued it all his life. The article concludes, as did the interview, when a large steamer passed beneath Jung's window. With "horns blowing and bells ringing," attendees of the International Congress of Psychotherapy stood on deck clamoring to see Carl Jung, "the greatest of all psychotherapists." Jung stepped out on his balcony to face two or three hundred wildly waving psychotherapists. Finally, he waved back—once—and went inside.

A nice little article, nice enough to win a prize in the *Tribune*'s travel story contest, but she found the encounter deeply disappointing—she was "too modest" to tell him in detail about her present book on spontaneous self-realization or to reveal the tremendous effects of her own Awakening. "I might have made a friend for life but to him I appeared to be a tongue tied young woman in a red hat." Claire regretted showing him her first book, *The Unpredictable Adventure*, because Jung found the jacket illustration of a nude woman on a centaur provocative; he became distracted by the words *grande amoureuse*.[34] "This was not what I wanted at all!"

Hooked on that theme, Jung failed to notice her hints to move him back to the substantive questions she had prepared in advance, which, in awe of this famous man's "giant intellect . . . flew out of her mind": "Will individuation prevent recurrence of war? Is there a way of contacting the collective unconscious other than through ecstasy? If a normal person wants contact with the collective unconscious, must there be a release of the personal unconscious first? What are the contents of a *normal* personal unconscious? Explain the Catholic and the Aristotelian idea of *intellectual* knowledge of God. Why do mothers reject children? Does this happen in Oriental or in Primitive cultures? How not to feel rejected if one's mother and father rejected one? Can all people achieve unification of the conscious and the unconscious?"[35]

Perhaps these questions give greater insight into Claire's state of mind than anything Carl Jung might have answered. Her personal questions on motherhood reveal the anguish she still suffered, failing to recognize the ways her parents had supported her throughout her life. She possessed a limited, even naive comprehension of Jung's model of psychic structure. She had started from scratch; mastering Jungian concepts would take years of study. And surely he answered some of her questions before the horns and bells interrupted their privacy. By the time she completed her book, published four years later, she had a clearer understanding of his theories, in part as a result of the interview. And she was better able to describe the spontaneous event itself.

In 1957, she wrote Jung another letter asking for permission to quote from his work and apologizing for seeming "stupid." Now, she assured him, she had confidence in her insights. In her search for the innate good in mankind and in herself, she discovered that only in luminous "rare moments of exaltation" could she unite with the creative principle in the cosmos. These unions released her "intuitive ethical esthetic loving spiritual self," which she defined as the "force of good in the universe." When "reason and intuition united in a great golden burst of glory," she wrote him, "I was made whole."[36]

But not *permanently* whole. The transformation was intense; but wholeness cannot exist on the human plane. Jung would have seen that moment of "enantiodromia"—the union of opposites—as temporary, attained periodically.

A most interesting characteristic of Claire's twelve years of bliss is their cyclical nature: after eight years of intense bliss, she entered a phase she called "purgation," a fall into a "state of nervous exhaustion." This emptying-out phase fostered a slow inner growth, "arid years" in preparation for a sudden elevation "to a shining plateau of quiet bliss and deepened conviction for the eternal verities." This elevated phase lasted two years, during which she began writing her second spiritual autobiography, *Discovery of the Self*, the search for a "road map to Enlightenment."[37] Here she relates examples of small ecstasies along with a deep understanding of the conscious manipulation of the unconscious; not a "how-to," but a guide for attaining moments of splendor through experiencing the sacred in all forms of art from symphony to paintings, from lectures to films.

In 1942, during Claire's period of self-examination of her writing skills, her friend Marian suggested that she was "fatally weak on construction and presentation," thus she had a hard time making "things sound realistic." This diagnosis, "a marvelous superstructure but no brick foundation," gave Claire new goals.[38] She vowed stringent self-discipline to leave her writing to "get cold" so she could see the flaws and vowed to achieve emotional distance by allowing time to pass between multiple drafts and revisions. She needed an editor. In terms of writing style both *Awakening to the Good* and *Discovery of the Self* are problematic. In terms of content, both were revolutionary for their times.

The lack of finesse of the two books, in narrative structure and style, reflects a convergence of the author's inner turmoil: an uncertainty of her passion colored by her enthusiasm for having attained altered states. The paradox manifests in the scattershot approach each book takes in the effort to tell the story and to understand the phenomena associated with the cycles as she lived through them. However, with her penchant for research and her natural inquisitiveness, she traversed the labyrinthine passages of the latest psychological theories extolled by Abraham Maslow, Aldous Huxley, F. S. C. Northrop, William Sheldon, Carl Jung, and others. She wrote toward an assimilation of their varied insights in order to validate her particular case. *Awakening to the Good* reproduces the process of her transformation, beginning with despair and the death of the ego, followed by anecdotes describing her lifelong series of mystical events, and ending with summaries of the psychological, poetic, biblical, and philosophical explanations of the human psyche. Two sections contain a series of poems that follow the description of the Great Awakening and the "Coda—Essay on the Whole Man," to comprise the final section, "Wholeness," which summarizes in verse the process of discovery the author has expounded in prose. Whereas the verse sections suffer in quality, the prose sections comprise a clear, energetic collage that juxtaposes research with event, mind with emotion, reason with mysticism, and science with art. Baffling, however, is the glaring omission of the Great Awakening itself. A four-page printed insert numbered 170 ½ a–d opens with an explanation: "Then the most incredible thing happened—the most frightening, beautiful, important experience of my entire life. I understood absolutely nothing of its meaning . . . *I did not even include it in this, my autobiography*. Was I too ignorant of its significance, too afraid that others would not believe it? Did I fear it indicated that I was queer or worse? I honestly do not know" (emphasis mine).[39]

A complete description of her rebirth of May 1950 follows. To omit the pivotal event of the book, the very reason she wrote it, seems remarkable. Perhaps she forgot to include it because of the difficulty in harnessing the cacophony of emotions and symbols and rendering them concrete.

Submitted as *The Search for Ultimate Reality*, the manuscript was rejected by Prentice Hall in January of 1956. As *The Mystical Awakening of a Confirmed Rationalist*, it was rejected by Macmillan the following November, and by Dodd Mead the following year. On June 11, she wrote Charles Gelatt that she had received signed contracts from a New York commercial firm that specialized in books on philosophy, psychology, comparative religion, and aesthetics. "But their reputation is not too good financially so I returned the contracts—reluctantly, I admit."[40] Possibly Claire came to regret that decision since, ultimately, she self-published it through Christopher Publishing House in Boston.

Her friend Edmund Sinnott, then dean emeritus of the Yale Graduate School, read the galleys, loved it, and "helped launch" the book. Sinnott, an eminent biologist and geneticist, erudite in religious and philosophical theories, called it "a moving account of how a keen and perceptive mind has met the ancient problem of the good and the evil in man through suffering, aesthetic insight, mystical experience and especially the unifying concepts of psychology."[41] He introduced her to his colleagues at Yale, philosopher F. S. C. Northrop, physicist Henry Margenau, and psychologist William Sheldon, whose works are quoted in the text. Her publisher excerpted Sinnott's letter, as well as one from Ruth Nanda Anshen, an editor of the World Perspectives series at Harper, extolling her for demonstrating the "principle of unity" and for evoking the "meaning of becoming and being." Sinnott urged Claire to send a copy of the book to Abraham Maslow, the prominent psychologist at Brandeis University, founder of the human potential and transpersonal psychology movements. Maslow "read the book at one sitting," praised it as "exciting and even fascinating": "I think you have done a wonderful job and I want to thank you for it." He backed his praise with concrete suggestions by including a list of the names and addresses of over one hundred academicians and researchers involved in the human potential movement—worldwide—she should write, send copies, and otherwise alert to her work.[42] Soon letters of praise poured in. In 1962, Maslow listed *Awakening to the Good* in the bibliography of his *Toward a Psychology of Being*.

Readers in the scientific community responded to the publication of *Discovery of the Self* with the same kind of enthusiasm. This "search for a road map to Enlightenment" attempts to devise a set of

14. Claire Myers Owens at a signing for *Discovery of the Self.* Photograph courtesy of the TWU Woman's Collection.

"rules" for the "modern independent seeker after self-actualization," and to identify a methodology that would make enlightenment accessible to a layperson.[43] "My system of rediscovering and developing the self, one's deeper, better, unused, nature might be amateur," she reflected.[44] "The whole point of such a discovery of the Self is that one realizes . . . how low one's own station is compared to the heights possible to mankind. . . . The reactions of readers were not praise for my book [*Awakening to the Good*] so much as for the wondrous laws of the human psyche that made such glorious experiences realizable. I could take no credit for anything. I had merely served as an instrument through which some strange impersonal power had elected to flow."[45]

Discovery, like its predecessor *Awakening to the Good*, is anecdotal, a collage of events reported and analyzed, juxtaposed with the research used for the analysis. It too explores the emotional impact of paranormal events, which continued to occur even as the author wrote *Awakening to the Good*. Each anecdote points to the inherent good of the human spirit and contributes to the author's pursuit of a method for discovering the true self, which ultimately leads to enlightenment. Each segment of research analyzes a particular psychological theory and its implications in regard to the author's personal experience.

Love is the answer and the question; the Enlightened soul lives in a state of unconditional love. A chapter called "Love and the Infant" describes the episode when Claire managed to quiet a continuously crying baby. Just being in the same room with mother and infant, she sensed that no one loved the baby "one iota."[46] Holding the baby, love poured forth from Claire's breast like mother's milk. The child stopped crying, smiled, and cuddled in her arms. Thus, love is the curative means for solving all dissension, a way of transcending the ego-situated self to reach the universal self.

"Love and Race" describes her friendship with a scientist who turned out to be Jewish, a fact she discovered while a guest in his home.[47] "When I was a child in the South, it was forbidden to allow a Catholic or a Jew in one's home or to enter theirs." Negroes were accepted and loved as servants, but she had been "imbued with prejudice against all other classes, races and religions. White Protestant and aristocratic Southerners were considered superior in blood and breeding." Reflecting on her surprise to discover his "race," she wrote: "A few years ago I undoubtedly would have felt a sense of shock in spite of myself. Today I felt nothing—blessedly nothing."[48] "Love and Color" similarly describes her unconditional love for her "Negro" cook, a woman who awakens in her a "blind devotion" and whom she knows she would protect with her life if need be against "the cruelty of racial prejudice."[49] Through this revelation, Claire proved to herself that she had shed all racial prejudices as a result of her Great Awakening and her subsequent search for enlightenment.

In his introduction to *Discovery of the Self*, Anthony Sutich, editor of the *Journal of Humanistic Psychology*, calls the book a realistic presentation of the "rough side" of the road to self, a portrayal of the ecstasies and agonies.[50] Writing *Discovery* created a state of mind in which ordinary episodes produced extraordinary effects. In the end, Owens declares that by relating her experiences she simply demonstrates how others can achieve happiness and enlightenment, for the discovery of the extraordinary lies in fully experiencing ordinary events. The self discovered—the good, compassionate, loving, creative self—centers in harmony with the universe, which encompasses both evil and good. Enlightenment, a psychological and religious state, transcends the dichotomous nature of the universe, a "place" where opposites cease to exist: "Finally the dichotomy . . . the painful duality between mind and body, . . . the conscious and unconscious, man and ultimate reality" finds resolution. Thus the Enlightened person attains what Evelyn Underhill called the Unitive Life, one that coalesces with the cosmic Self, with Reality, the life force, God. "To discover the self and develop it is to discover the secret of happiness, the meaning of life, the ultimate goal of living" the author concludes.[51]

Her chapter "Work" reports a visit with Marian Murray when they edited the very book she is writing. Unfortunately, they left untouched its most problematic feature: it pretends to have been written by Clairene Myers, the now deceased aunt of Claire Myers Owens, who takes up where her aunt left off and finishes the book. Both writers write in the first person. However, there seems to be no point in ascribing the book to a double author or in attributing her own experiences to an "aunt." This flaw notwithstanding, a reviewer found this "very personal story" to be engrossing and clear, despite the "sometimes superfluous adjectives or overflow of emotions." Ironically, the reviewer detects a difference in writing style after the aunt's death she called the "result of the author's skillful writing."[52]

While writing *Discovery of the Self,* Owens fell down the cellar stairs and broke her thigh. The accident plunged her into a state of despair, part of the cycle called the "dark night of the soul." She lay in the hospital in traction, immobilized for four and a half months. The "overworked nursing staff," was indifferent, sullen, rough. Dehumanized by the institutional system, they dehumanized the patients. "I lost my identity as a human being. . . . all contact with my true self, with ultimate reality." In a state of living death, her bones failed to mend. She grew weaker, thinner, and more depressed. She called out to God, asking why she had been "cast down so low." With the death of her spirit, she longed for physical death to end her misery. Then Thurston Owens stepped in.[53]

Demonstrating his quiet understanding of his emotionally distraught wife, he silently left a gift on her bedside table one morning while she slept. She awoke to find a set of Plato's *Dialogues.*[54] Socrates's dialectic method awakened her conscious and unconscious minds, simultaneously. "What a treasure! What clarity, what vigor!" It was the "noblest" book she had ever read; key to its nobility was its stimulation of both sides of the brain, which for Claire "almost induced another state of Enlightenment—by intellectual activation."

Almost, but not quite. For enlightenment is not so easily attained. Still, an unconscious transformation occurred, which allowed healing to begin. A birthday card to Thurston that year reveals her gratitude:

> Dear, dearer, dearest Thursty:
>
> Happy birthday! and 20 happier ones to come!
>
> How can words even begin to tell you how much you and your smiling face and steadfast spirit have helped me through this hospital ordeal. . . .
>
> In the early days I felt as if I had been shipwrecked in a stormy season. . . . Thursty was my strongest support. Without him I could not have carried on.
>
> Never in your life were you *needed* so terribly. I shall always need you—so take good care of my dear Thursty.
>
> Love and kisses—your Claire[55]

She was flooded with feelings of love, for everyone, including the hospital staff. She began to forget her own pain and attend to theirs. She asked the nurses personal questions about their private lives. Each shared the dilemmas they faced, pouring out their troubles. By the time she left the hospital they were coming in to perform favors above duty; they came to share the peace and tranquility of her room. "They smiled into my eyes, said good morning, and I felt cheerful." Her bones healed perfectly and she went home "to learn to walk again."

13

The Lady and Her Court

1963–1969

> She had a generosity of spirit that fed us. She was our inspiration. She'd been to the depths, and she'd been to the heights. She'd seen the landscapes—she knew where they lay.
>
> —Jean Houston

IF THE SEARCH FOR CERTITUDE, female equality, and creative expression motivated the utopian quest of Claire's youth, the search for intrinsic goodness, self-realization, and enlightenment informed Claire's quest for utopia during her later years. Using herself as a model to make her experience public, her personal search expanded to include the political and social advancement of humanity. With this shift, Claire's adolescent desire to "save the world overnight" resurfaced with a mature focus on spirituality as a step in the evolutionary process of the human species—one that would eliminate evil by excavating the natural goodness of every human being.

Dr. Jean Houston, founder of the Foundation for Mind Research, considers Claire Myers Owens the "key" to the human potential and transpersonal psychology movement.[1] Dr. Abraham Maslow, founder of the movement, considered Owens a valued friend; his inclusion of *Awakening to the Good* in the bibliography of *Toward a Psychology of Being*, reflected his high esteem of her work.[2] Prior to her Great Awakening, Owens's life and fiction were inseparable. Now with psychology as its central focus, the characters populating her autobiographical explorations became those women and men whose names graced the letterheads of journals, publishing houses, and institutions pioneering this new field.

"The scientists," as Owens referred to the various psychologists, psychoanalysts, anthropologists, biologists, theologians, and philosophers who researched the links between mind and spirit, psychology and religion, and right- and left-brain functions, performed the experiments, and wrote the theoretical books. Owens, through her lectures and books illuminating her Great Awakening, translated their theories in ways accessible for the lay public, expanding the scientific findings with personal revelations that synthesized experiential knowledge with scholarly research and scientific data. Hundreds of letters arrived in the wake of both *Awakening to the Good: Psychological or Religious?* and *Discovery of the Self* from readers searching for "small ecstasies" or "peak experiences" of their own, or finding solace in her descriptions of phenomena they had experienced but had found no way to validate or articulate.[3] Letters also arrived from those scientists who valued her work, praised her courage, and invited her to speak at their conferences and publish in their journals and anthologies. The exchange was mutual. Owens's ability to interpret their writings in the light of her spontaneous journeys into the mystical realms validated the findings of those whose work was theoretical and speculative rather than grounded in personal experience.

Abraham Maslow had a spontaneous, or "peak," experience of his own, but felt reluctant to detail it in books or lectures because he wished to respect the privacy of his family. For Owens, sharing her private experiences delighted her. Aldous Huxley wrote prolifically about his mystical journeys induced by mescaline, especially in *Doors of Perception*.[4] Owens's spontaneous awakening provided a contrast to his induced one; together they explored the similarities and differences of the two venues. Maslow and Huxley, along with other scholars and psychologists like Jean Houston, Anthony Sutich, Edmund Sinnott, William Sheldon, Raymond Prince—and later Kenneth Ring, Ken Wilber, Charles Tart, John White, and Raul daSilva—encouraged her to keep writing, keep speaking, stay visible. Still, there were disappointments. Even with letters of referral from this influential circle of scholars, she was unable to find a publisher for her next book, "Varieties of Self-Realization." But she succeeded as an important figure during these heady years of the human potential movement when many of the world's most gifted and renowned scholars believed they were on the verge of changing the world. In significant ways, their work has contributed to the paradigmatic shift in current popular trends in the area of spiritual studies.

Despite the explosion of commercialism in the "enlightenment industry" today, a wide audience has become interested in exploring the limitations of everyday consciousness, seeking something beyond mundane reality. That "something," for transpersonalists is, in Owens's words, the illumination of the "good within."

It is no accident that the human potential movement, with its emphasis on "ultimate human capacities," emerged in the aftermath of World War II, with Hitler's destruction of Eastern European Jewry and America's destruction of Hiroshima and Nagasaki.[5] Human ingenuity put to the test chose the pursuit of evil rather than good. Power meant violence; science meant obliteration. Humanity was no longer on the *verge* of blowing itself to pieces as had long been feared; it was in the *process*. The only way to change the world was to change human consciousness. "Political action, social work, this *ism*, that *ology*, are all incomplete unless accompanied by a new and elevated mode of awareness." If "*true revolution* is *revelation*," as John White observes, then true evolution is Enlightenment. But where does one begin?[6]

Psychology, still in its infancy in the West in the 1960s, finds its roots in philosophy and in science.[7] By the mid-1950s psychologists designated their history in terms of "forces." Humanistic psychology emerged as a "third force psychology," which provided a viable alternative to objectivist, behaviorist psychology, and to orthodox Freudianism. Abraham Maslow considered third force as revolutionary, provoking paradigm shifts in human thinking. Maslow defined humanistic psychology as "transitional, a preparation for a still 'higher' Fourth Psychology, transpersonal, transhuman, centered in the cosmos rather than in human needs and interest."[8] The third force spun out of Carl Jung's model of the unconscious, comprised of a personal unconscious and a "collective" or universal mind, which in religious language, paralleled the soul. Fourth force engaged that universal element, the soul, and applied methodical scientific approaches to sharpen and refine understanding of human experiences observed as "spiritual," or "transpersonal," thereby enriching both scientific and spiritual traditions. Anthony Sutich, founder of the *Journal of Humanistic Psychology*, organized a *Journal of Transpersonal Psychology*, to provide a forum for scholarly discussions of the expanding field.

In 1901, in his book *Cosmic Consciousness*, Dr. Richard M. Bucke, a Canadian psychiatrist who at age thirty-five "experienced an extraordinary moment of illumination," first introduced the concept of enlightenment as a "faculty entering the human race through evolution."[9] Among those he defined as having experienced "full cosmic consciousness" were Buddha, Krishna, Jesus, Dante, William Blake, and Bucke's friend and patient, the poet Walt Whitman. The term *cosmic consciousness* refers to a "suprasensory, suprarational level of mentation that transcends all other human experience, and creates a sense of oneness with the universe."[10] Since antiquity it has appeared under a variety of regional and ritual terms—*nirvana*, *satori*, *unio mystica*, *kairos*, to name a few. Bucke's findings became part of the literature on which Owens drew to contextualize her own cosmic moments of illumination. According to Bucke, moral elevation, intellectual illumination, charm and charisma, even physical transfiguration, accompanied the higher state. Bucke predicted that in time cosmic consciousness would become the norm for the whole race; indeed, to be without the faculty would become a mark of inferiority. Inevitably, his philosophy, published before the two world wars, became central to those seeking to reverse mankind's self-destruction and rebuild the world.[11]

Aldous Huxley's *The Perennial Philosophy* first popularized enlightenment and defined it as the core truth of the world's sacred traditions. His work unified multiple religious philosophies. Huxley's reputation as an intellectual made the quest for enlightenment "respectable," and brought public attention to the field and hope to "thoughtful people" searching for sanity in the midst of two world wars.[12]

Early in Owens's search for an intellectual explanation of the psychological phenomena she had experienced throughout her life, she looked to Huxley, a man whose writings were already familiar and with whom she had corresponded in the 1930s. This time when she wrote Huxley, now living in Los Angeles, she turned on her charm and asked for an interview.[13] "You, kind sir, are the subject of a chapter" in her new book discussing her awakening. She had read of his ecstatic episodes in *Doors of Perception* and wondered if he thought such events were determined by "our constitutional types," a question that revealed her familiarity with the findings of William Sheldon, the Yale psychologist she had met through Edmund Sinnott. Theories of Sheldon, Jung, and F. S. C. Northrop informed her letter, and she carefully let him know she had spoken with each in person. But, she flattered, his "brilliant, staggeringly erudite essays" and twelve of his books, which she read over the last twenty-five years, "nourished" her more than any others because he synthesized philosophy, religion, science, politics, and the arts. She told him he was "one of the few living men in this world capable of understanding" her book completely, and called him a "brilliant scholar" with whom she would be "honored" to confer. She offered to fly to Los Angeles; he wrote back that he would be in New York; she invited him to lunch. He accepted, happy to discuss these "strange and enormously important matters," and to learn from *her* ideas on the subject.

An account of their first meeting at the Women's University Club in New York's Biltmore Hotel appears in the draft for a poem called "Basic Encounters." Clearly Huxley dazzled her; passion flows forth:

> They sat looking, staring, drowning in each other's eyes
> From his eyes poured a hot black shining stream like lava from an
>   erupting volcano
> Threatening her very existence, threatening to overwhelm her
>   forever.[14]

Fortunately, she wrote a prose description of the same encounter where she captured the spirit of her reaction to Huxley, still rhapsodic, still passionate, less cloying in prose than in poetry:[15] "He came to tea with me at my club in NY. He was tall, unbelievably handsome with the beautiful tailoring only the English men achieve. We [discussed] the mystical experience he had after taking mescaline, which he'd written up in *Doors of Perception*. Never had I seen such vivid blue eyes in my life. They absolutely blazed at me like blue fire."

The room seems to "fill with great waves of desire, surging back and forth like a mighty ocean," leaving her confused, overwhelmed. A few years later Huxley and his new wife Laura joined her and Thurston for dinner in New Haven where "he had a play on at the Shubert, *The Genius and the Goddess*."[16] Evidently, she managed to control her physical attraction to this elegant, prolific man; they became good friends, corresponding regularly over a period of ten years about intellectual and philosophical trends, theories, and explorations of the day.

She sent him copies of her articles, and he sent lengthy and enthusiastic responses. Huxley used his influence with various editors, proffering advice to help Owens through the publishing maze. In one letter Owens reported the response of two editors who "held an hour's conference" on *Awakening to the Good* and found the twenty ecstatic experiences "impressive, beautifully written and very important" but recommended she cut the descriptions of despair and the rational explanations of the mystical events. "This was a blow! Two years of research discarded!" When the book was finally published, she sent Huxley a copy and he responded, "You bring out the all-important fact that religion is primarily concerned with the immediacy of being."[17]

After his death, Laura, a psychologist, continued her and her husband's mutual interest in human potential; she founded Our Ultimate Investment, a nonprofit organization for the "nurturing of the possible human." Owens wrote Laura friendly letters requesting permission to quote from Huxley's books. In January 1964, Laura wrote thanking Claire for her copy of *Discovery of the Self*, assuring her Aldous would have loved it, had he lived to read it.[18]

In Abraham Maslow, Owens made another friend for life. Having introduced her through his mailing list to an international network of interested readers, he invited her to conferences, mailed her reprints of his publications, recommended journals and books—helped her educate herself. In response to her mailing, she received letters from scholars all over the world.

In Maslow's work with peak experiences and self-actualization, Owens recognized a man with a goal similar to her own: to guide people to "the good." "Self-actualizing people, those who have come to a high level of maturation, health, and self-fulfillment, have so much to teach us that sometimes they seem almost like a different breed of human beings," Maslow wrote in *Toward a Psychology of Being.*[19] He discerned in reports of peak experiences that "the whole of the world is seen as unity, as a single, rich, live entity." Owens's variety of peak experiences catalyzed by art—paintings, sculpture, dance, literature—as well as by love and nature, resonated with Maslow's findings. Furthermore, she must have taken great comfort in his explanation for the dichotomy between intellectuality and femininity, one of her lifelong struggles as portrayed in her fictional character, Tellectina/Femina. As Maslow explained: "Many brilliant women are caught up in the problem of making an unconscious identification between intelligence and masculinity. To probe, to search, to be curious, to affirm, to discover, all these she may feel as defeminizing, especially if her husband in his uncertain masculinity, is threatened thereby. Many cultures and many religions have kept women from knowing and studying . . . to keep them 'feminine.'"[20]

From the beginning, they were kindred spirits; their letters expressed gratitude on both sides. Several of Owens's letters to Maslow contained questions to clarify, or at times refute, points made in his books or articles, numbered, with invitations to answer right on the letter, which on two occasions Maslow did.

They first met face to face at the 1959 Association of Humanistic Psychology conference in Washington, DC that Owens attended at Maslow's invitation. Maslow introduced her to his circle of colleagues—many had appeared on that original mailing list—as if "she herself were the celebrity." It must have been her book describing those "small ecstasies," she would tell audiences in lectures recalling those early years. Owens attended many such meetings, urged by Maslow. Around midnight he would call her room and say: "Claire, wake up, throw on your clothes, come down to the lobby and talk to me. I've finished all my business affairs." Down she would go—delighted of course.[21]

Owens remembered with exceptional fondness Maslow's discussion of his daughters, which he incorporated into a conference speech. As he spoke, Owens witnessed "an emanation of love" which she understood after reading his essay in the first issue of *Transpersonal Psychology.* Here he spoke of being-love—the "love of a person in a state of being, not of becoming but being. That's the kind of love he had for his daughters."[22]

As their friendship deepened, barriers between them fell away. "You see, when a woman is on 'the path,' and has not yet attained the highest state of consciousness, she's accepted by men as an equal."[23]

Maslow had introduced Owens to Anthony Sutich, editor of two ground-breaking journals in humanistic and in transpersonal psychology, who subsequently wrote the introduction to *Discovery of the Self.* Owens held Sutich in high regard: "His life was more than courageous. I thought it was heroic. I sent him an article that he rejected. It may be the only letter of rejection I ever received that made me happy." Sutich cushioned his "no" with a constructive letter, which "revealed the nature of 'a man' and the 'nature of man'"—generous and understanding.[24]

Letters to these colleagues-become-friends contain anecdotes dealing with her personal life, inseparable from her professional quest. The anecdotes evince Owens's nearly obsessive focus on discovering, not just the self, but a methodology for reaching that center of soul she identified as the seat of universal knowledge, the source of Ultimate Reality. Although circumstances in her life had catapulted her there many times spontaneously, she longed to discover the route she could choose on her own to travel whenever she wished. A central thesis of both *Discovery of the Self* and "Varieties of Self-Realization" regards the highway to Ultimate Reality as the road to the self and the center of the universe as the center of self. But, as Lex Hixon pointed out years later, the place Owens discovered during that Great Awakening of 1950 transcended even the universe, even the cosmos; Owens's ecstasies hurled her into a realm beyond materiality. No wonder she spent the second half of her life investigating methods for returning at will.[25]

Thanks to Maslow, Huxley, and Sutich, Owens felt famous. Periodically, she would take some of the letters to show her friends at Yale: Henry Margenau, Edmund Sinnott, and William Sheldon. Only one man, a professor of comparative religion at Yale whom she never named, resented her success. When she showed him the letters, he turned on her, his face contorted with rage, "his eyes like black ice so deadly cold with hate" she feared he would strike her. "All right, young lady, you may have had mystical experiences and I haven't. But that does not make you any sort of authority on the psychology of religion." She had sat "gratefully and admiringly at his feet" for years; such professional jealousy hurt her deeply but now, enlightened to the "good" in others, she responded with compassion: "You shock me to the marrow of my bones. It was you who gave me encouragement . . . I shall be indebted to you forever."[26] Her response deflated his anger. She left his office, saddened but not undone. "Ordinarily I would have been terribly hurt or burst into tears."[27]

She had learned an important lesson; unfortunately, she would need it in the future. Indeed, Claire Myers Owens again was living a "parallel life," undergoing a period of crisis so taxing she had little strength to survive the vicissitudes of writing and publishing, lectures, travel, and conferences. Thurston, her once loving husband, had become irascible, fluctuating between bitter silence and harsh criticism. He refused to look at *Discovery of the Self* when it was first published; then "hooted with derision" when fan letters arrived. "For 26 years we had a good marriage but just this last year he tried to destroy me," she confided to a friend.[28] In retaliation, Claire acted mean and nasty to Thurston until she realized her behavior made things worse. She reversed her strategy and began to show kindness and consideration, to rebuild his ego, which she thought must have suffered from her professional gratification. She even gave him a lovely surprise party, inviting only his friends—none of her own—a tactic that seemed to smooth things between them for a while.

Unbeknownst to Owens, after her hospital stay and during her extended convalescence, Thurston had changed his will, leaving one-third of his estate to her and the other two-thirds to his daughters, Doree Owens Smedley and Alice Van Zandt Kennett. A letter she wrote to Thurston in 1967 expresses her horror at his betrayal; she attributed her husband's behavior to problems of aging.[29] At eighty-eight, his health declining, he suffered from arteriosclerosis and degenerative heart disease. These ailments, accompanied by dementia, affected his usual generosity. Outwardly their lives still looked privileged. But as Roxane Gay points out, at various times, "life is hard for nearly everyone," and people "might endure situations you can never know anything about."[30] Ironically, Claire found herself in a battle to protect her assets from their original source. On the verge of hysteria, Claire sought the advice of Charles Gelatt, whom she often referred to as her "prince charming." Gelatt used his influence, convincing Thurston he must not leave his wife destitute. For the next two years, Claire spent a great deal of time negotiating her rights to their money, reallocating their funds in codicil after codicil, with Gelatt advising her on each draft.[31]

Throughout their marriage both Claire and Thurston corresponded regularly with the Gelatt family; theirs was a special and admirable relationship.[32] In the 1960s, Charles Gelatt, an economist educated at the University of Wisconsin and a member of their board of regents for some twenty-seven years, took over his father's role as president of Northern Engraving where Thurston worked for most of his career. A "financial genius," he expanded the family business into an empire that included Microcard Corporation in West Salem, Wisconsin, and LaCrosse Trust, whose assets between 1957 and 1967 went from ten to twenty-five million dollars. In 1967, the Owenses wrote congratulating him: "Hurrah Hurrah millionaire Charles Gelatt!!!!"[33]

Gelatt possessed the rare quality of shrewd business acumen tempered by a kind and generous nature. He saw to it that Thurston received stock options and benefited from the company's growth, even long after Thurston retired. In 1965, three years after Thurston's retirement, Gelatt brought Claire and Thurston to LaCrosse for festivities in celebration of changes in the business structure; they were treated like "movie stars."

Throughout the sixties, double-digit inflation wreaked havoc with retirees on fixed incomes. Sensitive to the Owenses's financial constraints, Gelatt would inquire as to whether they needed a "raise" in their pension. Thurston would gratefully refuse. "The average rainfall is 10 inches below normal but our grass never was greener." At age eighty-five, he wrote Gelatt: "Early to bed and early to rise with no afternoon naps is good medicine. That's the only kind I take."

The Owenses carefully limited their expenses, but continued to enjoy a prosperous existence. They gave up membership in most of their clubs in New York and New Haven, though they remained members of the "Q" club where Claire retained membership for life. They kept their "part-time maid who cooked several good meals each week," served on Lenox china, as Thurston assured Charles: "Our vacations are bigger and better each year and like everything else more expensive. We are happier each year and hope that you and Jane [Gelatt's first wife] are the same." Gelatt offered them the use of his apartment at the Surf Club in Palm Beach, Florida. Ecstatic, Thurston sent his reply to "Lord & Lady Gelatt: Dear Honorables, we accept with tumultuous rejoices."

Gelatt twice increased the Owenses's pension payments and continued them for Claire after Thurston died, even when in 1971, she wrote offering to discontinue the monthly pension. At that time, Gelatt instructed her "to set up a separate savings account and put that money there" so that if at some time Northern Engraving were unable to continue the pension she would be used to living without it. Meanwhile, it would accumulate for future needs.

But at times Thurston worried about finances, and though he protested help, he kept Gelatt informed. During 1965 and 1966, he conveyed in a letter that they had spent more than they earned and in September of 1967, Thurston noted, his bank balance was "moving in the wrong direction." "Went to the Red Barn, Westport yesterday for lunch. Soups are extra. Onion soup 75 cents etc. etc. Never have been quite as happy!!!" Gelatt offered them a room at the Breakers Hotel in

Palm Beach, Florida, "a little expensive but a tradition." The Owenses accepted—his letter an answer to their prayers. They would spend January with the Gelatts in Palm Beach and then move to the Breakers the first two weeks of February, and then to the Brazilian Court, where the rents were probably cheaper, until the end of March. For the rest of both Claire and Thurston's lives, Northern Engraving carried their car expenses—including purchase, insurance, and repairs. After Thurston's death, Charles took great pains to see that Claire had access to apartments in either Miami or Palm Beach for the winter months; often she stayed with Gelatt and his family and friends.

Researchers in transpersonal psychology demonstrate that enlightened individuals tend to attract good because they radiate goodness. For the most part, Claire's circle of supportive friends, admirers, and colleagues expanded as she attended meetings, gave lectures, and published scholarly articles. A major breakthrough in her standing came with the publication in *Main Currents in Public Thought* of "The Mystical Experience: Facts and Values," written in response to an essay by Dr. Raymond Prince, professor of psychiatry at McGill University. Prince's article, "Mystical States and the Concept of Regression," coauthored by Dr. Charles Savage, roused Owens's ire because its central thesis purported that the mystical state was a form of "regression in service of the ego," and had "much in common with psychotic states." Owens knew better: "Are not Prince's conclusions based on superficial resemblances, leaving untouched the *values* of the experience?" she asked in her article, challenging an expert in his field.[34]

With the editorial guidance of Reverend Betty Bogert and Dr. Walter H. Clark, Owens crafted a brilliant rebuttal.[35] Her article, which drew a wide, positive response, represented a leap in the level of her writing, her professionalism, and in her ability to illuminate personal experience without relying on autobiographical narrative. While Prince equated mysticism with madness and drew parallels with psychedelic experiences, psychotic regressions, and hallucinations, Owens equated mysticism with evolutionary progress. Third force psychologists, she maintained, considered the mystic state to be "part of the whole process of self-realization . . . often a vital step in the actualization of [human] potentialities."[36] Owens refuted Prince's psychiatric delineation of the five characteristics of mystical or altered states of consciousness with a point-by-point rebuttal that scientifically demonstrated the values of transcendent experience. Deriving from the "deeper levels of the unconscious," mystical insight for a "balanced and mature individual" is "healthy and deeply beneficial" both to the individual and to society at large. Indeed, a primary danger afflicting society stems from the dichotomy "between the conscious and unconscious, which causes people to suffer from meaninglessness in life." The mystical state, Owens argued, releases unconscious energy, which opens the path to the discovery of "meaning, wholeness and individual self-realization." Freudians, like Prince and Savage, Owens pointed out, rely on a few superficial "similarities between mysticism and early infancy [and] believe they have said enough to damn this most intense of all human experiences." Owens's promotion of the Jungian model illuminated the nature of the mystical experience on an archetypal level and demonstrated the ways such "peak experiences" can lead to the regeneration of society by releasing "latent capacities to create a peaceful and just world."

Prince wrote her a cordial letter in response to her rebuttal and, as president of the R. M. Bucke Memorial Society, invited her to attend their annual meeting in Montreal that October, in 1967.[37] Clearly, he respected her point of view as a so-called lay voice. The Bucke Society, named in commemoration of Dr. Richard M. Bucke, focuses on the scientific study of religious experience. Their meetings limited attendance to three hundred people of myriad backgrounds and cultures, and included scientists along with a variety of religious clergy.

At that conference, Owens met Jean Houston, a pioneer scientist in the area of mind phenomenology, who became yet another trusted colleague-turned-friend. Dr. Houston, in collaboration with her husband Robert Masters, established the Foundation for Mind Research in New York City in 1965.[38] When Owens read about their experiments in the Bucke Society newsletter, she wrote asking for "details" and enclosed a reprint of "Mystical Experiences: Facts and Values." Houston and Masters's work pertained to her search for scientific explanations of religious and mystical experience. She mentioned her own book-in-progress on the "self-actualization of famous persons," to be introduced by Edmund Sinnott.

For Claire Myers Owens, meeting Jean Houston at that October conference was something of a "peak experience" in itself. Returning to New Haven, Owens read Houston and Masters's 1966 *Varieties of Psychedelic Experience: A Classic Guide to the Effects of LSD on the Human Psyche*, and "could hardly lay it down." "As you are well aware," she wrote Houston, "it is honest, skeptical, informative, and profound, a classic." Her own involuntary awakening paled in contrast to their induced variety, like a "wild flower" compared to "a well-cultivated specimen." "Man has improved on nature. You have," she enthused, at a time before the controversial discussions of LSD had fully developed.[39]

Houston at twenty-nine had already attained stature in her field through her publications and her successful foundation, formidable accomplishments for such a young scholar. Owens marveled at Houston's strength and focus: what had first provoked her interest in philosophy? she asked. What made her choices in career possible? Her own religious beliefs? "Your husband must be exceptional," Owens speculated, "not to resent your brilliant intellect and worldly recognition." Surely as a couple they presaged future generations, which Owens predicted would "rise above conventional male-female relationships." Masters and Houston represented the potential Owens had sought to fulfill in her early relationships: a two-career family, a partnership.

Houston agreed to read the "Varieties of Self-Realization" manuscript, which, like her own, alluded in its title to William James's *Varieties of Religious Experience*. Houston praised the first ten chapters in a letter that Owens excerpted to include with submissions to publishers: The "lyrical yet tough-minded" writing evokes "the most vital and evolutionary options of our time." She predicted that for many, "reading this book will be the experience of being born anew."[40]

Overwhelmed by the enthusiasm of "so brilliant and erudite a mind," Owens dedicated the book to Houston, who was "stunned to find [her] name among those on the dedication page" and felt "honored beyond [her] deserts."[41] Houston offered to submit it to her editor at Holt. If Holt turned it down, she promised to send it to Viking and Harper and Row. She called it a "splendid achievement." Owens thanked Houston profusely. "My books," she confided, "seem to require assistance to launch from notables in the field."[42]

"Notables" did their best. Edmund Sinnott sat by the hour in Owens's third-floor study dissecting every sentence. "It is a masterpiece," he told her while they worked on "Varieties." "I am happy to sit at your feet and learn."[43] But Owens insisted his books "reveal nobility."[44] Nevertheless, she wrote Houston, since the publication of *Discovery of the Self*, many people sought her counsel. She seemed to be living out Teilhard de Chardin's prediction of a *homo progressivus* or "new being": strangers who believe in a similar future for mankind "may meet and experience total acceptance that cuts across differences in age, sex, race or religion." She felt that way when first meeting Houston in Montreal.

In his introduction to "Varieties," Sinnott emphasized its prophetic implications "toward a new era . . . the next step in evolution."[45] A biologist himself, he explained, "most scientists believe the existence of the self to be scientifically unverifiable"; however, he considered the self to be "the controlling factor of consciousness," integrating the personality toward "goodness, truth, beauty, love and wholeness." Sinnott concurred with Owens that human nature inherently loved the beautiful, a radical, controversial suggestion for a biologist.[46]

Owens's book contradicts the tenet of Judeo-Christian culture that casts humanity as innately evil. Instead she portrays human nature as innately good, offering psychological explanations of biblical allegories to prove it. Half-a-century after her intuitive insight at age ten, when spinning in the wind she was released from the notion of "evil she never felt," she had developed the intellectual and emotional skills to propose theories as to why.

Sinnott found Owens's book unique in its examination of the nature of matter, society, God, and humanity, and its investigation of the interior lives of Thoreau, Beethoven, Leonardo, Whitman, Socrates, and Plato, along with less famous subjects. The wealth of examples includes expanded studies of Edna St. Vincent Millay, Wordsworth, and many of the writers Owens had used as exemplars in her earlier works. Her biographical approach allowed for a study of the inner development of this wide variety of artists, tracing their methods for self-discovery and creative expression. The book would open readers to an "entirely new field of thought" concerned with the most profound problems confronting humanity at that time.[47]

Indeed, the problems affecting society Owens set forth in "Varieties of Self-Realization" remain as relevant today as they were in the 1960s. Materialism and affluence, the culprits of social decline, had been designated as "the good" by both liberals and conservatives on the political front. The good life was defined as two cars and two vacations a year and an ever-larger income. Technology threatened to "dehumanize" its users. America, having achieved the highest living standard on earth, showed an "increase in mental illness, crime and political corruption, rape and murder . . . and the degeneration of society in general. What had gone wrong?"[48]

Owens attributes this decline to the dominance of reason in Western culture for the last three hundred years, causing "a dissociation of man's conscious mind from his deeper unconscious." The resulting "split personality" cuts off "the area of the mind from which springs love of the good"—the deeper unconscious. Drawing on Jung's writings, Owens believed the "treasure house of man's better nature," was called "the self." By actualizing one's potentials, one could reach the self and live the "good life," which means the creation of ethical, moral, universal, and eternal values.[49] The seat of the self in the Jungian scheme, the unconscious mind, contains the "collective unconscious . . . [the] matrix of the good."[50]

Chapters explore methods for reaching these regions and cite autobiographical and biographical examples of transformation. Owens establishes several potential catalysts for achieving a higher consciousness and experiencing bliss: connections between nature and the cosmic rhythm, love as "rehearsal of self-realization," the seven arts—music, dance, sculpture, painting, architecture, drama, and poetry—and philosophy and reason, balanced by intuition.

Although in earlier books Owens discussed mystical awakenings of such famous artists and philosophers as Beethoven, Thoreau, Dante, Leonardo, and Whitman, in "Varieties" she details their life histories. Owens parallels Beethoven's musical development with phases in his psychological condition, calling the highest expression of his genius an expression of a "fully realized consciousness." Indeed, Beethoven himself stated that "art exists to communicate states of consciousness," and he demonstrated this superbly in his last quartets, which differ from the customary form of the quartet.[51] Owens maintained that the four-movement sonata actually corresponds to psychological processes: a conflict, a slow meditative movement, a passage that prepares for a vigorous final resolution, and the resolution itself.

Beethoven invented a form to express his own experiences of suffering. The movements of his symphonies were not stages of a journey, as many critics believed; rather, they radiated from a "central experience of mystical unity."[52] Humor is part of spiritual bliss, Owens contended, in the same way that humor is part of childlike innocence and purity. "Is not this what Jesus meant when he said, 'Except ye become as little children ye shall not enter into the kingdom of heaven'?" Thus, in pure joy lies the kingdom of heaven and the path to the divine.

The most significant aspect of attaining self-realization lies in the "dark night of the soul." Jung saw the unconscious as a self-regulating mechanism. In the stages of the journey toward enlightenment, the "dark night" follows the greatest heights of ecstasy as part of our natural instinct toward balance. "Even the greatest of composers may descend from the mountain." Beethoven, who wrote his greatest masterpieces after he became deaf, believed "suffering to be a gift of God and only from it could arise spiritual growth or the greatest art." In the end, Beethoven's *F-Major Opus 35* reflects "man at peace."[53] If she had not experienced it herself, Owens contended, she would not have recognized the stages in Beethoven's life.

Returning once again to her own experiences early in life—frolicking in the wind, dancing in the sun on the Long Island beach—Owens investigates the use of dance as a vehicle of mystical release for both observer and performer. "The mysterious joy of one's own muscular motion to the beat, beat, beat of measured dance music stirs the blood, lifts the heart, quiets the mind, allows the music to sweep through the whole body washing away inertia and hostility, renewing languishing hope and forgotten dreams."[54] Not only dance but all art provides stimulation for "the good" because of humanity's attraction to beauty. Artists from Leonardo to Kandinsky, Klee, and Mondrian, demonstrate that symbols erupt from the unconscious, which Owens calls "eternal verities."

Drawing on Sinnott's theories, Owens claims "man's response to beauty has a biological basis." Protoplasm, the basic stuff of life is "goal-seeking" in its tendency to seek beauty.[55] "There is an actual relationship between the organized patterns we call beautiful and the organized pattern existing in the protoplasm composing every human body." Beauty, for Sinnott "vibrates on the same wave length as the protoplasm." So our hunger for beauty is part of our biological goal-seeking, a natural urge like hunger, "we do not yet understand [but that] should be recognized as a basic fact and life's most characteristic quality."[56]

Jean Houston considered this period of Owens's life, her sixties and seventies, "a direct extension of her [1930s] novel."[57] In *The Unpredictable Adventure*, the Seven Siren Islands enfold Tellectina in their beauty; her exposure to the seven arts arouses her emotions, acting as foreplay to her erotic awakening. In "Varieties," Owens explores the effects of these same arts as stimuli to spiritual awakening. The arousal of the senses precedes the elevation of the spirit. The novel explores the depths and heights of culture in search of certitude. "Varieties" explores individuation as a lifelong process in search of certitude.

When the deeper levels of the unconscious are released, the stages of self-realization unfold. People who actualize their finest potentials know truth, "possess certitude," attain wholeness, wherein lies the promise for the salvation of the human race.[58] In the end, Owens looks toward a utopian future when humanity learns to become "good, loving and peaceful." Out of the "irresistible collision" of two opposite forces—the conscious and unconscious mind, symbolized by the philosophies of the West and the East—will evolve a "new good" that will "bring the eternal into the now."

"Today," she concluded, the world stands at the "crossroads between atomic destruction or the miasma of madness," and the actualization of our finest potentials. Humanity of tomorrow, the youth of today, possess the power to usher in an age of reason and science, peace and plenty, guided by love of the "good life and good society" in the ethical rather than the materialistic sense.[59]

In March of 1968, when Holt rejected "Varieties," Houston sent the manuscript to other publishers who ultimately rejected it as well. Owens was baffled: her two self-published books were used in several university psychology courses; her colleagues recognized the significance of her work. Why, she wondered, did editors reject it?

Those two self-published autobiographical studies addressed the connections between spirituality and psychology in creative and unprecedented ways; for editors of her day, they fell through the cracks. She seemed to be working in unchartered territory, which is why she proved of such high value to the humanistic psychologists whose goal was to invent a new genre of psychology.

"Varieties," less autobiographical, more theoretical, still was not the work of a trained psychologist, nor a formally educated metaphysician, but based on her experience and research in other people's scholarship. Claire worked independently with a wide range of well-connected friends in her intellectual circle. Publishers likely preferred scholars with more traditional credentials creating more recognizable genres.

Despite her sense of failure in receiving the level of attention she had hoped for, her stature grew within the community of psychologists and scholars, and her powers matured and expanded. Frequent incidents of clairvoyance and extrasensory perception guided her choices and augmented her gifts of counsel.

Jean Houston's loyalty in Claire's behalf persisted: Houston called the book "a harbinger of things to come which are about two years around the corner. . . . So keep your chin up and don't fall before each punch. The book *will be* published."[60]

But it was not. And surely it should have been. Edmund Sinnott thought so, agreeing with Jean Houston. Meanwhile, Owens revised and strengthened the manuscript numerous times, paying typists for pristine copies, with carbons, resubmitting to publishers Houston recommended and contacted in advance. Unhappily, one draft got lost in the mail and eventually, after much ado on Owens's part, was returned to her, soaked and ruined; she had to pay a typist to completely retype the soiled, faded pages.

Editors' responses to her work did not reflect its true value or the importance of her contribution to the movement. According to Houston, Owens's unique, dynamic presence secured her significant place in the scientific community. "She was a fine writer with a penchant for the mystical along with an intense curiosity regarding the phenomenology of the mind," she reminisced in a 1996 interview. Like William Blake, Owens demonstrated an uncanny ability to connect with the mystical realms and a gift for articulating her excursions into the cosmic. Houston remembered Owens's moving, eloquent, descriptive passages as "vibrant, vivid, poignant."[61]

Owens's experience was "as broad as it was deep," Houston recalled. Highly educated, erudite, she made her personal experiences accessible to this audience of scholars and thereby contributed an element of authenticity to their scientific findings. The men loved her—that southern charm—but both women and men responded to her as an authentic source of the experience about which they wrote. "She was brought up in a fairy-tale kingdom," which gave her an "Alice-in-Wonderland winsomeness," an innocence that stood in stark contradiction to her aura of sophistication. Part of her charm and part of her mystery arose from this paradox of simplicity and polish, wit and serious purpose—her total commitment to her work, and the total joy she found within it. Her dignity, class, aristocratic bearing contrasted with her openness and vulnerability, especially about matters which, at the time, people were reluctant to discuss. They did not know how. And those who did, like Abraham Maslow, were not always willing to share such deeply personal, emotional moments; others feared being considered highly eccentric at best, demented at worst.[62]

Owens's presence exuded the "dynamism of the twentieth-century birth of women's liberation," Houston observed.[63] She brought into the 1960s and 1970s an aura of history, a sense of the excitement of those prior decades of radical change. Like Robert Harling's "steel magnolias," Owens was emblematic of the southern woman whose strength lies buried beneath a facade of fragile beauty. Like her contemporary Edna St. Vincent Millay, Owens was emblematic of those women of courage whose exuberance for life, for freedom, for exploration of uncharted territories brought the freshness, power, and energy that expanded women's roles for future generations. Though she did not participate in human rights movements of the 1960s and 1970s, Claire's journey was inward and upward rather than politically directed, as evinced in her several memoirs.

"She had a generosity of spirit that fed us. She was our inspiration," Jean Houston proclaimed, calling her an "evocateur" who roused "others to achieve their full potential. She'd been to the depths, and she'd been to the heights. She'd seen the landscapes, she knew where they lay" so when she noticed one of them going in a direction that did not seem appropriate, she would help them redirect their energies, reshape their focus. In this way, Houston defined her as a kind of shaman or guide to the researchers who frequented the transpersonal psychology conferences. "A shaman is one who pushes the membrane of the possible," one who explores huge domains and dimensions that other people do not have the time and energy to do. Owens had taken the time and energy to explore the infinite. "She knew the 'last page' of the story; she made us our maps."[64]

She also knew a great many people and was "a tremendous networker," Houston claimed. A tireless letter writer, she managed to help keep researchers aware of one another's works, inviting them to her home or club, offering to take the train to their homes or offices. "She'd get them talking at conferences and then you'd look over and she'd be there taking notes like mad," Houston observed.[65]

In January of 1969, Huston Smith and Walter Clark encouraged Karlis Osis of the American Society for Psychical Research to contact Owens and invite her to organize a class in New York City to lead others to mystical experiences.[66] She declined, claiming that hers had been spontaneous and she was still searching for a way to induce these mystical experiences for herself. In fact, she was in the throes of serious family problems.

The Owenses were still embroiled in the struggle to resolve their differences concerning Thurston's will. In March of 1969, Claire wrote Thurston that she was trying "to understand how emotionally torn a man might be between his wife and daughter," but she trusted they had worked things out so that "harmony and love from now on" could prevail. She signed her note, "Your devoted wife, who tries to do everything she can to make her 89-year-old husband happy and well," and asked him to keep it at his bedside.[67] Another note assured him that recent changes reflected the stipulations they had agreed on in 1963, when he was in "good condition." "Let's try to make our last years together happy and harmonious. We'll both live longer."[68] But she left nothing to chance, putting their discussions and Gelatt's suggestions in writing.

By April of 1969, Thurston was seriously ill again; his personality changes kept Claire in a state of turmoil. Gelatt came to New Haven to reason with Thurston and walk Claire through their maze of financial records. In person and in letters, Gelatt helped her through many turbulent and frightening periods, finally counseling her to arrange for power of attorney to prevent Thurston from his erratic compulsions to change his will. "I am now nurse, valet, chauffeur, secretary, business partner, housekeeper and cook," she wrote him, now that her household help had been reduced to only part-time employees. "A 90-year-old person requires 25 hours out of the 24." She felt "utterly alone."

Thus, she doubly appreciated Gelatt's counsel, warning that they might have to rely on a nursing home though he understood her reluctance. Ironically, years earlier when his father, Philo, was bedridden, Charles and Claire corresponded privately as he himself refrained to place Philo in an institution, and Claire supported his choices.[69]

In early June, she wrote Houston, everything was in turmoil. Her husband was chronically ill, and she had to take over their legal and financial affairs. "College women should rebel for their education teaches none of the facts of life they have to face sooner or later."

Spending her days with lawyers, bankers, and tax accountants wore her down because she knew "nothing of these things" but was learning, which added stress because her true interests lay elsewhere.[70]

H. Thurston Owens died on June 27, 1969, at Yale–New Haven Hospital, just three months short of his ninetieth birthday. He donated his body to the Yale Medical School. Never a religious man, he instructed Claire that he did not want a church service; therefore, she arranged a private memorial ceremony in their home.

Charles Gelatt, loyal as ever, delivered one of the eulogies, speaking poignantly of his lifelong affection and respect for "Uncle Thursty." William Gentry, a lawyer, spoke on behalf of the members the Quinnipiack. Ina Vestal delivered a touching eulogy as well: "Claire was Thurston's Beloved, his pride and his delight. He was her protector, her strength and her joy" she proclaimed, nostalgically recalling the beginning of their friendship when she came to the door of the house on Livingston Street with a big bouquet of her favorite flowers, lilies of the valley, as a tribute to Claire, "the author of a fine book."

Perhaps that explains Claire's willingness to honor Ina, despite her history of betrayal. Ina called Thurston a man with common sense, "capable, honest, artistic, a pleasure, a Story Book man." But "Story Books must end," she concluded, and quoted from Robert Frost's poem "Stopping by the Woods on a Snowy Evening," her salute to a man who "kept his promises"; she wished him a "peaceful sleep."[71]

Claire sent letters, typed by her friend Grace Sullivan, to the many acquaintances whose notes, food, or attendance at the memorial service made her "sad days endurable." Her loneliness after "so many happy years together" derived from no longer being "'first' in anyone's life or love." But the house was fragrant with roses, which comforted her during the long weekends alone with her memories.[72]

Jean Houston's letter of condolence must have brought Claire a distinct quality of comfort, for it alludes to the "other" life she lived, outside the social and business community she shared with her husband—the community of the mind and spirit she shared with colleagues. Though she could offer "no balm or solace," Houston wrote, perhaps there was comfort in the "assurance that there is no such thing as death but only the continuation of the 'Great Adventure' with its many sleeps and awakenings, its infinite transitions and passageways, its multiple realities and manifold possibilities." She hoped that knowing Thurston "has entered into another phase of his Becoming" would sustain her in months ahead.[73]

"The first six months after a husband dies, a woman feels off-balance. You walk around in a fog," Audrey Fernandez observed in a private conversation.[74] Adjustments for Claire involved her responsibility for the Owenses's complex financial holdings. Although she was left with enough to enjoy a comfortable lifestyle, details confused and frightened her. With her usual intensity, she focused squarely on the problem. Spending hours studying figures, meeting with financial advisors, lawyers, and trust officers, she corresponded regularly with her "prince" Gelatt. His expert advice, generosity, and loving concern guided her through the financial labyrinth for the rest of her life, allowing her to gain a sense of security along with top dollar from her investments. She felt grateful to have sufficient income and planned to stay in her big house for at least another year. She wrote Jean Houston, "The spaciousness and the quiet and especially the garden are a great solace to me in my new loneliness."[75]

14

The End Is the Beginning

1970–1976

Love, like a private sun,
Lights up the greyest days . . .
—Claire Myers Owens, "Love"

DESPITE THE DIFFICULT ADJUSTMENT, Claire did not sit around mourning for long; rather, she garnered her emotions and set them in a new direction. *Loneliness* is a relative term. She found Thurston's absence devastating after a life of support and companionship. All her life, she had considered love more necessary than food or air—without it she would "wither away like an autumn leaf."[1] Accustomed to considering her servants members of her family, she came to rely on the companionship of Margaret Griffin, her Irish Catholic cook, with whom she shared a deep rapport.

Shortly after Thurston Owens's death, his elder daughter, Doree Smedley, sent a sympathy letter to "Mrs. Owens" as she addressed her stepmother, eight years her senior. As it turned out, Doree, a writer and astute businesswoman, had much in common with Claire. Though they never met in person, they exchanged pictures and correspondence for the rest of Claire's life.[2]

Claire responded to Doree's first letter by sending her some of Thurston's family heirlooms. She complimented Doree's excellent book on honey and complained about her arthritic fingers hampering her writing. Doree's answer created a tangible bond between the two women, for Doree had suffered from rheumatoid arthritis, and she had experience in settling family estates. She implored Claire not to sell her home at that time—a shortage of construction along with spiraling inflation made residential property more valuable than "the best bonds or blue chip stocks." With mortgage rates at 9.5 to 10 percent, a buyer would fight for the lowest possible figure. "This is not a good time to buy or sell anything"—furniture, jewelry, or other valuables.

As it turned out, Doree was right. In subsequent letters, she extended further advice on settling the estate—even offering to loan her money, which Claire gratefully refused. Doree, along with her younger sister, Alice Van Zandt Kennet Rogers, had received a portion in trust; she was gracious, not the least greedy, and eager that the settlement go smoothly so lawyers would not end up with most of the Owenses' capital.

Doree took special interest in Claire's painful arthritic condition. "I can tell by your handwriting just how your middle fingers feel—tender, warm to the touch, sensitive and sore. The whole hand is rather stiff and awkward to use at all. I know because my own hands used to be like that." Eight pages of medical instructions and remedies follow Doree's assurance that Claire would regain full use of her hands. She even included a questionnaire designed to identify dietary habits that provoke the disease and analyzed Claire's responses in subsequent letters. But perhaps the most significant contribution Doree made to Claire's life was her willingness to unveil the mysteries surrounding Thurston's first marriage and the births of his daughters.

"Yes, father's marriage to my mother was a tragedy for both of them. A frightful mistake." Though they had known one another from childhood, their meetings were brief and only after their marriage did they discover "they were opposites in all respects." Thurston, practical and "neat as a pin," discovered the first Mrs. Owens, trained as a concert pianist, lived "in the clouds." Her things were in constant "disarray—her hair in wisps, her clothing hitched with safety pins. . . . a daily source of aggravation to him." Sadly, even when she dressed to please him, her slip would show, or she would have a hole in her stockings.

The marriage got off to a disastrous start. During the first year they conceived Doree; her maternal grandmother, "an impossible woman, neurotic, intrusive, and determined to break up the marriage," became an invalid and moved in with the newlyweds. Doree understood how disappointed her father had been after his own lonely, unhappy childhood. "The one thing he wanted above all else as a young man was someone whom he could have all to himself to love and be loved by." But he had married a "girl who irritated him with every breath she drew, [and acquired] a querulous invalid mother-in-law, and a squalling baby." Extenuating circumstances allowed them to separate when Doree was eight months old, and mother, grandmother, and child went to live in Europe for five years. When Thurston joined them in Europe, they reconciled, and Doree's mother immediately became pregnant, against doctors' advice. Shortly after their brief reunion, they separated, divorcing two years later. But Thurston never saw his second daughter. "I know that the only truly peaceful happy years that father ever had were with you. . . . You made up to him all the misery of the past," she wrote Claire. Curiously, Doree did not seem to resent her estranged father. Equally curious was Claire's scant information concerning her husband's unhappy past, prior to Doree's chatty disclosures. Nothing more was disclosed about Alice, nor is there evidence she ever contacted Claire.

Coincidentally, Doree and Claire shared a common interest in mysticism. Claire sent Doree a copy of her article "Mystical Experience: Facts and Values"; Doree called it a "splendid piece of work" and "a formidable task." Doree's research included extensive reading of Jung, Freud, and Eastern religions, along with the use of yoga as part of her recovery from arthritis. All of their letters were energetic and deeply intellectual, but not until 1971 did they begin calling one another by their first names.[3]

In some ways, Doree provided the transition Claire needed for closure on the Thurston portion of her life. The first couple of months after Thurston died, Claire, now seventy-three, remained at home writing letters, refusing social invitations, considering her future. She wanted more than "cocktail parties and matinees."[4] She wanted to define a new way of living; she had the wisdom to "rush in where fools feared to tread" in order to do so.

Because she considered her spontaneous mystical awakening to have been her most beautiful experience, she continued to search for a method that would allow her to replicate the event and reach a higher state of consciousness. She read the latest research in her field. Her praise for the work of Jean Houston and Robert Masters was prodigious: "YOU ARE A GENIUS. Maybe you both are," she wrote Houston in December of 1969, having read their latest book. "I am still staggered by the immensity, originality, and importance of your work and the profundity of my own experience which you induced . . . I long to work for you. May I? You are the wave of the future."[5]

With her freedom to travel restored, she would take the train to New York and submit to the series of experiments Houston and Masters conducted at their Foundation for Mind Research. In part, she was curious; in part, she was searching for relief from her crippling arthritis. "She was in terrible pain all the time, not just in her hands," Houston explained. "But it affected her writing and typing skills"; the relaxation sessions with Houston eased her pain. She loved a particular audiovisual machine that used polarized light to create images that would dissolve and flow into each other. "She would put her hands up against the screen and the energy from the light would heal the pain and tension," Houston recalled.[6]

After one light session, Houston took Claire on a guided meditation during which Claire saw an image of her father in a field of Texas wildflowers and later an archetypal image of a wise old man. "He looks exactly like Michelangelo's painting on the ceiling of the Sistine Chapel—the one of God in swirling draperies, pointing a finger at Adam." Only Adam was not there; rather she saw herself as "a small white figure wearing red," her favorite color. Houston instructed her to listen to the figure's nonverbal communication. Claire put her hand on his knee, and he silently spoke: "You must not expect me to bring you to self-realization again as I did before. You must work for it this time."[7]

And work for it she did. Experimenting with various approaches and philosophies ultimately brought her to Zen, which she saw as her karma. Although sitting in meditation hurt her knees and back, she intended to adapt the method to her own needs and then move on—typical behavior for Claire. All her life she would embrace a philosophy, master it, retain what worked, drop what failed, and move on to her next challenge. She had no intention of becoming a part of the Zen tradition or community; rather, she sought to make Zen a part of her own. But in the beginning she needed appropriate training.

Roshi Philip Kapleau, founder of the Rochester Zen Center, whom she met at a seminar in Pennsylvania the Labor Day weekend following Thurston's death, told her of a group of Yale students looking for a place to meditate.[8] "I had this big empty house," she would tell audiences in lectures that traced her journey. "So I opened my home to these students." Several times a week, six to twelve young men and women came to sit. When she opened the door to them the first time, she was horrified to find the "great unwashed" standing on her front porch. The year was 1970, and this was Ivy League territory. "Unwashed" was in, along with long hair, beards, love beads, sandals, bell-bottoms, and flowered granny dresses, emblems of hippie fashion. Mind expansive techniques offered by Zen meditation and philosophy helped many youth of the counterculture transcend their drug addictions and mediate their disillusionment with an overly materialistic establishment and unethical world politics, especially the Vietnam War.

The timing was karmic indeed, since Thurston Owens would not have allowed such an unkempt-looking group—even Yalies—to enter his home. Claire, concerned about her conventional neighbors' reactions, went from door to door describing the sittings as "discussion group meetings" from Yale. In this neighborhood, inhabited by many Yale alumni and faculty, people could hardly object. She never mentioned Zen or meditation—"they would have been completely mystified by that." But when Claire opened her door, she opened her heart, and the students became her closest friends—many for the rest of her life.

Once again, Claire Myers Owens stood in the center of change. Her last two decades paralleled her first two; she lived in pursuit of a better world and a better self. Freedom for women coming of age in the 1920s and 1930s meant sexual and intellectual liberation; in the 1970s and 1980s, for a liberated elderly woman, freedom meant transcendence of the worldly realm and access to the eternal. Her rigorous search for good within paralleled youth culture's rallies for human rights and freedom. But sexuality for Claire remained part of her southern charm and demeanor. Her dignity and grace measured against her youthful enthusiasm; her "winsomeness," made her erotically irresistible, even to some men forty years younger.

When Dwain Wilder rang the doorbell at 286 Livingston, he had arrived twenty minutes early for his first sitting. Describing his first encounter with Claire, he recalled "an immediate electricity." They fell into a conversation and "when she found out I was from Texas, well, within twenty minutes we just spilled out our hearts to each other. No one else had arrived, and then people would come in and she was ignoring them and opening the door and pointing them upstairs for the sitting."[9] His first impression was that here stood the most beautiful woman he had ever laid eyes upon. As for the issue of age, he claimed, "the only thing I thought about age was that if she was twenty years younger or I was twenty years older we would have had a raging affair—that's the only thing I thought about age. Somehow I sensed that we were twenty years out of range of each other. So I must have thought that she was fifty or sixty. I was about thirty."[10]

Claire remembered Dwain asking her age shortly after they met. "How old do you think?" she replied smoothly. "Oh, about fifty," he answered. "Fifty is a nice age. I always feel a permanent forty."[11] He was twenty-nine and she was seventy-three. During the ensuing years, Dwain laughingly recalled, "She would be insulted if I underestimated her age by not enough years!" He took it upon himself to call her by her first name; all of the others called her Mrs. Owens, as she preferred. "More dignified."

Claire's memories of their early days together differ slightly from Dwain's. As Claire tells it, she noticed Dwain across the room during a zazen (meditation) session, when their eyes met and a spark ignited that "flamed and later flared until we were both almost consumed. . . . [We] laughed at everything, at nothing, smiled into each-others' eyes, were

15. Dwain Wilder, c. 1971. Claire's younger love. Photograph courtesy of the TWU Woman's Collection.

tender, considerate, wounded at every imagined slight. We scarcely dared to be alone . . . [or] dared to touch. Incredible as it seemed, passion boiled underneath the surface of propriety. I feared a volcanic explosion any moment."[12]

Members of the Zen group they formed a few years later in Rochester, New York, recall they did nothing to disguise their feelings for one another. Claire thought they were "circumspect in the presence of others. But when alone he would stand looking down into my eyes . . . as if a stream of golden light flowed from his eyes into mine. . . . Never had the charisma of a man so overwhelmed me."[13]

Well, never since Aldous Huxley, George Wanders, or Carton Moore-Park. Once again, she felt like an "inexperienced high school girl." Dwain asked her what she intended to do about her sex life now that her husband was gone. "Oh, sublimate it, I reckon," she replied, reverting to a southern idiom. He assured her that would not be necessary if they followed their "natural instincts."[14]

"Good lord," she thought, "is he blind?" Did he not notice the lines in her face, her white hair? She warned him that the disparity in their ages would feel like incest if they took their erotic feelings to a physical level. She worried that she and Dwain would appear ridiculous in the eyes of his peers. Endlessly, she pondered their dilemma: if she consented to an affair, she would have to tell him her real age or he would feel betrayed when he found out; however, if she told him there were forty years difference between them, she might lose him forever.

Silently she railed against society's double standards, reviving her feminist vision: When men in their sixties married girls in their twenties, they were congratulated. The current women's liberation movement that declared men and women equal in everything seemed not to apply. "Men had always supported mistresses and no one laughed. But then men had always arranged life for men's benefit. Every woman knew that."[15]

Claire did not realize that Dwain did not care. He thought not in terms of years but of connections, companionship. Their discussions, laughter, and inexplicable passionate spark mattered more to him. He came earlier and earlier to the yoga sessions and stayed late after the others left. One day he declared his love, not just with his eyes but "verbally, explicitly." Claire walked around for days in a state of ecstasy. Her dilemma deepened: "It is abnormal, unhealthy," she chided herself. "I don't care . . . Love is love wherever it occurs." She could not sleep or eat; she floated on a "rosy cloud of rapture."[16] She felt compassion for those older women who fall hopelessly in love with younger men and end up losing everything. She was seized by an urge to give Dwain everything: her car, house, money, body, life. But she refused to allow her emotions to destroy her; rather, she felt "nourished, rejuvenated" by their love. His presence in their "make-shift zendo" (meditation room), in the guest bedroom on the second floor, enveloped and penetrated her entire "body, mind and heart like a powerful fragrance."

Once, when he rescued her from a stumble, her "whole being melted, suffused with ineffable sweetness."[17]

Dwain and Claire went to the Greasy Spoon and ate chili; to avant-garde movies "where sex was made degenerate not beautiful"; to guitar concerts; and for rides in his convertible "where the roar of the engine drowned out all conversation and the wild wind reduced [her] elegant coiffure to a wreck." Privately, she called herself a love-sick idiot. Dwain continued to date and have sex with girls his own age who "seemed to have emotional problems," which he discussed with Claire. Rather than love, she thought his chief interest lay in helping them and that he "displayed a slight messianic complex." She feared marriage to any of these emotionally disturbed girls would wreck his life, and she told him so.[18]

After several months, Dwain began to evince signs of conflict regarding this "filial but dangerously passionate" involvement with an older woman. They both felt caught in whirlwind forces beyond control. Drawing on theories from Carl Jung, Claire told Dwain that his feelings were common to all men; what appeared to be incestuous represented the longing for the mother as a symbol of "man's desire for union with the deepest level of his unconscious, a desire to return to the cosmic source." The incestuous feeling represented a "vehicle of psychological rebirth." While Dwain looked dubious, she took comfort in her "beautiful" explanations.[19]

In letters to Jean Houston, she confided her discomfort in this "very serious situation."[20] Referring to Dwain as the "tall handsome charming young man from Texas," she described his cheerful disposition interrupted by days of frustration and panic. He had been married once and had two "unsatisfactory" affairs; Claire's heart bled when she saw him suffer. She tried to help him prevent a nervous breakdown, teaching him to combine Houston's theory of the four integral levels of consciousness[21] with zazen to obtain a spiritual, therapeutic experience. She assured him his life would be informed by the "eternal truths of the deep unconscious" and offered to sacrifice to help him, "like a mother who must give up her only beloved son in order to save him." For if he achieved enlightenment he might lose interest in her as a "mother substitute." Then they could "evolve into the new beings of which [Teilhard de] Chardin speaks where we love everyone regardless of age, sex or status."

The following month she reached a psychological breakthrough. In dreams and in zazen, she saw the old wise man image she first saw during her session with Jean Houston. But her way to him was blocked by buildings. Her breakthrough came when she envisioned herself pushing aside two skyscrapers; they turned out to be "mere children's blocks," and she emerged on the other side, enfolded in a golden light, standing before the figure. A young man in dark clothes and a dark hat appeared in silhouette, which she believed to be the personification of the conscious mind. She realized her longing for a son, for his undivided love and attention, had been latent in her unconscious, overwhelming her when she met Dwain. His need for "mother love with a little spice added" had been equally overpowering for him.[22]

She told Dwain she knew their relationship was "bad for him," and that they should just be "mild friends." Naturally, both of them realized this was merely an intellectual decision; it had no effect on either of their feelings. She tried to prepare herself for the time when their intense relationship would end; but again her decisions had little bearing on her emotions. To her chagrin, Dwain began to "cool off first." She took it as a good sign—"all sons are more eager to be free of close ties to their mothers" than mothers of their sons. But both of them suffered horribly. "We would sit and talk about it from six to nine in the evening, without dinner." Eventually, he brought "his current girl friend to the meditation group, which meant the queen bee (myself) would be dethroned. I found it very humiliating and asked him to wait another few weeks before bringing her again."[23]

Then she had an image during zazen in which a pair of hands presented a broken heart to the wise old man/God figure. Her rational mind declared it for the best, but her feelings and body felt the opposite. She maintained pride in her decorum: "I never got angry or cried in his presence. I attempted to appear pleasantly indifferent." But

Dwain's intuitive nature made her doubt she deceived him. Nothing eased the pain until she recognized their drifting apart as a healthy natural process. She compared him to a tree whose long roots had grown all through her body, which filled her with serenity and acceptance. She seemed to have reached an interpretation of their connection as organic, natural.[24]

Synchronistically,[25] she read Edgar Cayce's warning to beginning meditators that erotic passion may be aroused to an extreme degree of intensity. In India the energy that shoots through the seven chakras or psychic centers, known as Kundalini (energy stored at base of the spine, released through meditation), can be dangerous without proper guidance from an enlightened teacher.[26] Claire tempered her torrid emotional upheaval with such rational and intuitive insights—and off she went on another adventure.

The group continued to meet several times a week. In between, the students stopped by to visit and pour out their troubles. Some had used drugs. Most came from prominent homes with parents distressed to see their children turn from Christianity. Two Jewish members, a girl from Yale and another from Vassar, practiced Zen because they considered psychoanalysis an obstacle to enlightenment. Claire believed that to be whole, one must use both reason and intuition, that each supports the other in achieving a deeper level of clarity. This theory led to her later work with left- and right-brain functions applied to all aspects of understanding.

The group of Yale students held deep intellectual discussions before and after their sittings, comparing the values of their respective generations. Youth inspired Claire; she mentored them, told her life stories, animating social history. "Did your generation rebel against anything?" they asked, and she would tell them how she left home at twenty in rebellion against traditional roles for women, and of her parents' outrage at her taking jobs doing social work or clerking in bookstores: "Southern ladies did not do such things. To be a lady was the highest ideal." She tried to explain the paradox embedded in the widely accepted values of her time that required women, especially southern women, to take degrees in domestic science and then forbade them to do their own housework. One girl protested, "I've never heard of such a thing!"[27]

However, when one student remarked that the Old South sounded like the dark ages, Claire's answers revealed her acceptance of her unique past: "Like all societies the deep South was a mixture of good and bad. It taught dignity and self-confidence, integrity and honor, hospitality and graciousness." But, she explained that her father's adherence to Jeffersonian ideals of democracy measured against her mother's puritanical and Baptist standards and her grandmother's nostalgia for antebellum traditions left her conflicted. "It required many years for me to realize that my family, church, school and even my grandmother were actually trying to instill ethics into me."[28]

She saw this young generation as way ahead of her own, with their beginning at a point it had taken her a lifetime to achieve. And yet, she had rebelled against similar issues: domination over women, sexual double standards. Her generation "rebelled within the framework of existing society" rather than developing a counterculture. She explained how she had participated in the rebellious 1920s fashions by cutting her hair short and wearing short skirts, the opposite of their fashion protest of long hair and ankle-length skirts. She had "demonstrated" her protests by smoking in public, drinking at speakeasies, and exploring sexuality without marriage. Her generation worked for the money that gave them independence, while this generation took financial support even as they expressed hatred of their parents.[29]

Late into the night, the group analyzed the effects on society of materialism, the generation gap, the values of Zen, and the self-realization movement, which "some day might prevent the world from destroying itself."[30] Without mentioning the word *feminism*, Claire's innate regard for gender bias informed her values. "What about love?" one pretty girl demanded, and Claire, sighing, reflected: "Ah yes, we women have placed romantic love as the chief value of our lives. That is why we have suffered so much."[31]

"Mrs. Owens," one young man remarked, "you were certainly many years ahead of your time. The counterculture has just now caught up with you. In many ways you are more like us than we are ourselves."[32]

Eight months after the Zen group began meeting at her home, some of the members decided to further their study under the direct guidance of Roshi Philip Kapleau at the Zen Center in Rochester, New York. That spring Claire accompanied them on a visit. She toured the center and its "large impressive zendo" with a gold figure of Buddha on the alter surrounded by flowers and fruit offerings below. Zen followers tended to speak of "vibrations," and while Claire claimed she never knew exactly what that meant, "that zendo certainly emanated something—not holy exactly—but indescribable—different."[33]

That afternoon she met Audrey Fernandez, a tall, attractive, well-dressed woman in her forties who became her friend for life. Roshi drove Claire and Audrey out to the country estate of one of the prominent members of the center. The following day they attended the annual picnic on the grounds of the estate of another member. The young people eagerly encouraged Claire to join them. "We need older people here, Claire" they told her, not realizing she bristled when they dropped the formal address of Mrs. Owens. "We are all so young and inexperienced. We don't know nothin' about nothing." Claire, flattered by their attention and enchanted with the atmosphere Zen life offered, remained convinced she would never leave New Haven.[34] When the school year ended in June, Dwain urged Claire to sell her house and move with them.

"What! Leave my beautiful home where I lived for thirty-two happy years with my husband! Give up my friends and my three devoted servants! They are irreplaceable!" He should go; though she would miss him terribly, moving was "absolutely out of the question."

"But I *need* you, Claire. The young people at the Center need you. The Center is where you belong." He offered to find her a suitably elegant apartment and come back and move her belongings himself, after he settled. She laughed, told him he had lost his mind. Still, she called Charles Gelatt for financial advice; he told her the deciding factor must be "her happiness." But he recommended she make "absolutely certain" she wanted to move before she placed her house on the market.[35]

In a letter to Dwain written shortly after he left, she inquired, "How many blocks did you say it was from 1400 and 1600 East Ave. to the Center, please kind sir?" referring to the apartment buildings he had described. Lonely without her young friends, she wrote: "286 and I miss all of you terribly but I am getting a little rest. It was a beautiful 8 months—richly rewarding I hope to everyone." She signed, "Affectionately, Claire O," though she still loved him intensely.[36]

Letters to Jean Houston at the time bear witness to her drastic readjustment: "Did you read of Abe Maslow's death?" she asked sadly that June. She was ever grateful for Houston's contribution to her well-being in the face of so many losses—Maslow's death, her new friends moving away. Thanks to Houston's "wisdom and generosity," her fingers were better. The relaxation techniques worked. In July, she offered to relieve Houston of the "burden" of helping her market "Varieties of Self-Realization." Not wanting to impose further, Claire thought she might write McGraw-Hill or Norton or Putnam, which had published many Jungian authors. Or perhaps she would just use Christopher again and publish it herself, though the cost had increased to $5,000 and her money was still tied up in Thurston's estate. She thanked Jean Houston for a noble job.[37]

Perhaps Claire's karma put her in the path of young men and women; or perhaps the subject of her interests appealed to a younger generation. In either case, along with the graduate students from Yale, several other younger men came into her life as a result of her published work. These young men—John White, Kenneth Ring, Ken Wilber, Charles Tart, Raul daSilva—were then and are now, actively involved in the human potential and transpersonal psychology movement on various levels.

In the course of researching his first book, *The Highest State of Consciousness*, John White discovered Claire Myers Owens's book *Awakening to the Good* and her article "Mystical Experience—Facts and Values." The focus of White's research in consciousness studies of human development paralleled Owens's focus.[38] When he noticed she lived in New Haven, White called her. They felt an affinity by phone and made a lunch date. John White, whom Claire described as "tall, dark and very handsome," picked her up at home, and they went

16. Dr. Kenneth Ring, 1978. Courtesy of Dr. Ring.

to lunch at the top of the Klein Biology Tower, which offers a lovely, panoramic view of New Haven.

John White reminisces: "We spent an hour or so talking. I was working for the New England Telephone Company at that time, and overstayed my lunch hour, but it was such a delight to meet this lovely lady. Thereafter, we got to be good friends . . . and colleagues." She visited his home in Cheshire once, met his wife and children; shortly thereafter, she moved to Rochester and they stayed in touch by phone and by letter.[39]

White and Owens became literary collaborators, agent and author as well as friends. He helped her publish *Zen and the Lady* in 1979, and he reprinted *Awakening to the Good* in 1983 as *Small Ecstasies*, for which he wrote the foreword.[40] In her will, she designated John White her literary executor and made him heir to her published works.

As she began to consider moving to Rochester, she fretted endlessly, dialoguing with her "two selves" concerning the pros and cons:

17. John White, c. 1970. Courtesy of Mr. White.

the hassles of relocation, finding a new grocer, dentist, physician, lawyer, trust officer, hairdresser. She loved this "beautiful little state with its magnificent woodlands . . . dreaming blue hills, sparkling little brooks."[41] She would miss her friends of thirty years: Lucy Hammer, a state senator from 1961 to 1973, with whom she shared a deep aversion to cooking; Louise Ames, a prominent child psychologist with a prolific publication record; Lois Triffin; and, of course, Ina Vestal, despite their history of conflict.[42] She wept, prayed, meditated, and chastised herself for daring to trade all the wonderful things she had for an uncertain future. She reviewed her assets with a new appreciation: the

18. Raul daSilva, 1975. Courtesy of Mr. daSilva.

elegant Lawn Club, the prestigious Quinnipiack with the "best food in town." She walked the grounds of her garden, touching the forsythia bushes, the poplar, the white pine and gigantic oaks, the dogwoods that lit the green garden with white blossoms, the hemlock hedge Thurston had planted for her across the front, the park across the street where she and Thurston had walked happily among the trees and down along the Mill River. She stood at the front window and watched the "rays of late afternoon sun touch the East Rock palisades to a luminous red."

"I live in a beautiful green bower of trees—how could I ever abandon it?" Her cook Margaret Griffin pleaded, "Oh Mrs. Owens, I thought I was going to take care of you the rest of your life." When they both realized Margaret could not leave her own family to follow her employer, they put their arms around each other and cried. "How could I live without her?" Claire wondered, calling her a fine noble woman.[43] She walked around her home, seeing it with new eyes: the eighteenth-century decor, the crystal chandeliers, the Hepplewhite sideboard with its glossy mahogany luster, the sweeping red damask draperies. But a faint voice reminded her that Zen eschews attachment to material things. Perhaps leaving would release her into an even higher dimension of spirituality. In the end, loneliness won. "I am so utterly alone. I long for a 'flight of the alone into the Alone,'" she thought, quoting a mystic whose name she had forgotten.[44] With her new Zen family, she would rebuild her life and pursue her spiritual quest. "*I cannot do it alone.* And without it, my life will be an empty nothingness."[45]

She flew to Rochester and looked at the apartments Dwain had described. He had decided to marry his girlfriend; the timing made her decision all the more painful and conflicted. But when Dwain met her at the airport, "his face was shining like the harvest moon." He flung his arms about her and kissed her "soundly." Then he introduced her to Cindy. That night, after a strained dinner at the home of friends from the Center, Dwain and Cindy came into her room to say good night. When Cindy departed, Dwain "caught me in his arms, pressed my breast fiercely against his chest, his heart pounding wildly, and kissed me full on the lips with pent-up passion again and again. Such a wave of desire and love and unutterable sweetness flooded my body, my mind and heart, my whole being. . . . This was exactly what we had been longing to do for a whole year. It seemed so right, so inevitable, the culmination of something, a fulfillment, the end of our affair."[46]

She withdrew murmuring, "No, no, my dear darling . . . not ever again. . . . But I'm glad. Just this once." When he left, she sobbed herself to sleep. But in the morning she urged Dwain to marry Cindy, if he must marry at all, because she was "far superior" to his former girlfriends, who she said would have wrecked his life. She visited the Sutton Park high-rise apartment at 1400 East Avenue and found it to her liking: the bedroom and living room, large and well proportioned, graced by a wall of glass facing east that flooded the whole apartment with morning sunshine. With a heavy heart, she signed the lease for number 317.[47] Yet she knew it was the right thing to do, exchanging "an eleven room house with four baths and three servants" for a simple lifestyle. And though she felt ambivalent about Dwain's decision to marry, she knew it was best for him.

She flew back to New Haven and put her house on the market. The timing was far from ideal with interest at 8 percent and a depressed market. In May 1969, the house had been appraised for $67,500; by the summer of 1970, Claire, with the approval of Charles Gelatt, offered her beloved property at a mere $60,000. Thurston's gross estate amounted to nearly $200,000, and she had $136,471 left, after she settled their liabilities and his two daughters received their trust funds.[48] With Gelatt's generous continuation of Thurston's pension, Claire had enough money to live comfortably, either in New Haven or Rochester.

She spent the summer allowing "strangers" to walk through her home as she sorted through her cherished belongings, arranged for an estate sale and auction, and bid her lifelong friends good-bye. In July, Charles Gelatt came to visit and consult further on her financial investments. Ever the lady, Claire arranged for him to stay at the "Q" club and offered to give a cocktail party in his honor. By that time, eight couples had looked at the house, but no one had made an offer; she hoped the house would sell when Yale faculty returned for the fall semester. In August, her cousin Laura Lee Jacobson came to visit and help with the packing. Claire began to feel a sense of completeness through her sense of "family" connections and wrote Dwain how "amazing and wonderful" it was to find a "sister" in her cousin; a "brother" in Gelatt, and a "son" in him.[49] "If we were all blood relations I doubt if the feeling could be any deeper or more intense." The house sold in October, after Claire moved out, to a Mrs. Thatch who bought it for $47,000—a steal at the time, for Livingston Street was then, is now, and always had been "the most beautiful" and prestigious street in New Haven.[50]

On October 1, 1970, Dwain arrived by bus to drive them to Rochester in her car. He looked "ravishingly beautiful—not handsome—beautiful" in his blue coat and tie that "accentuated the blueness of his eyes. His hair was washed and combed, his face well-shaven." She invited him to one of her clubs for dinner and to prove she was not old-fashioned, she also invited the "rich homosexual" from whom Dwain had rented a room during graduate school. They had a delightful evening. That night Dwain stayed in her guest room, the one they had used as a zendo all those months. "Early next morning we sallied forth on the greatest adventure of our lives—of my life at any rate."[51]

Alone in that house, did they consummate their love? According to Claire's memoirs, they did not. Not then, not before, and not later as their relationship deepened, though the eroticism between them deepened as well. However, an undated letter to Dwain with a heading typed, "PRIVATE!!! CONFIDENTIAL * DESTROY AFTER READING PLEASE FOR YOUR EYES ONLY" referred to their "*beautiful secret* not to be mentioned or discussed with anyone—ever." Although "it" would not and should not happen again, paradoxically "it" had constituted the reassurance she needed to finalize her moving plans.[52]

If anything intimate had occurred between them at an earlier time, it would have been during that weekend in Rochester, for the note further stated that she would not have left that check with the apartment manager, had "this totally unexpected unplanned beautiful incident not occurred." She wondered if he was as "astounded" as she had been. "Nothing must ever be allowed to interfere with your normal happy healthy life with a sweet girl and wife your own age." She hoped he was not, in retrospect, disturbed by the incident—warm, comforting, and strengthening—something they both needed: "I mean our mother-son relation."[53] Modesty generates ambiguity: Did they? Did they not? Dwain Wilder, in a 1996 interview, balked at a definite answer, leaving their love story veiled in mystery, defined by discretion.[54]

Their drive back to Rochester remained one of her most thrilling memories: a "glorious Indian summer day—hot sun, cool dry air that acted like an elixir." Wrapped in their intimate private world "inside a little glass house on wheels," she relished every golden minute of the eight-hour trip. When she arrived, exhausted but blissfully happy, she was shattered by Dwain's eagerness to reunite with Cindy. The "silver cord" between them severed, she began to question the wisdom of selling her house at a loss. She wondered if she had wrecked her life completely and spent the night feeling the roots of her new life cut the very minute she had arrived. In the ensuing months, Claire and Cindy "struggled valiantly to become friends"; she was glad that Dwain loved Cindy. As a woman, she "did not want to see any woman marry without being loved by her husband. . . . It was all very confusing."[55]

Claire invited Cindy and Dwain to join her for dinner at the Manhattan Restaurant in Rochester, but her attempt to host a warm, friendly evening turned out a "miserable failure." She wondered what she could have done to hurt Cindy, "the last thing she wanted." In a May 26, 1971, letter, she enclosed a check for fifty dollars and instructed Cindy to buy herself a wedding gift "from Claire with love." In another letter, she offered to pay for their wedding reception and assured Cindy that Dwain was not her only young male friend: "I have several others and also girlfriends. I am devoted to them." She wrote Cindy that although she and Dwain shared a fondness, they felt like "nephew and aunt" and she wanted Dwain to marry because it was "the only way to human fulfillment of a certain kind. . . . But I have never seen a happy marriage happen all by itself." Success takes "constant thoughtful and constructive work."[56] In the long run, wisdom prevailed. She kept her distance from Dwain and focused on her "true" motives for moving—a new sangha (spiritual community) surrounded by youthful friends, a sense of belonging, and a commitment to extensive Zen practice.

By the following spring, securely settled in her apartment, she became deeply involved in Zen Center activities. Finding its six- to eight-hour sessions strenuous, she achieved ample psychic rewards; she was firmly on the path. Once, after six hours of zazen, she beheld a vivid image of a large golden teapot three feet wide with undulating pale blue lines "like small eels dancing on their tails." Then the teapot slipped to the floor and became flat like one of Dali's melted watches. She had reached what Jean Houston called the "sensory level" or third integral level of consciousness. She wrote a poem on meditation, "The Seven Wonders of the Inner World," and an article called "Zen in the Light of Modern Psychology," which Philip Kapleau asked to publish in *Zen Bow*, the Center's bimonthly literary journal.[57]

The "Dwain situation," she wrote Houston, "had evolved into a warm affectionate relationship. Nothing dire happened at any time and his fiancée is a dear." Dwain asked her three times to move to his same apartment house so they could live as a "tribal family." She refused, choosing "to be alone, free and quiet." She took from Zen what she needed, using it as a "good but arduous technique for inducing self-realization." She was happy with her rigorous schedule, rising at 4:30 a.m. to write, meditating until 9:30 p.m. for "three whole days." Everyone was "simply marvelous" to her: the five doormen, the three garage attendants, two managers, and the superintendent and his wife, a nurse. "They read my books too and even contributed money to the Center voluntarily. Not Zenists. I just love them all, they are so kind."[58]

Claire seemed fulfilled and happy. Accepted as a voice of distinction in the field of transpersonal psychology, though she had no formal credentials, her lectures elicited overwhelming affection from both professional audiences and lay groups. Her original awakening experience converged with her current quest to repeat it. She brought Zen techniques into psychological theory and she brought psychology to Zen, despite Roshi Kapleau's rejection of her infusion of rational explanation into their practices.

Philip Kapleau's book *The Three Pillars of Zen* reflects his studies in Japan.[59] He practiced under two of the great Zen masters of the time, Harada-roshi and Yasutani-roshi, coming to awakening while studying with Yasutani-roshi. His three pillars, as the book's subtitle suggests, consist of teaching, practice, and enlightenment. As Geoff Lister explains, the actual practice techniques consist of "zazen, the unique meditative tradition of Zen; *teisho*, or public talk by the teacher; and *dokusan*, or private interview with the teacher. The unique combination of these three elements creates an energetic, dynamic quality, unique to Zen—the 'flavor of Zen.'"[60]

As Kapleau writes in his preface to the 1964 edition, "Zen is a religious practice with a unique method of body-mind training whose aim is awakening, that is, Self-realization." His goal to "convey the religious character and spirit of Zen [appeals] to the heart no less than to the mind."[61]

Kapleau dedicated his book to his teachers Harada-roshi, the Sōtō master Yasutani-roshi, and to Nakagawa-roshi, who "selflessly taught the truth of the Dharma [the nature of the universe] for the welfare of all beings."

Such sentiments aligned with Claire's determination to discover the good in mankind as a path to self-realization. Nevertheless, because Claire used Zen as only one element on her path, a contentious relationship evolved between her and the Roshi. Kapleau's leadership required adherence to strict guidelines for practice, which rubbed against Claire's determined usage of the lessons of his wisdom to enrich her own goals. Claire needed freedom while Kapleau preferred a more structured approach. Thus, Claire believed that Kapleau resented her need for independence, especially her inclination to incorporate his teachings into her interest in transpersonal psychology. As Dogen Zenji, founder of Sōtō Zen, put it: "To study Buddhism is to study the self, to study the self is to forget the self."[62] Using Zen to transcend the self into oneness with the "light," Claire believed she would unveil the secret to the mysteries of self-realization.

Several important essays she published during the 1960s and 1970s record her progress in learning to articulate the difference between spontaneous and induced awakenings.[63] She had come to understand her own Great Awakening in 1950 as a moment of spontaneous enlightenment or self-actualization. Now, through Zen, she designed a complex comparison between the steps of the two processes. When spontaneous awakenings occur, the actualization of the self is attained first. "The onslaught is so sudden and violent . . . the nervous system becomes exhausted and requires periodic rests. Purgation and dark night of the soul are stages in the enlightenment process that bring rest from the exaltation of living in a perpetual ecstatic state." But they cause untold hours of distress. One feels desolate and depressed after a long period of utter bliss.

"The induced variety, attained through a concentrated program of meditation techniques, reverses the stages of the process: the dark night of the soul precipitates the rigorous search for relief."[64] Thus, the highest state is attained last, and the changes are gradual, requiring several years—a lifetime for some. The nerves adjust to the physical changes, and the transformation, though similar in scope to the spontaneous variety, is less traumatic and more peaceful. Meditation, along with the study of Eastern philosophy and religion, induces enlightenment beneficial for the devotee of mysticism far more than those few lucky people on whom mystical insight descends unsought. The self-realization ethic is essential to the formation of a "new society," that ever-elusive utopian tomorrow Owens and her colleagues in the human potential movement dreamed was near, and crucial. "Self-knowledge—the essence of soul or unconscious—is the key to survival of the individual and of the planet."

Such is the path of mystics and of saints; such is the journey for self-discovery that became central to the humanistic and transpersonal psychology movements and which merged religion and psychology, science and mysticism. The path to self-realization is a search for the divine within, for according to John White, "Self-realization is God-realization."[65]

In 1972, Charles Tart, professor of transpersonal psychology at the University of California, Davis, invited Philip Kapleau to contribute a chapter on Zen to his anthology *Transpersonal Psychologies.* Kapleau handed the opportunity over to Owens who, a bit disconcerted by such an enormous task, accepted. When she expressed doubt concerning her competence for the project, the Roshi told her, "Your work can be your practice." She claimed, as she often did while describing some newly realized insight, "I did not believe a word of it." Unfortunately, Kapleau came to resent her time-consuming devotion to producing her chapter for the highly-regarded anthology. Writing this chapter proved to be the most difficult exercise in her career, and the most exhilarating. Roshi was right; her work became "joyous play" as she experienced harmony between her conscious and her unconscious mind.[66]

The results, a clear, well-organized study, parallels Zen and Western psychology. Its publication put her in the company of leading spirituality experts. The book as a whole, erudite, scholarly, and interdisciplinary, attempts to bridge the gap between orthodox Western psychology and a number of transpersonal psychologies integral to specific spiritual disciplines, with two chapters on Buddhism, one by Claire Myers Owens and the other by Daniel Goleman, a graduate of Harvard with a PhD in personality and clinical psychology.[67] The essay underscores Owens's long-term interest in integrating Western science and culture with spirituality.

Owens's chapter opens with the question, "Is Zen a psychology, a philosophy or a religion? Or a lifestyle that actualizes man's noblest potentials?" For Owens, the path to enlightenment had been religious and psychological, spiritual and scientific. Clearly this interdisciplinary approach fit her experience and vision, allowing her to articulate her discoveries in a Zen context.

Nevertheless, the difficulties she encountered writing and editing this chapter took its toll; ill much of the time, Claire battled stomach cramps and digestion problems. Letters from her brother in Temple brought further disturbing news of illness and financial loss. Despite their differences concerning the settlement of their mother's estate years earlier, Claire demonstrated compassion and love for her brother in his time of need: "I am mailing you my two diamond rings to do with as you see fit. They are the only jewelry of value I have. Let Ruby wear them a while or sell them immediately as you wish." One appraiser valued them together to be worth $4,500 retail; another valued them at $3,800. She hoped they would help.[68]

For the next two years they stayed in touch, exchanging family news, checking on one another's health. In January of 1974, Coren wrote his last letter to "Clairene" expressing concern for her welfare. He felt lucky at "almost 80" because he was still working and fortunate to have his wife, Ruby, a "truly wonderful person," looking after him.[69] Coren died on May 22, 1974, and was buried at Hillcrest Cemetery in Temple; Claire remembered both Ruby and her niece, Sue Allen Harris, in subsequent drafts of her will.[70]

On November 12, 1972, she drove to the Zen Center to take Roshi a box of special dates and to drop off a section of her manuscript for him to check for accuracy.[71] She felt too weak to attend the zazen in the third-floor zendo. Dwain, there for the sitting, expressed his concern about her weakness; she told him that on the seventh, election night, she had vomited all night everything she had eaten. She was not feeling much better five days later.

"Why didn't you call me?" he asked angrily.

"What, at 2 in the morning?"

"What difference would that make? If you're sick you call me no matter when it is and I'll come."[72]

He drove her home, offering to stop for soup and fruit. She declined the food, but accepted the ride. In the garage, he put his arms around her and they laughed. Upstairs he fixed her tea and made her bed. He felt guilty for neglecting her, but he had been busy getting married, having a baby, and moving to a house.[73]

Claire had not been alone. No sooner did Dwain disappear from her daily life, than a new young man affiliated with the center, Larry McSpadden, took over as surrogate. The "only living person" who could decipher her handwriting, Larry volunteered to type her drafts. Their sessions would last whole afternoons: "We talked, worked on my manuscript, laughed a lot, discussed Zen seriously, cooked lunch together, and it was a beautiful delightful harmonious buoyant 4 hours. . . . To reproduce the hours would be like writing a symphony. . . . It does not seem possible that two human beings could have such delightful harmonious joyous rewarding hours together. He is 22 or 23 and I'm you know what 76."[74]

Such afternoons made her feel eternally young, innocent, and creative. With Claire's young male friends, sexual tension was balanced by the harmony of their mutual interests. Her relationship with Philip Kapleau proved far more complex. Although some contemporary Zen masters endorsed the psychology of Zen, Kapleau, a fundamentalist, did not. He believed Zen to be a purely religious discipline, not to be diluted with rational thinking or psychological theory. Owens, on the other hand, approached Zen as a tool for achieving enlightenment. Kapleau expected his followers to observe his teachings; dissent equaled heresy. All too often, giving him sections to check for accuracy resulted in battles of the will. Owens had rejected fundamentalism since early childhood. Now butting heads with Kapleau's "narrow-mindedness" kept her in a state of agitation.

"I try to see things his way," she reflected, wondering if Kapleau was right to argue that other disciplines would "dilute" Zen. "My rational mind could not accept Zen training until it verified its principle by the psychology of Jung, Maslow, etc. And I could not accept my own beautiful spontaneous experience until I consulted Jung, Underhill etc." The important issue for Owens was her dream that all people could experience self-realization—not through Zen alone: After all, it was not Zen sweeping America, but "the self-realization movement in general."[75]

Beginning with a letter from Charles Tart saying he was happy with her chapter, 1973 was a good year.[76] Kapleau eventually accepted Owens as a voice of dissension; he invited her to join him in an April trip to Montreal—four days with all expenses paid—where he was to lecture on "Art in Zen and Zen in Art" during the museum's Japanese and Chinese art exhibit.[77] Flattered, though bewildered, she accepted. The trip proved a delightful adventure for the two of them. Dr. Raymond Prince, the psychologist at McGill University whose essay she had so effectively refuted, took her to lunch at the Ritz. She admired Prince's research on the way "meditation of various forms has turned the young people away from psychedelics." Prince invited her to speak the following October at the Bucke Society conference held at McGill.[78]

Owens imbued Kapleau with her expertise on art; nervous, he insisted she sit in the front row during his lecture. Owens was twice mistaken for his wife, once at his lecture and once on the plane returning home. When she promised not to tell people at the center, he laughed and asked, "Why not?" Owens felt the strain between them resolved, to some extent. Charles Gelatt teased her when he heard the story: If he did not know she was "well versed in the rules of romance," he would be worried. "Perhaps I should, however, worry about Mr. Kapleau." Owens was seventy-seven; Kapleau, in his late fifties. Owens protested; she loved her freedom and financial autonomy and was glad she did not have "to marry to be supported."[79]

Her writing and lectures appealed to many religious denominations: In September, she lectured on Zen Buddhism to Christian church members in Rochester, a lecture she delivered again to a Baptist church the following year. A Presbyterian church in Rochester asked her to lecture on Zen and paid her a fee. While communicating with Charles Tart regarding her chapter, he asked her to write a "whole book" on spontaneous self-realization for a series he would edit. She reopened her research on the spontaneous realizations of Whitman, Beethoven, Dante, and Goethe while she considered the offer. Though she did not write the book, the completed manuscript of "Varieties of Self-Realization" might have served their purposes. When *Transpersonal Psychologies* was released, Claire wrote "Charley" to tell him it was "splendid," and that his chapter contrasting Western psychology with spiritual psychology was worth the price of the whole book. "You have clarified, simplified, and summarized these two important attitudes toward life as no one ever has before."[80]

In October 1973, Owens returned to Montreal to deliver her lecture, "Self-Realization, Induced and Spontaneous." Dr. Prince had asked her to compare self-realization induced by meditation with the spontaneous mystical experience. Using recent research on left- and right-brain functioning, she discussed self-realization as a part of a "greater whole" in the evolution of the species toward "the reconciliation of science and religion." Whereas some religions "object to having science invade their private domain, others feel that there may be only one way to save the world from destroying itself and that is on the cultural level through the integration of science and religion."[81] She quoted Carl Jung for support in her theory that "the tragic dichotomy between conscious and unconscious has caused our present world crisis."

Confronting the very source of dissension between herself and Kapleau, she told the three hundred scientists in the audience that most scientists could not accept a religious philosophy without first satisfying their rational minds, perhaps through psychology. She herself could not accept Zen training without first discovering a rational explanation through her study of Carl Jung, William James, Jean Houston and Robert Masters, Abraham Maslow, Aldous Huxley, and Evelyn Underhill. Nor could she have accepted her own "Great Awakening experience" until she found rational explanations for it.

Philip Kapleau conveyed his anger at the subject of her talk. "Am I finished?" she wondered. Although she was frightened of being forced to withdraw from the Zen Center, she remained true to her convictions. On December 22, 1973, Kapleau lured her to a Sunday morning teisho. "Like the naive idiot I am," she wrote in her journal, "I thought he was concerned for me when he made sure I would be there." However, Kapleau advocated aspects of Zen methodology Owens found destructive. She interpreted his teachings as an attack on her beliefs. "Compliment others by insulting them; children should have their ego tamed at all times. Speakers on Zen might mention this." When she left she smiled at him and said, "I got the message."[82]

"It was not meant for you but for everyone," he insisted. But she knew better. She abhorred the Zen principle of belittling people: "It may work for some temperaments, but why make people suffer unnecessarily?" She found "kindness, gentleness, and encouragement more productive of the good." The incident left her feeling betrayed. "I have built my life around the Zen Center of Rochester. I am too old to make a drastic change now. What am I to do?"[83]

In 1975, The Association for Transpersonal Psychology published "Kenneth Ring's Annotated Reading List," a bibliography comprised of selections dealing with what Professor Ring called "non-ordinary states of consciousness." Claire found his comments "so astute, so generous, yet gently skeptical and humorous that they revealed a very unique mind." Naturally, she wrote Ring, then professor of transpersonal psychology at the University of Connecticut at Storrs, and told him so, and they too became friends.[84] Their mutual intellectual obsession with the burgeoning body of literature and research in the field of transpersonal psychology drove their lengthy communications—letters and Ring's visits to Owens's apartment.

A unique relationship, based on similar histories, emerged. Both had been married three times when they met; both were highly receptive to the sexual energies of the opposite sex. They held similar views about life. For both, life was an adventure and if it was unpredictable, well, so much the better. Laughter—Mount Ghaulot—was life's highest peak. In their earliest communications, Ring seemed to intuit a kindred spirit and asked to come visit during his summer break. Delighted, Owens put him up at a nearby inn as her guest. "Unity through Self," the story of their first visit appears in *Zen and the Lady*.[85] She describes Dr. Ring as "about forty, attractive and instantly friendly." She served him lunch, and they spent their first day talking nonstop, a pattern that persisted throughout their friendship. Ideas are electrifying and intellectual stimulation is highly erotic, and yet there was never anything erotic between them.[86]

Claire had a penchant both for attracting men and for being attracted to them. Raul daSilva recalls their first meeting in 1975, in the mail room of their apartment building at 1400 East Avenue. "As I was opening my mailbox . . . I felt a slight tap on my shoulder. Turning around to respond, I was surprised to see a tall woman with a big smile and a large red hat. 'My name is Claire Myers Owens,' she said with an air of confidence. 'We are supposed to meet.' Because of my pursuit of consciousness studies, I would take such an 'out of the blue' introduction in stride and with interest." A lasting friendship evolved; Raul was around forty-two, and Claire around seventy-nine.[87]

Despite her vexing confrontations with Kapleau, life in Rochester was filled with friends Claire considered family: Audrey Fernandez, Margaret Lee Braun, Marion Rigney, Barbara Percy, and Raul daSilva, all with whom she spent Thanksgiving, Christmas, New Year's, Easter, Mother's Day, and many hours of intimate and intellectual conversation. She and Dwain remained friends, along with his wife, Cindy, and daughter, Lara, Claire's godchild. Larry McSpadden, Craig Learned, Geoffrey Lister—young men affiliated with the Zen Center—loved to drop by the apartment and devote hours helping her with minor chores while engaging in lengthy philosophical discussions, arousing her erotic energies and their own, and leaving her to wonder why she allowed herself to become so fascinated by their youthful attentions. One by one, they would find a girl their own age and marry, inviting Claire to the wedding, urging her to wear the long, flowing "passionate pink" evening gown from her New Haven wardrobe.[88]

15

"Grande Amoureuse"

1976–1983

Abandon yourself recklessly to the passion of living. . . . Be the grand[e] amoureuse.

—Aunt Sophistica

Claire Myers Spotswood, *The Unpredictable Adventure*

ON THE MORNING OF FEBRUARY 11, 1976, Claire Myers Owens awakened amazed to feel "little fountains of joy bubbling up" in her chest. "Hail to the rising sun!" she wanted to shout, "like some early pagan." She noticed the myriad flower arrangements decorating her room at the Brazilian Arms Hotel in Palm Beach, Florida. Red roses from her former cook Margaret Griffin, spring flowers from Charles Gelatt, a lovely bouquet from Dwain and Cindy Wilder. Then she remembered: today was her eightieth birthday. "I have never been happier in my life . . . My body may be eighty but I feel twenty-five." She flung her pink pajamas on the bed and stood before the bathroom mirror, scrutinizing her naked body. "Tall and slender . . . no lumps or bumps in the wrong places though my front leaves a few things to be desired. The legs are still shapely but the arms are thin and ugly. And the face—lines—but there could be more. Hair grey—but it could be white."[1]

She studied her face, "suffused with a pink glow," an inner radiance from deep sleep. That same glow used to appear after a long swim in the ocean or a night of making love with her husband or after prolonged zazen. She found it amusing that such diverse activities as deep sleep, swimming, sex, and zazen all produced the same external glow but with different results. Zazen transformed character and life focus. It awakened that which she had sought for so long—"the good."

"How is it possible for any woman to look like this at eighty?" she wondered. "Has zazen discovered the fountain of youth?" She dressed and strolled through the morning sunshine to breakfast on the hotel patio. Every atom of her body felt alive and tingling, and yet stillness pervaded the core of her being, an art she learned through Zen meditation. "It allows all the richness of one's being to rise to the surface like cream." She sat at her table in utter peace and reflection. "Never . . . in all my eighty years have my senses been so alive, my thinking so clear, my love of people . . . so universal, intuitive insights so quick and my body so eager and buoyant."[2]

On returning to her room, she was overcome by the irresistible urge to write a new book. Every morning for a month from nine o'clock in the morning to noon or one, she wrote "by hand and by machine faster than human fingers are designed to move." Never had her writing flowed so easily, without a plan, without outlines, and without signs of arthritic cramping and stiffness. As Roshi Kapleau suggested, she was "living zazen." Writing was a joy; her work had become her practice. "I walked through my days with a singing heart, active mind, healthy body, love and spiritual fulfillment and sweet yearning."

Life during her eighties could not have been richer. Each winter she flew to Florida, often as a guest of Charles Gelatt. Her steady correspondence continued with New Haven friends and colleagues. Figures from the Zen community and from the transpersonal world filtered in and out of her daily life. John White, her literary agent and advisor, offered her a "generous fee" to lecture on the "Joys of Aging" for the Phenix Society—a spiritual group in New Haven for people over forty—on September 23, 1978. Claire arranged a visit with Lucy Hammer and her husband Torval in Branford and a lunch with Louise Ames during her stay. She treasured their friendships, but she wrote them, now eighty-two, "travel is too strenuous for me." This trip, she feared, would be her "swan's song."[3]

Kenneth Ring met her plane in Hartford and drove her to New Haven; both Ring and Owens called their excursion a "delightful adventure"—taking four hours to drive the fifty miles to Madison near New Haven.[4]

Her lecture was a huge success: "The minute I stopped speaking, the psychiatrist who had been making the tape recording jumped up on the stage and hugged and kissed me and said, 'It was beautiful.'"[5] A rush of men and women followed; never had she been "kissed and hugged so much by so many people." Several women called it "positively inspiring"—one looked her in the eye and said, "I want you to know that this is the high point of my life."[6] People responded to Claire as to a beloved prophet. Professor Ring offered an important insight: though not preceded by illness or physical trauma, Owens's 1950 Awakening seems to have been similar to a near-death experience (NDE). People who experience NDEs often become charismatic following their incident. "Claire," he observed, "was radiant."[7] Her presence attracted the same kind of love she emanated from within. Yet she felt shocked to elicit such warm, enthusiastic responses. On Friday, the first day of the meeting, not a single copy sold of either *Awakening to the Good* or *Discovery of the Self* and no one had taken any of the brochures on display. By Saturday noon—her talk was 9–10 a.m.—all the books were sold, and the sixty brochures had disappeared. She spent Saturday afternoon signing autographs. People would come up and say, "I love you," smiling with tears in their eyes.[8]

In her letter thanking "Dear Kind Ken" for his unselfish efforts in her behalf, she credited him for her success. "Be personal and you'll be a great hit," he had advised her.[9] She did a good job so as not to disappoint him or John White. But the response she received confirmed her belief that Philip Kapleau's adherence to the Zen method of withholding praise was wrong. Encouragement and compliments were the greatest incentive to doing better work. Such hard-won wisdom she frequently passed on to her younger friends to use in their parenting, teaching, and love relationships.

Through the years, as Ken Ring encountered difficulties with a girlfriend, spouse, or child, Owens became mentor and "wise old woman." When Ring's daughter Kathryn suffered an asthma attack, Owens gently reprimanded him regarding his involvement with an "immature woman" who could not provide Kathryn proper maternal support. "It is none of my business but I feel great empathy especially since she has no mother. . . . Can't you next time fall in love with a nice middle aged woman?"[10]

Fundamentally, the roots of their mutual admiration lay in their utmost respect for one another's life work.[11] In 1977, when Ring read the completed manuscript for *Zen and the Lady*, which begins at the end of her marriage and traces her journey from New Haven to Rochester, he wrote a letter, which Owens excerpted and sent to publishers: "Claire, I hope that I am expressing more than enthusiasm in rendering this judgment, but I don't see how your book can miss. The story of your last seven years is a beautiful tale, artfully told." He called her candor regarding her young men "extraordinary and marvelous," her book imbued with "momentous transpersonal experiences."[12]

Ring compared her "beautiful search for self-realization" to Carl Jung's *Memories, Dreams, Reflections*. Both books are "suffused with wisdom," Ring observed. However, where Jung is remote, Owens is intimate; where Jung is arrogant, she is humble. The difference, he believed, was that while wisdom is "abundant" in both books, Owens reveals wisdom "through love." Of all of his acquaintances, Ring felt Owens was "the only one who . . . has truly arrived 'on the other shore.'"[13]

Naturally, Ring did not mean to imply that Owens's book was equal in scope or depth to Jung's; after all, Jung's theories revolutionized depth psychology, which explores the relationship between the conscious and the unconscious, and made the concept of archetypes paradigmatic. Owens's book's remarkable qualities lay in her loving portrayal of friends and colleagues who became characters in her story, though she changed some of their names. "People," as Ring put it, "abound."[14] Omitted from that excerpt was Ring's question regarding the Roshi's response. "I hope he will finally agree that it is not too full of psychology." But, he assured, in this case "CMO was right."[15]

The people abounding in "Snowbound," Owens's fictional name for Rochester, include the members of her sangha at the Zen Center and participants in the transpersonal movement. Going back to her roots as a southern belle reared to believe a girl was a "flat failure socially unless she was besieged by male admirers," the men in her life and in her books always seem central. Owens openly admitted she had been "flirting with every personable male from seventeen to seventy from the time [she] was ten."[16] *Zen and the Lady* captures the spirit of her female relationships as well. Audrey Fernandez, "Blanch" in the book, remembers that many of their mutual acquaintances assumed Audrey and Claire related as daughter to mother. "Claire always said I was like a sister. But I think I was like her mother."[17] According to Fernandez, by the end of her life Owens had resolved her conflicted feelings about her mother. In the last several years, through intense and prolonged zazen, dichotomies between her masculine and feminine principles vanished and transformed her anger and hurt into love and compassion.

In many ways, Owens and Fernandez lent an air of middle-class respectability to the center. Whenever money needed to be raised or support sought from Rochester's wealthy residents, the two women went out on a mission. Both slender and tall at five foot eight, Owens, dressed in a pink or red designer suit and matching hat from her New Haven years, accompanied by Audrey, equally stylish in earth-tone colors, stood out among the long-haired youth clad in jeans, granny dresses, and sandals. "We were presentable, more a part of the establishment."[18] Fernandez found Owens's demeanor remarkable: "When she moved here she must have been seventy-four. But she never seemed old. She had such an expansive spirit. She never seemed confined by her body the way many older people are, hunched at the shoulders. She had a good physique, held herself well, and *just did not seem old.* She always thought of herself in her forties."[19]

Beyond appearance, Fernandez and Owens shared a keen intellectual approach to Zen, an approach Philip Kapleau abhorred. Fernandez, working on a master's degree in Chinese language and literature at the University of Rochester, possessed formidable erudition in Zen literature and philosophy. They traded books and articles and spent endless hours discussing ideas. Both women took issue with

19. Claire with Susan Stone and Audrey Fernandez at Susan's wedding. Zen Center, 1978. Courtesy of the author, gift from Audrey Fernandez.

authoritative, patriarchal perspectives of Zen and supported women's rights: Audrey identified as an "ardent member of the Woman's Liberation Movement," while Claire found the movement of the 1970s and 1980s too negative, too full of biases against men. Having lived her life in search of equality, having published a solidly feminist novel, and written two others, she took offense at the style of the movement but not at its content. "Intellectually, I knew men had exploited women from the beginning of time but I found them so interesting that emotionally I forgave them—almost."[20] But not quite. Owens commanded respect from men and women, held herself with dignity, but the advice she gave her youthful friends in the sangha broke down the barriers between generations and genders.

The young men asked frank questions about the kind of lovemaking women liked, and she would answer them, frankly. Although there was no promiscuity at the center, couples lived together. "That was the modern form of 'engagement.' They did not call it an 'affair'; it was a 'relationship.' They did not 'make love,' they 'had sex'—much more truthful. The young people came to me for counseling about sex, neuroses and every other variety of problem."[21]

Margaret Lee Braun felt a deep bond with Claire, who "loved to talk about men and women. It was nice to have an older person to talk to and she really cared." Claire believed that women put too much emphasis on love and got hurt. She had learned from her own experiences that, "Your lovers are people like you. But you marry your opposites."[22]

"She liked to encourage affairs of the heart," Geoffrey Lister recalls. When he was getting married she advised, "You do not criticize your mate. You emphasize and praise the good qualities and the good events that you have together and the rest will wash away. She did this with Thurston, and it worked." Making life work took willpower; "it was just that *will*" that made things work.[23]

She spoke of Thurston fondly to Geoffrey, but to Audrey, already married, she told of their difficulties. Yet, even in her eighties, Claire showed a "great enjoyment of men, of flirting, of her power to attract." Fernandez observed: "There was an extra quality when men were involved. With women she could be more straightforward, as if she told herself, 'I don't have to use my wiles with you.' But men were a challenge—that's how she was brought up, and there was always an extra sparkle."[24]

A source of affirmation, validation, and inspiration for the men and women in the Zen community, she had a way of focusing her attention that made them feel important, a way of "taking younger people and raising them up." During dharma dialogues, people speak before the group and tell about their experiences on the Zen path. Often responses were sharp, intended to "blister." But Claire, with her deep respect for people she might even disagree with, would respond with encouragement: "Oh, don't you realize how wonderful what you're doing is?"[25]

For Audrey, Claire's poise was self-revelatory: "Her courtesy made me realize just how discourteous I could be." Claire was not the only one at odds with Kapleau; "some said Roshi set people against each other." Claire stood up to him without showing disrespect, validating others and herself. She taught her young friends to search for the truth within: "It doesn't have to be what the Roshi said, but what you experience yourself."[26]

Zen and the Lady captures the tension and struggle at the Zen Center, the camaraderie and the competition, the personal and the public side of the participants. Zen practice requires demanding discipline; Zen dramatizes the pain of the experience along with its ample rewards. Owens's frail physical condition made zazen difficult. The zendo was kept very cold, and she worried she would become ill, which would mean three weeks in bed with fever. Despite the requirements that they all go barefoot, she wore stockings, and no one reprimanded her—"a concession made for age." She found the blows from the *keosaku* stick across the shoulders particularly humiliating given her upbringing in the South where striking a woman was beneath contempt. All Zen practice diminishes the ego so as to release the inner or True Self. After months of practice, Claire was ready for her long *sesshin* (extended meditation). On the third day of her first four-day sesshin, sitting on her cushion in the zendo at five in the morning, she was rewarded for her discomforts. She beheld "an endless parade of colored images. They passed across the blank wall . . . like continuous motion pictures. . . . I saw a figure of Buddha, then a Buddha with the Roshi's face, the Virgin Mary with the infant Jesus in her arms. A green forest with monkeys cavorting about, many buildings, a stage with actors. A light like a small flashlight played across all these scenes. And once I beheld a small golden dragon."[27]

No one had prepared her for this astonishing phenomenon. "My body shook uncontrollably and I was wracked with deep continuous sobs." Every time she attempted to use a Kleenex, a monitor would mutter, "No moving." Swallowing the mucus flowing from her nose seemed unbearable, and even the threat of a blow from the keosaku stick was no match for her solid sense of dignity. She risked the pain of a lashing, defied the rules, and wiped her nose. The parade of archetypal images continued for twelve hours as she "beheld a group of Egyptians and Jews dressed in Biblical garb . . . walking around and around a well gazing at me intently."[28] When her group broke for dinner, Owens immediately began to analyze the experience as described by Jung, Masters and Houston, and Stanislav Grof. The Roshi dismissed her excitement, calling them *makyo* (illusions), and warned they could become obstacles on her path.

At the end of the fourth day, the members streamed out of the zendo laughing, crying, kissing, overwhelmed with love, joy, and enormous bursts of energy. Owens went home and read everything she could find to explain in scientific terms the nature of the images and their source. Despite Zen constraints against rational explanations of mystical phenomenon, only by satisfying her conscious mind could she take satisfaction in the beautiful visions. When people criticized her need to explain that which they considered ineffable, Owens would say, "Well, that's just fine if you feel that way but I have to know."[29] This time Aldous Huxley's *Heaven and Hell* provided the answers, which she found as exciting as the mystical experiences themselves. "My conscious mind and my unconscious, reason and intuition, the masculine . . . and feminine principle were functioning together harmoniously. I felt whole, beautifully whole as nature intends us to be. The incredible claims of the greatest mystics were biologically possible and scientifically explicable."[30]

Two particular instances stand out. The first occurred during a seven-day sesshin when the vision of a "detached black hand outlined in light" appeared, faded, and was replaced by the vision of a fern leaf, detached from its bush, enameled in white and studded with jewels—amethysts—her birthstone. The brown wooden wall before her suddenly turned to brown gauze. "I could distinctly see the coarse threads that composed it. Suddenly I saw right through this gauze wall! I beheld two men sitting on cushions on the other side and the legs of . . . the monitor as he walked down the aisle with the keosaku stick." She had read of Hindu yogis who made such claims and had "never believed a word of it." Now she herself could see through the solid wooden wall. Later she confirmed the validity of the vision she had seen.[31] But when she went home, her rational mind demanded explanations, and she complied. Her path to enlightenment, like the path her dual protagonist Tellectina/Femina walked many years earlier, journeyed in search of the resolution of all dialectic, all oppositions, all dichotomies, which she considered the source of all evil.

The second primary incident, though there were many minor ones, echoed her earliest childhood ecstasies catalyzed through communion with nature. Walking along a path in Florida after a deep sleep, she noticed that "everything in nature vibrated with a new beauty, colors became more vivid," awareness became so intense she feared she would explode with joy. A particular palm tree mesmerized her as she sat at the patio table during breakfast. "It was as if a door suddenly opened into another dimension of existence, as if a barrier had melted away, as if a veil had been lifted. I saw that palm tree in a different light, saw into the nature of the thing itself, into its true essence. It possessed a numinous quality. . . . I sensed the primal unity of all things."

A silent voice spoke: "IT IS ENOUGH. THAT—TREE—IS—ENOUGH. I DON'T NEED ANYTHING ELSE IN THE WORLD. NOT THINGS. NOT THE WORLD. NOT PEOPLE. NOT EVEN THE LOVE OF MEN. I AM FREE."[32]

When she returned to her apartment, an inner experience occurred and she beheld herself standing on top of a great mountain where an "excess of light" blasted her. She described it, invoking Emerson: "The falseness of man-made values. . . . fell off me like shackles from my legs and I stood on the mountain top naked and free and unafraid."[33]

In 1974, after four years of steady commitment to Zen, she experienced the feeling that her dependence on Buddha as teacher fell off her shoulders "like a heavy cloak." Now, two years later, her dependence on people, on all material reality fell away as well. During that visit to Florida in the winter of 1976, she sensed that all her struggles had ended, all her seeking had been satisfied, all dualities abandoned. "i NEED NOTHING. I—HAVE—EVERYTHING. EVERYTHING IS—IN MY MIND. EVEN UNIVERSAL MIND—IS IN MY MIND. I AM—CONTENT."[34]

Whereas many members of the Zen community found the idea of a novelistic autobiography about their sangha enticing and flattering, others objected, seeing it as too personal, too sexual, too erotic. The only aspect of *Zen and the Lady* that could be considered scandalous dealt with the details involving her relationship with Dwain, whom she calls Dexter, and the two young men who followed, with whom she also felt erotic ties: Larry McSpadden, or Lance, and Craig Learned, or Haig. While there is no explicit sex in the book, and Owens is careful to assure readers these intense relationships were never consummated, the idea of an older woman having romantic connections with younger men was simply too much for the Zen community to handle. Yet, they had observed Claire and accepted the unusual nature of her friendships as part of the atmosphere of their special group. Dwain admits they did nothing to hide their feelings in public, though they never resorted to open displays of affection. Raul daSilva recalls that the first time he met Dwain, Claire introduced Dwain as her "lover."[35]

The way Owens portrays their love in *Zen and the Lady* captures its erotic, sexual, and romantic nature. But it is not illicit. And though the various relationships are unusual, must they be found offensive? Owens wrote all of her books to expand the notion of human potential and to explore life-style possibilities. *Zen and the Lady,* in addition to its being a spiritual autobiography, reveals an honest self-portrait of a "grande amoureuse."

"Edwin," a prominent member in his forties, found the idea of a book about the center disturbing. He did not want to see an erotic relationship portrayed in a Zen setting. He did not want to see their center novelized. Edwin, who had written his own book, adamantly objected to Owens's. "Women shouldn't write books about religion," he argued, displaying his overt sexism. Before *Zen and the Lady* was published, he came to Owens's apartment and berated her, insisting she forego publication. The harangue lasted for hours. Owens sat in utter silence, unable to speak a word in her own defense. "Edwin was an English intellectual who had an inferior sense of himself as he came from the working class and class is more visible in England. Claire had an upper-class presence," Audrey Fernandez explained, so perhaps some of his resentment arose from the divergence of their backgrounds. Claire admired him, so she "just sat and took it, but her blood pressure went up twenty points and stayed that way for a year."[36] To bring it down, she began using relaxation techniques and massage therapy, in addition to her usual zazen. Audrey, who helped Claire through the crisis, believes her reticence when confronted by open hostility was a result of her southern Christian upbringing. Vestiges of early admonitions to act like a "lady"—courtesy, respect, a noblesse oblige—prevailed during the attack. Since she felt unable to react with anger, she turned the anger against herself. Anger turned inward becomes depression. Just as Ina Vestal's betrayal thirty years earlier had resulted in a long bout of depression and physical illness, so this diatribe against her work created depression, which she overcame by using her advanced abilities of spiritual and emotional transcendence.

In the end, she held herself up in dignity just as she had always done and courageously published and promoted the book. However, because of Edwin's attack, she fictionalized and obscured many of the characters' identities.[37]

Fernandez observed, "Claire had the courage to write her experiences, her own truths as she lived them because of her stable and secure childhood." In a sense, the same set of values that dictated the decorum of repression buttressed her strength of character. Coren Myers encouraged his daughter's independence and self-definition in subtle ways even though he tried to block some of her decisions. While he endorsed the southern code of gender roles, he "winked at her precocity." Although Susan Myers found her daughter's ways less amusing, she quietly rebelled against restrictions of her own creativity. She expressed her intellectual and ethical values through her civic work, church leadership, and the formation of her gourmet club—the Cordon Bleu. In the end, Audrey believed, Claire came to realize that her upbringing was a source of her courage.

"She had a way about her that encouraged risk-taking in others," Margaret Lee Braun recalled. Meeting Claire at the start of a seven-day sesshin, Margaret, who at the time had a "fear of feeling captive" for seven days, told Claire she planned to attend a four-day sesshin instead. "Oh," Claire responded, "don't just put your toes in the water. Come on in all the way!" and she waved at Margaret and "glittered" off.[38] Margaret had not realized she was being cautious. Like Aunt Sophistica in *The Unpredictable Adventure*, Claire recognized caution and tried to dissuade it: "Do *not* be careful," Aunt Sophie had advised Tellectina. "Be wise and rush in. . . . Abandon yourself recklessly to the passion of living. . . . Be the grand[e] amoureuse."[39]

Claire's wise counsel brought comfort to many. Charles Gelatt's second wife, Paula, had experienced a mystical awakening in 1975 that had created a chasm between her and Charles. Claire found herself in the precarious position of guiding Paula through the trauma of her "beautiful experience" while at the same time offering support to Charles. Paula wrote Claire that 1977 had been "filled with turmoil as well as hard work and rewards. [Charles] was used to being in charge and I have blossomed. It couldn't work."[40]

The Gelatts separated that summer; Paula went to live in Florida, and Charles stayed in Wisconsin. Claire wrote Charles to remind him that he had "virtually predicted it. Divorce is always painful for everyone." He was attractive to women and would soon have an interesting companion. "What can I do for you? Is there anything at all—will you please call on me?" That December she sent him a large book on Spain for his birthday and two others for Christmas.[41] The end of the Gelatt marriage was not unusual under these circumstances since profound character change often occurs in the "awakened" person. That Claire and Thurston managed to weave the changes into their life together attests to the self-discipline Claire called "will."

Larry McSpadden moved to Indiana, married, started a family, and sold insurance. Craig and Halcyon Learned moved to Pennsylvania but visited often and wrote warm, loving letters. Dwain and Cindy Wilder separated in 1977 and divorced in 1978. Claire made it a point to encourage them to stay together if possible, but supported them both with fine letters in the end. On February 22, 1978, she wrote Dwain from the Brazilian Court Hotel in Palm Beach, commiserating on his sad situation, assuring him he had the strength, common sense, wisdom, and compassion to cope, but warning "it will hurt down deep. I know of nothing that is so devastating as a broken marriage."[42] She urged him not to lose self-esteem because often the trouble is "simply a misfit of two people" and advised him not to suppress his feelings; inhibited emotions would punish him with "psychosomatic ailments."

She cautioned, "Be natural"—weep, swear, break dishes, walk miles. "At least you and I have Zen and meditation to help and guide us," she consoled, urging him to keep up his practice as it awakens all the best qualities.

She had learned from Adele Davis's book *Let's Get Well* that she had developed diverticulosis and high blood pressure by not expressing hurt and anger; hence the importance of "blowing off steam." Her thirty-two year marriage taught her that "when things go wrong between two people, it is always the fault of both." She advised Dwain to acknowledge what he did wrong. Craig Learned called it the CMO method—forgetting her "old ego" long enough to put herself in her husband's place, telling him his virtues, showing concern for his suffering. "Often [Thurston's] annoying traits disappeared without my ever having to mention them. In a disagreement, one must analyze oneself," Craig recalled her telling him.

Although much of her advice sounds motherly, Claire expressed genuine gratitude for the appreciation shown by Larry, Craig, and Dwain. "I simply am astounded that all you young men should be so kind and affectionate. I don't understand it but I love it. Your love nourishes me as I hope mine nourishes you." In closing her letter to Dwain, she sent love to "Dear darling little Lara and Cindy too." They were her family—all of them. She took their friendship and love as a personal responsibility, giving as she received.

Zen and the Lady was not the last book this "grande amoureuse" would write. "Meditation and the Lady" followed. Owens began writing the latter while the former was in press with Baraka Books, Ltd., a small publisher in New York. John White negotiated the contract and hired Reid Boates, a publicist at Anchor Press, to market it. When *Zen and the Lady* appeared in 1979, Owens was flooded with phone calls from ecstatic readers and from journalists asking for newspaper interviews. "Fortunately meditation diminishes the ego" for she was "showered with praise" for months. She "hardly had time to brush her teeth."[43]

Lex Hixon, author of *Coming Home: The Experience of Enlightenment in Sacred Traditions*, invited her to appear as a guest on his radio program, *In the Spirit*, broadcast from New York City.[44] *A.M. Rochester* scheduled a special Claire Myers Owens Week of interviews by Matt Rinaldi, a local TV talk show host. Kenneth Ring arranged the interview they had planned to do two years earlier in preparation for a documentary film Raul daSilva wanted to produce and direct. All three interviews provided a meaningful opportunity for Owens to look back over her life with the benefit of skilled guides leading her to new levels of self-understanding.

At the time Kenneth Ring conducted his interview with Owens, he was completing research for his book *Life at Death*, the first full-length empirical investigation of near-death experience, which involved interviews with over one hundred NDE survivors. Although this interview had nothing to do with his book, it benefits from Ring's vast experience.[45] The central question with which Ring planned to open the interview was designed to elucidate Owens's views about her mystical experiences in the context of her life, rather than allowing incidents from her life to "seep out" between her views. He prompted her, saying he would begin with a question like:

> Mrs. Owens, how did an indulged daughter of the Old South ever wind up, in her eighties, hanging out in a Zen Center (instead of on the Riviera)? This would provide an entree into your girlhood, your break from your family . . . and pretty soon in your tale, you'd begin to work in your experiences, and your suffering, and all the things you've read, and then your first book (novel), and then your real first book, and the reactions to that. . . . Soon people would begin to see . . . what an extraordinary human being you are.[46]

This approach results in a capacious portrait of Owens's life and art presented as a charming repartee; as in their personal relationship, they had intellectual fun. Owens wrote Ring: "You are superb in that tape—your warm attractive voice and your wonderful heart-warming laughter. You won't believe it, but I was unaware at the time that we laughed. I am sure all the women who hear it will fall in love with Ken Ring. It shows your brilliant mind, your warm heart and your generosity. . . . —your own unusual personality was revealed."[47] Typically, Owens's praise focused on Ring's skills rather than her own. At eighty, she still knew how to charm others.

Raul daSilva loved it; he planned to film a Ring and Owens documentary. Ring not only revealed his own skills and personality, he captured Owens's charm and complexity. By the end of their three-hour dialogue, Owens seems to have discovered what she meant in 1935 when she described her quest to reach Mount Certitude. At age eighty-three, "The Lady" achieved the summit of a life that had been filled with peak experiences.

If Ring's interview is the most comprehensive of the three, Lex Hixon's is the most penetrating of Owens's mysticism.[48] Hixon's drive to understand and describe the mysteries surrounding psychic phenomena motivates his relentless push for a clear definition of the nature and significance of Owens's Great Awakening, which he focuses on as the pivotal moment that launched her on the path to Zen. Having read her books, Hixon detected the "primordial" in her accounts of merging with the light that resonates with descriptions of religious enlightenment.

He led her down the path of her journey, carefully probing her proclivity for ecstatic experiences until he came to that moment in New Haven. He wanted her to explicate how it felt to merge completely with the "golden light." She explained that she felt drawn into it, into its power, as if it meant to obliterate her. She became part of this power and it became part of her. The feeling was "ineffable," the greatest ecstasy ever, followed by intuitive insights into the nature of the universe. "I saw it was good, others were good, I was good. After feeling that the world was so evil I could not bear to live in it, it was a remarkable insight." She described a sense of the oneness of everything and a deep penetrating love of mankind manifested in the goodness. Owens stressed that the important thing is not the experience, but its effect on daily life, and its power to "change the world."

Hixon pressed Owens for a description of "the nature of the golden light." Owens did not know, had never read a clear definition. Ramakrishna, the nineteenth-century Indian mystic, described it as radiating light, she suggested. Visionary artists portray Jesus crowned with light. In fact, Owens observed, light radiated all around John White's head when he lectured to the Phenix Society. But she did not know if that light was subjective or objective.

Perhaps, Hixon suggested, it transcends subjectivity and objectivity. Perhaps it is the very "ground of being."

Owens hedged here. "I am shy to say that, and yet I suppose that's what it is—a manifestation of the infinite. As Ken Wilber says, if we open the doors to it, it is 'already always there—we put up the barriers.'" She could accept Hixon's definition, but with reluctance because Owens hesitated to state that she had seen some form of God; it seemed too tremendous a claim.

But Hixon persisted:

> HIXON: You said the universe appeared later, but in the golden light there was no universe, no cosmos.
>
> OWENS: I just don't know to tell you the truth. I try to understand yet . . .
>
> HIXON: Let's pursue this in the spirit of inquiry. It seems to me the golden light transcended the universe and the cosmos and was more fundamental than any limited spiritual experience along the path.

Here, Hixon referred to Owens's "small ecstasies." "Sometimes you say you encountered it; others times that you merged with it. But if you merged with it, you became the ground of being." This, Hixon argued, differs from merely encountering the light as in a vision or as a voice. Merging with the light is transformative. But what is the light?

"Buddhists describe it as a void that contains everything," Owens explained, comparing it to a manifestation of a Zen adage: form is emptiness; emptiness is form. "[The light] is so overpowering one is humbled in its presence, and I don't like to claim too much."

But Hixon had detected a paradox he sought to untangle. Hixon wanted to know, with all his heart and soul, the *exact* nature of the Ultimate. He pursued this quest relentlessly, finding new ways to phrase the same question. But all she could tell him was that it was good. Hixon believed that Owens's experience expands the meaning of the Ultimate and affirms its existence. "It is experiences such as the one Claire Myers Owens had in New Haven that religions are made of," he insisted. If one could say there is God in everyone, the whole "framework of reality is essentially God or Good"—just by adding or subtracting an *O*.

Owens agreed: "That is what I experienced. When you experience the Ultimate Good, you are experiencing God . . . the highest experience of which people are capable."

He pressed further: She had reached enlightenment, if only temporarily, and "enlightenment offers freedom from our attachments to the cosmos." Paradoxically, the cosmos represents material reality, from which we must seek freedom. Yet when Owens merged with that golden light, there was no cosmos: cosmic energy is vast but limited; God is limitless.

Owens could not seem to unlock the mystery Hixon found so compelling. She searched to explain but she did not have the words, and furthermore, she embraced the mystery. All her life she had sought to explicate, but this conundrum she accepted. Owens sought a compromise. "I am still working on that." Maybe she had not "risen to that level" of understanding. Scientists coin words; she simply used their words. Hixon objected: this was the problem. We must take the language from the experience and not try to fit the experience to the language. Her case was significant: she was an actual "experiencer," an authentic mystic. "Ninety percent of what is written about religion is speculative. Whereas you have had the experience and it is authentic." In Owens's case, she had felt herself disappear, merge into the Good. This, Hixon argued, made her report unusual; Hixon considered it her responsibility to express the event with more clarity because "understanding it takes it to a different level."

As she composed a new answer, her voice grew weak, tired. Hixon's relentless press for the ultimate truth, the definitive explanation of the experience of enlightenment, pushed Owens to the limit of her physical strength. She gathered all of her energy to make a final attempt to please her interviewer and satisfy his desire to break through to a new level of understanding:

> Yes, I feel that. I feel very responsible. I feel undeserving. Why me? Why have I had these beautiful experiences? I felt I was an instrument, used. And I've tried to live up to it. The last three months—I've never worked so hard in my life. I've seen people asking for help and guidance, answering questions. When I compare myself to somebody like Buddha, I haven't gotten very far. But compared to the average person, seeking and searching all their life as I have . . . it is my duty to help them all I can.

In a poem she wrote near the end of her life, she describes the experience of Ultimate Reality as arriving to "beyond within," that sacred place where all dichotomies merge, and good prevails. At the end of the Hixon interview, Owens tried to convey this ineffable truth, and Hixon reluctantly accepted what he considered a less than adequate explanation.

His resolve to force Owens to define what lay beyond the cosmos provoked his determined questioning. And if she knew the answer, she had no words to describe its essence. "I see what you mean," she said kindly, but confused. Owens had reached the limits of her claims. "Well, what else do you want me to say? What else do you want to say?" Hixon was silent. Owens's voice turned charming, "It was a lovely interview. Thank you." Hixon found his voice and thanked her for being "one of the older sisters of humanity."

The following week she wrote Hixon and told him she had felt his presence in her apartment the whole week after he left.[49] They exchanged letters and books and remained on good terms. His intentions had been honorable; speaking to mystics living half their lives outside material reality, Hixon had learned to press for words where no words yet existed. Inventing a language could create a new reality. His interview succeeded because each of them had the courage to speak, the strength to chase down the truth, and the integrity to stick to each unique interpretation. However, for Owens, the interview bordered on ordeal and left her depleted.

The highlight of fame for Owens was her guest appearance on *A.M. Rochester*, a local TV talk show hosted by Matt Rinaldi.[50] The technical crew arrived on a Monday morning and taped five fifteen-minute sessions to appear five days in a row. The first segment opens with Owens seated on her striped damask sofa in her living room. Fresh red-and-gold Gerber daisies sit on the table to her right, with a copy of *Zen and the Lady*, flanked by a red gloxinia, resting on the coffee table. A wall of books provides a suitable background to Owens, elegant in a tasteful deep coral dress with a matching, loose-fitting jacket. The rich russets and reds set against her perfectly coifed silver hair provide a warm luminescence. Her face glows with joy and youthful energy. Her voice and manners tell the story of her journey; she has traveled far and wide from the small Texas town of her roots. Not a trace of southern dialect remains in her speech. Rather, she sounds almost British, aristocratic, her elocution seasoned by her years in New York and Connecticut.

"I had been living an ordinary married life with a good marriage, a beautiful home, three devoted servants, minks, diamonds, trips to Europe, parties the way everybody does," she begins, unaware of the intrinsic irony. "And I enjoyed it, I don't mind telling you." What broke her magic bubble was World War II in its savage brutality, the atom bomb, crime in the streets, political corruption. She "lost complete faith in Western culture—there was something dreadfully wrong with the people who were running the world."

So, once again, she launches into her story of spontaneous enlightenment which lasted twelve years.

"Twelve years? Only twelve?" Rinaldi responds on cue.

"Oh yes, I thought it would last forever. But only great spiritual figures like Buddha or Jesus attain permanent enlightenment."

"What is enlightenment?" Rinaldi asks, directing his questions with the skill of a talk show host who knows the level of his audience.

"The highest state of consciousness," which can be reached only through the use of both sides of the brain. Owens explains the different capacities of the left and right hemispheres and opens the discussion to Western reliance on the left lobe, which controls rationality.

"Ah," Rinaldi responds, "you mean science does not have all the answers?"

"Science does *not* have all the answers," she confirms, laughing gaily as if discussing the latest fashion or a trip to the theater. Yet, science has verified two modes of knowing—intuitive, or experiential, and rational are located separately in the right and left lobes of the brain. The interview, friendly and informative, proceeds with its focus on Zen meditation as a method for integrating the two halves in the process of seeking wholeness.

More than Owens's personal life and experiences, the interview reveals her extensive knowledge of complex philosophical, theological, and psychological literature, which she presents in simple, direct language—a "lay scholar" who chats and bubbles about the nature of life and the universe as she explores the various themes of her book, which one reader called a "spiritual story for people of all religions."

"The fundamental truths in Zen are the fundamental truths in all religions," Owens reflects. Its core and heart is meditation, which can be used within or outside any religious system. Zen, simplified, teaches basic human eternal truths that transcend culture, time, and place, she explains with energy and dignity.

Each segment closes with a pitch for *Zen and the Lady* and where to buy it. The Matt Rinaldi show sold out her books at all four book shops in the area and left them with many orders to fill. "I can't imagine why life is so good to me," she told Rinaldi. "I try to deserve it."[51]

The three interviews exhausted her. She needed a week to recover after each. She was slowing down, but still writing. Despite her arthritic fingers and failing eyesight, she wrote in longhand, page after barely legible page of manuscript for "Meditation and the Lady." In addition, she continued to work on the enormous project of her full-length "Autobiography," which she dedicated to Ken Wilber. Raul daSilva put her in touch with Barbara Percy, a typist who became Owens's hands and eyes during the final years.[52] Under Owens's influence, Percy became interested in meditation. They had long discussions about their Christian roots, though Percy maintained her ties to Christianity whereas Owens had severed hers long ago. They often went to lunch, took long rides in the country, with Percy driving Owens's cherry-red 1969 Buick, the one Charles Gelatt had insisted she let Northern Engraving purchase. Percy inherited the Buick when Owens died. "She wrote every day of her life. It was an exercise," Percy recalled.

"Meditation and the Lady" expands prior themes of meditation. The book remains unfinished, though she worked on it through the remaining days of an active life.

No matter her own physical condition, she continued to be available to other seekers experiencing the traumatic aftermath that often accompanies mystical awakenings and other psychospiritual phenomena. No one could have been more appreciative of her wisdom and guidance than Helen Nelson. Among the first forty subjects Professor Ring interviewed for his book *Life at Death*, Nelson proved one of the most fascinating. Ring noticed parallels between her own and Owens's life stories and gave Nelson a copy of *Awakening to the Good*. Ring wrote Owens that Nelson was "rhapsodic over it, carrying on something fierce." In fact, subsequent to reading the book Nelson experienced moments of epiphany and Kundalini to the extent that she began to fear she was losing her mind. She could call Claire at any time of the day or night, and Claire would help her find ways to harness the massive power of emotions and make sense of the baffling intuitive insights that transformed her life. She remained grateful long after Claire's death.[53]

Now internationally renowned figures with impressive publishing histories, Ken Wilber, Charles Tart, Kenneth Ring, and John White corresponded with Owens during their early years, when they could afford to let their vulnerabilities show to this woman forty years their senior. They used words like *glowing* or *radiant* to describe her presence, her creative energy, her wisdom. She used words like *brilliant* and *genius* to describe them. Ken Wilber read her poem on old age in the journal *Phoenix* in 1980, and asked to reprint excerpts in *ReVision: A Journal of Consciousness and Change*, which he edited.[54] "Your poem, more than any other . . . moved me, actually pushed me into that state of non-grasping, non-attachment that meditation does. . . . You are a real gift, and a walking monument to the power and beauty of Spirit."

In 1982, when *ReVision* faced "potentially fatal financial problems," he wrote to ask if some of her "millionaire friends" could contribute. He did not want to offend her, but he needed to raise $20,000. Owens, far from offended, enclosed a check for one hundred dollars with a note saying she wished it were thousands but she was not rich. As to those "millionaires," she wished they were the kind who would support *ReVision*, but they would not be familiar with a movement concerned with actualizing human potentials or Zen or a higher consciousness.

"I myself have never had much money," Wilber confided.[55] He left graduate school in biochemistry in order to write *The Spectrum of Consciousness* when he was twenty-three. In order to support himself, he washed dishes and bused tables for three years. Even by the time he wrote the *Atman Project*, he had to work manual jobs. "I've never really talked about this to anyone, mostly because I managed to survive somehow." Wilber, who described himself as "a simple Zen monk," became one of the most respected transpersonalists in the world, as did Ken Ring and Charley Tart. Ring's extensive scientific validation of near-death experience has contributed to the transformation of the field from its status as paranormal or weird to its current stature as a viable discipline of mind phenomenology. John White, editor and author of multiple books, is a leading figure in the New Age community. He is a master networker, tireless lecturer and organizer, a seeker of self-realization, and a traveler on the path devoted to discovering "the good."

As early as 1973, Owens had begun preparations for her inevitable death. Since her Awakening and her intellectual insights into the nature of immortality, she had no fear of dying. She kept her will updated so that her friends would benefit from her material assets. Periodically, she would write out detailed instructions for Dwain and Cindy, or Audrey, or John, concerning the disposal of her personal property, funeral arrangements, and the disposition of published and unpublished manuscripts. On January 28, 1973, Dwain and Cindy received notice that she had willed all the personal property in her apartment to them. Her preparations probably followed an illness, but her letter was ten years and four months early.

In August 1977, Owens bought a certificate of deposit for Lara Wilder for $1,500 and sent Dwain and Cindy detailed information concerning Lara's savings account numbers. "At my advanced age I might pop off any minute and I'd feel more comfortable if you had this information in your possession."[56] She wanted Lara's money to yield as much interest as possible—she was putting Gelatt's financial lessons to use.

Claire returned to Denton in the spring of 1979, making her first visit to the College of Industrial Arts, now Texas Woman's University, since her graduation in 1916. Elizabeth Snapp, the newly appointed director of libraries, encountered Claire, "dressed to the nines" and wearing a "beautiful large red hat." According to Elizabeth, Claire appeared to be walking to the Little Chapel in the Woods.[57] "I knew I had to meet this fascinating woman."[58]

TWU was in the process of building the new Blagg-Huey Library, and Elizabeth had begun to add to the Woman's Collection and its archive. Upon learning Claire was an author, Elizabeth "asked her immediately if she would be interested in having copies of her new book and other writings in her own archival collection." Over the next four years, the two women talked often. Claire sent copies of her books, audios of her speeches, and reviews of her work to the library. Thus, the Claire Myers Owens Collection, one of their earliest, was established.

"I knew I treasured her friendship," Elizabeth later wrote, "but I learned after her death that our friendship was truly a deep one on both sides." Claire had instructed her attorney to ask Elizabeth to pack up her remaining papers and personal library in order to "bring them home to the TWU Collection." Claire had provided funds for that task as well, so Snapp travelled to Rochester in 1983. "I was honored to do just that, staying with Audrey Fernandez for a week and having an opportunity to visit her beloved Zen Center."[59]

In 1980, Claire wrote Dwain, now divorced, asking him to take charge of her cremation, with details for the procedure she wished him to follow. Echoing her motto beneath her senior picture in her high school year book, "fresh and sweet as the first flower," she added,

"I have told [the Zen Center] I wished my ashes to be distributed over some lovely trees and grassy place so I can come up as a little yellow crocus." Audrey would take care of her household things, but he should take anything he wanted. "When you see this letter I shall have said my last good-by to you and thanked you for all the beauty and love you brought into my life."[60]

As Claire had sorted through her papers and prepared the boxes for shipping, she confided to John that she was reluctant to include her first book, *The Unpredictable Adventure*. Perhaps it was still "too risqué"; she did not wish to offend southern sensibilities. John's letter offered reassurance: "Times have changed enough so that it won't shock people. . . . It shows your contribution to freeing the human mind from religious dogma." He praised her for being "nursemaid" to the higher race he believed would emerge out of the "current upheaval" of the planet. "You've done your part, and I love you for it."[61]

Around this time, Louise Ames submitted Owens's name for *The World Who's Who of Women*. Owens appears in the 1982 edition, with the photograph taken at age eighty-two for the jacket of *Zen and the Lady*: still beautiful, the dimple on her right cheek predominant, her face unlined, her demeanor elegant in a straw hat.[62]

During these final years of her life, John White and Raul daSilva concur, Claire had reached a level of enlightenment few attain. She had the powers of clairvoyance and extrasensory perception; she projected a sense of calm assurance. Raul tells stories of Claire's ability to know which streets were congested by accidents so that on their way out to dinner, they would miss traffic jams. On one occasion, Raul recalls, she "knew" where to find a specific audio tape he had misplaced: "Look in your sock drawer," she told him during one of their probing discussions.

Her world had expanded beyond racial and religious divisions. Raul daSilva is of Puerto Rican and Jewish ancestry, and Kenneth Ring, like Abraham Maslow, is Jewish by birth. Though the demographics of the Zen Center during the 1970s and 1980s may not have been particularly diverse in race or religion, Claire's consciousness had expanded to include human beings as universal souls.

"She wasn't a saint," White explained; she was a mystic who had reached a level often described as bodhisattva,[63] or one who strives to inspire and instruct others on the path toward enlightenment. Her lifelong quest to awaken "the good" in the human spirit allowed her to reach the summit of Mount Certitude, which imbued her presence with a sense of wonder and mystery.[64]

In December 1982, Charles Gelatt sent Claire a check for $870 to cover the round trip airfare to Florida for her and two companions. In January, after their visit, he wrote advising her to get a certificate from her doctor verifying her eye condition. If she was legally blind, she was due an extra $1,000 per year deduction on her income tax, and the bank could file for refunds for prior years dating back to 1979. Sell "AT&T and General Motors," he added, and "reinvest in a tax free fund which now yields 9.75%." In March 1983, she wrote Gelatt to thank him for his hospitality during her Florida visit. In her letter, however, she let him know that Fred Pederson, a longtime executive for the firm, had deeply offended her. "I cried bitterly that night after our last dinner in Florida. I don't object to teasing about having been an opera singer or polo player but how can a man as kind, intelligent and sensitive as Fred imagine that to add the third category 'a madam who was willing to oblige on Saturday night' is beyond my comprehension." Of course, she realized Pederson meant his teasing remarks as a joke, which she did not find amusing in any sense. "Tell him it is not funny, it hurts deeply . . . [and] not to say such things to me or any other woman."[65] She may not have called herself "feminist," but she never ceased promoting the dignity of women, never ceased demanding respect for herself and for others.

Two months later, Claire died quietly in her apartment. Charles Gelatt was her friend and protector until the very end, as were the members of the sangha, all her true family.

Saturday, May 7, 1983, marked the beginning of a seven-day sesshin at the Rochester Zen Center. May 8 was Mother's Day, which Claire traditionally celebrated with Audrey and Joe Fernandez and their three children.[66] During the week, she sent Audrey a pink azalea plant with a note saying she would not join them for Mother's Day dinner this year because she did not feel up to it—she had lost her appetite and found it hard to digest what she managed to eat. Audrey called to express concern and offered to bring Sunday dinner over the night before. Claire declined, but mentioned that Margaret would be coming by Saturday at four o'clock for tea.

Looking back on that conversation, piecing together Claire's final hours, Audrey realized that Claire had planned her death with as much attention and consideration for others as she displayed throughout her life. Her condition had deteriorated, and her quality of life was in steady decline. Her mind still alert, the misery of Thurston's final days formed lucid memories. She could not bear the thought of further burdening her dear friends. True to her nature, she took control of her death just as she had always taken control of her life. She decided to end her own suffering in a way that would cause the least suffering to others.

Audrey felt overwhelmingly sad that she hadn't been able to help her or to be with her those final hours:

> I didn't want her to die alone. I went there on Wednesday night and made her supper. I felt that she shouldn't have done it; she shouldn't have chosen her time to go. She should have waited. . . . I can see that she was an extremely brave woman and did *not* want to go to a nursing home, did not want to become unconscious, did not want people to have to physically care for her. She saw this helplessness as inevitable, and she saw it clearly, so I do admire her for what she did. There was a lot of pain. She recognized it was time to go. She called it diverticulosis. I think she suspected cancer and didn't want it to be diagnosed. After Claire died, I kept her portrait up in my bedroom for six months, and it was just awful because I thought of all the things I didn't say to her.

Claire did not want to be found on her deathbed by her true love, Dwain Wilder, nor did she wish to burden Audrey with the discovery. Audrey had her hands full with her invalid husband, Joe, who was suffering from Alzheimer's disease. Margaret, on the other hand, was engaged, her wedding day set two weeks hence; her new life lay ahead. Unpleasant as it might be, perhaps Claire considered Margaret the person most able to withstand the shock of discovering her body. As for Dwain, by the time he left the seven-day sesshin, she would have been cremated. All that would be left was the memorial service and the disbursement of her ashes, the plans for which she had clearly spelled out to both Dwain and Audrey. As with many aging people in declining condition, Claire had access to many kinds of prescriptions. She managed to collect enough of her pain medication to comprise a lethal dose. Everything in the apartment was immaculate. Her finances were in order; her manuscripts safely stored in boxes, ready to be shipped to the Blagg-Huey Library at Texas Woman's University in Denton. Elizabeth Snapp would be among the first people notified by Claire's lawyer.

The last time Geoffrey Lister saw Claire she was terribly ill. "When I went into her bedroom, I could feel Thursty there. I never knew him, but I could feel that he was there and I knew it was him—as if he were coming back for her, as if he came back to help her through this last part."

Raul daSilva recalls that afternoon through a mystical veil: "I turned on my stereo to listen to some Beethoven when suddenly I felt Claire's passing into the next dimension." Powerful, almost atmospheric, he felt sudden remorse at having failed to bid her farewell when he had moved to Syracuse. "Filled with unbearable distress, I began to call the few people I knew who might know about Claire and soon enough was told she had passed the day before."[67]

Margaret arrived for tea that Saturday evening at four o'clock; she brought with her a gift of carrot ginger soup for Claire's supper. Claire's apartment door was chained. When Claire did not answer, Margaret called the manager and they cut the lock. The body was still warm.

On May 10, Audrey arrived at the Whitehaven crematorium carrying a huge yellow tulip. The morticians were shocked to see her, but she had promised Claire she would be present. Everything went according to plan—Claire's plan. "She'd requested that her body be kept for three days before it was cremated," Audrey explained. "Buddhists believe this leaves time for the mind energy to separate from the body. The funeral director thought I was insane, walking in with that yellow tulip and a little bell and a brass gong. I sat and chanted the *Prajna-paramita* and the *Kanveon* in English, Japanese, and Chinese." The purpose of this Buddhist ritual is to help the soul go to the next stage. The ritual symbolizes that form is emptiness and emptiness is form. There is no death; there is only change, only transformation. "I left when the process was over—it took about an hour and a half." Audrey recalled noticing a red damask box as she left the crematorium, which reappeared on the alter in the Buddha hall, in front of the great golden Buddha, the day of the memorial service.

It was a cool bright spring day. Everything was blooming and lovely against a gray sky. A large group of people assembled, primarily members of the Zen community. Barbara Percy wrote a tribute, which she read as a eulogy. Audrey Fernandez read Claire Myers Owens's poem, "Seven Wonders of the Inner World":

How can I,
How can anyone despair—
However weary our body—
Or weighed down by the strife
And suffering of the world—
When the provocative Spring breeze on our cheek
Is a kiss of promise,
When the burst of Spring blossoms
Renews the hope we feared had died,
When the misty greenness
Of new leafing trees
So young and tender,
So pure and perfect
Awakens the *beyond within*
When the unending expanse of sky
Filled with hundreds of majestic storm clouds
Built up like fabulous castles
Of white and gray and black

Suddenly reveals in its very midst
An unknown something, a current of energy,
A presence,
And the sunrise one morning
Flung like gold over a gray world,
Brings the *eternal into the now*;
How can we ever despair
So long as nature can restore us
To the rhythm of the universe?[68]

The "*beyond within*." Perhaps these are the words that could have described the state Claire had reached on her path to enlightenment, the description Lex Hixon had probed to obtain during their interview. Perhaps the beyond within best describes the pinnacle Claire achieved when she felt herself merging with the light that embraces all of "the good."

Geoffrey and Kathy Lister, Dwain Wilder, and Audrey Fernandez met one afternoon several weeks later in the Zen Center garden. They had the red damask box with them, Audrey recalled. "We took a little hand shovel and dug a hole and bowed and put the ashes under the dogwood tree. I felt renewed after doing this. I felt there was nothing but life, nothing but transcendence."[69]

Nothing, perhaps, but a river of light illuminating the beyond within, merging the eternal with the now.

20. Zen garden. Claire's ashes buried under the dogwood tree next to the Sitting Buddha. Courtesy of the author.

Notes • Selected Bibliography • Index

Notes

Introduction

1. Anne Brigman, *The West Wind, 1915*, published courtesy of the George Eastman Museum.

2. Claire Myers Owens, *Awakening to the Good—Psychological or Religious? An Autobiographical Inquiry* (Boston: Christopher House, 1958), 101–7.

3. Miriam Kalman Harris, "The Pressure of the Choices," in *All Sides of the Subject*, ed. Teresa Iles (New York: Teacher's College Press, 1992), 68–79.

4. Owens, *Awakening*, 41–47.

5. Anne Firor Scott, *The Southern Lady: From Pedestal to Politics, 1830–1930* (Chicago: University of Chicago Press, 1970), 10.

6. Scott, 4.

7. Georgina Hickey, review of *Women of the American South: A Multicultural Reader*, Christie Anne Farnham, ed., *Southern Cultures* 6, no. 3 (Fall 2000): 93.

8. Debby Irving, *Waking Up White, and Finding Myself in the Story of Race* (Cambridge, MA: Elephant Room Press, 2014), 124–27, Kindle.

9. Roxane Gay, *Bad Feminist* (New York: Harper Perennial, 2014), 12, Kindle.

10. Penelope Niven, *Carl Sandburg* (New York: Scribner, 1991), xi.

11. For previous accounts, see Harris, "Pressure," 68–79; Miriam Kalman Harris, "Claire Myers Spotswood Owens: From Southern Belle to Grand Amoureuse," *Southern Quarterly* 31, no. 1 (1992), 50–69; Miriam Kalman Harris, afterword to *The Unpredictable Adventure: A Comedy of Woman's Independence*, by Claire Myers Spotswood Owens (Syracuse, NY: Syracuse University Press, 1993), 459–95.

12. Ray Monk, "Life without Theory: Biography as an Exemplar of Philosophical Understanding," *Poetics Today* 28, no. 3 (Fall 2009): 527–70.

13. Sara Alpern, et. al., eds., *The Challenge of Feminist Biography: Writing the Lives of Modern American Women* (Champaign, IL: University of Illinois Press, 1992), 11.

14. Liz Stanley, "Biography as Microscope or Kaleidoscope? The Case of Power in Hannah Cullwick's Relationship with Arthur Munby," *Women's Studies International Forum* 10, no. 1(1987): 19–31.

15. Carol A. Kolmerton, *The American Life of Ernestine Rose* (Syracuse, NY: Syracuse University Press, 1999), xxii.

16. Judith P. Zinsser, "Feminist Biography: A Contradiction in Terms?" *The Eighteenth Century* 50, no. 1 (Spring 2009): 43–48, accessed December 18, 2016, https://muse.jhu.edu/article/372742.

17. Linda Wagner-Martin, *Telling Women's Lives: The New Biography* (New Brunswick, NJ: Rutgers University Press, 1994), 19.

18. Zinsser, "Feminist Biography," 43–48.

19. Claire Myers Spotswood Owens, with an Afterword by Miriam Kalman Harris, *The Unpredictable Adventure: A Comedy of Woman's Independence* (Syracuse, NY: Syracuse University Press, 1992); Miriam Kalman Harris. "Owens, Clair Myers." In *Handbook of Texas Online*. Texas State Historical Association. Article published June 15, 2010; last modified November 15, 2017. http://www.tshaonline.org/handbook/online/articles/fownz; Harris, "Pressure," 68–79; Harris, "Owens: Southern Belle to Grand Amoureuse," 50–69; Miriam Kalman Harris, "Rediscovery: Claire Myers Spotswood (Owens)," *Belles-Lettres* 5 (Winter 1990): 15; Miriam Kalman Harris, "Claire Myers Spotswood Owens: A Grande Amoureuse" (paper, National Symposium on "The Role of Women: The Past and the Road Ahead," Hardin-Simmons University, 1991, and "Women and Texas History," University of Texas at Austin, 1990). Miriam Kalman Harris, "Claire Myers Owens," "Jean Houston," and "Florida Maxwell-Scott" in *American Women Writers Series*, ed. Taryn Benbow-Pfalzgraf, (Detroit: St. James Press, 1999).

20. Cynthia Maude-Gembler (then acquisition editor, Syracuse University Press), repeating comment by Carol Farley Kessler, private correspondence with author, 1991. See Kessler, ed., *Daring to Dream: Utopian Stories by United States Women, 1836–1919* (Boston: Pandora, 1984.

21. Stanley, "Biography," 19–31.

22. Zinsser, "Feminist Biography," 43.

23. Carolyn G. Heilbrun, *Writing A Woman's Life* (New York: Norton, 1988), chaps. 2 and 5.

24. Emily Bingham, *Irrepressible: The Jazz Age Life of Henrietta Bingham*, (New York: Farrar, Straus and Giroux, 2015), 3–8. Thanks to my grandson Miles Harris Wucher for the "crown of rare jewels" metaphor.

25. Heilbrun, *Writing*, 59.

26. Jeanne Perreault, *Writing Selves: Contemporary Feminist Autography* (Minneapolis: University of Minnesota Press, 1995).

27. Kolmerton, *The American Life*, xxii.

1. Smug Harbor

1. Claire Myers Owens, interview by Kenneth Ring, 1979, Claire Myers Owens Manuscript Collection, Blagg-Huey Library, Texas Woman's University, Denton, TX, box 68, folder 1 (hereafter cited as CMO Collection).

2. CMO interview by Ring.

3. *History of Bell County* (Fort Worth, TX: Temple Junior Chamber of Commerce, 1958), 171.

4. Susan Myers to CMO, Feb. 19, 1919, CMO Collection, box 1, folder 12.

5. CMO interview by Ring.

6. For southern codes of behavior for women see Anne Firor Scott, *The Southern Lady: From Pedestal to Politics, 1830–1930* (Chicago: University of Chicago Press, 1970) and Bertram Wyatt-Brown, *Southern Honor: Ethics and Behavior in the Old South* (New York: Oxford University Press, 1982), 14, 34.

7. W. J. Cash, *Mind of the South* (New York: Knopf, 1941), 5.

8. CMO interview by Ring.

9. Miriam Kalman Harris, "Claire Myers Spotswood Owens: From Southern Belle to Grand Amoureuse," *Southern Quarterly* 31, no. 1 (1992), 50–69; Miriam Kalman Harris, afterword to *The Unpredictable Adventure: A Comedy of Woman's Independence*, by Claire Myers Spotswood Owens (Syracuse, NY: Syracuse University Press, 1993), 459–95; Scott, *Southern Lady*, 4.

10. Wyatt-Brown, *Southern Honor*, 226 and chap. 9.

11. CMO interview by Ring.

12. Susan Chandler, "100 Years Encouraging the Gentle Arts of Home," *Temple Daily Telegram*, March 9, 2014.

13. "Temple Woman's Report Criticizes Sanitation," *Fort Worth Star Telegram*, December 13, 1915, accessed March 1, 2017, http://www.genealogybank.com/doc/newspapers/image/v2:10EEA3CFD

14. CMO interview by Ring.

15. Rufus B. Spain, *At Ease in Zion: Social History of Southern Baptists, 1865–1900* (Nashville: Vanderbilt University Press, 1967), 126.

16. CMO interview by Ring.

17. Sarah Wilkerson-Freeman, "Stealth in the Political Arsenal of Southern Women: A Retrospective for the Millennium," in *Southern Women at the Millennium: A Historical Perspective*, eds. Melissa Walker, Jeannette R. Dunn, and Joe P. Dunn, (Columbia and London: University of Missouri Press, 2003), 47.

18. Wyatt-Brown, *Southern Honor*, 14 and chaps. 1 and 2.

19. Matthew L. Downs, "Clicking the Trinoculars into Position: A Conversation with Glenda Elizabeth Gilmore" in *The Historian Behind the History: Conversations with*

Southern Historians, eds. Megan L. Bever and Scott A. Suarez (Tuscaloosa, AL: University of Alabama Press, 2014), 168.

20. Claire Myers Owens, "Amanda Mann," or "To Be Herself," CMO Collection, box 18.

21. Genealogies, CMO Collection, box 11. Letter from Cousin Mary, 1930, CMO Collection, box 2, folder 1.

22. Owens, "Amanda Mann."

23. Owens, "Amanda Mann."

24. Claire Myers Owens, *Zen and the Lady* (New York: Baraka Books Ltd., 1979), 30–32.

25. "To Coren Lee" by Emma S., CMO Collection, box 76, folder 12.

26. Coren Lee Myers to Susan Myers, June 19, 1899, CMO Collection, box 76, folder 6.

27. Laura Allen to Mrs. C. L. Myers, April 10, 1899, CMO Collection, box 1, folder 1.

28. Photographs, CMO Collection, boxes 65 and 66.

29. CMO interview by Ring.

30. CMO interview by Ring.

31. CMO Collection, box 40, folder 2.

32. CMO Collection, box 40, folder 2.

33. *History of Bell County*, 41 and 45.

34. CMO interview by Ring.

35. CMO interview by Ring.

2. A Bundle of Contradictions

1. CMO Collection, box 1, folder 1.

2. Temple High School yearbook, 1913. I wish to thank Nancy Williams, research librarian at the Temple Public Library, for assisting me in locating their Temple High School yearbooks 1912–16, City Directories, and guides to area cemeteries.

3. CMO Collection, box 49, folders 1, 2.

4. Will, CMO Collection, box 9, folders 5–8.

5. CMO Collection, box 40, folders 1, 2.

6. CMO Collection, box 40, folders 1, 2.

7. John Bowker, *World Religions* (London: Doring Kindersley, 1997), 172. In Islamic mystical tradition, Sufis seek a close, personal, intense union with God, and believe that God and soul are identical. Barbara G. Walker, *The Woman's Encyclopedia of Myths and Secrets* (New York: Harper and Row, 1983), 961. Sufi poets claimed the universe was held together by feminine forces.

8. CMO Collection, box 40, folders 1, 2.

9. CMO Collection, box 40, folders 1, 2.

10. Virginia Woolf, *A Writer's Diary* (New York: Harcourt Brace Jovanovich, 1954), 23. Owens placed a vertical line here in ink. In the Ring interview, she explained, "When I was fourteen, I wrote in my diary, 'I want to be a writer,'" underlined in ink.

11. Claire Myers Owens, interview by Kenneth Ring, 1979, CMO Collection, box 68, folder 1; "Miss Mary and Mr. Charles," CMO Collection, box 11, folder 3.

12. Letters from Pierrot, CMO collection, box 1, folder 18.

13. CMO interview by Ring.

14. Debby Irving, *Waking Up White, and Finding Myself in the Story of Race* (Cambridge, MA: Elephant Room Press, 2014), 127, Kindle.

15. Reference to Hans Christian Andersen and the Brothers Grimm (Jacob and Wilhelm), well-known nineteenth-century writers of folklore and fairy tales.

16. Claire Myers Spotswood Owens, *The Unpredictable Adventure: A Comedy of Women's Independence*, (Syracuse, NY: Syracuse University Press, 1993), 17–18.

17. Anne Firor Scott, *The Southern Lady: From Pedestal to Politics, 1830–1930* (Chicago: University of Chicago Press, 1970), 4.

18. Owens, *Unpredictable Adventure*, 22–23.

19. Owens, *Unpredictable Adventure*, 20.

20. Owens, *Unpredictable Adventure*, 24.

21. CMO to Mrs. C. L. Myers, CMO Collection, box 1, folder 3.

22. CMO Collection, box 40, folders 1, 2.

23. Scott, *Southern Lady*, 25.

24. CMO Collection, box 40, folders 1, 2.

25. CMO Collection, box 11, folder 4.

26. CMO interview by Ring.

27. CMO Collection, box 11, folder 4.

28. CMO Collection, box 40, folders 1, 2.

29. CMO interview by Ring.

30. CMO interview by Ring.

31. Temple High School yearbooks, Temple Public Library.

3. Rote Hill

1. Joyce Thompson, *Marking a Trail: A History of Texas Women's University* (Denton: TWU Press, 1982), 2, 4.

2. Thompson, 163. In 1934, L. H. Hubbard recommended a change in curriculum to shift the emphasis from technical and vocational to liberal arts. At this time, the board of regents voted to change the name College of Industrial Arts to Texas State College for Women (TSCW), which it remained until 1957, when it became Texas Woman's University (TWU).

3. Thompson, 1.

4. Thompson, 2.

5. Thompson, 4–5.

6. Thompson, 3.

7. Thompson, 3, 36.

8. *The Daedalian*, 1917.

9. Claire Myers Owens, "Autobiography" (unpublished manuscript), CMO Collection, box 19.

10. CIA was the acceptable abbreviation for the College of Industrial Arts. However, due to contemporary connotations, I have refrained from using it except in direct quotes.

11. Owens, "Autobiography."

12. Claire Myers Owens, "Gaily Bedight" (unpublished manuscript), CMO Collection, box 26.

13. Claire Myers Owens, interview by Kenneth Ring, 1979, CMO Collection, box 68, folder 1.

14. CMO interview by Ring.

15. Claire Myers Spotswood Owens, *The Unpredictable Adventure: A Comedy of Women's Independence*, (Syracuse, NY: Syracuse University Press, 1993), 54.

16. Owens, *Unpredictable Adventure*, 54.

17. Owens, *Unpredictable Adventure*, 46.

18. Owens, *Unpredictable Adventure*, 47.

19. Miriam Kalman Harris, afterword to *The Unpredictable Adventure: A Comedy of Woman's Independence*, by Claire Myers Spotswood Owens (Syracuse, NY: Syracuse University Press, 1993), 470. This paragraph is taken from my analysis of the Tellectina/Femina split. For other versions, see Miriam Kalman Harris, "Rediscovery: Claire Myers Spotswood (Owens)," *Belles Lettres* 5, Winter (1990):15; Miriam Kalman Harris, "The Pressure of the Choices," in *All Sides of the Subject*, ed. Teresa Iles (New York: Teacher's College Press, 1992), 73; Miriam Kalman Harris, "Claire Myers Spotswood Owens: From Southern Belle to Grand Amoureuse," *Southern Quarterly* 31, no. 1 (1992), 61–62.

20. *Handbook of Texas Online*, s.v. "Ousley, Clarence N.," article published June 15, 2010, https://tshaonline.org/handbook/online/articles/fou02.

21. In the CMO Collection, there is no record of correspondence between the two women; however, Clare Ousley is mentioned in the "Autobiography," in "Gaily Bedight," as "Marion," and in "Mrs. Oppidan," as "Marian."

22. My discussion of Clairene's and Clare's college careers is based on information from the 1914–16 editions of *The Daedalian* and from artifacts within the CMO Collection.

23. CMO Collection, box 11, folder 5.

24. Sex trafficking, in today's vernacular, refers to an illegal business of kidnapping underage teen girls and drugging, beating, and raping them before selling them into sexual slavery.

25. Owens, "Autobiography." (Sec also Owens, *The Unpredictable Adventure*, chap. 3. This character is named Tommy.)

26. Raewyn W. Connell and Rebecca Pearse, *Gender: In World Perspective*, 3rd ed., Short Introductions, (Cambridge, UK: Polity, 2014), 211–16, Kindle.

27. Owens, *The Unpredictable Adventure*, 57–58.

28. Lillian Faderman, *Surpassing the Love of Men: Romantic Friendship and Love between Women from the Renaissance to the Present* (New York: Morrow, 1981).

29. Owens, *The Unpredictable Adventure*, 59–60.

30. Robbie McKnight letter, CMO Collection, box 1, folder 4.

31. Owens, "Autobiography." So-called "soft" anti-Semitism, like racism, was common parlance of the culture.

32. Claire Myers Owens, *Awakening to the Good: Psychological or Religious?* (Boston: Christopher Publishing, 1958), 60–61.

33. Owens, *Awakening*, 60–61.

34. CMO interview by Ring.

35. Alden Evans letter, CMO Collection, box 1, folder 5.

36. Owens, *Unpredictable Adventure*, 63.

37. CMO interview by Ring; see also Owens, *Unpredictable Adventure*, 67–68 for scene depicting Tellectina and her mother, Mrs. Christian, discussing Tina leaving Smug Harbor.

38. Elizabeth Snapp and author, email discussion, March 6, 2017. "If Claire graduated from college in 1916 and her mother started The Homemakers Club in 1914 it is no wonder she did not want to go home, become a teacher, marry, and face the peer pressure of a traditional life in Temple Texas!" Exactly.

39. Owens, "Gaily Bedight."

40. CMO interview by Ring.

41. CMO interview by Ring.

42. Owens, "Gaily Bedight" and "Autobiography."

43. Owens, "Gaily Bedight."

4. Be Wise

1. Joseph Campbell, *The Hero with a Thousand Faces*, Bolligen Series (Princeton, NJ: Princeton University Press, 1949, 1973), 69. In-depth analysis of archetypal hero's journey in chapter 7.

2. Claire Myers Spotswood Owens, *The Unpredictable Adventure: A Comedy of Women's Independence*, (Syracuse, NY: Syracuse University Press, 1993), 72.

3. Claire Myers Owens, interview by Kenneth Ring, 1979, CMO Collection, box 68, folder 1.

4. Claire Myers Owens, *Awakening to the Good: Psychological or Religious?* (Boston: Christopher Publishing, 1958), 41–46.

5. Cheris Kramarae and Paula A. Treichler, eds., *A Feminist Dictionary* (London: Pandora, 1985), 300–301.

6. The "woman question" as used by "classical Marxists refers to the question of women's historical status and role within current social arrangements." It is separate from the feminist question, "directed at the cause of sexual inequality between men and women and of male dominance over women." Kramarae and Treichler, *Feminist Dictionary*, 496. See also Elaine Showalter, *Sexual Anarchy: Gender and Culture at the Fin de Siecle* (New York: Penguin, 1990), 47, 56; Eleanor Marx and Edward Aveling, "The Woman Question," *Westminster Review*, (1886), accessed on June 16, 2016 from The Marxists Internet Archive, http://www.marxists.org/archive/eleanor-marx/works/womanq.htm.

7. Showalter, *Sexual Anarchy*, 38.

8. Nancy Milford, *Savage Beauty: The Life of Edna St. Vincent Millay*, (New York: Random House, 2001).

9. Claire Myers Owens, "Gaily Bedight" (unpublished manuscript), CMO Collection, box 26, p. 90.

10. Letter from Alden Evans, July 13, 1916, CMO Collection, box 1, folder 5.

11. Owens, "Gaily Bedight," 90.

12. Owens, "Gaily Bedight," 90–91.

13. Owens, "Gaily Bedight," 92.

14. Owens, "Gaily Bedight," 94.

15. Jacob Riis, *How the Other Half Lives* (New York: Scribner, 1890).

16. Owens, "Gaily Bedight," 95.

17. Owens, "Gaily Bedight," 95.

18. Owens, "Gaily Bedight," 96–97.

19. Simone de Beauvoir, *The Second Sex* (New York: Vintage, 1974), 715.

20. Owens, "Gaily Bedight," 97.

21. Owens, "Gaily Bedight," 97, 99–100.

22. Owens, "Gaily Bedight," 103.

23. Owens, "Gaily Bedight," 105.

24. Owens, "Gaily Bedight," 107.

25. Letter, Alden Evans, CMO Collection, box 1, folder 5.

26. Letter, Alden Evans, CMO Collection, box 1, folder 5.

27. Owens, "Gaily Bedight," 109–10.

28. Owens, "Gaily Bedight," 112–13.

29. CMO interview by Ring.

30. Owens, "Gaily Bedight," 133.

31. CMO interview by Ring.

32. CMO interview by Ring.

33. Owens, "Gaily Bedight," 116.

34. Janet L. Freedman, *Reclaiming the Feminist Vision: Consciousness-Raising and Small Group Practice* (Jefferson, NC: McFarland, 2014), 618–23, Kindle.

35. Owens, "Gaily Bedight," 118.

36. CMO interview by Ring.

37. CMO interview by Ring; Owens, *Awakening*, chap. V.

38. Letter, Alden Evans, January 12, 1917, CMO Collection, box 1, folder 7; Claire Myers Owens, "Among the Alabama Hill Folk," CMO Collection, box 37, folder 4.

39. Letter, Alden Evans, January 12, 1917, CMO Collection, box 1, folder 7; Claire Myers Owens, "Among the Alabama Hill Folk," CMO Collection, box 37, folder 4.

40. Letter, Alden Evans, January 12, 1917, CMO Collection, box 1, folder 7; Claire Myers Owens, "Among the Alabama Hill Folk," CMO Collection, box 37, folder 4.

41. Letter, Alden Evans, January 12, 1917 CMO Collection box 1, folder 7.

42. Letter, Alden Evans, March 15, 1917, CMO Collection, box 1, folder 7.

43. Letter, Alden Evans, March 15, 1917, CMO Collection, box 1, folder 7.

44. Letter, Alden Evans, March 24, 1917, CMO Collection, box 1, folder 7.

45. Letter, Alden Evans, March 24, 1917, CMO Collection, box 1, folder 7.

46. Letter, Alden Evans, March 24, 1917, CMO Collection, box 1, folder 7.

47. Owens, "Gaily Bedight," 125.

48. Owens, "Gaily Bedight," 126.

49. CMO interview by Ring.

50. Owens, "Gaily Bedight," 127.

51. William L. O'Neill, *Echoes of Revolt: The Masses, 1911–1917* (Chicago: Ivan R. Dee, Inc., 1989), 17. Few magazines compare to the legendary influence of the *Masses*, the Greenwich Village literary and political journal, which flourished briefly in the early 1900s, large in "importance and excitement." See Leslie Fishbein, *Rebels in Bohemia: The Radicals of The Masses, 1911–1917*, with Foreword by Frank Freidel (Chapel Hill: University of North Carolina Press, 1982) and Daniel Aaron, *Writers on the Left, 1912–1940* (New York: Oxford University Press, 1961). Of note, Edna St. Vincent Millay "stood by the editors of *The Masses* when they were up against charges for treason in 1918." Milford, *Savage Beauty*, xiii.

52. Owens, "Gaily Bedight," 120.

53. Owens, "Gaily Bedight," 129.

54. CMO interview by Ring. Owens discussed her reaction to World Wars I and II with Kenneth Ring and described the ways World War II contributed to her "dark night of the soul," which climaxed with her Great Awakening, 1949–59.

55. Owens, "Gaily Bedight," 131a.

56. CMO interview by Ring.

5. Nithking

1. Claire Myers Owens, interview by Kenneth Ring, 1979, CMO Collection, box 68, folder 1; Claire Myers Owens, *Awakening to the Good: Psychological or Religious?* (Boston: Christopher Publishing, 1958), 71.

2. Claire Myers Owens, "Gaily Bedight" (unpublished manuscript), CMO Collection, box 26, p. 142.

3. Owens, "Gaily Bedight," 147–48.

4. Owens, "Gaily Bedight," 157; CMO interview by Ring.

5. Janet L. Freedman. *Reclaiming the Feminist Vision: Consciousness-Raising and Small Group Practice* (Jefferson, NC: McFarland, 2014). Freedman references Peggy McIntosh, "White Privilege and Male Privilege: A Personal Account of Coming to See Correspondences through Work in Women's Studies" (working paper, Wellesley College Center for Research on Women, 1988), accessed March 1, 2017, http://www.collegeart.org/pdf/diversity/white-privilege-and-male-privilege.pdf.

6. Letter, Robbie McKnight, CMO Collection, box 1, folder 17.

7. Lee Virginia Chambers-Schiller, *Liberty, A Better Husband: Single Women in America, The Generations of 1740–1840* (New Haven: Yale University Press, 1984), 18. See chap. 1.

8. Chambers-Schiller, 1, 24.

9. Nancy Woloch, *Women and the American Experience*, (New York: Knopf, 1981), 281–86.

10. Leslie Fishbein, *Rebels in Bohemia: The Radicals of The Masses, 1911–1917* (Chapel Hill: University of North Carolina Press, 1982), 81.

11. Fishbein, 81; see also Daniel Aaron, *Writers on the Left, 1912–1940* (New York: Oxford University Press, 1961). Fishbein calls them New Intellectuals; Aaron designates them Young Intellectuals.

12. Fishbein, *Rebels in Bohemia*, 4.

13. Fishbein, *Rebels in Bohemia*, 81. Women and sexuality, chap. 5.

14. Caroline F. Ware, *Greenwich Village, 1920–1930* (Cambridge, MA: Riverside, 1935), 5.

15. Frank Freidel, foreword to *Rebels in Bohemia*, by Leslie Fishbein (New York: Oxford University Press, 1961), xii.

16. Owens, "Gaily Bedight," 148–50.

17. Owens, "Gaily Bedight," 149–50.

18. Dorothy M. Brown, *Setting a Course: American Women in the 1920s* (Boston: Twayne, 1987), 178, 213–14, 218.

19. CMO interview by Ring.

20. CMO interview by Ring.

21. CMO Collection, box 1, folder 10.

22. Letter, Leo Saidla, CMO Collection, box 1, folder 10.

23. Letter, Leo Saidla, CMO Collection, box 1, folder 10.

24. Owens, "Gaily Bedight," 178.

25. Woloch, *Women*, 408.

26. Woloch, 408.

27. Owens, "Gaily Bedight," 181.

28. Letter, Susan Myers, CMO Collection, box 1, folder 9.

29. Letter, Susan Myers, CMO Collection, box 1, folder 9.

30. Letter, Susan Myers, CMO Collection, box 1, folder 28.

31. Letter, author unknown, possibly Carton Moore-Park, CMO Collection, box 1, folder 11; Barbara G. Walker, *The Woman's Encyclopedia of Myths and Secrets* (San Francisco: Harper & Row, 1983), 549, 207. Walker identifies Lorelei as "anciently identified with a Water-siren or River-goddess who lured men to death by drowning." A nineteenth-century German writer transformed Lorelei into a maiden who threw herself in the river reappearing as a spirit, singing "fatal songs to passing boatmen." Carton/Chester calls Sibyl Daphne, the virgin of Greek myth saved from rape by Apollo by transforming herself into a laurel tree.

32. CMO interview by Ring.

33. Owens, *Awakening*, 72.

34. Owens, "Gaily Bedight," 202.

35. Owens, "Gaily Bedight," 211.

36. Claire Myers Owens, "Autobiography" (unpublished manuscript), CMO Collection, box 19.

37. Owens, "Autobiography."

38. Edward Carpenter, *Love's Coming of Age: A Series of Papers on the Relation of the Sexes* (Manchester: Labour Press, 1896), 61–62.

39. Owens, "Gaily Bedight," 222–23.

40. Owens, "Gaily Bedight," 231.

41. Owens, "Gaily Bedight," 230. In 1921, Marie Stopes opened Britain's first birth control clinic, Holloway, in London.

42. Letter, Leo Saidla, CMO Collection, box 1, folder 13.

43. Letter, Leo Saidla, CMO Collection, box 1, folder 13. Also contains two French postcards.

44. Letter, Susan Myers, CMO Collection, box 1, folder 12.

45. Letter, Susan Myers, CMO Collection, box 1, folder 12.

46. Letter, Alden Evans, CMO Collection, box 1, folder 8.

47. Letter, Alden Evans, CMO Collection, box 1, folder 8.

48. Letter, Alden Evans, CMO Collection, box 1, folder 14.

6. New Chimera

1. Claire Myers Owens [Claire M. Spotswood, pseud], "Our Cooperative Colony," CMO Collection, box 37, folder 34.

2. Owens, "Our Colony," 1.

3. Owens, "Our Colony," 1–2.

4. Owens, "Our Colony," 3.

5. Owens, "Our Colony," 5.

6. Owens, "Our Colony," 3.

7. Owens, "Our Colony," 4.

8. Owens, "Our Colony," 4.

9. Owens, "Our Colony," 4–5.

10. Claire Myers Owens, "Gaily Bedight" (unpublished manuscript), CMO Collection, box 26, p. 7–8.

11. Letter, Susan Myers, CMO Collection, box 1, folder 12.

12. Owens, "Our Colony, 10.

13. Owens, "Our Colony," 7.

14. Owens, "Our Colony," 13.

15. Owens, "Our Colony," 13.

16. Owens, "Our Colony," 16.

17. Owens, "Our Colony," 18.

18. Claire's "poor feet" resulted from these chilblains.

19. Owens, "Our Colony," 22.

20. Claire Myers Owens, "Wherein Two Can Live as Cheaply as One and the Only Bill Is the Grocery Bill," CMO Collection, box 37, folder 34.

21. Claire Myers Spotswood Owens, *The Unpredictable Adventure: A Comedy of Women's Independence*, (Syracuse, NY: Syracuse University Press, 1993), 94–128 (chap. V).

22. Owens, *Unpredictable Adventure*, 94–128 (chap. V).

23. Historian Linda Gordon uses "voluntary motherhood" to describe women's demands to assert control over their own sexual lives. See Linda Gordon, *Woman's Body, Woman's Right: Birth Control in America*, revised and updated edition (London: Penguin Books, 1990).

24. Owens, *Unpredictable Adventure*, 111.

25. Owens, *Unpredictable Adventure*, 113.

26. Owens, *Unpredictable Adventure*, 116.

27. Owens, "Gaily Bedight," 267.

28. Owens, "Gaily Bedight," 272.

29. Owens, "Gaily Bedight," 269.

30. Owens, "Gaily Bedight," 298.

31. Owens, "Gaily Bedight," 374.

32. Owens, "Gaily Bedight," 273.

33. Owens, "Gaily Bedight," 323.

34. Adrienne Rich, "Conditions for Work: The Common World of Women," in *Working It Out*, eds. Sara Ruddick and Pamela Daniels (New York: Pantheon Books, 1977), xiv–xxiv.

35. Owens, "Gaily Bedight," 293.

36. Owens, "Gaily Bedight," 291–94.

37. Owens, "Gaily Bedight," 295.

38. Owens, "Gaily Bedight," 303.

39. Owens, "Gaily Bedight," 320.

40. Owens, "Gaily Bedight," 334.

41. Owens, "Gaily Bedight," 340.

42. Nancy Woloch, *Women and the American Experience*, (New York: Knopf, 1981), 408; see also Miriam Kalman Harris, afterword to *The Unpredictable Adventure: A Comedy of Woman's Independence*, by Claire Myers Spotswood Owens (Syracuse, NY: Syracuse University Press, 1993), 473.

43. Letter, Leo Saidla, February 23, 1920, CMO Collection, box 1, folder 15.

44. Letter, Leo Saidla, February 23, 1920, CMO Collection, box 1, folder 15.

45. Letter, Leo Saidla, CMO Collection, box 1, folder 12.

46. Letter, Leo Saidla, CMO Collection, box 1, folder 12. The Mann Act proscribed the interstate transport of women or children for immoral purposes. *Encyclopedia of the American Judicial System*, vol. 1 (New York: Scribner, 1987), 125b.

47. CMO, "Gaily Bedight," 364.

48. Claire Myers Owens, interview by Kenneth Ring, 1979, CMO Collection, box 68, folder 1.

49. CMO interview by Ring.

50. Letter, Coren Lee Myers, May 29, 1920, CMO Collection, box 1, folder 16.

51. Letter, Coren Lee Myers, July 12, 1920, CMO Collection, box 1, folder 16.

52. Claire Myers Owens, "Autobiography" (unpublished manuscript), CMO Collection, box 19.

53. Letter, Leo Saidla, CMO Collection, box 1, folder 25.

54. Letter, Leo Saidla, CMO Collection, box 1, folder 25.

55. Letter, Leo Saidla, August 8, 1920, CMO Collection, box 1, folder 15.

56. Letter, Philippe, August 26, 1920, CMO Collection, box 1, folder 18.

7. Rivers of Light

1. Jeanne Perreault, *Writing Selves: Contemporary Feminist Autography* (Minneapolis: University of Minnesota Press, 1995).

2. Mary Karr, *The Art of Memoir* (New York: HarperCollins, 2015), 239, Kindle.

3. Virginia Woolf, *A Room of One's Own* (London: Harcourt Brace Jovanovich, 1929), 97.

4. Karr, *Art of Memoir*, 240, Kindle.

5. Claire Myers Owens, *Awakening to the Good—Psychological or Religious? An Autobiographical Inquiry* (Boston: Christopher House, 1958), 98.

6. Claire Myers Owens, "Gaily Bedight" (unpublished manuscript), CMO Collection, box 26, pp. 367–68.

7. *Women in Congress, 1917–2006* (Washington, DC: History, Art & Archives, U.S. House of Representatives, Office of the Historian, 2007), "I'm no Lady; I'm a Member of Congress: Women Pioneers on Capitol Hill, 1917–1934," http://history.house.gov/Exhibitions-and-Publications/WIC/Historical-Essays/No-Lady/Introduction/.

8. Owens, "Gaily Bedight," 367–68.

9. Karr, *Art of Memoir*, 292, Kindle.

10. Telegram from Carton, December 31, 1920, CMO Collection, box 1, folder 18.

11. CMO Collection, box 1, folder 18.

12. Photograph, CMO Collection, box 66, folder 2.

13. Owens, *Awakening*, 72.

14. Claire Myers Owens, "Autobiography" (unpublished manuscript), CMO Collection, box 19.

15. Owens, "Gaily Bedight," 348.

16. Owens, "Gaily Bedight," 345. This anecdote compiled from the novel, short stories, and autobiographical writings.

17. Owens, *Awakening*, 71.

18. Owens, *Awakening*, 72.

19. Owens, *Awakening*, 73.

20. Owens, "Autobiography."

21. Owens, *Awakening*; Algernon C. Swinburne (1837–1909), "Hertha"; Ralph Waldo Emerson (American, 1803–82), *Essays, First Series* (Boston: Houghton, Mifflin, 1903).

22. Owens, *Awakening*, 73.

23. Owens, *Awakening*, 73–75.

24. Owens, *Awakening*, 77.

25. According to *Webster's Third Edition International Dictionary* (1986), a "sack suit" is a man's suit with a single- or double-breasted jacket with a straight, unfitted back.

26. Owens, *Awakening*, 78.

27. Owens, *Awakening*, chap. 7. This chapter tells the whole incident, as does the "Autobiography."

28. Owens, "Autobiography." Claire and Carton hid from public view most of the time they were together. However, in this story, they appear together at a private party without any self-consciousness regarding their adulterous relationship.

29. Owens, *Awakening*, 79.

30. Owens, *Awakening*, 79.

31. Owens, *Awakening*, 80.

32. Owens, *Awakening*, 83.

33. Owens, *Awakening*, 83–84.

34. Owens, *Awakening*, 84.

35. Claire Myers Owens, interview by Kenneth Ring, 1979, CMO Collection, box 68, folder 1. In the interview, Owens recalled, "The party was evil but the poem ("Hertha") was good."

36. Owens, *Awakening*, 85; Emerson, *Essays*. Quotes from "Intellect," "Self-Reliance," and "Over-Soul."

37. CMO interview by Ring.

38. *Santa Teresa In Ecstasy* (1645–52), a sculpture by Gian Lorenzo Bernini in the Cornaro Chapel, Santa Maria della Vittoria, Rome. Claire often refers to Santa Teresa in her writing, comparing her own experiences to that depicted by Bernini.

39. Claire Myers Owens, "Belle Randolph" (unpublished manuscript), CMO Collection, box 26; a.k.a. "Sons and Husbands" (unpublished manuscript), CMO Collection, box 17; a.k.a. "Love Is Not Enough" (unpublished manuscript), CMO Collection, box 18.

40. Owens, "Belle Randolph," 51.

41. Owens, *Awakening*, 94–100.

42. James Branch Cabell (1876–1948) was best known for his Jurgen series of fantasy novels. His novel *Donmei: A Comedy of Woman-Worship*, (New York: McBride, 1930), influenced Owens's choice of a subtitle for *The Unpredictable Adventure: A Comedy of Woman's Independence*.

43. Owens, "Autobiography."

44. Claire Myers Owens, "Concerning Women's Soft Domination," CMO Collection, box 35, folder 4.

45. Owens, "Soft Domination," 1.

46. CMO, box 35, folder 4.

47. Owens, "Gaily Bedight," 356a.

48. Claire Myers Spotswood Owens, *The Unpredictable Adventure: A Comedy of Women's Independence*, (Syracuse, NY: Syracuse University Press, 1993), 47.

49. Letters, Claire Myers to Christopher Morley, CMO Collection, box 35, folder 16 and box 37, folder 41.

50. Peggy McIntosh, "White Privilege and Male Privilege: A Personal Account of Coming to See Correspondences through Work in Women's Studies" (working

paper, Wellesley College Center for Research on Women, 1988), accessed March 16, 2017, http://www.collegeart.org/pdf/diversity/white-privilege-and-male-privilege.pdf.

51. Betty Friedan, *The Feminine Mystique* (New York: W. W. Norton and Co., 1963).

52. Owens, "Autobiography."

53. Letter, writer unknown, CMO Collection, box 1, folder 19.

54. Owens, "Autobiography."

55. Letters, CMO Collection, box 1, folder 26. All are undated; all signed "Devotedly, C" or "My dear love! C," if signed at all. The handwritten ones are nearly illegible. There are two typed letters, one six pages long and the other two pages.

56. Letter, CMO, CMO Collection, box 1, folder 27.

57. Owens, "Autobiography."

58. Owens, "Autobiography"; Owens, *Awakening*, 87.

59. Owens, *Awakening*, 89.

60. Owens, "Autobiography."

61. Letter, Leo Saidla, CMO Collection, box 1, folder 20.

62. Letter, "Pierrot," CMO Collection, box 1, folders 20 and 21. "Pierrot's" letter in folder 20 is dated 1925 in pencil, presumably by Claire. "Pierrot" indicates "Pierrette" has been "gone for three full weeks."

63. Owens, *Awakening*, 87–93.

64. Owens, *Awakening*, 89–90.

65. Owens, "Autobiography."

66. Owens, "Autobiography."

67. Owens, "Autobiography."

68. CMO Collection, box 51. Dauber and Pine Book Shop opened as a secondhand bookshop in 1922 at 83 Fourth Avenue, near Eleventh. It moved to expanded quarters in 1925, at 66 Fifth Avenue, between Twelfth and Thirteenth Streets. "More writers frequent it than any other," noted *Publishers Weekly* (1935, p. 5). Today, The New School is at this site.

69. Owens, "Autobiography"; see Josh Rahn, "Modernism," In *The Literature Network*, 2011. http://www.online-literature.com/periods/modernism.php.

70. Owens, "Autobiography."

71. Owens, "Autobiography."

72. Edna St. Vincent Millay, "Figs from Thistles: First Fig," *Poetry Magazine: A Magazine of Verse* 7 no. 3 (June 1918): 130, https://www.poetryfoundation.org/poetrymagazine/poems/14095/first-fig.

73. Jean Houston, phone interviews by author, May 1, 1996; December 12, 1996; December 17, 1996.

74. Owens, "Autobiography."

75. Jean Houston, phone interviews by author, May 1, 1996; December 12, 1996; December 17, 1996.

76. Carroll Smith-Rosenberg, *Disorderly Conduct: Visions of Gender in Victorian America* (New York: Alfred A. Knopf, 1985), 277–80.

77. Owens, "Autobiography."

78. Owens, "Autobiography."

79. Owens, "Autobiography."

8. If It's Predictable . . .

1. Claire Myers Owens, "Autobiography" (unpublished manuscript), CMO Collection, box 19; Claire Myers Owens, "Celebrities on Parade," CMO Collection, Bookstore Brevities series, box 37. Sir Thomas Glen-Coats, a Dauber and Pine customer, was a wealthy British designer of yachts who purchased books about American economics.

2. CMO Collection, box 1, folder 22.

3. Owens, "Autobiography."

4. CMO to parents, September 19, 1928, CMO Collection, box 1, folder 22.

5. Claire Myers Owens, "A Dangerous Thing," CMO Collection, box 37, folder 10; "Evening Dress in a Bus," box 37, folder 13; "Latest Style in Crime," box 35, folder 13.

6. Katherine Angell (a.k.a. White), fiction editor for the *New Yorker* from 1925 to 1960; Arthur Kober, "Audition," *New Yorker*, October 6, 1928, 88–89.

7. W. Gibbs to CMO, October 18, 1928, CMO Collection, box 37, folder 10.

8. Claire Myers Owens, "Evening Dress in a Bus," CMO Collection, box 37, folder 13.

9. Kober, "Audition," 88.

10. Cartoon, *New Yorker*, October 6, 1928, 72.

11. CMO, Bookstore Brevities series, CMO Collection, boxes 35, 36, 37.

12. Carroll Smith-Rosenberg, *Disorderly Conduct: Visions of Gender in Victorian America* (New York: Alfred A. Knopf, 1985), 281–83.

13. Smith-Rosenberg, 281–83.

14. Susan Faludi, *Backlash: The Undeclared War against American Women* (New York: Crown Publishers, Inc., 1991), x–xi.

15. Claire Myers Spotswood Owens, *The Unpredictable Adventure: A Comedy of Women's Independence*, (Syracuse, NY: Syracuse University Press, 1993), chap. 5.

16. *U.S. History: Pre-Columbian to the New Millennium*, s.v. "Flappers," accessed March 17, 2017, http://www.ushistory.org/us/46d.asp.

17. CMO letter to Hansen, February 17, 1929, CMO Collection, box 52, folder 1.

18. Carton Moore-Park (1877–1956). In 1926, William Rudge published a limited edition of Samuel Levy Bensusan's *The Gospel According to Saint Luke*, illustrated by

Moore-Park. Other publications include *An Alphabet of Animals* (Blackie, 1899), *A Book of Birds* (Blackie, 1900), *A Book of Elfin Rhymes* (Gay and Bird, 1900), *A Country-Side Chronicle* (Heinemann, 1907), *A Dog Book* (Grant Richards, 1902), *Parnassus in Tennessee* (1922), *Reynard the Fox* (Macmillan, 1920), and *Wild Folk* (Little, Brown, 1930). He is identified as a "portrait and animal painter, lithographer, and writer of New York" on the OCLC database catalog.

19. Claire Myers Owens, "Adventures in a Bookshop: Celebrities on Parade," CMO Collection, Bookstore Brevities series, box 37, folder 1.

20. Claire Myers, Owens, "Adventures in a Bookshop: Fame and *Faux Pas*," CMO Collection, box 27, folder 1.

21. Claire Myers Owens, Alabama series, CMO Collection, box 37, multiple folders.

22. Claire Myers Owens, "Among the Alabama Hill Folk," CMO Collection, box 37, folder 4.

23. Claire Myers Owens, "Among the Alabama Hill Folk," CMO Collection, box 37, folder 4.

24. Claire Myers Owens, "Among the Alabama Hill Folk," CMO Collection, box 37, folder 4.

25. Claire Myers Owens, "The Magic Kindergarten," CMO Collection, box 37, folder 23.

26. Owens, "Autobiography."

27. Owens, "Autobiography."

28. CMO Collection, box 53, folder 2.

29. Edgar Allan Poe, "Eldorado," in *The Poems of Edgar Allen Poe*, ed. Killis Campbell (New York: Russell & Russell, Inc., 1962), 128–29.

30. Owens, "Autobiography."

31. Joseph Campbell, *The Hero with a Thousand Faces* (Princeton, NJ: Bollingen, 1949, 1973), 49–59.

32. Campbell, *Hero*, 69.

33. Claire Myers Owens, "Autobiography."

34. Campbell, *Hero*, 71.

35. Owens, *Unpredictable Adventure*, 75.

36. Owens, *Unpredictable Adventure*, 71–72.

37. Smith-Rosenberg, *Disorderly Conduct*, 287–88.

38. Claire Myers Owens, "Gaily Bedight" (unpublished manuscript), CMO Collection, box 26, title page.

39. Campbell, *Hero*, 97.

40. Smith-Rosenberg, *Disorderly Conduct*, 289.

41. Campbell, *Hero*, 97.

42. Owens, *Unpredictable Adventure*, 201–2.

43. Owens, *Unpredictable Adventure*, 178.

44. Owens, *Unpredictable Adventure*, 204.

45. Owens, *Unpredictable Adventure*, 208.

46. Owens, *Unpredictable Adventure*, 211.

47. Owens, *Unpredictable Adventure*, 212–13.

48. Owens, *Unpredictable Adventure*, 221.

49. Kim Chernin, *Reinventing Eve: Modern Woman in Search of Herself* (New York: Harper and Row, 1987), 73.

50. Owens, *Unpredictable Adventure*, 221.

51. Owens, *Unpredictable Adventure*, 226–29.

52. Chernin, *Reinventing Eve*, 77.

53. Campbell, *Hero*, 109–26.

54. Chernin, *Reinventing Eve*, 96.

55. Miriam Kalman Harris, afterword to *The Unpredictable Adventure: A Comedy of Woman's Independence*, by Claire Myers Spotswood Owens (Syracuse, NY: Syracuse University Press, 1993), 476–78; see also Miriam Kalman Harris, "Claire Myers Spotswood Owens: From Southern Belle to Grand Amoureuse," *Southern Quarterly* 31, no. 1 (1992); Miriam Kalman Harris, "The Pressure of the Choices," in *All Sides of the Subject*, ed. Teresa Iles (New York: Teacher's College Press, 1992), 68–79.

56. Owens, *Unpredictable Adventure*, 271–72.

57. Owens, *Unpredictable Adventure*, 274.

58. Owens, *Unpredictable Adventure*, 273.

59. Owens, *Unpredictable Adventure*, 277–78.

60. Campbell, *Hero*, 109.

61. Owens, *Unpredictable Adventure*, 272.

62. Owens, *Unpredictable Adventure*, 285–86.

63. Owens, *Unpredictable Adventure*, 287.

64. Chernin, *Reinventing Eve*, 86.

65. Owens, *Unpredictable Adventure*, 329.

66. Campbell, *Hero*, 189.

67. Carolyn G. Heilbrun, *Writing a Woman's Life* (New York: W. W. Norton, 1988), 89.

68. Owens, *Unpredictable Adventure*, 442–45.

69. Rachel Brownstein, *Becoming a Heroine* (New York: Viking, 1982), xxv.

70. Burton Rascoe to CMO, February 9, 1935, CMO Collection, box 54, folder 8. He begins this letter: "Keep your pants on. You are going places and are going to do things."

71. Chernin, *Reinventing Eve*, 25.

72. Muriel Rukeyser (1913–1980), American poet, feminist, and political activist.

73. CMO letters to Rascoe, June 8 and June 21, 1935, CMO Collection, box 54, folder 8.

74. Marian Murray, "Her First Book Will Be Published in September: Woman author tells of hard work and success," *Hartford Daily Times*, May 18, 1935, in CMO Collection, box 58, folder 2.

75. CMO Collection, box 54, folder 8.

76. Randolph Bartlett to CMO, October 19, 1935, CMO Collection, box 54, folder 10.

77. CMO Collection, box 58, folder 2.

78. CMO to Paul de Kruiff, October 8, 1935, CMO Collection, box 54, folder 10.

79. H. L. Mencken to CMO, December 27, 1935, CMO Collection, box 6, folder 37.

80. Richard Aldington to CMO, June 26, 1935, CMO Collection, box 6, folder 1.

81. CMO to Burton Rascoe, CMO Collection, box 53, folder 2.

82. Aldington to CMO, CMO Collection, box 6, folder 1.

83. Joan Acocella, "Metamorphoses: How Angela Carter Became Feminism's Great Mythologist," *New Yorker*, March 13, 2017, 72.

84. Aldous Huxley to CMO, November 27, 1935, CMO Collection, box 6, folder 32.

85. C. Hugh Holman, *A Handbook to Literature*, 4th ed. (Indianapolis: ITT Bobbs-Merrill, 1985), 11.

86. Carol Farley Kessler, *Charlotte Perkins Gilman: Her Progress toward Utopia with Selected Writings* (Syracuse, NY: Syracuse University Press, 1995), 7–9.

87. E. S. Cumbie to CMO, July 22, 1937, CMO Collection, box 54, folder 10.

88. Owens, "Autobiography."

89. Owens, "Autobiography."

90. CMO Collection, box 54, folder 9 and box 55, folder 4.

9. Parallel Letters/Parallel Lives

1. CMO Collection, box 2, folder 2.

2. Claire Myers Owens, "Autobiography" (unpublished manuscript), CMO Collection, box 19.

3. Kim Chernin, *Reinventing Eve: Modern Woman in Search of Herself* (New York: Harper and Row, 1987), 19.

4. Owens, "Autobiography."

5. Owens, "Autobiography."

6. CMO to Mother, 1911 box 1, folder 3

7. Claire Myers Owens, "Gaily Bedight" (unpublished manuscript), CMO Collection, box 26, 81.

8. Owens, "Autobiography."

9. Owens, "Autobiography."

10. Jonathan Cape & Harrison Smith to CMO regarding her tentative title, "Puritan's Progress," February 20 and November 4, 1931, CMO Collection, box 53, folder 1.

11. Owens, "Autobiography."

12. George Wanders to CMO, May 17, 1931, box 2, folder 3.

13. George Wanders to CMO, May 17, 1931, box 2, folder 3.

14. Owens, "Autobiography."

15. Owens, "Autobiography."

16. In "Belle Randolph," Claire used fictional names for some but not all of her characters.

17. Claire Myers Owens, "Belle Randolph" (unpublished manuscript), CMO Collection, box 26, pp. 177–78.

18. Owens, "Autobiography."

19. Owens, "Autobiography."

20. Owens, "Autobiography."

21. Owens, "Autobiography."

22. Owens, "Autobiography."

23. CMO to parents, July 2, 1931, CMO Collection, box 2, folder 4.

24. Owens, "Belle Randolph," 148–49.

25. CMO to parents, July 26, 1931, box 2, folder 4.

26. CMO to attorney, n.d., 1932, CMO Collection, box 2, folder 8.

27. Owens, "Belle Randolph," 193.

28. George Cram Cook started the Provincetown Players in Provincetown, Massachusetts, in 1915. With the support of Eugene O'Neill and John Reed, they moved to 139 MacDougal Street in Greenwich Village in November 1916. See Don B. Wilmeth with Tice L. Miller, *Cambridge Guide to American Theater* (New York: Cambridge University Press, 1996).

29. Owens, "Belle Randolph," 212.

30. Owens, "Belle Randolph," 214.

31. Owens, "Belle Randolph," 214.

32. Owens, "Belle Randolph," 152.

33. Owens, "Belle Randolph," 213–16.

34. Owens, "Belle Randolph," 232.

35. CMO to parents, August 3, 1931, CMO Collection, folder 2, box 5.

36. CMO to parents, August 18, 1931, CMO Collection, box 2, folder 4.

37. Owens, "Belle Randolph," 234.

38. Owens, "Belle Randolph," 271–83

39. Owens, "Belle Randolph," 288–89.

40. Owens, "Belle Randolph," 294.

41. Lenore E. Walker, *The Battered Woman* (New York: Harper & Row, 1979); Del Martin, *Battered Wives* (Volcano, CA: Volcano Press, 1976); see also, Miriam Kalman Harris, *Rape, Incest, Battery: Women Writing Out the Pain* (Fort Worth: Texas Christian University Press, 2000).

42. C. J. Newton, M.A., "Domestic Violence: An Overview," *Mental Health Journal*, February 2001, https://www.facebook.com/note.php?note_id=97660852648.

43. Owens, "Belle Randolph," 297.

44. Owens, "Autobiography."

45. Owens, "Autobiography."

46. CMO to parents, August 31, 1931, CMO Collection, box 2, folder 4.

47. CMO to parents, September 10, 1931 CMO Collection, box 2, folder 5.

48. Owens, "Belle Randolph," 306–13.

49. Claire Myers Owens, prologue to *Awakening to the Good: Psychological or Religious?* (Boston: Christopher Publishing, 1958).

50. Claire Myers Owens, *Awakening to the Good: Psychological or Religious?* (Boston: Christopher Publishing, 1958), 107.

51. Owens, "Belle Randolph," 184–88.

52. Owens, "Belle Randolph," 184–88.

53. Sigmund Freud, *Beyond the Pleasure Principle*, (New York: Bantam, 1959).

54. CMO to parents, CMO Collection, box 2, folder 5.

55. CMO to "Winny," CMO Collection, box 2, folder 6. Claire spells both Winnie's names with an "ie" ending, but this letter is signed "Winny," written to "Dear Clair."

56. CMO to parents, December 30, 1931, CMO Collection, box 2, folder 5.

57. Owens, "Belle Randolph," 441.

58. Owens, "Belle Randolph," 436–37.

59. Peter Milhado, "Men with a Mother Complex," *Don't Tell Me Who I Am . . . Let Me Guess* (blog), July 24, 2012, http://drpetermilhado.com/men-with-a-mother-complex accessed March 20, 2017.

60. Harris, *Rape, Incest, Battery*, xv–xxv. The various narratives and introductions illuminate themes related to abuse.

61. CMO to parents, May 24, 1932, CMO Collection, box 2, folder 7.

62. George Wanders to Claire's parents, May 7, 1932, CMO Collection, box 2, folders 7. 8, 9, 14.

63. CMO to parents, May 24, 1932, CMO Collection, box 2, folder 7.

64. George Wanders to CMO, February 24, 1932, CMO Collection, box 2, folder 7.

65. Owens, *Awakening*, 109–10.

66. Owens, *Awakening*, 109–10.

67. Owens, *Awakening*, 109–14.

68. CMO to George Wanders, multiple letters, CMO Collection, box 2, folder 8.

69. Susan Myers and CMO Correspondence, CMO Collection, box 2, folder 15.

70. Claire Myers Owens, "Sons and Husbands" (unpublished manuscript), CMO Collection, box 17, p. 594; a.k.a. "Belle Randolph." Notes 62 and 63, text taken from "Sons and Husbands," dated 1935, an earlier version than the "Belle Randolph" submitted to the Thomas Jefferson Prize.

71. Owens, "Sons and Husbands," 611.

72. Owens, "Belle Randolph," 476.

73. Owens, "Belle Randolph," 480.

74. Owens, "Belle Randolph," 507.

75. Owens, "Belle Randolph," 536.

76. CMO to attorney, box 2, folder 8; see also unfinished story, "The Worst Thing in the World," CMO Collection, box 37, folder 39.

77. Penelope Washbourn, *Becoming Woman: The Quest for Wholeness in Female Experience* (New York: Harper & Row, 1977), 71.

78. Owens, *Awakening*, 112.

79. Washbourn, *Becoming Woman*, 71.

80. Washbourn, 73.

10. "The Wolfe" at the Door

1. Claire Myers Owens, "Belle Randolph" (unpublished manuscript), CMO Collection, box 26; a.k.a. "Sons and Husbands" (unpublished manuscript), CMO Collection, box 17; a.k.a. "Love Is Not Enough" (unpublished manuscript), CMO Collection, box 18.

2. M. Farouk Radwan, "Inferiority Complex (Alfred Adler's Theory)," https://www.2knowmyself.com/Inferiority_complex_Alfred_adler.

3. "Who was Alfred Adler?" North American Society of Adlerian Psychology, http://www.alfredadler.org/alfred-adler.

4. Owens, "Belle Randolph."

5. Owens, "Belle Randolph."

6. Claire Myers Owens, foreword to "Sons and Husbands" (unpublished manuscript), CMO Collection, box 17.

7. Burton Rascoe to CMO, December 11, 1936, CMO Collection, box 53, folder 2.

8. Burton Rascoe to CMO, December 14, 1936, CMO Collection, box 53, folder 2.

9. Harrison Smith to CMO, July 1937, CMO Collection, box 53, folder 3.

10. Harrison Smith to CMO, July 1937, CMO Collection, box 53, folder 3; Donald MacCampbell to CMO, CMO Collection, box 53, folder 4.

11. Harrison Smith to CMO, July 1937, CMO Collection, box 53, folder 3.

12. Donald MacCampbell to CMO, 1940, CMO Collection, box 53, folder 4.

13. Donald MacCampbell to CMO, 1940, CMO Collection, box 53, folder 4.

14. Donald MacCampbell to CMO, 1940, CMO Collection, box 53, folder 4. MacCampbell's remarks sound like satire today.

15. CMO to Rascoe, 1940, CMO Collection, box 53, folder 7. See Willa Cather, *Song of the Lark* (Cambridge, MA: Riverside Press, 1915); reprint with revisions and Cather introduction, 1937.

16. CMO to Rascoe, 1940, CMO Collection, box 53, folder 7.

17. Note on cover page, CMO "Belle Randolph," 1942 submission for Thomas Jefferson Southern Award, CMO Collection, box 26.

18. CMO to Rascoe, CMO Collection, box 53, folder 4.

19. Cather, *Song of the Lark*, v.

20. Carolyn A. Carney and Miriam Kalman Friedman, eds. "A Collection of Stories by Claire Myers Owens" (unpublished manuscript). Owens's short story collection includes The Woman's Hotel Series.

21. Claire Myers Owens, "Autobiography" (unpublished manuscript), CMO Collection, box 19.

22. Owens, "Autobiography"

23. Owens, "Autobiography"

24. Owens, "Autobiography"

25. Owens, "Autobiography"

26. Owens, "Autobiography"

27. CMO/Carton Moore-Park correspondence, CMO Collection, box 2, folder 15.

28. CMO/Carton Moore-Park correspondence, CMO Collection, box 2, folder 15.

29. CMO/Carton Moore-Park correspondence, CMO Collection, box 2, folder 15.

30. CMO/Carton Moore-Park correspondence, CMO Collection, box 2, folder 15.

31. CMO/Carton Moore-Park correspondence, CMO Collection, box 2, folder 15.

32. CMO/Carton Moore-Park correspondence, CMO Collection, box 2, folder 16.

33. CMO/Susan Myers correspondence, CMO Collection, box 2, folder 15.

34. CMO/Susan Myers correspondence, CMO Collection, box 2, folder 15.

35. CMO/Susan Myers correspondence, CMO Collection, box 2, folder 15.

36. CMO/Susan Myers correspondence, CMO Collection, box 2, folder 15.

37. Claire Myers Owens, "Dauber & Pine Bookshops, Inc.: A Rendezvous of the Famous," *Publishers Weekly*, vol. CXXVI, no. 2 (November 17, 1934): 1824–28, in CMO Collection, box 51.

38. Claire Myers Owens, "Schulte's Book Store, Inc.: Where They Cater to All—From the Collector to the 5-Cent Bargain Hunter," *Publishers Weekly*, vol. CXXVIII, no. 4 (July 17, 1935): 214–17, in CMO Collection, box 51.

39. Laura Allen to CMO, June 14, 1935, CMO Collection, box 2, folder 15.

40. Laura Allen to CMO, June 14, 1935, CMO Collection, box 2, folder 15.

41. Laura Griffin to Laura Allen, May 8, 1932, CMO Collection, box 76, folder 9.

42. Braxton Griffin to Laura Allen, May 5, 1932, CMO Collection, box 76, folder 9.

43. Fannie Cobb Monroe to Cousin Mary, July 28, 1935, CMO Collection, box 76, folder 10.

44. Susan Myers to CMO, 1936, CMO Collection, box 2, folder 16.

45. Owens, "Autobiography."

46. Owens, "Autobiography."

47. Susan Myers to CMO, April 1, 1936, CMO Collection, box 2, folder 16. C. L. Myers died on Sunday, March 29, at two o'clock in the afternoon and was buried the following day, according to the *Temple Daily Telegram*, March 30, 1936, page 1. The dates do not correlate since Claire's journey took two days and two nights.

48. Owens, "Autobiography."

49. Owens, "Autobiography."

50. CMO to Thomas Wolfe, December 2, 1935, CMO Collection, box 8, folder 34. Compiled from the "Autobiography" and from various short stories, CMO Collection, box 37, folders 14 and 32.

51. Carney and Friedman, "Collection of Stories."

52. Owens, "Autobiography."

53. Susan Myers to CMO, 1936, CMO Collection, box 2, folder 16.

54. Obituary of Laura Smith Allen, CMO Collection, box 11, folder 19.

55. CMO Collection, box 11, folder 16.

11. Expiedway Ten

1. H. Thurston Owens obituary, *New Haven Register*, July 1969, CMO Collection, box 75, folder 15.

2. Horne family genealogies and obituaries, 1974, CMO Collection, box 75, folders 13–15. Eventually, the family dropped the *e* from their name.

3. CMO Collection, box 75, folder 15.

4. CMO/Doree Owens Smedley correspondence, CMO Collection, box 7, folders 20, 21.

5. Claire Myers Owens, "Autobiography" (unpublished manuscript), CMO Collection, box 19.

6. Owens, "Autobiography."

7. Claire Myers Owens, *Awakening to the Good: Psychological or Religious?* (Boston: Christopher Publishing, 1958), 115–16.

8. Thurston Owens/Gelatt family correspondence, CMO Collection, box 75, folders 2–8; CMO/Gelatt family correspondence, CMO Collection, box 6, folders 13–28.

9. Owens, "Autobiography."

10. Owens, *Awakening*, 116.

11. Owens, "Autobiography."

12. Owens, "Autobiography."

13. Owens, "Autobiography."

14. CMO/Smedley correspondence, CMO Collection, box 7, folders 20, 21.

15. Owens, "Autobiography."

16. Owens, "Autobiography."

17. Claire Myers Owens, interview by Kenneth Ring, 1979, CMO Collection, box 68, folder 1.

18. Owens, *Awakening*, 116.

19. Henry S. Harrison, *Harrison's Illustrated Guide: Greater New Haven* (Real Estate Educational Foundation, 1995), 179. In the 1990s, "more Yale graduate students, faculty and staff live[d] here than anywhere else."

20. Owens, *Awakening*, 117.

21. Owens, *Awakening*, 117–23.

22. Owens, "Autobiography."

23. Elizabeth Mills Brown, *A Guide to Architecture and Urban Design* (New Haven, CT: Yale University Press, 1976).

24. Owens, "Autobiography."

25. Owens, "Autobiography."

26. Harrison, *Harrison's*, 179.

27. Harrison, 179.

28. "Quinnipiack Club Member's Guide: The First One Hundred Years, 1871–1971", reprinted 1987.

29. Owens, "Autobiography."

30. CMO Radio Scripts Collection, box 39, folders 2, 3.

31. Owens, "Autobiography."

32. Owens, "Autobiography."

33. Owens, "Autobiography."

34. Marian Murray to CMO, October 12, 1944, CMO Collection, box 2, folder 25; Margaret Daniels to CMO, October 20, 1944, CMO Collection, box 2, folder 25.

35. C. D. Myers to CMO, March 9, 1938, CMO Collection, box 2, folder 19.

36. CMO to C. D. Myers, July 9, 1938, CMO Collection, box 2, folder 19

37. CMO to Susan Myers, July 9, 1938, CMO Collection, box 2, folder 19.

38. Adrienne Rich, "What Does a Woman Need to Know? 1979," in *Blood, Bread, and Poetry: Selected Prose 1979–1985* (New York: Norton, 1986), 4.

39. Owens, "Autobiography."

40. Susan Allen Myers obituary, CMO Collection, box 11, folder 19. See chapter 1 for Susan's accomplishments. Author went to visit the grave, and descriptions are author's.

41. Owens, "Autobiography."

42. Owens, "Autobiography."

43. Rolia Campbell to CMO, January 23, 1939, CMO Collection, box 2, folder 20.

44. Laura Griffin to CMO, March 14, 1939, CMO Collection, box 2, folder 20.

45. C. D. Myers/CMO correspondence, CMO Collection, box 2, folder 28.

46. C. D. Myers/CMO correspondence, CMO Collection, box 2, folder 28.

47. In fact, Germany had invaded Poland on September 1, 1939.

48. Owens, "Autobiography."

49. Owens, "Autobiography."

50. CMO to Burton Rascoe, 1940, CMO Collection, box 53, folder 4.

51. Owens, "Autobiography."

52. Roxane Gay, *Bad Feminist* (New York: Harper Perennial, 2014), 19, Kindle.

53. CMO to Burton Rascoe, 1940, CMO Collection, box 53, folder 4.

54. CMO to Burton Rascoe, 1940, CMO Collection, box 53, folder 4.

55. CMO to Pearl S. Buck, January 20, 1941, CMO Collection, box 53, folder 5.

56. CMO to Van Wyck Brooks, December 29, 1941, CMO Collection, box 53, folder 5.

57. CMO journal, CMO Collection, box 48, folder 4.

58. CMO journal, CMO Collection, box 48, folder 4.

59. CMO to Rascoe, 1940, CMO Collection, box 53, folder 4.

60. CMO journal, CMO Collection, box 48, folder 4.

61. CMO journal, CMO Collection, box 48, folder 4.

62. CMO journal, CMO Collection, box 48, folder 4.

63. Anne Sexton, *The Complete Poems* (Houghton, Mifflin, 1982), 77; see also Carolyn G. Heilbrun, *Writing a Woman's Life* (New York: W. W. Norton, 1988), 113–14.

64. Claire Myers Owens, "Mrs. Oppidan" (unpublished manuscript) and "Mrs. Oppidan is Moved" (unpublished manuscript), CMO Collection, box 26. I am grateful to the late Stanley R. Harris for solving the mystery of "Oppidan" as an anagram for *p' in a pod.*

65. Owens, "Mrs. Oppidan" and "Mrs. Oppidan is Moved."

66. CMO/Doubleday, 1944, CMO Collection, box 53, folder 7; CMO journal, CMO Collection, box 40.

67. CMO/Doubleday, 1944, CMO Collection, box 53, folder 7.

68. CMO journal, CMO Collection, box 40.

69. Owens, "Autobiography."

70. Owens, "Autobiography."

71. Owens, "Autobiography."

72. "Aldous Huxley: Visionary Experience," audio cassette, CMO Collection, box 68, folder 7.

73. Owens, "Autobiography."

74. Owens, "Autobiography."

75. Owens, "Autobiography."

76. Owens, "Autobiography."

77. Owens, "Autobiography."

78. Owens, "Autobiography."

79. Owens, "Autobiography."

80. Owens, "Autobiography."

81. Owens, "Autobiography."

82. Claire Myers Alexander (CMO), "File . . . for Friendship," *Today's Woman*, January 1946; "You're Grown Up If You Can Take Criticism," *Today's Woman*, August 1946; Claire Myers Owens, "Why You Start Things and Don't Finish Them," *Today's Woman*, October 1947; "Those Little Interruptions," *Today's Woman*, July 1948, CMO Collection, box 51.

83. *New Ocean House Daily News*, Swampscott, MA, 1947–1949, CMO Collection, box 51.

84. "Channel Bookshop Installs Rental Library of Prints," *Publishers Weekly* 51, no. 2, January 11, 1947, section 1, 160–62 in CMO Collection, box 51.

85. "Lady Glen-Coats Will visit Owens['s] for Holiday Week," *New Haven Register*, December 6, 1946, CMO Collection, box 58, folder 4.

86. *Washington Times-Herald*, March 24, 1947, 9, CMO Collection, box 58, folder 4.

87. CMO to Dorothy Ann Rutherford, 1947, CMO Collection, box 2, folder 28.

88. CMO interview by Ring.

89. Psychogram, CMO Collection, box 11, folder 7.

90. "AAUW Art Group to Meet," *New Haven Register*, April 26, 1949, CMO Collection, box 58, folder 4.

91. "AAUW Hears Talks in Yale Gallery of Art," *New Haven Register*, November 9, 1949, 37, CMO Collection, box 58, folder 4.

92. Owens, "Autobiography."

93. Owens, "Autobiography."

12. Awakening—Discovery of the Self

1. Claire Myers Owens, "Autobiography" (unpublished manuscript), CMO Collection, box 19.

2. CMO to Ina Vestal, December 2, 1949, CMO Collection, box 2, folder 28.

3. Whereas there is no copy of Ina's letter in the archive, there is a partial copy of a draft Claire wrote back to Ina. It is unclear whether Ina actually mailed her letter to *Today's Woman* magazine; both Claire and Thurston believed she had. Nor is there evidence as to whether Claire ever sent her response to Ina.

4. Claire Myers Owens, interview by Kenneth Ring, 1979, CMO Collection, box 68, folder 1.

5. CMO interview by Ring.

6. Claire Myers Owens, *Awakening to the Good: Psychological or Religious?* (Boston: Christopher Publishing, 1958), 21–23.

7. Owens, *Awakening*, 24.

8. Owens, *Awakening*, 24–26.

9. Owens, *Awakening*, 31.

10. Claire Myers Owens, "A Case of Spontaneous Self-Realization," *Human Dimensions*, vol. 4, no. 2, 1975, 43–52, in CMO Collection, box 51. Also described similarly in *Awakening*, 31–34.

11. CMO interview by Ring; see also CMO, interview by Lex Hixon, 1979, CMO Collection, box 68, folder 8, audiocassette.

12. Owens, *Awakening*, 38.

13. Owens, "Spontaneous Self-Realization," 47.

14. Owens, "Spontaneous Self-Realization," 47.

15. Owens, *Awakening*, 170½. A similar discussion of Owens's Great Awakening is also mentioned in "A Case of Spontaneous Self-Realization" and her interview with Kenneth Ring.

16. Little had been written on this topic prior to the 1970s. See Stanley R. Dean, *Psychiatry and Mysticism* (Chicago: Nelson-Hall, 1975).

17. The sessions began in October 1949, before the Awakening. Insights from journals: psychiatric sessions, 1950–1951, CMO Collection, box 40, folder 3; dreams, 1952 and 1981, CMO Collection, box 40, folder 4.

18. Owens, *Awakening*, 170.

19. CMO interview by Ring.

20. Roger Porter and Dan Reisberg, "Autobiography and Memory," (MLA Convention, Autobiography and Neuroscience, Chicago, December 29, 1995). By permission of Dr. Porter, email to author, October 30, 1996, and April 30, 2018, 1.

21. Porter and Reisberg, "Autobiography and Memory," 8, 14.

22. Carolyn G. Heilbrun, *Hamlet's Mother and Other Women* (New York: Ballantine, 1990), 30–31.

23. Mary Karr, *The Art of Memoir* (New York: HarperCollins, 2015), 292, Kindle.

24. Porter and Reisberg, "Autobiography and Memory," 15.

25. Kim Chernin, *Reinventing Eve: Modern Woman in Search of Herself* (New York: Harper and Row, 1987), 112.

26. Claire Myers Owens, "Gaily Bedight" (unpublished manuscript), CMO Collection, box 26, 88.

27. Owens, "Spontaneous Self-Realization," 50.

28. Psychiatric sessions, CMO Collection, box 40, folder 3.

29. Owens, "Autobiography." Owens's search for understanding prompted her to write her autobiographical novels.

30. "State AAUW Contest in Arts Is Made Known," *New Haven Register*, January 13, 1952, 3, CMO Collection, box 58, folder 6.

31. Owens, "Autobiography."

32. CMO to Carl Jung, 1954, CMO Collection, box 6, folder 33.

33. "Tourists Abroad," *New York Herald Tribune*, Paris Edition, 12 August 1954, CMO Collection, box 52, folder 3; CMO, "Horns Blowing, Bells Ringing," in *Jung Speaking*, eds. William McGuire and R.F.C. Hull (Princeton, NJ: Princeton University Press, 1977), 237–39.

34. Owens, "Autobiography."

35. CMO, questions for Jung, CMO Collection, box 48, folder 8. Questions paraphrased to avoid repetition.

36. CMO to Carl Jung, 1957, CMO Collection, box 6, folder 33.

37. Claire Myers Owens, *Discovery of the Self* (Boston: Christopher Publishing House, 1963).

38. Psychiatric sessions, CMO Collection, box 6, folder 53.

39. Owens, *Awakening*, 170 ½ a.

40. CMO/Charles Gelatt family correspondence, June 11, 1956, CMO Collection, box 6, folders 12–28.

41. Edmund Sinnott, quoted on front of book jacket, Owens, *Awakening*.

42. Maslow to CMO, April 30, 1958, CMO Collection, box 6, folder 35.

43. Owens, *Discovery*, 134–35.

44. Owens, *Discovery*, 137.

45. Owens, *Discovery*, 27.

46. Owens, *Discovery*, 149.

47. Jewish colleague is unknown; probably not Maslow, since they first met at a conference.

48. Owens, *Discovery*, 183–90. She considers Jews a separate "race" and Negroes a different "color."

49. Owens, *Discovery*, 196–203. In "Love and Color," race refers to the color of her cook's skin.

50. Anthony Sutich, introduction to *Discovery of the Self*, by Claire Myers Owens (Boston: Christopher Publishing House, 1963), 7–8.

51. Owens, *Discovery*, 334.

52. *Writer's Notes and Quotes* (Fullerton, CA, June 1964).

53. Owens, "Autobiography"

54. Plato, *Collected Dialogues* (New York: Pantheon, 1961).

55. Birthday card, CMO to Thurston Owens, CMO Collection, box 75, folder 3. October 23 was Thurston's eighty-fourth birthday; Claire was then sixty-seven.

13. The Lady and Her Court

1. Jean Houston, phone interviews by author, May 1, 1996; December 12, 1996; December 17, 1996.

2. Abraham Maslow, *Toward a Psychology of Being* (New York: D. Van Nostrand Company, 1962, 1968).

3. In *Awakening to the Good: Psychological or Religious?* (Boston: Christopher Publishing, 1958), Owens referred to the twenty "rapturous incidents" and "ecstatic experiences" she struggled to articulate. Later she coined the term "small ecstasies" to denote temporary glimpses into higher or "cosmic consciousness."

4. Aldous Huxley, *Doors of Perception* (New York: Harper & Row, 1956).

5. Charles Tart, ed., *Transpersonal Psychologies* (New York: Harper & Tow, 1975), 2.

6. John White, ed., *What is Enlightenment?: Exploring the Goal of the Spiritual Path* (Paragon, 1995), xii; John White, ed., *The Highest State of Consciousness* (Anchor, 1972), ix.

7. Tart, *Transpersonal*, 4n. Tart's introduction defines *spiritual* and *religious*, with *spiritual* designating an individual's meaning of life, God, ethics, and morality.

8. Maslow, *Psychology of Being*, iii–v.

9. White, *Enlightenment*, 1–10.

10. Stanley Dean, ed., *Psychiatry and Mysticism* (Chicago: Nelson Hall, 1975), 7.

11. *Ibid.* Dean, Psychiatry, 7.

12. White, *Enlightenment*, 27.

13. CMO/Huxley correspondence, CMO Collection, box 6, folder 32.

14. Claire Myers Owens, "Autobiography" (unpublished manuscript), CMO Collection, box 19.

15. "Aldous Huxley to Tea," CMO Collection, box 7, folder 2.

16. "Aldous Huxley to Tea," CMO Collection, box 7, folder 2.

17. CMO/Huxley correspondence, CMO Collection, box 6, folder 32.

18. CMO/Huxley correspondence, CMO Collection, box 6, folder 32.

19. Maslow, *Psychology of Being*, 62, 71.

20. Maslow, 88.

21. CMO interview by Ring.

22. CMO lecture at the Association of Humanist Psychology Conference, Boston, November 9, 1979, audio cassette, CMO Collection, box 68, folder 6.

23. CMO lecture at the Association of Humanist Psychology Conference.

24. Owens, "Autobiography."

25. CMO interview by Lex Hixon, recorded, later edited for radio program In the Spirit, September 1979, in CMO Collection, box 68, folder 7. See CMO/Hixon Correspondence, CMO Collection, box 6, folder 29.

26. Claire Myers Owens, *Discovery of the Self* (Boston: Christopher Publishing House, 1963), 163–64.

27. CMO interview by Ring; interview by Hixon.

28. CMO to anonymous friend who was going through a bitter divorce, CMO Collection, box 3, folder 21.

29. CMO/Thurston Owens correspondence, CMO Collection, box 3, folders 18–20.

30. Roxane Gay, *Bad Feminist* (New York: Harper Perennial, 2014), 17, Kindle.

31. Thurston's actions were likely a symptom of dementia and guilt concerning his two daughters.

32. CMO/Gelatt family correspondence, CMO Collection, box 6, folders 12–28; Thurston Owens/Gelatt family correspondence, CMO Collection, box 75, folders 2–8.

33. Thurston Owens/Gelatt family correspondence, CMO Collection, box 75, folder 6.

34. Raymond Prince and Charles Savage, "Mystical States and the Concept of Regression," *Psychedelic Review*, no. 8, 1966, 59–75; Claire Myers Owens, "The Mystical Experience: Facts and Values, *Main Currents in Modern Thought* 23, no. 4, March/April 1967, 93–99. Both articles reprinted in John White, ed., *The Highest State of Consciousness* (New York: Anchor Books, 1972).

35. CMO/Betty Bogert and Walter H. Clair correspondence, CMO Collection, box 6, folder 4.

36. Owens, "Mystical Experience," 93.

37. CMO to Raymond Prince, May 25, 1967, CMO Collection, box 7, folder 2.

38. CMO/Jean Houston correspondence, CMO Collection, box 6, folders 30–31.

39. CMO/Jean Houston correspondence, CMO Collection, box 6, folders 30–31.

40. CMO/Jean Houston correspondence, CMO Collection, box 6, folders 30–31.

41. Claire Myers Owns, "Varieties of Self-Realization" (unpublished manuscript), CMO Collection, box 26. Owens dedicated the book "To Jean Houston with Gratitude and Affection for Her Understanding and Invaluable Assistance."

42. CMO/Houston correspondence, CMO Collection, box 6, folders 30–31.

43. Edmund Sinnott, formerly a biologist at the University of New Hampshire, was dean of the Yale Graduate School, emeritus, and former director of Sheffield Scientific School of Yale University; CMO to Jean Houston, February 8, 1968 CMO Collection, box 6, folder 30.

44. CMO to Jean Houston, February 8, 1968 CMO Collection, box 6, folder 30.

45. Edmond Sinnott, introduction to "Varieties" (unpublished manuscript) by Claire Myers Owens, CMO Collection, box 26.

46. Sinnott, introduction.

47. Sinnott, introduction.

48. Owens, "Varieties," 6–7.

49. Owens, "Varieties," 9, 26.

50. Owens, "Varieties," 14.

51. Owens, "Varieties," 82–83.

52. Owens, "Varieties," 83.

53. Owens, "Varieties," 84–85.

54. Owens, "Varieties," 38–39.

55. Owens, "Varieties," 15, 137.

56. Owens, "Varieties," 137–38.

57. Jean Houston, phone interviews by author, May 1, 1996; December 12, 1996; December 17, 1996.

58. Owens, "Varieties," 411.

59. Owens, "Varieties," 413.

60. CMO/Houston correspondence, CMO Collection, box 6, folders 30–31.

61. Jean Houston, phone interviews by author, May 1, 1996; December 12, 1996; December 17, 1996.

62. Houston, phone interviews by author.

63. Houston, phone interviews by author.

64. Houston, phone interviews by author.

65. Houston, phone interviews by author.

66. CMO/Karlis Osis correspondence, CMO Collection, box 6, folders 30–31.

67. CMO to Thurston Owens, CMO Collection, box 3, folder 20.

68. CMO to Thurston Owens, CMO Collection, box 3, folder 18.

69. CMO/Gelatt family correspondence, CMO Collection, box 7, folders 13–28.

70. CMO/Houston correspondence, CMO Collection, box 6, folders 30–31.

71. Obituary, eulogies, and letters to friends, CMO Collection, box 75, folder 15.

72. Obituary, eulogies, and letters to friends, CMO Collection, box 75, folder 15.

73. Obituary, eulogies, and letters to friends, CMO Collection, box 75, folder 15

74. Audrey Fernandez, conversation with author, February 1, 1991.

75. CMO/Houston correspondence, CMO Collection, box 6, folders 30–31.

14. The End Is the Beginning

1. Claire Myers Owens, *Zen and the Lady* (New York: Baraka Books Ltd., 1979), 8.

2. CMO/Doree Smedley correspondence, CMO Collection, box 7, folders 20–21. All further quotes from letters in these folders.

3. CMO/Doree Smedley correspondence.

4. Claire Myers Owens, interview by Kenneth Ring, 1979, CMO Collection, box 68, folder 1.

5. CMO/Jean Houston correspondence, CMO Collection, box 6, folders 30–31.

6. Jean Houston, phone interviews by author, May 1, 1996; December 12, 1996; December 17, 1996; see also Owens, *Zen*, 39–41.

7. Owens, *Zen*, 39–41.

8. Owens, *Zen*, 11.

9. Audrey Fernandez, Geoffrey Lister, Marion Rigner, Barbara Percy, Dwain Wilder, Margaret Lee Braun, interview in Rochester, New York, with author, February 1 and 2, 1991.

10. Fernandez et al., interview with author.

11. CMO, *Zen*, 21.

12. CMO, *Zen*, 20.

13. CMO, *Zen*, 20–21.

14. CMO, *Zen*, 22.

15. CMO, *Zen*, 23.

16. CMO, *Zen*, 22–23.

17. CMO, *Zen*, 24.

18. CMO, *Zen*, 25–26.

19. CMO, *Zen*, 26.

20. CMO/Houston correspondence, March 5, 1970, CMO Collection, box 6, folder 31.

21. Jean Houston, *A Passion for the Possible: A Guide to Realizing Your True Potential* (New York: HarperSanFrancisco, 1998). Houston refers to the four levels of consciousness as Physical/Sensory, Psychological/ Historical, Mythic/Symbolic, and the Spiritual/Unitive. Email, Betty Rothenberger to author, May 12, 2017.

22. CMO/Houston correspondence, April 16, 1970, CMO Collection, box 6, folder 31.

23. CMO/Dwain Wilder correspondence, CMO Collection, box 8, folder 33.

24. CMO/Dwain Wilder correspondence, CMO Collection, box 8, folder 33.

25. Synchronicity is a concept psychologist Carl Jung developed to designate a meaningful coincidence, seemingly without obvious cause.

26. Owens, *Zen*, 26–27.

27. Owens, *Zen*, 29–32.

28. Owens, *Zen*, 35–36.

29. Owens, *Zen*, 37, 50.

30. Owens, *Zen*, 50.

31. Owens, *Zen*, 37.

32. Owens, *Zen*, 50.

33. Owens, *Zen*, 54–55.

34. Owens, *Zen*, 55.

35. Owens, *Zen*, 56–57.

36. CMO/Wilder correspondence, June 13, 1970, CMO Collection, box 8, folder 33.

37. CMO/Houston correspondence, July 4, 1970, CMO Collection, box 6, folders 30–31.

38. John White and Raul daSilva, interview with author, New Haven, CT, November 5, 1995.

39. John White and Raul daSilva, interview with author, New Haven, CT, November 5, 1995.

40. John White, ed., *Small Ecstasies*, Inner Visions Series #2 (San Diego: ACS Publications, 1983).

41. Owens, *Zen*, 61.

42. Lucy Taylor Hammer, Connecticut state senator for the Twelfth District from 1961 to 1973, received her MA from Yale in 1941. Louise Bates Ames, received her PhD from Yale in 1936 and was cofounder and director of the Gesell Institute of Child Development in New Haven and author of the syndicated news column, Parents Ask.

43. Owens, *Zen*, 60.

44. Plotinus, c. 204–270 CE.

45. Owens, *Zen*, 58–61.

46. Owens, *Zen*, 63.

47. Owens, *Zen*, 64.

48. Documents pertaining to the settlement of H. Thurston Owens estate, CMO Collection, box 63, folder 2; miscellaneous legal documents, CMO Collection, box 64, folders 10–15.

49. CMO/Wilder correspondence, August 18, 1970, CMO Collection, box 8, folder 33.

50. Comment made by unnamed neighbor to author, 1995.

51. Owens, *Zen*, 65.

52. CMO/Wilder correspondence, n.d., CMO Collection, box 8, folder 33.

53. CMO/Wilder correspondence, n.d., CMO Collection, box 8, folder 33.

54. Dwain Wilder, in Rochester interview with author, 1996.

55. Owens, *Zen*, 69.

56. CMO/Wilder correspondence, May 26, 1971, CMO Collection, box 8, folder 33.

57. Owens, *Zen*, 250–60.

58. CMO/Houston correspondence, CMO Collection, box 6, folders 30–31.

59. Philip Kapleau, *The Three Pillars of Zen*, 25th Anniversary Updated and Revised Edition (New York: Anchor Books, 1989).

60. Email conversation with author, July 23, 2018; Phone conversation with author, July 25, 2018.

61. Kapleau, *The Three Pillars of Zen*,

62. "What Is Zen," accessed April 4, 2017, http://www.zen-buddhism.net.

63. Claire Myers Owens, "The Mystical Experience: Facts and Values, *Main Currents in Modern Thought* 23, no. 4, March/April 1967, 93–99, reprinted in John White, ed., *The Highest State of Consciousness* (New York: Anchor Books, 1972; Claire Myers Owens, "Self-Realization—Induced and Spontaneous," *Journal of Altered States of Consciousness* 2, no. 1, 1975, 59–73; Claire Myers Owens, "A Case of Spontaneous Self-Realization," *Human Dimensions* 4, no. 2, 1975, 43–52. For additional comments on spontaneous awakenings see also Claire Myers Owens, "Comments on Haven's Religious Implications of Consciousness-Changing Drug," *Journal for the Scientific Study of Religion* IV, no. 2, Spring 1965, 246–48.

64. Owens, Self-Realization, 59–73.

65. John White, interview with author in New Haven, 1995.

66. Claire Myers Owens, "Zen Buddhism," in *Transpersonal Psychologies*, ed. Charles Tart (New York: Harper & Row, 1975), 154–202.

67. Daniel Goleman, "The Buddha on Meditation and States of Consciousness," in *Transpersonal Psychologies*, ed. Charles Tart (New York: Harper & Row, 1975), 204–30. The Goleman chapter first appeared in the *Journal of Transpersonal Psychology* 4, nos. 1 and 2, 1972.

68. CMO to Coren Douglas, September 14, 1972, CMO Collection, box 3, folder 24.

69. Coren Douglas to CMO, January 1974, CMO Collection, box 3, folder 24.

70. Wills, codicils, and notes, CMO Collection, box 64, folders 11–15.

71. CMO journal, CMO Collection, box 40, folders 4–5.

72. CMO journal, CMO Collection, box 40, folders 4–5.

73. CMO journal, CMO Collection, box 40, folders 4–5.

74. CMO journal, CMO Collection, box 40, folders 4–5.

75. CMO journal, CMO Collection, box 40, folders 4–5.

76. CMO/Charles Tart correspondence, CMO Collection, box 8, folders 1–10.

77. Owens, *Zen*, 133.

78. CMO/Raymond Prince correspondence, CMO Collection, box 7, folder 2.

79. CMO/Gelatt family correspondence, CMO Collection, box 6, folders 12–28.

80. CMO/Tart correspondence, CMO Collection, box 8, folders 1–10.

81. Owens, "Self-Realization—Induced and Spontaneous," Montreal, October 21, 1973, audio cassettes, CMO Collection, box 68, folder 2.

82. CMO journals, CMO Collection, box 40, folders 4–5.

83. CMO journals, CMO Collection, box 40, folders 4–5.

84. CMO/Kenneth Ring correspondence, CMO Collection, box 7, folders 3–12.

85. Owens, *Zen*, 239–45.
86. Kenneth Ring, interview with author in Storrs, CT, June 1989.
87. Raul daSilva phone conversation and email with author, July 6, 2017.
88. Owens, *Zen*, 279.

15. "Grande Amoureuse"

1. Claire Myers Owens, *Zen and the Lady* (New York: Baraka Books Ltd., 1979), 273–74.
2. Owens, *Zen*, 273–75.
3. CMO/Hammer correspondence, CMO Collection, box 4, folders 2–3; CMO/Ames correspondence, CMO Collection, box 6, folder 2.
4. CMO/Gelatt family correspondence, CMO Collection, box 6, folders 12–28.
5. Claire Myers Owens, "Joys of Aging," presented to the Phenix Society in Madison, CT, September 23, 1978, CMO Collection, audio cassette, box 68, folder 5.
6. CMO/Gelatt family correspondence, CMO Collection, box 6, folders 12–28.
7. Kenneth Ring, interview with author in Storrs, CT, June 1989.
8. CMO/Gelatt family correspondence, CMO Collection, box 6, folders 12–28.
9. CMO/Ring correspondence, CMO Collection, box 7, folders 3–13.
10. CMO to Ring, November 6, 1977, CMO Collection, box 7, folder 4.
11. CMO to Ring, November 6, 1977, CMO Collection, box 7, folder 4.
12. Ring to CMO, June 6, 1977, CMO Collection, box 7, folder 5.
13. Ring, interview with author in Storrs, CT.
14. Ring to CMO, June 6, 1977, CMO Collection, box 7, folder 5.
15. Ring to CMO, June 6, 1977, CMO Collection, box 7, folder 5.
16. Owens, *Zen*, 34.
17. Audrey Fernandez, interview with author in Rochester, NY.
18. Fernandez, interview with author in Rochester, NY.
19. Fernandez, interview with author in Rochester, NY.
20. Owens, *Zen*, 115.
21. Owens, *Zen*, 212–13.
22. Margaret Lee Braun, interview with author in Rochester, NY. See the similar advice she gave to Dorothy Anne Rutherford in her letter of 1947 (chapter 11, note 85). "Choosing a mate was different from choosing a lover. A lover can be a soul mate; but a husband may not be."
23. Geoff Lister, interview with author in Rochester, NY.
24. Fernandez, interview with author in Rochester, NY.
25. Audrey Fernandez, Geoffrey Lister, Marion Rigner, Barbara Percy, Dwain Wilder, Margaret Lee Braun, interview in Rochester, New York, with author, February 1 and 2, 1991.
26. Fernandez, interview with author in Rochester, NY.

27. Owens, *Zen*, 94–97.

28. Owens, *Zen*, 99.

29. Claire Myers Owens, interview by Kenneth Ring, 1979, CMO Collection, box 68, folder 1.

30. Owens, *Zen*, 102.

31. Owens, *Zen*, 125.

32. Owens, *Zen*, 286–87.

33. Owens, *Zen*, 291.

34. Owens, *Zen*, 297.

35. Dwain Wilder, interview with author in Rochester, NY. Raul daSilva, multiple phone interviews with author.

36. Fernandez, interview with author in Rochester, NY.

37. Fernandez, interview with author in Rochester, NY.

38. Braun, interview with author in Rochester, NY.

39. Claire Myers Spotswood Owens, *The Unpredictable Adventure: A Comedy of Women's Independence*, (Syracuse, NY: Syracuse University Press, 1993), 73–74.

40. CMO/Gelatt family correspondence, 1977, CMO Collection, box 6, folders 12–28.

41. CMO/Gelatt family correspondence, 1977, CMO Collection, box 6, folders 12–28.

42. CMO to Wilder, February 22, 1978, CMO Collection, box 8, folder 33.

43. CMO to Paula Gelatt, CMO Collection, box 6, folders 12–28.

44. CMO/Lex Hixon correspondence, CMO Collection, box 6, folder 29.

45. CMO, interview by Ring, six audio tapes, CMO Collection, box 60, folder 1.

46. CMO/Ring correspondence, CMO Collection, box 7, folder 5. Ring's reference to UPA as Owens's first book, not her first "real" book, refers to her embarrassment that her novel was risqué and reflected youthful naiveté. Dr. Ring had not read the book and was unaware of the great accomplishment it represents.

47. CMO/Ring correspondence, CMO Collection, box 7, folder 5.

48. CMO, interview by Lex Hixon, August 1979, one audio cassette, CMO Collection, box 68, folder 7.

49. CMO to Hixon, n.d., CMO Collection, box 6, folder 29.

50. AM Rochester, videotape, CMO Collection, box 67.

51. AM Rochester, videotape, CMO Collection, box 67.

52. Barbara Percy, interview with author in Rochester, NY.

53. Helen Nelson, telephone interview with author, January 1997.

54. CMO/Ken Wilber correspondence, CMO Collection, box 8, folders 27–32.

55. CMO/Ken Wilber correspondence, CMO Collection, box 8, folders 27–32.

56. CMO/Ken Wilber correspondence, CMO Collection, box 8, folders 27–32.

57. Mary Carolyn Hollers George. "Little Chapel in the Woods." In *Handbook of Texas Online*. Article published June 15, 2010. http://www.tshaonline.org/handbook/online/articles/ccleb. This nonsectarian chapel, considered one of the state's architectural masterpieces, was dedicated by Eleanor Roosevelt on November 1, 1939.

58. Elizabeth Snapp, email message to author, May 12, 2017, and numerous conversations over the years.

59. Elizabeth Snapp, email message to author, May 12, 2017, and numerous conversations over the years.

60. CMO to Wilder, CMO Collection, box 8, folder 33.

61. CMO/White correspondence, CMO Collection, box 8, folder 33.

62. *The World's Who's Who of Women* (Marquis, 1982).

63. White and daSilva, interview with author, New Haven, CT.

64. White and daSilva, interview with author, New Haven, CT.

65. CMO/Gelatt family correspondence, CMO Collection, box 6, folders 12–28.

66. Fernandez, et al., interview with author in Rochester, NY. Unless otherwise noted, the account of Owens's final hours and her cremation comes from this interview.

67. Raul daSilva phone interview and email with author, July 6, 2017. In this recent conversation, daSilva recalled this mystical event in much the same words as recorded in 1996.

68. Owens, *Zen*, 250–51 (emphasis mine); entire poem (seven sections), 250–60. Owens lacked the "gift" of poetry, though she had a poetic spirit beautifully released in her narratives. She described one of her poems as "prose crying to be poetry." Audrey Fernandez's reading of this poem at the Owens memorial brought closure and comfort to mourners because Claire's own voice was "there" to reassure them she had found peace through Zen, meditation, and the "joys of aging."

69. Fernandez, interview with author in Rochester, NY.

Selected Bibliography

Aaron, Daniel. *Writers on the Left, 1912–1940.* New York: Oxford University Press, 1961.

Alpern, Sara, Joyce Antler, Elisabeth Israels Perry, and Ingrid Winther Scobie, eds. *The Challenge of Feminist Biography: Writing the Lives of Modern American Women.* Champaign, IL: University of Illinois Press, 1992.

Beauvoir, Simone de. *The Second Sex.* New York: Vintage, 1974.

Bingham, Emily. *Irrepressible: The Jazz Age Life of Henrietta Bingham.* New York: Farrar, Straus and Giroux, 2015.

Brown, Dorothy M. *Setting a Course: American Women in the 1920s.* Boston: Twayne, 1987.

Brown, Elizabeth Mills. *A Guide to Architecture and Urban Design.* New Haven: Yale University Press, 1976.

Brownstein, Rachel. *Becoming a Heroine.* New York: Viking, 1982.

Cash, W. J. *Mind of the South.* New York: Alfred A Knopf, 1941.

Chambers-Schiller, Lee Virginia. *Liberty, A Better Husband: Single Women in America. The Generations of 1740–1840.* New Haven: Yale University Press, 1984.

Campbell, Joseph. *The Hero with a Thousand Faces,* 21st ed. Princeton: Princeton University Press, 1973.

Carpenter, Edward. *Love's Coming of Age: A Series of Papers on the Relation of the Sexes.* Manchester, UK: Labour Press, 1896.

Carney, Carolyn A., and Miriam Kalman Friedman, eds. "A Collection of Stories by Claire Myers Owens." Unpublished manuscript.

Cather, Willa. *Song of the Lark.* 1915. Reprint, Cambridge, MA: Riverside Press, 1937.

Chernin, Kim. *Reinventing Eve: Modern Woman in Search of Herself.* New York: Harper and Row, 1987.

Connell, Raewyn A., and Rebecca Pearse. *Gender: In World Perspective*, 3rd ed. Short Introductions. Cambridge, UK: Polity Press, 2014. Kindle.

Dean, Stanley, ed. *Psychiatry and Mysticism*. Chicago: Nelson Hall, 1975.

Downs, Matthew L. "Clicking the Trinoculars into Position: A Conversation with Glenda Elizabeth Gilmore." In *The Historian behind the History: Conversations with Southern Historians*, edited by Megan L. Bever and Scott A. Suarez, 164–78. Tuscaloosa, AL: University of Alabama Press, 2014.

Faderman, Lillian. *Surpassing the Love of Men: Romantic Friendship and Love between Women from the Renaissance to the Present*. New York: Morrow, 1981.

Faludi, Susan. *Backlash: The Undeclared War against American Women*. New York: Crown Publishers, 1991.

Fishbein, Leslie. *Rebels in Bohemia: The Radicals of The Masses, 1911–1917*. Chapel Hill: University of North Carolina Press, 1982.

Freedman, Janet L. *Reclaiming the Feminist Vision: Consciousness-Raising and Small Group Practice*. Jefferson, NC: McFarland, 2014. Kindle.

Freud, Sigmund. *Beyond the Pleasure Principle*. New York: Bantam, 1959.

Gay, Roxane. *Bad Feminist*. New York: Harper Perennial, 2014. Kindle.

George, Mary Carolyn Hollers. "Little Chapel in the Woods." *Handbook of Texas Online*. http://www.tshaonline.org/handbook/online/articles/ccleb.

Gordon, Linda. *Woman's Body, Woman's Right: Birth Control in America*, rev. ed. London: Penguin, 1990.

Harris, Miriam Kalman. Afterword to *The Unpredictable Adventure: A Comedy of Woman's Independence* by Claire Myers Spotswood Owens. Syracuse, NY: Syracuse University Press, 1993.

———. "Claire Myers Spotswood Owens: From Southern Belle to Grande Amoureuse." *Southern Quarterly* 31, no. 1 (Fall 1992): 50–69.

———. "The Pressure of the Choices." In *All Sides of the Subject*, edited by Teresa Iles, 68–79. Columbia University: New York: Teachers College Press, 1992.

———. *Rape, Incest, Battery: Women Writing Out the Pain*. Fort Worth: Texas Christian University Press, 2000.

Harrison, Henry S. *Harrison's Illustrated Guide: Greater New Haven*. Real Estate Education Foundation, 1995.

Heilbrun, Carolyn G. *Hamlet's Mother and Other Women*. New York: Ballantine, 1990.

———. *Writing a Woman's Life*. New York: W.W. Norton, 1988.

Hickey, Georgina. Review of *Women of the American South: A Multicultural Reader* edited by Christie Anne Farnham. *Southern Cultures* 6, no. 3 (Fall 2000): 93. Accessed January 18, 2017. http://www.southerncultures.org/content/masthead.

History of Bell County. Fort Worth: Temple Junior Chamber of Commerce, 1958.

Holman, C. Hugh. *A Handbook to Literature*, 4th ed. Indianapolis: ITT Bobbs-Merrill, 1985.

Houston, Jean. *A Passion for the Possible: A Guide to Realizing Your True Potential*. New York: HarperSanFrancisco, 1998.

Huxley, Aldous. *Doors of Perception and Heaven and Hell*. New York: Harper & Row, 1956.

Irving, Debby. *Waking Up White and Finding Myself in the Story of Race*. Cambridge, MA: Elephant Room Press, 2014. Kindle.

Jung, Carl G. *Archetypes and the Collective Unconscious*. Translated by R. F. C. Hull. Princeton: Princeton University Press, 1982.

Kapleau, Philip. *The Three Pillars of Zen*, 25th anniversary rev. ed. New York: Anchor Books, 1989.

Karr, Mary. *The Art of Memoir*. New York: HarperCollins, 2015. Kindle.

Kessler, Carol Farley. *Daring to Dream: Utopian Stories by United States Women: 1836–1919*. Boston: Pandora, 1984.

Kolmerten, Carol A. *The American Life of Ernestine Rose*. Syracuse, NY: Syracuse University Press, 1999.

Kramarae, Cheris, and Paula A. Treichler, eds. *A Feminist Dictionary*. London: Pandora, 1985.

Maslow, Abraham. *Toward a Psychology of Being*. Princeton, NJ: Norstrand, 1968.

Milford, Nancy. *Savage Beauty: The Life of Edna St. Vincent Millay*. NY: Random House, 2001.

Millay, Edna St. Vincent. "First Fig." *Poetry: A Magazine of Verse* 7, no. 3 (June 1918): 130. Accessed July 3, 2018, https://www.poetryfoundation.org/poetrymagazine/poems/14095/first-fig.

Monk, Ray. "Life without Theory: Biography as an Exemplar of Philosophical Understanding." *Poetics Today* 28, no. 3, (Fall 2009): 527–70.

Niven, Penelope. *Carl Sandburg*. New York: Scribner's, 1991.

O'Neill, William I., ed. *Echoes of Revolt: The Masses 1911–1917*. With an introduction by Irving Howe and an afterword by Max Eastman. Chicago: Ivan R. Dee, 1989.

Owens, Claire Myers. "A Case of Spontaneous Self-Realization." *Human Dimensions* 4, no. 2 (1975): 43–52.

———. *Awakening to the Good: Psychological or Religious?* Boston: Christopher Publishing House, 1958. Republished as *Small Ecstasies.* Edited by John White. San Diego: ACS Publications, 1983.

———. *Discovery of the Self.* Boston: Christopher Publishing House, 1963.

———. "Horns Blowing, Bells Ringing." In *Jung Speaking: Interviews and Encounters*, edited by William McGuire and R. F. C. Hull, 237–39. Princeton: Princeton University Press, 1977.

———. "The Mystical Experience: Facts and Values." In *The Highest State of Consciousness*, edited by John White, 135–52. New York: Anchor, 1972.

———. "The Psychology of Zen in Transpersonal Psychologies." In *Transpersonal Psychologies*, edited by Charles Tart, 153–202. New York: Harper and Row, 1975.

———. *Zen and the Lady.* New York: Baraka Books Ltd, 1979.

Owens, Claire Myers Collection. Woman's Collection, Blagg-Huey Library. Texas Woman's University, Denton.

Owens, Claire Myers Spotswood. *The Unpredictable Adventure: A Comedy of Woman's Independence.* New York: Doubleday, 1935. Reprint, with an Afterword by Miriam Kalman Harris, Syracuse, NY: Syracuse University Press, 1993.

Perreault, Jeanne. *Writing Selves: Contemporary Feminist Autography.* Minneapolis: University of Minnesota Press, 1995.

Rich, Adrienne. "Conditions for Work: The Common World of Women." In *Working It Out.* Edited by Sara Ruddick and Pamela Daniels. New York: Pantheon Books, 1977.

———. "What Does a Woman Need to Know? (1979)." In *Blood, Bread, and Poetry: Selected Prose, 1979–1985*, 1–9. New York: W.W. Norton, 1986.

Riis, Jacob. *How the Other Half Lives.* New York: Scribner, 1890.

Ring, Kenneth. *Life at Death: A Scientific Investigation of the Near Death Experience.* New York: Coward, McCann & Geoghegan, 1980.

Scott, Anne Firor. *The Southern Lady: From Pedestal to Politics, 1830–1930.* New York: Harper and Row, 1970.

Sexton, Anne. *The Complete Poems.* Boston: Houghton, Mifflin, 1982.

Showalter, Elaine. *Sexual Anarchy: Gender and Culture at the Fin de Siecle.* New York: Penguin, 1990.

Smith-Rosenberg, Carroll. *Disorderly Conduct: Visions of Gender in Victorian America.* New York: Alfred A. Knopf, 1985.

Spain, Rufus B. *At Ease in Zion: Social History of Southern Baptists, 1865–1900.* Nashville: Vanderbilt University Press, 1961.

Stanton, Domna C. *The Female Autograph.* New York: New York Literary Forum, 1984.

Stanley, Liz. "Biography as Microscope or Kaleidoscope? The Case of Power in Hannah Cullwick's Relationship with Arthur Munby." *Women's Studies International Forum* 10, no. 1(1987): 19–31.

Stopes, Marie Carmichael. *Married Love: A New Contribution to the Solution of Sex Difficulties.* London: Putnam's Sons, 1923.

Tart, Charles, ed. *Transpersonal Psychologies.* New York: Harper and Row, 1975.

Thompson, Joyce. *Marking a Trail: A History of Texas Women's University.* Denton: TWU Press, 1982.

Wagner-Martin, Linda. *Telling Women's Lives: The New Biography.* New Brunswick, NJ: Rutgers University Press, 1994.

Walker, Barbara G. *The Woman's Encyclopedia of Myths and Secrets.* San Francisco: Harper & Row, 1983.

Walker, Lenore. *The Battered Woman.* New York: Harper and Row, 1979.

Ware, Caroline. *Greenwich Village 1920–1930.* New York: Universal Press, 1935.

Washbourn, Penelope. *Becoming Woman: The Quest for Wholeness in Female Experience.* San Francisco: Harper & Row, 1977.

White, John, ed. *The Highest State of Consciousness.* New York: Anchor, 1972.

———. *What is Enlightenment? Exploring the Goal of the Spiritual Path.* St. Paul, MN: Paragon House, 1995.

The World's Who's Who of Women. Marquis, 1982.

Wilkerson-Freeman, Sarah. "Stealth in the Political Arsenal of Southern Women: A Retrospective for the Millennium." In *Southern Women at the Millennium: A Historical Perspective*, edited by Melissa Walker, Jeannette R. Dunn, and Joe P. Dunn. Columbia: University of Missouri Press, 2003.

Wilmeth, Don B., *Cambridge Guide to American Theater.* With Tice L. Miller. New York: Cambridge University Press, 1996.

Wolfe, Thomas. *Look Homeward Angel.* New York: Scribner, 1929.

Woloch, Nancy. *Women and the American Experience*. New York: Knopf, 1981.

Woolf, Virginia. *A Writer's Diary*. New York: Harcourt Brace Jovanich, 1954.

———. *A Room of One's Own*. London: Harcourt Brace Jovanovich, 1929.

Wyatt-Brown, Bertram. *Southern Honor: Ethics and Behavior in the Old South*. Oxford: Oxford University Press, 1982.

Zinsser, Judith P. "Feminist Biography: A Contradiction in Terms?" *The Eighteenth Century* 50, no. 1 (Spring 2009): 43–48. Accessed December 18, 2016. https://muse/jhu.edu/article/372742.

Index

Italic page numbers denote illustrations.

Photograph courtesy of Robert H. Friedman, PhD

Miriam Kalman Friedman, whose scholarly work in women's studies has focused on women's life stories, has taught English and creative writing at various universities, including University of Texas at Dallas, University of Houston, and Texas Christian University. She was professor of English at Tarrant County College. She has received fellowships from the American Association of University Women, the National Endowment of the Humanities, and the Salzburg Global Seminar. Currently retired from teaching, she has written plays that have been produced in Houston community theater festivals. Her publications include a reprint of Claire Myers Spotswood Owens's 1935 novel, *The Unpredictable Adventure: A Comedy of Woman's Independence*, published by Syracuse University Press in 1993; and *Rape, Incest, Battery: Women Writing Out the Pain*, published by Texas Christian University Press in 2000. She resides in Houston, Texas, and is married to Dr. Robert Friedman, her high school sweetheart and true love. Their combined family includes five children, seven grandchildren, and two great-grandchildren.